D1008663

THE
EMPLOYMENT
OF
TEACHERS

Some Analytical Views

Edited by

DONALD GERWIN

University of Wisconsin, Milwaukee

McCutchan Publishing Corporation
2526 Grove Street
Berkeley, California 94704

ISBN: 0-8211-0610-4
Library of Congress Catalog Card Number: 73-20854

© 1974 by McCutchan Publishing Corporation

Printed in the United States of America

Editor's Preface

There seems to be a widespread feeling that the demands for quick solutions to educational problems have led to hurriedly developed programs based on inadequate research. Thomas K. Glennan, Jr. ("National Institute of Education: A Personal View," *Educational Researcher*, II (March 1973), pp. 13-16), Director of the National Institute of Education, has said, "One of the most important goals of the Institute is to resist the temptation of hasty action and to restore to education programs and their implementation in the field the kind of scientific rigor that we consider essential to more fundamental areas." This problem seems no less applicable to the particular area of educational administration to which this volume is addressed, the employment of teachers. Many observers will agree that research in the area has tended to be descriptive, somewhat lacking in empirical support, and overly concerned with cookbook remedies. The situation seems to be much the same whether the topic is a relatively new one, such as collective negotiations, or a well-established one, such as teaching careers.

At the same time the need for sophisticated, analytical thinking is increasing because of rapid and fundamental changes occurring in the nature of the employment relationship. In the last few years we have seen teacher shortages turn to oversupply, administrative paternalism give way to collective bargaining, and relatively abundant financial resources dwindle because of inflation and taxpayers' revolts. More-over, it appears that teachers are giving up their traditional nonparti-sanship in favor of political involvement.

The existence of this situation undoubtedly comes as no surprise to most readers of this volume. What is new and exciting is that it may be changing. A solid core of analytical research concerning the employment relationship has begun to emerge. My purpose is to bring it, or at least examples of it, to the attention of interested scholars, practitioners, and students. These groups need to know who is doing the research, the kinds of problems being studied, and the methods of analysis being used. There is also a need to appraise the utility of these works and to suggest directions for future research. This last point cannot be overemphasized. It is not my contention that researchers armed with relatively sophisticated intellectual tools automatically hold a key to the truth. The literature is filled with examples of analytical frameworks applied to problems for which they were not suited, of problems bent to fit a model's constraints, and of conceptual tools misused because they were inadequately understood.

Strictly speaking, analytical modes of thinking employ some bor-rowed or original conceptual framework to break a problem down into parts, explain the behavior of the parts, and assemble an explan-ation of the whole. The conceptual frameworks used in the research presented here run the gamut along several dimensions. Some are primarily concerned with explaining or predicting behavior (Alutto and Belasco's decisional participation schema); others are directed toward recommending changes in behavior (Levin's application of cost-effectiveness analysis to teacher selection). Some are relatively broad in scope (Herzberg's motivational theories, which are used by Sergiovanni); others (Drotning and Lipsky's categories for under-standing the causes of collective bargaining impasses in public educa-tion) are highly specialized. The overwhelming majority are verbal frameworks, but a few are stated as formal mathematical models (Holtmann's linear programming approach related to compensation). Some—the labor market theory used by Kershaw and McKean—are time-tested points of view, but others, for example, the information processing theories of decision making that I used, are relatively new. To be sure, some of the frameworks might be better classified as taxonomies. A few papers have much in common with traditional descriptive research, but in general these explicitly contribute to the development of analytical frameworks in their problem areas.

What are the problems treated here? The volume has been divided into four sections reflecting the areas in which most of the analytical work seems to have been done. The first deals with teaching careers, specifically the variables influencing the flow of teachers into, within, and out of the school system. The second part looks at research into more efficient compensation practice, as well as work identifying the causes of the size and components of the wage package. The third section on organizational behavior inquires into individual and group issues such as conflict, job satisfaction, attitude consensus, and participation in decision making. The last section deals with facets of collective bargaining such as the structure of the bargaining relationship and impasse procedures. Most of these articles in examining some aspect of the employment relationship quite properly assume, either explicitly or implicitly, that the actors are the school administration, or school board, and the teachers. There are exceptions, however, which help to provide a more balanced view. Garbarino, for example, is concerned with the impact of state regulations on collective bargaining. Luttbeg and Zeigler, Cole, and to some extent Corwin analyze interpersonal relationships among teachers. Gerwin's work gets at the influence of other school systems in compensation decisions. This volume contains no research on the relationship between teachers and students in the classroom, how-ever.

Teacher employment issues are now receiving the attention of scholars in a number of disciplines; they are no longer reserved for educational administration. This is healthy since the problems are too complex to be viewed in just one particular way. Accordingly, a conscious effort has been made to be eclectic in the selection of papers within the bounds of a quality constraint. The disciplines turning out to be most pertinent are educational administration (Bolton, Brown, Charters, Sergiovanni, Sarthory), industrial relations (Drotning and Lipsky, Garbarino, Hellriegel *et al.*, Kasper), behav-ioral science (Alutto and Belasco, Cole, Corwin), economics (Holt-mann, Kershaw and McKean, Levin), management science (Gerwin), and political science (Luttbeg and Zeigler). Perhaps this eclectic view will produce a more balanced compendium, one filled with new insights for researchers and administrators trained in one approach or the other. For example, the works of Drotning and Lipsky and Sarthory are complementary, and they have much to offer each other.

The commitment to delve into the conceptual frameworks' utility is manifested in at least two ways. In virtually all cases the papers that have been selected incorporate some kind of empirical data as a check. More important, original contributions by practitioners have been included to provide an opportunity for the expression of personal views on problems, solutions, and trends in certain areas and to appraise certain papers from the practical rather than the academic side. Emphasis is placed on inquiring into the extent to which recommendations for change will work in practice, on evaluating whether or not actual situations have been understood, and on suggesting how the work can be made more realistic. Much less attention is paid to theoretical and methodological issues. These contributions will, I hope, suggest areas where further research needs to be done and give practitioners some clues as to applicability in their situation. A warning is, however, in order. It was not feasible to have all points of view represented by having, say, a teacher, an administrator, and a school board member each comment on a specific study. Seven of the volume's eighteen contributions are commented upon but by only one commenter, and one of these involves previously published material of a noted academic. The remaining six are original pieces from individuals who are currently or in the past have been associated with the administration's or a school board's point of view. The teacher's frame of reference is not represented. Geographically, the contributions are from three states: Wisconsin (3), Pennsylvania (2), California (1). Two large city districts and four suburban systems are represented. Knowing these biases should allow the reader to put the practitioners' comments in proper perspective.

This volume represents an effort to gather together some analytical treatments of issues concerning the employment of public school teachers. Further, a commitment has been made to a multidisciplinary view and to the appraisal of these works from the practical side. I hope this approach will benefit researchers, students, and practitioners in educational administration and related areas.

Contributors

Joseph A. Alutto, School of Management, State University of New York, Buffalo.

James A. Belasco, School of Business, California State University, San Diego

Charles S. Benson, School of Education, University of California, Berkeley

Dale L. Bolton, Department of Educational Administration, University of Washington, Seattle

Alan F. Brown, Ontario Institute for Studies in Education, University of Toronto, Toronto, Ontario

W. W. Charters, Jr., Center for the Advanced Study of Educational Administration, University of Oregon, Eugene

Stephen Cole, Department of Sociology, State University of New York, Stony Brook

Ronald G. Corwin, Department of Sociology, Ohio State University, Columbus

John E. Drotning, School of Industrial and Labor Relations, Cornell University, Ithaca, New York

Wendell French, Department of Management, University of Washington, Seattle

Joseph W. Garbarino, Graduate School of Business Administration, University of California, Berkeley

Donald Gerwin, Graduate School of Business, University of Wisconsin, Milwaukee

Lawrence Grant, Whitefish Bay Public Schools, Milwaukee, Wisconsin

Don Hellriegel, Department of Management Science and Organizational Behavior, Pennsylvania State University, University Park, Pennsylvania

A. G. Holtmann, Department of Economics, Florida State University, Tallahassee

Hirschel Kasper, Department of Economics, Oberlin College, Oberlin, Ohio

Joseph A. Kershaw, Department of Economics, Williams College, Williamstown, Massachusetts

Carroll L. Lang, Department of Educational Administration, California State University, Northridge

Henry M. Levin, School of Education, Stanford University, Stanford, California

David B. Lipsky, School of Industrial and Labor Relations, Cornell University, Ithaca, New York

Norman R. Luttbeg, Department of Government, Southern Illinois University, Carbondale

James H. Lytle, Pennsylvania Advancement School, Philadelphia, Pennsylvania

Roland N. McKean, Department of Economics, University of Virginia, Charlottesville

Richard B. Peterson, Department of Industrial Relations, University of Washington, Seattle

Joseph A. Sarthory, Department of Educational Administration, Kansas State University, Manhattan

Thomas Sergiovanni, Department of Educational Administration, University of Illinois, Urbana

Slack Ulrich, Northridge Lakes Development Corporation, Milwaukee, Wisconsin

A. William Vantine, Abington Heights School District, Clarks Summit, Pennsylvania

Robert Wegmann, Department of Sociology, University of Wisconsin-Milwaukee, Milwaukee

Harmon Zeigler, Department of Political Science, University of Oregon, Eugene

Contents

Editor's Preface   iii

I / Teaching careers   1
Introduction   2
1 / A Cost-Effectiveness Analysis of Teacher
    Selection   *Henry M. Levin*   6
2 / The Effect of Various Information Formats on
    Teacher Selection Decisions   *Dale L. Bolton*   16
COMMENT / The Teacher Selection Process in Practice
    Carroll L. Lang   35
3 / A Perceptual Taxonomy of the Effective-Rated
    Teacher   *Alan F. Brown*   41
COMMENT / Brown's DPRT: A Means of Effectively
    Evaluating Teachers   *Lawrence Grant*   58
4 / Some Factors Affecting Teacher Survival in School
    Districts   *W. W. Charters, Jr.*   66

II / Compensation   93
Introduction   94
5 / Salary Differences and Salary Reform
    Joseph A. Kershaw and *Roland N. McKean*   99
COMMENT / The Money We Spend and What Happens
    to It   *Charles S. Benson*   134

6 / Linear Programming and the Value of an Input
   to a Local Public School System
   A. G. Holtmann   141
7 / An Information Processing Model of Salary
   Determination in a Contour of Suburban School
   Districts   *Donald Gerwin*   152
8 / Formulating Salary Policy in Suburban School
   Districts   *Donald Gerwin*   184
COMMENT / The Fiscal-Professional Conflict:
   A Professional View   *Slack Ulrich*   204
9 / The Effects of Collective Bargaining on Public
   School Teachers' Salaries   *Hirschel Kasper*   216

III / Organizational Behavior   239
Introduction   240
10 / Patterns of Organizational Conflict
   Ronald G. Corwin   244
COMMENT / The Role of Organizational Conflict
   in a Large Urban School System
   James H. Lytle   266
11 / Attitude Consensus and Conflict in an Interest
   Group: An Assessment of Cohesion
   Norman R. Luttbeg and *Harmon Zeigler*   273
12 / Factors Which Affect Satisfaction and Dissatis-
   faction of Teachers   *Thomas Sergiovanni*   294
13 / A Typology for Participation in Organizational
   Decision Making
   Joseph A. Alutto and *James A. Belasco*   311
COMMENT / Teacher Participation in Educational
   Decision Making   *Robert G. Wegmann*   325

IV / Collective Bargaining and Related Issues   335
Introduction   336
14 / Professional Negotiations in Education
   Joseph W. Garbarino   340
15 / The Outcome of Impasse Procedures in New York
   Schools under the Taylor Law
   Joseph E. Drotning and *David B. Lipsky*   359
16 / Structural Characteristics and the Outcome of
   Collective Negotiations   *Joseph A. Sarthory*   376

17 / Teacher's Strike: A Study of the Conversion of
      Predisposition into Action   *Stephen Cole*   387
18 / Collective Negotiations and Teachers: A Behavioral
      Analysis   *Don Hellriegel, Wendell French,*
      and *Richard B. Peterson*   410
COMMENT / Thoughts on Collective Negotiations and
      Teachers   *A. William Vantine*   434

Tables

Table   Page

1-1	Means and standard deviations for samples of Negro and white sixth graders	10
1-2	Output in student verbal score for each additional unit of teacher verbal score and experience	10
1-3	Estimation of earnings functions for Eastmet teachers	11
1-4	Relative costs of increasing student verbal achievement	12
2-1	Variables involved in the study	21
2-2	Results of seven 2x2x3x3 analyses of variance for four dependent variables	24
2-3	Practical significance of the optimum recommended format analysis of marginal means on time variable	30
3-1	Classification of administrators' perceptions of teachers	48
3-2	Priorities in personnel judgments	50
3-3	Detailed analysis of the content of administrators' perceptions of teachers for each of three subgroups	52
4-1	Survival data for male and female Oregon teachers, 1962 cohort	73
4-2	Rate of survival by age group, male and female Oregon teachers	74
4-3	Rate of survival by teaching level and age group, male and female Oregon teachers	76
4-4	Rate of survival by school system size, male and female Oregon teachers	77
4-5	Rate of survival by school system size and age group, male and female Oregon teachers	79
5-1	Example of three-step salary schedule	125
6-1	Value of one additional unit of various inputs in the Detroit high schools	147
6-2	Number of teachers available and the number of teachers needed in the Detroit high school system	149
7-1a	Range violations	160
7-1b	Range adherences for positions six and seven	160
7-1c	Settlement positions	160
7-2	Old policy vs. new policy	162
7-3	Statistics for comparing actual and predicted increases	174
7-4	Error measure percentages	176

7-5	Characteristics of North Side School Districts	182
7-6	Bamin increases and across-the-board increases	182
7-7	B. A. minimum salaries	183
8-1	Policy positions	191
8-2	Board's and teachers' proposals	195
9-1	Estimated number of agreements with school districts by organization and nature of representation, 1967	219
9-2	Simple correlations among the variables estimated in equation (1)	224
9-3	Regression coefficients (and standard errors) for alternative models of determinants of teachers' salaries	226
9-4	Alternative parameter estimates (and standard errors) of the determinants of teachers' salaries relative to those of entering policemen	229
9-5	Residuals from equation (5) for selected states	233
9-6	Alternative combinations of salary increases and teachers covered yielding an increase in average state salaries of 4 percent	234
9-7	Selected data on teacher representation and average salaries	238
10-1	Rank-order correlations between organizational characteristics and indexes of tension and conflict	254
11-1	Comparison of the three attitude sets in the area of mandate for actions by leaders, teachers' organizations, and the OEA	281
11-2	Comparison of the three attitude sets in the areas of expectations and satisfaction with leadership's actions	283
11-3	Comparison of the attitude sets in the area of orthodox values	286
11-4	Comparison of the attitude sets in the area of the norms of teachers' political participation	289
12-1	Percentages and values of chi-squared for the frequency with which each first-level factor appeared in high attitude sequences as contrasted with low attitude sequences for the total group	301
12-2	Percentages and values of chi-squared for the frequency with which each second-level factor appeared in high attitude sequences as contrasted with low attitude sequences for the total group	303
13-1	Decisional situations	314
13-2	Distribution of subjects by decisional condition	315
13-3	Analyses of decisional deprivation, equilibrium, and saturation groupings	318
13-4	Levels of deprivation	320
13-5	Summary of relative and organizational characteristics	321
15-1	Use of impasse procedures under the Taylor Law, 1969	362
15-2	Use of impasse procedures under the Taylor Law, January to September 1970	363
15-3	Cost of impasse procedures in New York State, 1969 and 1970	368

15-4	Education and occupation of PERB fact finders and mediators	371
16-1	Factors distinguishing between impasse and nonimpasse districts	381
17-1	Percentage supporting the strike by five nonteaching statuses (New York sample)	390
17-2	Percentage supporting the strike by political affiliation and social support (New York sample)	391
17-3	Percentage supporting the strike by index of militant predisposition and social support (New York sample)	391
17-4	Percentage supporting the strike by type of school and union membership (aggregate data)	394
17-5	Percentage calling in sick by IMP score and attitudes of friends toward the strike (New York sample)	395
17-6a	Percentage calling in sick by IMP score (New York sample)	396
17-6b	Percentage calling in sick by number of cross-pressure-producing statuses (New York sample)	397
17-7	Fear and action on April 11—only those believing the strike justified (New York sample)	398
17-8	Index of militant predisposition, fear, and action on April 11 (New York sample)	399
17-9	Index of militant predisposition, type of school, and action on April 11 (New York sample)	400
17-10	Percentage of friends favoring the strike action on April 11—only those who were afraid (New York sample)	402
17-11	Fear of losing respect of colleagues and action on April 11—for those low on IMP and having more than 50 percent of their friends favor the strike (New York sample)	403
17-12	Fear of losing respect of colleagues and action on April 11—for those high on IMP and fearing sanctions from supervisors (New York sample)	404
17-13	Index of militant predisposition, fear of loss of respect, action on April 11 (New York sample)	405
18-1	Mean levels of satisfaction for all respondent teachers in descending order by satisfaction factor	422
18-2	Mean levels of attitudes toward collective negotiations in descending order of negotiation factors for all respondent teachers	423
18-3	Degree of correlation in descending order between satisfaction factors and support of teacher strikes by respondent teachers	426
18-4	Support of teacher strikes by sets of socioeconomic factors	428

Figures

Figure		Page
2-1	The interaction effect of instruction (I) and documents (D) on time	25

2-2   The interaction effect of instruction (I) and documents (D) on discrimination, as measured by variance of estimates on the Teacher Evaluation Instrument   26

2-3   The interaction effect of interview information (A) and documents (D) on certainty of estimates on the Teacher Evaluation Instrument   27

2-4   The interaction effect of masking (M) and documents (D) on consistency of estimates on the Teacher Evaluation Instrument   28

3-1   Perceptual preoccupations of administrators asked to consider eighteen combinations of staff members   54

3-2   Discriminating power of administrators' perceptions of teachers   55

4-1   Survival curves for male and female Oregon teachers, 1962 cohort   70

4-2   Survival data and fitted curves for male and female Oregon teachers (semilog coordinates)   72

4-3   Rate of survival by age at employment of male and female Oregon teachers, 1962 cohort   75

4-4   Rate of survival by school system size, male Oregon teachers, 1962 cohort   78

4-5   Survival curves for male and female Missouri teachers, 22-26 years of age, 1951-1953 cohort (semilog coordinates)   81

4-6   Observed survival curve for 1947-48 cohort, Champaign County, Illinois, and curve expected for comparable Oregon cohort (semilog coordinates)   84

4-7   Survival curves for male and female University of Illinois graduates entering employment in 1937-1939, Group I, and 1940-1942, Group II (semilog coordinates)   86

7-1   Outline of the model   158

7-2a   Fox Point—Bayside   163

7-2b   Glendale—River Hills   164

7-2c   Mapledale—Indian Hills   166

7-2d   Nicolet   168

7-2e   Shorewood   169

7-2f   Whitefish Bay   170

7-2g   Common constraints   172

8-1   Sources and content of information   189

11-1   Nature of the analysis   275

12-1   The continuum assumption   295

12-2   Herzberg hypothesis   295

12-3   Basic design features of the content analysis   300

18-1   Conceptual model of factors related to teachers' attitudes toward collective negotiations   412

18-2   Simplified system of relations between the legal context and social-psychological context   418

I / TEACHING CAREERS

INTRODUCTION

In this section we focus on three steps in the development of a teacher's career vis-à-vis his school system; entering, working within, leaving. Two of the chapters deal with teacher selection, one with teacher evaluation, and one with separation. These categories are the traditional ones used in school personnel texts. The significant difference is that, instead of emphasizing the structure and functioning of the personnel activity, these chapters tend to focus on the analysis of decision making. Bolton's contribution is the obvious example since he concentrates on the teacher selection decision. Levin suggests standards he feels should be used in the same kind of choice. Brown is concerned with the criteria used in teacher evaluation decisions, and his methodology is based on having subjects make such choices. As will be suggested, Charters' research may be viewed as investigating the influences on a teacher's decision to participate in the school system. Research into teaching careers, Charters points out,[1] has been overly descriptive and lacks an explanatory focus. It is possible that decision process analysis, as exemplified here, may provide one means of shifting the balance.

Levin investigates which teacher characteristics should be emphasized in the selection decision in order to improve the attainment of educational objectives. His conceptual framework for attacking this problem is cost-effectiveness analysis, a technique that utilizes economic reasoning to make explicit the costs and benefits of alternative proposals for achieving some ends. An excellent introduction to cost-effectiveness in education is provided by Cohn[2]. Levin deals with the traditional methodological pitfalls of this approach by making some simple assumptions concerning goals (students' verbal scores on standardized tests) and shape of cost functions (linear), and also by judicious use of already available data. Within this framework two proposals are examined: recruiting teachers with higher verbal scores versus recruiting teachers with more years of experience. His call for salary schedule reform to attract teachers with the characteristics the analysis shows to be most effective should be considered in light of the next section's discussion of augmenting the single salary schedule. The chapters by Kershaw and McKean, Benson, and Holtmann are most enlightening in this regard.

Bolton studies teacher selection by analyzing the effect on the outputs of certain inputs to the decision-making process. His dependent variables refer to aspects of the specified choice which is made, while his independent variables characterize the format of the input information. This framework permits him to question whether the form in which interview data is presented to the decision maker affects the consistency of his choices and whether various degrees of data summarization influence feelings of certainty about the outcome. These and other issues are explored in an imaginative simulation in which subjects, who are principals, get information on the hypothetical context in which their choices are to be made and data on fictitious applicants with controlled personality traits. Bolton's simulation is not just a research vehicle; it has practical value for administrators interested in improving information formats for teacher selection. Further, as indicated by Bolton[3], it has potential as an experiential learning device for individuals who normally make this type of decision. Practitioners, however, must deal with a multiplicity of other influences on teacher selection which it was not Bolton's intention to study. Drawing upon his past experience, Lang complements Bolton's effort by discussing some of these factors.

Examining the way a teacher's career progresses while he or she is in a school system implies a commitment at some point to look into the subject of teacher evaluation. Unfortunately, evaluation criteria generally acceptable to administrators and teachers have not been forthcoming. McNeil and Popham[4] report this is true even for the most carefully researched dimension, teaching effectiveness in the classroom. Accordingly, it is useful to develop a better understanding of the ways in which evaluation decisions actually are made. Brown looks for the standards used by principals in discriminating between teachers by employing an instrument known as the Discriminant Perception Repertory Test (DPRT). This methodology, related to the kinds of comparisons administrators often make, is particularly useful for uncovering actual as opposed to stated evaluation criteria. Out of Brown's research has emerged the beginning of a conceptual framework based on four general classes of criteria used in practice. This facilitates learning whether principals are using appropriate standards such as classroom effectiveness measures. It permits research into the variables associated with the use of different sets of criteria. Brown's provocative findings on the relationship between leadership style and evoked criteria is a case in point. Grant, in his comments, emphasizes another possible advantage. The DPRT might be used by administrators and teachers to prepare an evaluation instrument that reflects their real values rather than those to which they pay lip service.

Charters' paper adds a new dimension to research on the separation of teachers from school systems. Traditional work has examined the determinants of turnover rates. He demonstrates the utility of also inquiring into the reasons why teachers remain. Using the theory of stochastic processes, he makes some simple assumptions about flows of teachers within and out of a district. His analytical tool, derived from these assumptions, is the survival curve, which indicates the proportion of a cohort of teachers who stay in a district over time. Charters' attention is focused on the curve's parameter, the survival rate, estimated using data from a large sample of Oregon teachers. His investigation of the variables influencing the survival rate leads to a better understanding of the role played by personal attributes versus school characteristics in separation decisions. From a practical viewpoint Charters' findings can be used as guidelines by administrators intent upon hiring a solid core of teachers committed to the district. A significant research question also raised is whether a unifying framework can be found to incorporate the complementary views of survival and turnover research. March and Simon's[5] theory of an employee's decision as to whether or not to continue to participate in an organization is a logical choice. It should be possible to adapt their theory to an educational setting using the findings of survival and turnover research and then to conduct tests on the resulting combined view.

The comments in this section are by Carroll L. Lang and Lawrence Grant. Dr. Lang is assistant professor of education, California State University, Northridge. He has served as Director of Personnel in the Simi and Pomona unified school districts in California and as a supervisor in the Los Angeles city schools. He is the author of *Teacher Recruitment; Problems, Promises and Proven Methods,* published by Prentice-Hall. Dr. Grant is principal of the high school in Whitefish Bay, a suburb of Milwaukee, Wisconsin. His previous appointments include assistant principal in Kenosha, Wisconsin, and mathematics teaching in Newington, Connecticut. He has published in *The Bulletin* of the Wisconsin Secondary School Administrators' Association and served on various committees for national and state professional associations. Dr. Grant received his D.Ed. in Educational Administration from the University of Illinois.

Notes

1. W. W. Charters, Jr., "Some 'Obvious' Facts about the Teaching Career," *Educational Administration Quarterly,* III (No. 2, Spring 1967), 183-93.

2. Elchanan Cohn, *The Economics of Education,* Lexington Books (Lexington, Massachusetts: D. C. Heath, 1972).

3. Dale L. Bolton, "Simulating the Process for Selection of Teachers," in

Dale L. Bolton (ed.), *The Use of Simulation in Educational Administration* (Columbus, Ohio: Charles E. Merrill, 1971), pp. 88-148.

4. John D. McNeil and W. James Popham, "The Assessment of Teacher Competence," in Robert M. W. Travers (ed.), *Second Handbook of Research on Teaching*, (Chicago: Rand McNally, 1973), pp. 218-44.

5. James G. March and Herbert A. Simon, *Organizations* (New York: John Wiley, 1958).

1 / A Cost-Effectiveness Analysis of Teacher Selection

Henry M. Levin

INTRODUCTION

It has been widely recognized that the educational systems of the
large cities have failed to teach effectively or motivate significantly
large numbers of disadvantaged youngsters.[1] The recent public
response to these failures has been to increase spending for the
schools in order to compensate for disadvantages in the backgrounds
of their students. Indeed, the Elementary and Secondary Education
Act of 1965 alone has provided over $1 billion a year in additional
school expenditures for students from low-income families. Given
these infusions of dollars, school districts, state governments, and the
U.S. Office of Education have been increasingly concerned about
how to get the most impact out of the additional financial support.
These governments have been looking to cost-effectiveness analysts
for the answers, and the response has been a profuse outpouring of
cost-effectiveness studies.[2] Interestingly, each of these studies has
examined the relationship between total costs and a hypothetical set
of outcomes without examining the particular programs on which
the money was spent. That is, the process by which education is
produced has been ignored, and only a gross relation between dollar
expenditures and outputs has been surveyed. The internal efficiency
of different educational strategies has not been explored.

Reprinted from *The Journal of Human Resources*, V (No. 1, Winter 1970),
24-33.

Yet the educational decision maker is faced with the problem of how to spend additional resources in the most effective way possible. In doing this, he is handicapped by some formidable obstacles. First, there is little unanimity on what schooling output is or on how to measure a multidimensional array of outcomes. Second, there is almost no theory which describes the relations between schooling inputs, the educational process, and schooling outcomes. And third, there is even a great deal of vagueness on what should be considered as schooling inputs. For example, it has been suggested that students contribute to the education of fellow students and that teachers' attitudes may be more important than other characteristics of teachers. Finally, even student performance on standardized achievement tests is so confounded by the student's own social class, his abilities, and his general environmental milieu that it has proven very difficult to measure school effects separately from those caused by other influences.[3]

The result of all this confusion is that additional funds for education have been expended in very traditional ways, most particularly on reductions in class size and the addition of remedial specialists. This very unimaginative route is taken despite the plethora of alternatives that are available: new instructional technologies, radically different curricula, and different types of teachers represent possibilities that have been scarcely considered while schools do more of what they have always done with reduced class sizes and a few additional specialists. Unfortunately, the cost-effectiveness studies undertaken thus far have done little to delineate the most effective strategies for any particular objective (for example, raising reading scores). Indeed, one study has stated this shortcoming quite honestly: "A key part of this final analysis, which is missing completely from this study, is the analysis of how differences in program inputs can affect the direct measures of achievement."[4]

COST-EFFECTIVENESS AND TEACHER SELECTION

If one were to attempt to help the school decision maker spend his money more efficiently, where would we start? An obvious place to begin would appear to be teacher selection, for teachers' salaries represent about 70 percent of current operating expenditures for the elementary and secondary schools. Thus, we might want to ask two questions:

1. Which teachers' characteristics show a relation to a goal that most of us would accept for the schools, that is, student performance on a standardized test of verbal achievement?

2. What does it cost the schools to obtain teachers with different characteristics?

Given answers to these two questions, we wish to ascertain whether we can obtain teachers with more effectiveness per dollar of expenditure.

The first question might be answered if we were to estimate a production function of the form:

$$(1) \qquad A = F(X, Y, Z_1, \ldots, Z_k)$$

where A is the achievement score for an individual, X represents a vector of social class and background influences which affect achievement, Y represents a vector of nonteacher characteristics for the schools, and $Z_1, \ldots, Z_k$ represents a vector of teacher attributes. Ordinarily the assumption is made that F is convex to the origin and continuous throughout its domain (and that the first order partial derivatives are positive and the second order partials are negative).

Corresponding to question 2 would be budget constraint

$$(2) \qquad B = P_1 Z_1 + P_2 Z_2 + \ldots + P_k Z_k)$$

which in this case would apply only to the teachers' costs, where $P_1, \ldots, P_k$ denote the prices of teacher characteristics $Z_1, \ldots, Z_k$ respectively. Let us call this a teachers' quality budget constraint, since we are assuming that teacher-student ratios are constant and that the question before us is that of obtaining teachers of a better quality for a given teachers' budget.[5] While we are using this example only for illustrative purposes, this approach does have the advantages of keeping the problem down to a manageable—but still meaningful —size.

Assume that we wish to maximize (1) subject to constraint (2). The solution to this problem would require obtaining each type of teachers' quality Z_i until its additional contribution to achievement $(\partial A / \partial Z_i)$ relative to its price (P_i) were equal for all Z_i $(i=1, \ldots, k)$. That is:[6]

$$(3) \qquad \frac{\partial A / \partial Z_1}{P_1} = \frac{\partial A / \partial Z_2}{P_2} = \ldots = \frac{\partial A / \partial Z_k}{P_k}$$

What if the school decision maker has no knowledge of production relations (1) or the relative prices (P_i) in (2)? This is certainly likely to be the case in the present instance where the knowledge gap is so great. Yet, assume that the decision maker does indeed wish to maximize (1). Then, as cost-effectiveness analysts, we would like to give him information as to which teacher characteristics represent "best buys" in improving achievement scores within the confines of a limited budget.[7]

PRODUCTION ESTIMATES

What follows are the results from admittedly early representations of (1) and (2) which I believe yield insights into the teacher selection problem. Eric Hanushek has estimated educational production functions for black and for white sixth graders in metropolitan schools.[8] Using standardized achievement scores as measures of output and other data on inputs from the Survey of Equal Opportunity data, Hanushek estimated relations similar to (1) for whites in 471 elementary schools and for blacks in 242 elementary schools in the metropolitan North. Thus, the analyses were cross-sectional single equation estimates for 1965-66 done separately for black and for white students where the school was the unit of analysis. That is, student and teacher data were averaged for each school. While Hanushek specified these functions using social class and other variables as arguments, we will discuss only the net estimated relationships between teacher characteristics and student verbal score.

In general, Hanushek found two teacher characteristics that were consistently related to the verbal scores of sixth graders. These two traits were the number of years of teacher experience and teacher's verbal score. The means and standard deviations for these variables are shown in Table 1-1 and the estimated payoffs to each characteristic are displayed in Table 1-2.[9]

Thus, for each additional point of teacher verbal score, the Negro students showed an increment of .175 points and the white students an increment of .179 points in student verbal score. For each additional year of teacher experience, the test scores of Negro students were about .108 points higher and the test scores of white students were about .060 points higher.

TEACHER COSTS

The relative prices for teacher characteristics are taken from my estimates of earnings functions for teachers.[10] In this work I esti-

TABLE 1-1. Means and standard deviations for samples of
Negro and white sixth graders

	Negro		White	
	Mean	Stan. dev.	Mean	Stan. dev.
Student verbal score	26.68	4.20	35.70	4.54
Teacher verbal score	23.98	1.80	24.77	1.43
Teacher experience (years)	11.29	4.00	11.88	4.56

Source: Eric Hanushek, "The Education of Negroes and Whites" (Ph.D. diss.,
Department of Economics, Massachusetts Institute of Technology, 1968), pp. 39
and 75.

mated the relationship between teachers' salaries and teachers' characteristics. The estimates were derived for four metropolitan regions
considered as labor markets, and the data were derived from the
same source as that used by Hanushek.

Table 1-3 shows the annual dollar return to teachers for specific
characteristics within an eastern metropolitan region. While this
result represents a linear function for an aggregate sample of teachers, results are available for nonlinear forms of the equation and by
sex and race of teacher analyzed separately. For illustrative purposes,
however, this equation will suffice.

Among this large sample of almost 3,000 teachers, about $24 of
annual salary was associated with each additional point of teacher's
verbal score; males were receiving about $400 more than females;
and each additional year of college training was worth almost $400
to a teacher. Teachers with nonacademic majors were receiving about
$160 more than were their counterparts who majored in elementary

TABLE 1-2. Output in student verbal score for each additional unit
of teacher verbal score and experience

	Additional points of student verbal score	
	Negro	White
Each additional unit of teacher verbal score	.175	.179
Each additional year of teacher experience	.108	.060

Source: Estimated from results on pp. 37 and 73 in Hanushek, "The Education
of Negroes."

education or academic subjects; graduates of teacher colleges were receiving less than graduates of other institutions. For each additional year of teaching experience, teachers were receiving about $79, and there were also higher returns to each successive certification level and to dissatisfaction with the racial composition of one's students ("discrepancy on proportion white").

What is of particular interest to us is that the approximate annual cost to the schools of obtaining a teacher with an additional year of experience was about $79 and that of obtaining a teacher with an

TABLE 1-3. Estimation of earnings functions for Eastmet teachers

Teacher characteristics	Slope coefficient	Statistic t
Verbal score	$ 23.98	5.6
Female	−398.59	10.1
Years of schooling	396.04	17.8
Miscellaneous major	159.73	3.5
Graduate of teacher college	−125.73	3.0
Years of experience	78.91	36.0
Certification level	564.09	23.1
Discrepancy on proportion white	18.27	2.3
Mean salary	7,084.56	
Standard deviation	1,679.76	
R^2 (corrected for degrees of freedom)	.80	
R	.65	
Sample size	2,921	

additional point on the verbal score was about $24, ceteris paribus. Combining these estimates with the results in Table 1-2, we obtain the approximate costs of raising student test scores with two strategies: recruiting and retaining teachers with more experience, and recruiting and retaining teachers with higher verbal scores.

SOME FINDINGS

Accordingly, Table 1-4 shows the relative costs of improving student performances under alternative recruitment strategies.[11] It is important to emphasize the relative costs of each strategy rather than the absolute ones.[12] In terms of relative costs, for a given test score gain for Negroes it appears that obtaining teachers with higher verbal scores is about one-fifth as costly as obtaining more teacher experience, and the teachers' verbal score route is ten times as efficient as teachers' experience per dollar of expenditure for increasing the verbal scores of white students. The obvious policy implication is that school districts are obtaining too much experience as against verbal proficiency.[13] Accordingly, the schools should try to increase the recruitment and retention of verbally able teachers while paying somewhat less attention to experience. How much trade-off should be made is not evident given our linear results.[14]

Another interesting observation is that teacher experience appears to be twice as effective per dollar of expenditure for Negro students as it does for white ones. Giving equal weight to

TABLE 1-4. Relative costs of increasing student verbal achievement

	Approximate cost for increasing a student's verbal score by one point	
Strategy	Negro	White
Teacher's verbal score	$ 26	$ 26
Teacher experience	128	253

point gains for whites and Negroes, the schools might wish to assign their more experienced teachers to the schools attended by Negro students for higher total yields. What might explain this phenomenon? One possible interpretation is that a more experienced teaching staff and low teacher turnover show greater benefits to Negro than to white students because of the lesser stability of the Negro home. It is well known that Negro students are far more likely to come from "broken homes" (one where one or both parents are absent) than are white students. That is, stability and continuity of the school environment may have their greatest impact on those students characterized by the least stable home environments.[15]

The overriding implication of this analysis is that school salary policies should provide financial incentives that will attract and retain teachers with greater verbal skills, a policy that would represent a distinct break from tradition. On the other hand, it is suggested that the schools grant too large a reward for experience. The result of reducing salary increments for experience and implementing them for verbal performance would appear to attract a more capable teaching staff with regard to the production of student achievement.

Of course these two strategies could not be considered as true alternatives if the teachers with higher ability were also those with greater experience. In fact, this is not the case. The zero-order correlation between experience and verbal ability for the several thousand teachers in Eastmet was not significantly different from zero. There was a significant pattern among the newer teachers, however. That is, the teachers with the highest verbal facility were those with no teaching experience, the new entrants to the profession. Unfortunately, it appears that many of the most highly endowed of these individuals leave the schools within three years so that the stock of teachers with three years or more experience shows significantly lower test scores than those with less than three years' experience.[16] This finding is consistent with the fact that the schools do not reward such proficiencies while other employers do. It seems reasonable that this adverse retention could be reversed by a more competitive salary policy, one that did account for the teacher's verbal facility.

These findings are not the final answer by any means. They are meant to be illustrative rather than definitive. There are grounds for expecting specification biases on both the production and cost sides. Yet, it would take [such] enormous biases—all in the same direction—to offset our finding that it appears far more efficient to improve student achievement by raising teachers' verbal score than by increasing teacher experience.

Notes

The author is grateful to Donald Keesing, Stephan Michelson, Samuel Bowles, and Eric Hanushek for comments. The research was supported by the Brookings Institution and the Stanford Center for Research and Development in Teaching. An earlier version was presented at the 34th Annual Meeting of the Operations Research Society of America, Philadelphia, November 8, 1968.

1. These failures have been so well recognized that they are topics of the daily press. For some insights, see Christopher Jencks, "Is the Public School Obsolete?" *The Public Interest* (Winter 1966), pp. 18-28.

2. Some of the most extensive are: Thomas I. Ribich, *Education and Poverty* (Washington: The Brookings Institution, 1968); Robert Spiegelman *et al.*, "Cost-Benefit Model to Evaluate Educational Programs, Progress Report," Stanford Research Institute, March 1967, and "A Benefit/Cost Model to Evaluate Educational Programs," Stanford Research Institute, January 1968; Clark C. Abt *et al.*, "Design for an Elementary and Secondary Cost Effectiveness Model," Contract OEC-1-6-001681-1681, Report on the Mathematical Design Phase for U.S. Office of Education, February 1967; Jacob J. Kaufman *et al.*, "An Analysis of the Comparative Costs and Benefits of Vocational Versus Academic Education in Secondary Schools," Contract OEG-1-6-000512-0817, Preliminary Report for the U.S. Office of Education, October 1967.

3. The sparsity of knowledge in all of these areas is demonstrated in James

S. Coleman *et al., Equality of Educational Opportunity* (Washington, D.C.: U.S. Department of Health, Education, and Welfare, 1966), ch. 3; and Samuel S. Bowles and Henry M. Levin, "The Determinants of Scholastic Achievement," *Journal of Human Resources* (Winter 1968), pp. 3-24. For a discussion of the problems in doing cost-effectiveness analysis in education, see Samuel S. Bowles, "Towards an Educational Production Function," paper presented at the Conference on Research in Income and Wealth, University of Wisconsin, November 15, 1968; and Henry M. Levin, "Cost Effectiveness Evaluation of Instructional Technology: The Problems," paper prepared for the Commission on Instructional Technology (Washington, D.C., November 1968).

4. See Spiegelman *et al.*, "A Benefit/Cost Model," p. 54.

5. The elimination of class size as a parameter of achievement is based on the fact that no rigorous study has shown a consistent relation between class size and achievement within the ranges of class size under consideration. For evidence that even drastic reductions in class size and student-teacher ratios show little effect on standardized achievement scores, see David J. Fox, "Expansion of the More Effective School Program," Evaluation of New York City Title I Educational Projects 1966-67 (New York: Center for Urban Education, 1967), pp. 32-44.

6. The derivation of this solution is assumed to be familiar to the reader. Others may refer to Paul A. Samuelson, *Foundations of Economic Analysis* (Cambridge, Mass.: Harvard University Press, 1961). For a formal proof, see H. Hancock, *The Theory of Maxima and Minima* (New York: Dover Press, 1960).

7. The approach taken here is similar to that suggested by Glen Cain and Harold Watts in "Problems in Making Inferences from the Coleman Report," Discussion Paper 28-68 (Madison: Institute for Research on Poverty, University of Wisconsin, 1968).

8. Eric Hanushek, "The Education of Negroes and Whites" (Ph.D. diss., Department of Economics, Massachusetts Institute of Technology, 1968).

9. These estimated payoffs represent approximate slope coefficients for linear relationships between student's verbal score and the specific teacher characteristics, extracted from an equation in which other relevant explanatory variables were also included in the relationships. Teacher's degree level and other traits showed no statistically significant association with student achievement. See Hanushek's discussion of possible specification biases in "The Education of Negroes."

10. Henry M. Levin, "Recruiting Teachers for Large-City Schools" (Washington, D.C.: The Brookings Institution, 1968), mimeo. To be published by Charles E. Merrill.

11. These costs were obtained by applying the teacher's experience and verbal score salary coefficients from Table 1-3 to the production coefficients in Table 1-2. It was assumed that the additional effort would have to be maintained for the first five years of schooling in order to obtain the sixth grade results shown in Table 1-2. Therefore, the present values in Table 1-4 represent additional expenditures for the previous five years compounded at a 5 percent rate of interest and divided by an average class size of thirty in order to obtain a per student figure.

12. The additional costs are probably biased downwards because the original salary data from which costs are estimated did not include fringe benefits.

13. The high payoff to verbal score is not very surprising given the relatively

modest intellectual performances—on the average—of teachers in the elementary schools. In fact, while school salary schedules provide higher remuneration for more experience, they offer no incentives to those with greater verbal proficiency. The dull and superior are treated as equals. As long as the general market for college graduates rewards verbal performance while the schools do not, we can expect that individuals with greater verbal skills will opt for nonteaching careers. See Levin, "Recruiting Teachers," chs. 3, 6, and 7.

14. That is, our production estimates do not satisfy the conditions of the second order partial derivative set out for equation (1), above.

15. On the other hand, experience of teachers is related to the social class of the student body. That is, the schools characterized by the highest teacher turnover or the least teacher experience are those attended by children who are drawn from the lowest social strata. If the social class of the students is less adequately measured for Negro than for white students, the relatively higher student achievement that is apparently attributable to teacher experience may merely reflect the higher social status of Negro students in schools with low teacher turnover. It is obvious that the teacher experience-student achievement relation between races needs further investigation before we can be more nearly certain of its proper interpretation.

16. See Levin, "Recruiting Teachers," ch. 3. One notable exception to this pattern is that the few teachers who entered the profession during the depression years, 1930-1940, showed test scores as high as those of the new teachers.

2 / The Effect of Various Information Formats on Teacher Selection Decisions

Dale L. Bolton

Among the important decisions made by educational administrators are those concerning the selection of teachers. Each teacher represents a potential gain or loss to the school system in terms of goal accomplishments. Therefore, the teacher selection process provides an opportunity for an educational administrator to make a major contribution to the improvement of a school system. In addition, it affords an example of the decision process in which the process itself can be studied systematically and the results generalized to many administrative tasks.

The decision to select a teacher from a number of applicants is the culmination of a series of preliminary decisions which constitute the selection process. So crucial is the selection of a teacher to the quality of the educational program that it seems obvious that this decision should be made with the utmost certainty regarding its utility. Yet such decisions are frequently intuitive and arbitrary, and, despite a certain amount of theory development, a lack of empirical data has left the teacher selection process a highly subjective one. Under such conditions, reliability and discrimination may be extremely low, and decision makers may feel relatively uncertain regarding their choices. Of

Reprinted from *American Educational Research Journal,* VI (No. 3, May 1969), 329-47.

major concern, then, is whether conditions can be specified which will increase the reliability, discrimination, and feelings of certainty regarding decisions made in selecting teachers.

Fundamental to this study was the view that teacher selection decisions are based on information, and this information may be available to decision makers in various formats. Since the format of the information may affect decisions, the general problem was to find an information format that would not adversely affect teacher selection decisions as far as the following dependent variables were concerned: (a) amount of time needed to make decisions, (b) fineness of discriminations made, (c) feeling of certainty regarding the decisions, and (d) consistency in estimating decision outcomes.

To determine whether the format of information affects decisions made in the selection of teachers, it was necessary to simulate an educational situation in order to manipulate and control variables. The four independent variables manipulated in the simulated situation were: (a) amount of instruction provided on how to process information (two levels: instruction, and no instruction), (b) number of written documents presented (two levels: multiple and single), (c) degree of masking of information (three levels: considerable, partial, none), and (d) interview information (three levels: filmed audiovisual, tape-recorded audio, none).

SIGNIFICANCE OF THE VARIABLES

A number of research studies influenced the selection of variables for this study. From the views of Miller,[1] suggesting the need to group data because of the limits of accuracy with which individuals can judge more than one attribute simultaneously, came the idea of using a summary document and masking nonexceptional data. Springbett's studies[2] of selection in the armed forces and industry indicated that the order in which information is received affects the select-reject decision, but he did not provide information regarding the ranking process or the estimate of consequences of selection. Likewise, Springbett found that appearance in the first two or three minutes of the interview affects final outcome in 85 percent of the cases. The study reported here controlled the order of receipt of information; in addition, the inclusion of the controlled interview variable was influenced by Springbett's studies.

Barrett, who also was interested in the effect of the interview on selection decisions,[3] found that interviews tended to be weighted heavier than objective data by psychologists; but neither he nor Springbett sought information regarding the relative effect of the content of the interview as compared with appearance. However, the results of a study by Giedt[4] caused him to warn that interviewers should be careful to avoid being misled by appearance and expressive cues and should continue to rely heavily on what is said in the interview. Giedt's study was conducted on psychological patients and needed replication in an educational setting. Sydiaha conducted experiments which indicated that empathic processes tended to introduce errors in interviews by causing individuals to "attribute characteristics to others which, in fact, the others failed to attribute to themselves."[5] Sydiaha, therefore, argued for putting selection decisions on a strictly actuarial basis.

Levine and McGuire noted that, in a medical situation, one or two significant cues early in the information collection stage can distort the diagnosis.[6] This again suggests a format for the written information which will capture and not distort information; it also suggests the need to provide instructions regarding the processing of information. Drake indicated that many companies report improvement in judgments following training regarding interviewing theory and techniques.[7]

The independent variables of the study reported here were chosen because of their relationship to the way an administrator might use his time and how information might be processed. The use of a single summary document or partially masked information (i.e., exceptional data rather than the total data available) might allow clerical help or data processing equipment to transform information into a more useful format and therefore permit the administrator to use his time in actual decision making rather than cumulating and collecting information.[8] However, giving the decision maker instructions regarding how to process information might facilitate decisions to the extent that it would nullify the benefits of mechanical or clerical manipulation of information.

If interview information is found to be beneficial, then it must be retained for the purpose of assisting in decision making. If, however, administrators do not benefit from interview information, perhaps Sydiaha's argument for actuarial decisions would be further strengthened and the interview should still be retained—but for purposes other than decision making (for example, to provide the applicant with information regarding the teaching situation, to help the applicant to make a decision, or to begin orienting the prospective teacher to the expectations of the school organization).

The four dependent variables were selected because of their potential tangible gains for a school district. One of them is concerned with the reliability of decisions (i.e., the *consistency* with which predetermined organizational outcomes are predicted). Unless outcomes of decisions are consistently predicted, long-range goals will not be maximized because of the discrepancy between prediction and the actual outcome. Therefore, if selection decisions are not reliable, relative losses will occur to the school system because of the unaccomplished goals and purposes. (This is not to be construed as an argument against variability within a teaching faculty; if variability is a desired outcome, it should be planned for and predicted in the same manner as any other desired outcome.)

The need for making fine *discriminations* among teacher applicants is probably not as obvious as the need for consistency. However, as the quality of teacher applicants improves, and as pressures increase for minimum error in selection, the need to make subtle distinctions among teachers who are relatively homogeneous becomes more critical.

Unless decisions are both discriminative and consistent, there is little foundation upon which to accumulate evidence as to the validity of the decisions being made. There is no basis for using the outcomes of past decisions to improve future decisions; hence, decision making is likely to remain a vague, intuitive process.

The reason for interest in the *time* needed to make decisions seems obvious, in that a small amount of time saved on each of a large number of teacher selection decisions means a considerable saving of valuable administrator time for a school district. The time variable is a practical consideration in decision making and is independent of the "goodness" of the decision made.

It is much more difficult to relate *certainty* regarding decisions to such tangible measures as costs, but the interest in this dependent variable is due to the idea that decisiveness in an administrator is a good quality and that uncertainty can lead to indecision, vacillation, and wasted motion.

The significance of the four dependent variables is established then on a direct or indirect relationship to tangible gains for a school district. The question of the validity of the decisions, or the "goodness" of the decisions in terms of whether the "correct" teacher was selected, was omitted intentionally from this study. It is assumed that local school systems define teacher effectiveness according to specified local criteria; if so, the local systems will be able to specify the outcomes desired in terms of teacher behavior and to validate a procedure within the system.[9] It is also assumed that, if the decision maker can consistently discriminate among teacher applicants in a simulated situation, he should be able to consistently relate teacher applicants to criteria for selection specified by a local school district. This last assumption is worthy of empirical verification, however, and should be studied.

Because the experiment was conducted in a simulated situation, some of the variables that might ordinarily affect administrative decisions could be controlled, e.g., the assignment situation for the hypothetical vacancy, supervision situation, evaluation procedure, independence of decisions of the subjects of the experiment, physical conditions for the subjects, time of year for the decision, order of presentation of subjects, order of presentation of information regarding applicants, and the motivation of the subjects.

PROCEDURES

Descriptive and visual teacher selection materials prepared for use in the study included: (a) instructional materials for describing the hypothetical situation for which the applicants were considered (these included a synchronized slide-tape presentation plus a programmed text), (b) audio and audiovisual materials for simulating teacher interviews (color films and the sound track from the films), (c) written documents (transcripts, credentials, etc.) needed for describing fictitious teacher applicants, (d) materials for presenting instructions on how to process information (concise instructions and a short criterion test were given), and (e) a response device for completion by the subjects.

Fictitious applicants were created for the simulation of teacher selection. An attempt was made to create applicants whose personalities, characteristics, and experiences were distinct, yet similar enough to require a rather fine degree of discrimination to note the distinctions among them. The five factors of teacher behavior (for elementary teachers) identified by Ryans in the Teacher Characteristics Study[10] were used for dimensions around which to build the applicants' personalities. These factors can be identified by their first order dimensions as: (a) originality, (b) organization, (c) empathy, (d) sociability, and (e) buoyancy. The five factors were varied among the fictitious applicants in such a way that the personality of each applicant was obviously high on one factor. Two other factors were less obvious (but present), and two others were not evident.

The individuals used to portray the fictitious applicants in the filmed interviews were selected from University of Washington education majors. The actresses were selected on the basis of the extent to which they "fit" one of the fictitious applicants whose traits they would display on the filmed interviews. Scripts were prepared to exhibit the designated characteristics, and the scripts were learned and rehearsed until a natural aura pervaded the interview. Information in the documents provided to the subjects was complementary to the interview information in that it portrayed the same characteristics.

The subjects used for this study were selected from three counties in the state of Washington. Districts were randomly chosen from these three counties, and the first nine were asked to participate. Since these districts had slightly more than the number of principals needed for the study, 144 were randomly chosen and randomly assigned by groups of four to each of the 36 treatments. The design was a completely randomized 2 x 2 x 3 x 3 fixed model treatment arrangement with measures on all four of the dependent variables. Table 2-1 shows the variables involved in the study and the levels of the independent variables. It should be noted here that, although the design included four dependent variables, the analysis consisted of separate analyses of variance for each dependent variable rather than a single multivariate analysis of variance.

All subjects in the experiment were first given information via slides, tape, and programmed instruction describing the hypothetical situation in which selection decisions were to be made. Characteristics of the community, school district, school, and vacancy were

TABLE 2-1. Variables involved in the study

Independent variables		Dependent variables
Variables	Levels	
1. Instruction	a. Instruction	1. Time (total time taken)
	b. No instruction	2. Discrimination (by groupings, and
2. Documents	a. Multiple	by estimated consequences)
	b. Single	3. Certainty (regarding ranking, and
3. Masking	a. Considerable	regarding estimated conse-
	b. Partial	quences)
	c. None	4. Consistency (regarding ranking,
4. Interview	a. Audiovisual	regarding estimated conse-
	(filmed)	quences
	b. Audio (tape	
	recorded)	
	c. None	

described. The purpose of providing a complete description of the hypothetical situation was to: (a) remove the subjects from their own situation and place them in a controlled situation; and (b) allow the subjects to determine criteria appropriate for selection in the given situation.

The general experimental task performed by each subject was to examine eight fictitious applicants for a hypothetical teaching position and make decisions regarding the appropriateness of each applicant for the position. Each subject was asked to: (a) estimate how each applicant would be evaluated on a Teacher Evaluation Instrument (TEI) at the end of one year of teaching, (b) rank order the eight applicants according to their desirability for the hypothetical position, (c) make a statement about the certainty of his judgments regarding the estimates on the TEI and the rank order by indicating how willing he would be to bet that his judgments were correct, and (d) group the eight applicants according to selected attributes or characteristics.

The above tasks were completed during the morning session of the experiment. For purposes of measuring the consistency of the decisions, a retest was administered in the afternoon in the following manner.

Five of the eight applicants presented in the first session were repeated in the afternoon session. These five applicants were made to appear different by modifying certain minor data, e.g., age, birthplace, height, and weight. Changes in makeup, hairpieces, and clothes altered appearances during the filmed interview. The other three applicants used during the first session were decoys and were replaced by considerably different applicants during the afternoon session. The decoys appeared late in the order of presentation in the first session and early in the second session to aid in forming the impression that the second set was an entirely new set of applicants. It was assumed that the insertion of the decoys did not affect the decisions regarding the five applicants on whom repeated measures were taken.

On completion of the experiment, the following information was available on each subject:

1. Time required for each subject to complete the decision (T).

2. A ranking of the five applicants in set one (R1) and set two (R2).

3. A measure of certainty regarding the ranking (C1).

4. An estimate of consequences of selecting each of the five applicants in set one (E1) and in set two (E2).

5. A measure of the subjects on selected characteristics (G).

The data for time needed to complete the decisions were examined, and it was determined that it was not necessary to transform the data prior to analysis. An analysis of variance (ANOVA) for the 2x2x3x3 factorial experiment was completed for the main and interaction effects of the four independent variables.

Separate ANOVA's were completed for each certainty measure, testing for both main and interaction effects.

Prior to using an ANOVA for determining the consistency of the decisions of the subjects, some derived scores were computed. First, a correlation was computed between R1 and R2 for each subject. These correlations were transformed by Fisher's r to z transformation and the z scores used for the ANOVA. This analysis allowed statements to be made regarding the effects of the independent variables on the consistency of the decisions regarding the rankings of teacher applicants.

Another analysis of consistency was made by computing a correlation between E1 and E2 for each subject, transforming the rs to z scores and using the resultant z scores for the ANOVA. This permitted statements regarding the effects of the treatment variables on the consistency of the decisions regarding estimations of consequences.

To determine the ability of a subject to discriminate finely among applicants, the groupings of the teacher applicants on the selected attributes (G) were used. If one subject grouped the eight applicants into eight groups on a given attribute, e.g., scholarship, and another subject used three groups, then the first subject was considered to discriminate more finely. The average number of groupings on the attributes selected was used as a discrimination score for an ANOVA of the effects of the independent variables on fineness of discrimination.

A second measure of discrimination was obtained by computing the variance of the 16 applicant scores on each item of the TEI. The mean of these variances (i.e., $\Sigma s_i^2/Q$, where s_i^2 $[i = 1, \ldots, Q]$ is the variance of the 16 applicant scores on the ith item and Q represents the number of items on the TEI) was used as a discrimination score; the greater the variance, the more discriminating the individual; the smaller the variance, the less discriminating the individual. The discrimination scores were then used in the ANOVA, and tests of significance were made for the main and interaction effects.

Several post analyses were made of the data. Where means were compared, orthogonal comparisons were made by a Newman-Keuls test. Also an orthogonal comparison was made of an interaction effect. On one interaction effect where it was desirable to make comparisons that were not orthogonal, Scheffé's test was used.

RESULTS

The analyses of variance for the experiment are presented in Table 2-2. Since each analysis included the same independent variables, the sources of variation are the same for all seven analyses. Table 2-2 indicates results that were significant at the .05 and .01 levels.

It will be noted in Table 2-2 that 105 F tests were computed. Where such a large number of tests were computed, the reader should be aware of the possibility that some of these apparently significant Fs may have occurred by chance. This experiment needs to be replicated to fully confirm these results. The most suspect are the interactions that occurred at the .05 level. Accounting for 30 of the

TABLE 2-2. Results of seven 2x2x3x3 analyses of variance for four dependent variables[a]

			Dependent variables					
			Discrimination		Certainty		Consistency	
Source of variation	df	Time	Group-ing	Est. cons.	Rank-ing	Est. cons.	Rank-ing	Est. cons.
I: Instructions	1	.01						
D: Documents	1	.05			.05			
M: Masking	2	.01			.05			
A: Interviews	2	.01			.01	.01	.05	
I x D	1	.05			.05			
I x M	2							
I x A	2							
D x M	2							.05
D x A	2						.05	
M x A	4							
I x D x M	2							
I x D x A	2							
I x M x A	4							
D x M x A	4							
I x D x M x A	4				.05			
Within cells	108							
Total	143							

[a]Table entries are maximum probabilities

nonsignificant Fs were the "grouping" measure of discrimination and the "ranking" measure of consistency. The former proved to have such a small variance (less than .5 where the average number of groups was slightly less than three) that there was very little possibility for significant differences. The latter measure, conversely, had so much within cell variance (probably due to the fact that the rs were computed on such a small n) that no significant differences occurred. One further comment might be made regarding the interactions. No attempt was made to interpret the four-way interaction found, partly due to the fact that it was at the .05 level and partly because of the extreme difficulty of interpretation.

Instruction on how to process information, under these experimental conditions, reduced the amount of time it took to make decisions. Instructions also interacted with documents by reducing the time for multiple documents and by increasing the discrimination of the subjects' estimates on the TEI. (See Figure 2-1 and Figure 2-2.)

Therefore, regardless of the format of the information, there would be a time benefit from giving information-processing instructions to principals who are engaged in the selection of teachers. However, increased discrimination would result from instructions

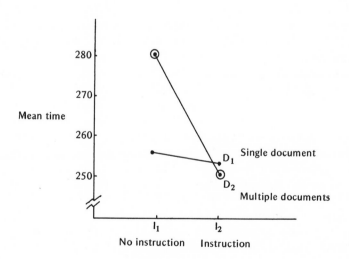

Figure 2-1
The interaction effect of instruction (I)
and documents (D) on time

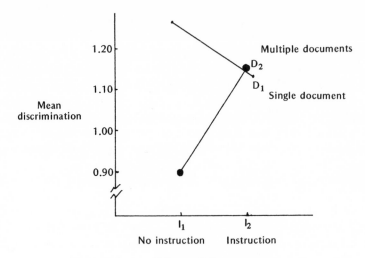

Figure 2-2
The interaction effect of instruction (I)
and documents (D) on discrimination,
as measured by variance of estimates
on the Teacher Evaluation Instrument

only where multiple documents were used (which happens to be the more normal procedure at present although the advantages of the single document are indicated in the following section).

The single document reduced the time required to make decisions and increased the amount of discrimination in making estimates on the TEI. However, documents interacted with interview information by depressing the certainty of estimates on the TEI for the audio interview information obtained by the multiple document treatment. See Figure 2-3 for a plotting of this interaction.

Documents also interacted with the masking information as far as consistency was concerned in estimation on the TEI. See Figure 2-4 for a plotting of this interaction. This interaction may be due to chance since no main effects or other interactions were significant for the 15 F tests computed for this ANOVA. When multiple documents were used, the most consistency was obtained with considerable masking; when the single document was used, it yielded the most consistency with no masking. These results appear to be compatible with a general notion that too much information (or information in an unmanageable form) is confusing and precipitates incon-

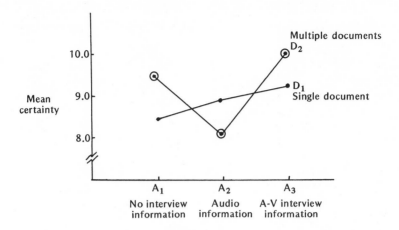

Figure 2-3
The interaction effect of interview information (A)
and documents (D) on certainty of estimates
on the Teacher Evaluation Instrument

sistent responses, while too little information precipitates random behavior.

The main effects of the document variable indicate the advantages of the single document for saving of time and for increasing the discrimination of decision makers. The interaction effect with the interview information is difficult to explain, but since it is primarily concerned with the relationship of the multiple documents with audio information (a case which is not commonly used and is not recommended as part of the optimum information format), this should not cause concern. The interaction between documents and masking, although quite possibly due to chance, points to a potential advantage of the single document (or of masking, if multiple documents were used) as far as consistency is concerned.

The degree of masking of information had a main effect of reducing the time needed to make decisions and of decreasing the discriminations made in the estimates of consequences on the TEI. Also, as indicated in the prior section, masking reduced the consistency of the single document.

An increased amount of masking provided the advantage of saving time; however, the increased masking reduced discrimination. Of the two of these effects, discrimination is probably more important as

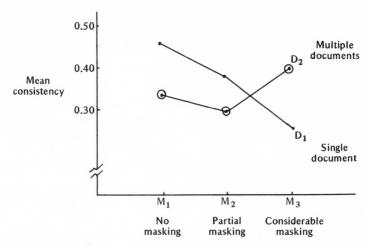

Figure 2-4
The interaction effect of masking (M) and documents (D)
on consistency of estimates
on the Teacher Evaluation Instrument

far as risk and potential loss is concerned. As indicated above, the documents-masking interaction points to the advantages of either the single document with no masking or of the multiple documents with masking of nonexceptional data.

The analysis of the effect of the interview information indicated that audiovisual and audio information increased the time needed to make decisions but increased the discrimination on the estimation of consequences on the TEI. In neither of these cases was there a significant difference between the results of the audiovisual and the audio treatments.

The results also indicate that there was more certainty expressed with the audiovisual information than with the audio on both measures of certainty, but only with the measure of certainty regarding the ranking of applicants was the mean certainty of the audiovisual greater than with no interview information. The interaction of interview information with documents (where certainty was measured by the estimation on the TEI) indicated that the audio information depressed the certainty scores with the multiple documents.

The main effects of the interview variable indicate that there are advantages to having audiovisual information as far as discrimination and feelings of certainty regarding decision making are concerned; however, there is a concomitant loss in time. The advantages of the main effects appear to outweigh the disadvantages of loss in time. The comparisons of the three types of information indicate that the only advantages of the audiovisual interview information over the audio interview information (on this set of dependent variables) is in the relatively higher feelings of certainty. However, the interview-documents interaction indicates a relative disadvantage to audio interview information presented in combination with multiple documents.

DISCUSSION OF THE RESULTS

The implications of the results of this research project for practice in the selection of teachers are as follows. If principals or personnel directors involved in selection of teachers are of a similar nature to the subjects used in this study, their decisions regarding the selection of teachers will be affected by the format of information about applicants. Further, one would expect that the format which would yield optimum results (as far as time, discrimination, consistency, and certainty are concerned) would consist of the format found optimum in this study, *viz.,* instructions regarding the processing of information, a single summary document, no masking of information, and interviews that include visual as well as audio stimuli.

Although the changed format is recommended on the basis of the statistically significant differences that were found in the experiment, one might reasonably raise the question regarding the practical significance of the new format. The analysis of the data with respect to such a question is not nearly as clear as the statistical comparisons of treatments.

An analysis of marginal means does provide some information for this question, however. Differences between marginal means of categories within each variable could be considered as a percentage of the present practice or as a percentage of the grand mean. Table 2-3 illustrates this analysis for the time variable, and provides the following information:

1. The difference in marginal means for the two categories of the instruction variable is 18.2 minutes.
2. This 18-minute period represents a gain of 6.8 percent time, if considered as a percentage of the present practice, i.e., no instruction. As a percentage of the grand mean, it represents a 7.0 percent gain. Note that there is a very slight difference in these two percentages.

TABLE 2-3. Practical significance of the optimum recommended format analysis of marginal means on time variable

	t	d	d/p	d/m	t	g	g/p	g/m
			(percent)				(percent)	
No instruction (p)	268.1	18.2	6.8	7.0				
Instruction	249.9							
Single document	253.0	12.0	4.6	4.7				
Multiple documents (p)	265.0							
No masking (p)					271.5	23.9	9.2	9.2
Partial masking					257.8			
Considerable masking					247.6			
No interview					219.1	55.0	25.1	21.2
Audio interview					283.8			
A-V interview (p)					274.1			
Totals		30.2	11.3	11.7		78.9	28.9	30.5

t amount of time
d difference between recommended category and present practice
d/p ratio of d to present practice
d/m ratio of d to grand mean
g potential gain if *Time* is considered as only dependent variable
g/p ratio of g to present practice
g/m ratio of g to grand mean
Grand mean time = 259.0

3. The percentage gains in time for the document variable are 4.6 percent and 4.7 percent.
4. The change in format represented by the instruction and single document variables would mean a gain in time of 11.3 percent −11.7 percent, depending on which ratio is used.
5. Had time been the only dependent variable, there would have been a different format recommended, since masking required less time than no masking and since no interview required less time than either type of interview. However, because the results with the other dependent variables necessitated the recommendation of no masking and audiovisual (or audio) interviews, Table 2-3 shows only the potential gain that would have occurred if time had been the only dependent variable. In effect, this indicates the significance of the masking and interview variables (i.e., the reason they were included in the design as variables that might potentially influence the depen-

dent variables), while at the same time it demonstrates the potency of the design which uses multiple dependent variables. Had there not been the inclusion of the other dependent variables, and the necessity to find a format that was optimum for all of these variables, then considerably more time could have been saved.

6. As noted in Table 2-3, there was a potential gain of approximately 30 percent through the use of considerable masking and no interviews. The reader is reminded, however, that the use of masking and no interviews would seriously affect the discrimination and feelings of certainty.

The analysis of marginal means of the discrimination variable indicated the following:

1. The increased discrimination due to the single document represented a gain of approximately 14 percent.
2. The potential loss if considerable masking and no interviews had been used would have been approximately 50 percent.

The analysis of marginal means of the certainty variable indicated that there would have been a potential loss of approximately 15 percent if audio interviews had been used. Strangely, there would have been only a 9 percent loss of certainty had no interviews been used. These results suggest the need to investigate why the subjects felt more uncertain with audio interviews than with no interview information.

The analysis of marginal means of the consistency variable indicated that the single document with no masking was approximately 30 percent more consistent than the multiple document with no masking.

These analyses of marginal means give an indication of the percentage gain, but provide no information about the amount of overlap of the distributions represented by the marginal means. Such an analysis would simply compare the differences in the marginal means with the standard deviations of the distribution (in this case, the square root of the mean square within). This analysis was made and can be summarized as follows. The differences in marginal means were all less than one *s.d.*, except in the case where the potential gain due to no interview was considered (approximately 1½ *s.d.*). One must conclude that there was considerable overlap of the distributions and that the percentage gains cited represent average gains.

The results of this study support Miller's proposal for grouping data in a manageable form for making judgments,[11] in that the single document was found to have advantages; however, masking proved nonbeneficial when the single document was used. The short instructions also proved beneficial, supporting the studies in industry reported by Drake.[12] The results regarding interview information extend the work of Springbett, Barrett, and Giedt[13] to the area of selection in education.

IMPLICATIONS OF THE MATERIALS DEVELOPED

The implications of this research project, resulting from the materials developed, are considerable in relation to increasing the knowledge of decision-making processes. An optimum information format will allow experiments to be conducted in a simulated situation without fear that the results will be adversely affected by the manner of presenting information to subjects. This experiment, then, was necessary in order to utilize the simulated situation for testing hypotheses regarding certain elements of decision theory. For example, if one wants to describe the decision-making behavior of a particular individual (or a set of individuals), or if one desires to prescribe a manner in which a decision maker might behave more effectively, it is necessary to determine both: (a) the manner in which he predicts consequences, or at least what consequences he predicts, and (b) the value system he uses in the final choice. But how can the prediction of consequences be separated from the values attached to them? How does one know, by observing the choice of a particular alternative, whether the choice was made on the basis of a high prediction of consequences and a low value, or the reverse, or both a high prediction of consequences and a high value?

Interest in value systems has led students of decision making to devise descriptive and prescriptive decision-making models. One intent of these models is to assist people in making the consequences they predict and the values attached to them explicit, yet little work has been done to accomplish this intent.

One approach to the description of the decision-making process might be to place subjects in a precisely described choice situation in which the consequences can be accurately determined and known by the subject. For example, a betting situation in which the odds are known—as in coin flipping, rolling dice, or choosing combinations from a deck of cards—might be used. Subjects could be taught the probabilities of the alternatives chosen, i.e., the types of bets they made. However, such an approach would leave much to be desired because prediction of consequences would have been controlled, in a sense. Therefore, one could only infer that differences in behavior were due to differences in value systems rather than the way consequences were predicted. Inability to determine concomitantly the subject's manner of predicting consequences and his value system is a limitation in this situation; such a limitation might elicit behavior considerably different from behavior in a less-restricted decision situation.

An approach from which broader generalizations might be made is one in which the situation is described, but the decision maker must make choices on the basis of his own prediction of consequences and attachment of values to these consequences. An example is the simulated teacher selection situation described in this report. In this decision situation, subjects are not taught probabilities of consequences of choosing certain teacher applicants, but must make estimates of what will occur if each teacher is hired. In addition, they must make choices among the teachers. The estimates of what will occur when a teacher is hired become the subject's explicit expression of probable consequences, and the value system of the subject is implied by this expression and his choices among teachers.

The materials used to simulate the decision-making process for selecting teachers, then, provide a setting whereby descriptive and prescriptive theories of decision making may be tested. In addition, other variabes that have been controlled in this experiment—especially those dealing with situational factors and interview information—can be manipulated in future experiments to determine their contribution to decision making. The results of this project, in addition to providing some recommendations for the practices of selecting teachers, make possible the control of a very important variable (the format of information) in future studies of the decision-making process.

Notes

This research was supported by the U.S. Office of Education, Grant No. OEC 4-7-061349-0266, "Variables Affecting Decision Making in the Selection of Teachers." Director: Dale L. Bolton.

1. George Miller, "The Magical Number Seven, Plus or Minus Two: Some Limits on Our Capacity for Processing Information," *Psychological Review*, LXIII (1956), 81-97.

2. B.M. Springbett, "Factors Affecting the Final Decision in the Employment Interview," *Canadian Journal of Psychology*, XII (1958), 13-22.

3. R.S. Barrett, "The Process of Predicting Job Performance," *Personnel Psychology*, XI (Spring 1958), 39-55.

4. Harold F. Giedt, "Comparison of Visual, Content, and Auditory Cues in Interviewing," *Journal of Consulting Psychology*, XIX (1955), 407-16.

5. Daniel Sydiaha, "Interviewer Consistency in the Use of Empathic Models in Personnel Selection," *Journal of Applied Psychology*, XLVI (October 1962), 344-49.

6. Harold G. Levine and C. McGuire, "Role Playing as an Evaluative Technique," *Journal of Educational Measurement*, V (Spring 1968), 1-8.

7. Frances S. Drake, "The Interviewer and His Art," in Robert E. Finley (ed.), *The Personnel Man and His Job* (New York: American Management Association, Inc., 1962).

8. A number of sources have described the use of electronic data processing for personnel work in industry, e.g., Paul Duke, "Personnel Records: Along the Road to Automation," *Personnel*, XXXVI (May-June 1959), 31-40; S.O. Parsons and W.B.Wait, "Automation and Personnel Inventory," *Personnel Journal*, XXXVIII (April 1960), 413-17; E.D. Phelps and W. Gallagher, "Integrated Approach to Technical Staffing," *Harvard Business Review*, XLI (July-August 1963), 122-29. Perry M. Kalick gave a brief description of data processing in teacher selection ("Teacher Selection Methods in Sixty-two School Systems Affiliated with the Metropolitan School Study Council," which was a part of "Teacher Selection Methods," Government Report, U.S.O.E. Project No. 6-1665, Grant No. OEG 1-6-061665-1624, June 1967, p. 119.

9. Saul W. Gellerman ("Personnel Testing: What the Critics Overlook," *Personnel*, XL (May-June 1963), 23) presented a very clear argument for the view that there is no such thing as general validity for any test; its usefulness as a selection instrument has to be proven for every job of every company in which it is used, and periodically reproven, as well. The argument for multivariate data is straightforward. Many authors have made similar comments regarding the need to situationally define criterion variables in education, for example, see David G. Ryans, "Problems in Validating Teacher Selection Policies and Procedures," which was a part of "Teacher Selection Methods," Government Report, U.S.O.E. Project No. 6-1665, Grant No. OEG 1-6-061665-1624, June 1967, pp. 81ff.

10. David G. Ryans, *Characteristics of Teachers* (Washington, D.C.: American Council on Education, 1960).

11. Miller, "Magical Number Seven."

12. Drake, "The Interviewer and His Art," p. 130.

13. Springbett, "Factors Affecting the Final Decision in the Employment Interview"; Barrett, "Process of Predicting Job Performance"; Giedt, "Comparison of Visual, Content, and Auditory Cues in Interviewing."

COMMENT / The Teacher Selection Process in Practice

Carroll L. Lang

I have difficulty in confining my comments on the selection of teachers to the various information formats in the teacher selection process. The reason is, simply, that I have employed teachers for many teaching fields, for many kinds of assignments, under different kinds of time constraints, and during a time in history when there was a critical shortage of teachers. My problem was largely one of recruitment rather than selection. Conditions today are quite different, yet Bolton's study was made just at the end of the teacher shortage era. In spite of this limitation, the significance of selection was always foremost in my mind, and I make only a few apologies for the thousands of teachers I have recommended for employment during the years with the aid of principals and others associated with this responsibility.

While Bolton's article is a scholarly bit of research, it fails to consider one of the most significant variables in the selection process, namely that of assignment. The practitioner always keeps in his mind the ultimate placement of the teacher, for a teacher may be an outstanding success in one situation and a near failure in another regardless of the kinds and quality of information formats available for decision making.

This statement is supported by Kenneth Eugene Underwood ("An Analysis of Letters of Recommendation" [Ph.D. diss., Indiana University, Bloomington, 1961]). He identified twenty-five teachers most likely to be successful in the classroom and twenty-five least likely to be successful. These fifty new teachers were selected from a population of 1,200. Two years later he compared the evaluation reports of the two groups and found that the ones he predicted would become outstanding teachers did, as a group, perform better, but there was a large amount of overlap. That is, many in the lower group performed far better than had been predicted even for the top group. His conclusion was that placement is almost as important, if not as important, as predicted competence. A poor placement, then, may reduce the effectiveness of a good teacher.

My experience confirms the Underwood study. Early in the employment season offers of employment were sent to prospective applicants before principals had an opportunity to know their staff needs for the coming year. Once these offers were accepted, it became necessary to assign the teachers. Principals having vacancies were invited to come to the personnel office to review references. They could phone the applicant or those who wrote references for him, and they had access to the interview notes before making a decision.

One principal would spend hours reviewing references prior to making a decision yet was never at peace with the decision made; nor was the teacher eventually selected excited about the assignment. Another principal said he did not have time to come in and read the references; he trusted the decisions made in the personnel office. Teachers assigned to this principal were without exception pleased with their school and the principal was pleased with them.

This observation verifies a principle that people perform in proportion to the level of expectation one has for them. If we treat a person as he is, we demean him. If we treat him as we expect him to become, we ennoble him.

Bolton reports early in his study that teacher selection decisions are frequently intuitive and arbitrary and that the teacher selection process is highly subjective. I concur. He also believes that being subjective is not all bad when all constraints are considered and not just the ones identified in this report.

The Bolton study considered the following dependent variables, even though more exist in a real situation:
a. Amount of time needed to make decision.
b. Fineness of discrimination made.
c. Feelings of certainty regarding decisions.
d. Consistency in estimating decision outcomes.

He found it necessary to simulate an educational situation in order to manipulate and control variables. This was a reasonable design. The four variables manipulated were:

a. Amount of instruction on how to process information (two levels: instruction and no instruction).
b. Number of written documents presented (two levels: multiple and single).
c. Degree of masking information (three levels: considerable, partial, none).
d. Interview information (three levels: filmed, tape-recorded audio, none).

I find it difficult to respond to these variables for those concerned with the selection process vary in their skills of personnel appraisal perhaps as much as the variables mentioned. Expressed in other terms, the experiences of those reacting to the variables may effect the outcome of the study as much as the four variables under study, the training period notwithstanding. Again, reference must be made to assignment, for teachers must become a functional part of a staff; they cannot be considered as independent persons working in isolation and with clients having universally accepted value systems.

The second variable, the number of written documents, omits some significant considerations: How comprehensive is the single document? Who wrote it? What training and experience enabled the author to prepare a meaningful document? Within what framework was the information presented? Other questions could be raised. Again, pages of references or complete files from placement offices may contain little information of use to the selection committee. A good reader of references has developed a knack of reading between the lines, and some placement offices have completely open files, affording no confidential information. Frequently, references are opinion based rather than criteria based, and some data may be of value in consideration for one assignment and not for another. Bolton does not elaborate on the kinds or the content of written data and, for this reason, caution must be used in reacting to his work. I believe that some written information may be useful in the selection process, but the kind of data that is useful varies with the situation. Scholarship might be an example. When employing a person to teach a gifted class, academic history and achievement are probably more significant than they would be for an average class. Leadership styles, expectations for creativity or conformity, and extent of supervision experienced or anticipated may also vary with the situation. I have found that much information submitted on behalf of an applicant is useless unless the author of the information identifies the framework within which he is making his comments. This is also not considered in the Bolton report.

Bolton's description of masking information was interesting and effective. The practitioner views masking from another perspective. Too commonly both the applicant and the person or committee making the selection "wear masks." Another way of expressing this is that the presence or absence of a bit of information may influence a decision significantly. Obviously, when such significant information is masked, the outcome may be altered. The intent of a good selection process is to get at all of the relevant facts, to penetrate all masks worn by participants and the selection committee, and those appearing in the records. Bolton's use of masking could be included in a training program.

The decision-making process for the selection of teachers merits serious study. It will vary with the district and with the principals in a given organization. Whether we like it or not, it is politically expedient to consider certain local community mores. In theory one always wants to select the best applicant available. This is thoroughly defensible, but who describes what is "best" and who will be responsible for the selection? These are the questions the practitioner must ask. Equally important, is the selection to be made to meet immediate needs, or is it to have long-range significance?

Given below are some considerations that a practitioner sees in the selection process.

1. *The teaching job should be carefully defined.* As professionals we have been most casual about defining job responsibilities. Typically, we have been satisfied with describing the job as a third-grade position at a certain school. Supportive data about the socio-economic level of the clientele, its mobility, or its achievements, or the goals of the school or district are frequently unavailable.

I believe that teachers perform in six roles: (a) directors of learning, (b) counselors and advisers, (c) links with the community, (d) mediators of the culture, (e) members of a staff, and (f) members of a profession. Teachers should be advised of their responsibility within each of these roles, and know that evaluations will be based on these criteria. Such data may and should be obtained during the student teaching experience.

2. *The responsibility for selection should be clearly defined.* Committee and even community participation in the selection process is a current reality. When such persons are significantly involved in the selection process, responsibility is centered more in estab-

lishing a process and adhering to it than in making fine discriminations in professional competence. Expressed in other terms, persons who participate in personnel selection on a casual basis only are more likely to be influenced by superficial characteristics (such as appearance, conversation, ability) than by substantive and conceptual understanding of the role of the teacher and related concerns. The issue is not clear-cut, and this poses one of the problems of selection. If a principal or a committee from the school selects the teacher, they will try to make that teacher successful. Under such conditions, even a modest teacher may obtain excellent evaluations, for no other reason than to justify the individual or group decision. If, however, an unrelated individual or group makes the selection, there might be a reluctance to accept the fact that the judgment of teaching competence was not good. This places even the best teacher in a precarious position.

3. *Local conditions must be taken into account in the selection process.* Across the country there are requests for more black, Mexican-American, and other minority teachers. In many instances these requests are valid, but all too frequently there is an inadequate supply of such teachers. Selection committees must then determine how important it is to have minority teachers on the staff. On other occasions a school may have too many teachers from a given religious group or training institution or an unbalanced age distribution. On one occasion I placed a charming single teacher in a small school where the teachers were all married and had families. The young teacher left in midyear because she never felt a part of the group.

Variables in the selection process are numerous. While one may control variables in a laboratory situation, this is impossible in a real situation. Additional variables may enter the decision-making process of the practitioner.

It may be heresy, but we still have very little data to show that students learn more from one teacher than another. Coleman, for example, found that the quality of the child's home affects his learning more than the teacher. The new movement toward performance objectives, accompanied by levels of cognitive knowledge and levels in the affective domain and a concern for evaluation of process and product, may ultimately provide information that will materially assist in the selection process.

The current level of the act of selection is not highly developed. One reason is that we have not too clearly defined the role and expectations of the teacher; nor have we determined how we are to measure or evaluate them. We have not really assessed the out-of-school influence on the learner in the classroom or how the teacher is able to cope with it, either, and this also has implications for teacher selection, as does the fact that some teachers receive more support from the community than others. Bolton has made a contribution to the literature, but the practitioner needs more information than just the four variables involved in the study.

Few practitioners will read Bolton's work at the application and evaluation level of understanding. Perhaps this is a reflection upon the training of the practitioner; yet this is also a reality for the moment.

3 / A Perceptual Taxonomy of the Effective-Rated Teacher

Alan F. Brown

The intent of this paper is to show that:

1. Perceptual systems of school administrators are amenable to measurement, in terms of both (a) form, and (b) content,
2. Principals exhibit differences between those teacher behaviors they tend to notice and those they value (value is throughout used in the restricted sense of worth on the job, i.e., effectiveness),
3. Administrator's perceptions of teachers project the value systems of school administrators, and
4. Through their perceptions of teachers, administrators belie their own leadership styles, particularly with respect to system-centeredness and individual-centeredness.

Those four statements could have been called hypotheses. In the present context, they serve to spell out the otherwise diffuse but persistent purposes of this part of an ongoing study of the interpersonal perceptions of public school administrators.

PROJECTIONS AND PERCEPTIONS

In planning the attack on the foregoing hypotheses, the question one asks is, "How important, if at all, are the characteristics, if

Reprinted from *The Journal of Experimental Education*, XXXV (No. 1, Fall 1966), 1-10.

identifiable, of the perceptual systems, if any, used by school administrators, if ever?" Those four ifs suggested the research design.

Two decisions appeared early to become obvious. 1) Only some sort of projective tool with a reasonably ambiguous stimulus would elicit the kind of information to satisfy the ifs. One cannot discover a principal's perception of the effective-rated teacher simply by asking him. He will tell you, of course, but what he will tell you may be as vaporous as the typical set of aims of education, or he will repeat to you the value statements sanctioned by the system though not internalized by himself—probably first enunciated by his superintendent or professional development committee. 2) Since there is no more important single activity of an administrator than making personnel decisions, it was decided that one special form of this activity, that of personnel judgments, would form the base—though not the continuing focus—of the instrument.

We all tend to develop ways of trying to make some sense out of our interpersonal world. We form our own ways of distinguishing between persons, and of organizing our ideas about persons. Your way of perceiving others may differ from mine; that makes us two people and not one. It is a most human pastime, and one that, short of prejudicial discrimination, is for most of us quite harmless.

Therefore, much of this paper could be passed off as parlor games, except for the fact of that peculiar breed of educator known as the administrator. This man, whether known as a superintendent, director, supervisor, inspector, principal, or consultant, by the nature of his work is paid to make interindividual discriminations. He cannot escape it. Not only must he discriminate in a general way among several staff members, but also must he discern the particular strengths and the needs of individual teachers. In a recent textbook on administration interpersonal perceptions are considered crucial enough to have the first page of text open with this inclusion:

> Literally hundreds of times during the day, the administrator is perceived and his behaviour interpreted by the people around him. He, in turn, perceives others and interprets their behaviour. This perceiving is not usually a slow and deliberate process of observation. Often, such activities are fleeting and barely conscious but they help to make up the human atmosphere in which the person lives and functions and moreover, are crucial for administrative success.[1]

Similarly Lipham's[2] critique of administrative behavior research points specifically to the "dynamic variables of . . . selective interpersonal perception" as requiring considerable research and theoretical development during the years ahead.

One of the reasons why the administrator must be fairly discriminating in his interpersonal perceptions is because he makes what may be called personnel judgments: that is, judgments as to the relative effectiveness, or worth to the school system, of individual teachers. Elsewhere we have reported research indicating the sometimes startling but possibly predictable effects upon a teacher's output when she is appraised of such ratings;[3] here our attention may be said to center upon the evaluative process itself.

TO REVEAL A REPERTORY OF
DISCRIMINANT PERCEPTIONS

One of the purposes of the instrument, therefore, is to elicit from each subject a sample of the perceptions he characteristically uses when contemplating the individual differences among his professional associates. Another is to weigh each of these perceptions according to their relative importance to our subject's personnel judgments (i.e., importance to his implicit definition of the effective teacher).

The instrument is called the Discriminant Perception Repertory Test (DPRT) because it tries to elicit a subject's repertory of interpersonal perceptions in a form that permits their discriminating power to be tested. Its historical antecedents may be traced somewhat deviously to G.A. Kelly's Role Construct Repertory Test developed in his two volume work, *The Psychology of Personal Constructs*[4] and followed up in various forms by other writers, notably James Bieri.[5] Our Discriminant Perception Repertory Test developed here consists of (a) a grid six squares wide and eighteen deep, (b) eighteen write-in spaces, (c) six rating scales, and (d) an overlay sheet containing instructions. Administered in group, it takes about fifty minutes to complete.

Instructions ask the subject to identify on the overlay, which is not turned in, the three teachers at his school whom he considers— using his own criteria—to be the best or most effective teachers, and those he considers to be the three weakest or least effective teachers. In this phase the subject is forming personnel judgments. On the test these six teachers are represented simply by the letters A, B, C, D, E, and F, respectively. The subject is then asked successively to consider these persons, taken only three at a time, and to decide in what important way two of them are sufficiently alike to differentiate them from the third, and to write down each successive differentiating factor on the lines provided: one for each sort. There are twenty possible combinations of six persons considered only three at one sort. Combinations ABC (all effective) and DEF (all ineffective) are omitted. In this manner is formed a series of eighteen modes of perceiving others which, as a total picture, is assumed to be relatively characteristic of the subject. We head this list "Distinguishing Characteristics" on the test. No restrictions are imposed: characteristics may be repeated and have much or little to do with the teaching act. Here is the list of eighteen discriminant characteristics found on one subject's protocol in his words: considerate toward pupils, suspicious of others' actions, frequent lengthy detentions, conservative, lacks discipline in classroom, personally sensitive, greater expectancy of student improvement, interested in students as people, awareness of larger institutional goals, appearance, speech, less outspoken, sincerity with others, knowledge of subjects taught, formal training, rather quiet and withdrawing, experience, work. Note that just from inspection there would seem to be about three or four general factors underlying this man's eighteen-item repertory: we would take this pattern of perceptual modes to characterize this subject.

Finally, the subject completes an eighteen-item descriptive rating scale on each teacher in turn: ABCDE and F. For descriptive items, he simply uses the eighteen discriminating characteristics already entered in appropriate spaces and signified that he strongly agrees, agrees, disagrees, or strongly disagrees, that each successive item describes the person in question.

Scoring assigns weights of 4, 3, 2, 1 to the response categories. For each elicited item the "Discriminating Value" becomes the absolute difference between summed weights for ABC (effective-rated) and summed weights for DEF (ineffective-rated). For each subject, "Perceptual Discrimination" (PD) becomes the sum of his eighteen item-values. The "Discriminating Power" of an entire concept, such as "Stimulatingness," becomes the mean of the summed discriminating values of all items thereunder classified, across all protocols. For each subject, an estimate of the extent to which his own interpersonal perceptions were consistent and hung together, i.e., of his "Perceptual Integration" (PI), was the mean of the 163 intercorrelations yielded by his protocol.

From our earlier work on this instrument,[6] we would caution that perceptual discrimination and perceptual integration, although clearly representing two important properties of an administrator's perceptual system, are probably not polar concepts in the usual sense. That is, neither high nor low PI or PD scores, but rather those about midrange, seem "best" for a principal.

RELIABILITY AND VALIDITY

Our DPRT has produced a one-week test-retest reliability coefficient of .78. Measures of reliability based on internal comparisons (split-half and so on) would make no theoretical sense and accordingly, were not performed. Content validity is no doubt enhanced by the fact that all "items" are of the subject's own choosing; his wording—whatever you may read into it—is within his own perceptual field and therefore has meaning at least to himself. One estimate of a test's construct validity is the theoretical sense of its correlates; here the correlation of .74 between its two measures (PI and PD) makes sense. In a sense, the remainder of this paper may be interpreted as evidence of predictive validity, to distinguish between known groups.

PERCEPTUAL TAXONOMIES

Systems are built to be destroyed and taxonomies are assembled to become later torn apart. Those the writer shares with you are no exceptions. A taxonomy is just a special kind of system and taxonomic constructions follow a variety of methodologies. Ours classified under relatively few headings about 1,152 teacher-descriptions elicited from 64 principals. The classes were derived from content analysis of the descriptive words and phrases, that is, they are empirically derived. Certain criteria suggested themselves by the very nature of the material: e.g., *no* classification should be used

(a) which accounted for fewer than 8 percent of the statements in the total sample,

(b) which failed to discriminate between effective- and ineffective-rated teachers,

(c) which overlapped an existing classification, or

(d) which was not represented both positively and negatively, admitting of degrees along a continuum.

What administrators tended to perceive in teachers fell into four broad classes of teacher characteristics: 1) their pedagogy, 2) their orientations toward their job, 3) their interpersonal relations, and 4) their personality—in that order. Within each general class appeared two or more subclasses that, in dimensional form, admitted of degrees. The higher or more positive end of the scale, in each instance, represents to the administrator the greater degree of desirability in a teacher. The exception is the personality characteristics class, the subclasses of which are represented in frequencies too low to be defended as dimensions. Accordingly, "personality" is through-out used as a category although its dimensional nature resides actually in the nonused subclasses.

The subclasses that best account for our administrators' percep-tions of interpersonal differences between teachers, as well as approximately a dozen verbatim examples of the percepts that define each, are as follows:

Class A: Pedagogy

1. *Stimulatingness (STIM)*—lessons highly motivated, challenge pupils, stimulate pupils, dull and uninspiring, lack of ability to maintain interest, varied pace and varied approach, not so creative in teaching methods used, not so stereotyped in approach, inspire students, use of novelty and creativity, exciting use of visual aids, imagination, effective presentation of new material, paucity of illus-trated materials, drab,

2. *Organization (ORGA)*—effective planning, excellent routines, weak classroom routines, disorganized, classroom management good, lessons have an objective, precise units of daily [and] unit and long-range planning, superior organization, methodical and thorough in lesson planning, lack organizational ability,

3. *Discipline (DISC)*—good discipline, control, poor discipline, reasonably firm, consistent, too lenient, strict disciplinarians, forceful but unreasonable, permissiveness, oblivious to noise, expect a reasonable standard of behavior from children, master of the situa-tion with children,

4. *Knowledge of the Job (KNOW)*—university degree(s), know sub-ject, poor mastery of the subject field, no training in subject area, good qualifications, greater knowledge of teaching procedures, strong preparational background, ability to adapt instruction to age level, taken no courses lately,

Class B: Job Orientations

5. *Broad-Narrow Scope of the Job (SCOP)*—do realize goals in education, lack awareness of larger institutional goals, rigid concern for trivia, teach for the exam, enrichment, textbook orientation to course, willingness to experiment, afraid to try new methods [and] conservative, open minded, active in professional organization, extra-curricular interest in school as a whole,

6. *Positive—Negative Job Attitude (ATTI)*—well prepared, conscien-tious workers, lack drive [and] energy, show initiative and resource-fulness, are responsible and make sound decisions, accept responsi-bility, dependable, attend staff meeting, if given tasks will complete

them, teaching not taken seriously, flighty, do not feel need for self-improvement as teachers, discontented in jobs and complain about work frequently, job satisfaction [and] enjoy teaching, highly critical of administration, faith in administration to help,

Class C : Interpersonal Relations

7. *Consideration toward Others (CONS)*—sincerely interested in children, warm [and] interested in others, little ability in human relations, treat students with respect, attentive to individual differences, threatening [and] unkind, show hostility, real concern for problem children, knowledge of pupils' backgrounds, provide extra beyond-duty help to individual pupils,

8. *Rapport with Others (RAPP)*—rapport with colleagues [and] other teachers, get along well with other staff members, promote good staff morale, not liked by students, rapport with students, inclined to be critical of others on staff, inability to cooperate in staff groups, well liked by students, do not have cooperation of students, enjoy their confidence,

Class D: Personality Characteristics (PERS)

9. *Neuroticism*—emotionally stable, easily flustered, insecure, touchy or sensitive,

10. *Extra-Introversion*—sociable, very reserved, aloof, show enthusiasm, withdrawn,

11. *Dominance-Submissiveness*—dynamic [and] effective leaders, little leadership in school projects, forceful, authoritarian, dominant personality,

12. *Physical Appearance*—athletic type, neat and tidy, voice shrill or harsh,

Unclassed: Miscellaneous (MISC)

Children of their own, foreign to this country, intelligent, similar personal interests, teach the same subject or grade level, married, general statements such as "effective teacher" or opposite.

The above categories make up Table 3-1. Table 3-1, however can also provide the reader with data from which may be drawn inferences with respect to the relative importance, to the administrator, of each of his percepts. This is presented in two ways. First, Table 3-1 provides an estimate of an administrator's "Preoccupations" when asked to consider the similarities and differences among staff members; the estimate is the simple percept of all elicited items accounted for by any one of the ten perceptual dimensions. For example, number 6, *Job Attitude,* accounted for the largest number of items elicited. Since random expectation would suggest 10 or 11 percent per

TABLE 3-1. Classification of administrators' perceptions of teachers

General class		Preoccupation (percent mentions)	Discriminating power[a]
Class A	Pedagogy	35	54[b]
	a. Stimulatingness in teaching	9	61
	b. Organization	8	53
	c. Discipline	10	62
	d. Content and method knowledge	9	42
Class B	Job orientations	31	53
	a. Broad-narrow scope of the job	12	52
	b. Positive-negative job attitude	19	54
Class C	Interpersonal relations	17	48
	a. Consideration toward others	11	49
	b. Rapport with others	6	46
Class D	Personality characteristics	14	45
	a. Neuroticism		
	b. Extraversion-introversion		
	c. Dominance-submissiveness		
	d. Physical characteristics		
(unclassed)	Miscellaneous	3	37

[a]Power = mean discriminating value of all elicited percepts falling within each category. (A percept has "high" discriminating value when the difference between summed ratings on "effective" teachers and summed ratings on "ineffective" teachers is great.)

[b]Standard scores scaled to mean 50, standard deviation 10

dimension, number 6 suggests some indication of what is occupying any principal's perceptual system. Second, however, Table 3-1 includes a more useful index of the importance of the principals' perceptions in the column headed "Discriminating Power." As noted on the table, this is an estimate of the extent to which an administrator uses any particular concept to differentiate teachers whom he considers to be strong from those he finds weak.

We may never have any notion of the validity of an administrator's personnel judgments; nor may it ever be possible to elicit from him his actual criteria used in forming them. But, at least the principal is now able to tell us, projectively, the "correlates" of his personnel criteria. That is why we call this list, and the following tables, an "operational" taxonomy. It is not an armchair classification system; nor is it a classification of teacher-effectiveness criteria. It is simply a statistically organized list of notions that administrators use when mulling over the ins and outs of their personnel. But, because of their prior personnel judgment, this list is now operational in the sense that it suggests the power of each notion to "predict" his effectiveness criteria. For all we know, it may even be them. For example, though they mention Class D, *Personality*, 14 percent of the time (above the mean), this classification held an average discrimination value of 45 (below the mean), whereas, No. 3, descriptions of a teacher's *Discipline*, mentioned only 10 percent of the time, appears very highly associated with decisions as to her effectiveness (62, or 1.2 standard deviations above the mean).

And those in the faculties and schools of education take little solace from the fact that when administrators either commend or condemn a teacher's *Knowledge of the Job* (No. 4), they are not apt to confuse this notion with their judgment of the teacher's relative worth on the job.

A general observation at this point is that, of the four general classes—pedagogy, job orientation, interpersonal relations, and personality—the first two are the most closely allied with notions of teacher effectiveness. This is not surprising. Both are relatively task-oriented categories. Indeed, concepts of personality and interpersonal relations emerge as rather strong. What is more curious is that strictly pedagogical comments drew barely over one-third the total. Does this suggest administrators pay little attention to classroom practice? Or, perhaps, is it overt evidence finally that our subjects have accepted the changed role of the administrator from overseer of classroom practice to one holding a concern for the "whole teacher" as a person? Study of the research instrument itself would support the latter inference in that it permits the subject— through eighteen sorts—to see teachers as individuals. Its free choice leaves it unencumbered by pedagogical restrictiveness. All terms used herein are of the subjects' own choosing.

THE NOTICED AND THE VALUED

One of the hypotheses supposes that what principals tend most often to notice may not be the same as what they most highly value, when referring to teachers. Value, of course, is being here restricted to the sense of worth on the job or to the educational enterprise: i.e., effectiveness.

It would be possible to substantiate that directly by correlating the "Preoccupations" column and the "Discriminating Power" column in Table 3-1. This was in fact done with each of three subgroups separately in Table 3-3, but not with the whole lot. From what we know of the subgroup correlations, and can see by inspection, a low, positive, and probably nonsignificant correlation is indicated. What this seems to mean is that principals are not all of the time thinking about how good or bad a teacher is Mary Jones—whenever they are busy thinking of Mary Jones at all. A high correlation would conjure up visions of principals so goal-bound that teachers could only be considered in the same light.

PROJECTED VALUE SYSTEMS

The tendency of a person to disclose quite a lot about himself in his descriptions of others has been earlier established.[7] "Assimilative projection," it used to be called. In the present context, it would dictate that a principal and a teacher would tend to describe in different terms, and in a value system more akin each to his own, the overall characteristics of teachers.

Testing such a hypothesis with the Discriminant Perception Repertory Test is simply performed by using two samples, one of princi-

TABLE 3.2 Priorities in personnel judgments: Ten dimensions of teacher-behavior descriptions, ranked according to their power to discriminate between effective-rated and ineffective-rated teachers for three subgroups (N = 30)

Dimension	System-centered principal	Individual-centered principal	Teacher-prospect	Combined groups
Discipline	1	1	2	1
Stimulatingness	5	2.5	1	2
Job attitude	2	6	5	3
Organization	3	2.5	8	4
Scope	6	4	6	5
Consideration	8	8	3	6
Rapport	7	10	4	7
Personality	4	9	9	8
Knowledge of job	9	7	7	9
Miscellaneous	10	5	10	10

pals and one of teachers. The samples of principals was easy to obtain. All selected were supervising principals who are experienced men, judged by their superior numbers to be effective on the job and successful in the system. But for teachers we had to use a group who, though yet teachers, are due for first promotion imminently. Each of them has begun graduate work in administration and each is on his employer's active "Prospect List." That possibly slants their values differently from those of other teachers and perhaps to a point that is more akin to those of principals.

Even so, Table 3-2, which simply ranks the ten dimensions of teacher descriptions according to the discriminating values thereto attached by each subgroup, clearly differentiates principals from the teacher-prospects. The four categories ranking highest for the combined groups, included only two of the teachers' compared with three from each principal-group (similarly, three out of top five cf. four out of top five).

But, even more revealing, are the kinds of categories the teacher-prospect regards most closely with the "effective/ineffective teacher." He places the "Interpersonal Relations" categories (consideration, rapport) as third and fourth compared with seventh to tenth by the principals. Organization, on the other hand, ranks quite low (eighth, cf. third or second).

Turning from revelations of the teachers' values to those of the principals', one discovers that principals mainly want teachers to do a good job in the classroom and show a positive attitude toward the institution. ("Misc." is set aside for that inference).

But comparing relative priorities within the given set of categories tells only part of the story. The other part lies in studying the categories themselves. Consider two broad classes, "Interpersonal Relations" and "Job Orientations," into which comments fell with sufficient frequency and with sufficient discriminating power to require their inclusion in the taxonomy. The very presence of these two factors suggests that principals, who in the performance of their own administrative role must be concerned with breadth of scope, positive institutional attitude, and effective human relations, permit these concerns to dominate their perceptions of teachers—who perform quite a different institutional role.

PERCEPTUAL PATTERNS AND LEADERSHIP

Through their perceptions of teachers, administrators belie their own leadership styles. The characteristics of teachers that one principal will "see" is determined by the style of leadership this man

TABLE 3-3. Detailed analysis of the content of administrators' perceptions of teachers for each of three subgroups (N = 30)

General class and components	System-centered principals (N = 10)		Indiv.-centered principals (N = 10)		Teacher-prospects (N = 10)	
	Preoccupations (percent)	Discrim. value[a]	Preoccupations (percent)	Discrim. value[a]	Preoccupations (percent)	Discrim. value[a]
A. Pedagogy	41	52	37	59	28	52
a. Stimulatingness	13	52	9	61	4	68
b. Organization	12	56	9	61	2	42
c. Discipline	7	65	11	65	11	57
d. Knowledge of job	8	35	8	48	11	43
B. Job orientations	31	57	32	49	29	52
a. Scope	11	50	10	53	14	52
b. Job attitude	20	60	22	48	15	53
C. Interpersonal relations	18	47	13	42	20	56
a. Consideration	11	45	10	46	12	56
b. Rapport	7	50	3	31	8	56
D. Personality	9	55	13	38	20	41
a. Neuroticism	3	77	4	41	7	38
b. Extra/intro	2	91	3	41	4	34
c. Dominance	2	25	3	36	4	58
d. Physical	2	31	3	36	4	46
E. Miscellaneous	1	31	5	49	3	31
Raw Mean[b]	5.74		3.66		4.47	
Raw standard deviation	0.39		0.70		0.94	
Correlation: preoccupations X Discrim. Value[c]	.55		.14		.04	

[a] Standard scores scaled to mean 50, standard deviation 10
[b] All mean differences are significant (well beyond .01 level)
[c] Only the correlation of .55 is significant. Differences between the three correlations (using Fisher's z) show significance between .55 and each of the two smaller, but not between the two smaller correlations.

typically adopts. If his outlook is system-centered, he appraises teachers at a different level, and according to other criteria, relative to a principal whose chief outlook is individual-centered. Or, so naive observation would lead one to suppose. But testing such a theory is no simple matter. In an earlier attempt[8] we learned that teacher-principal similarities in "objectively-tested" values and attitudes bore no relation to principals' personnel judgments of teachers. Nor, perhaps, should they so long as a teacher's score on an attitude scale differs from his superior's perception of that same teacher's attitudes.

In the present study, we used two "judges" to select the subjects. As judges, these two men hold central office supervisory positions, come into quite close contact with elementary school principals and their problems, and have—through graduate study and subsequent institute work—a highly developed working knowledge of the criterion terms. System-centered principals were to be those whose dominant evident interests lay in the efficient operation of his administrative unit—in a smooth-running school; nomothetic types who showed structure-initiation. Individual-centered principals were those who showed a sensitivity to individual differences among staff members—a more diagnostic outlook; idiographic types strong on consideration. To be sure, several principals are both, several neither, several something else altogether. The writer asked for, and received, ten subjects high on "System," low on "Individual," and ten the opposite. The ten "Teacher-Prospects" had been studied previously. The DPRT protocols from these thirty subjects supplied the data for Table 3-3.

The vastness of the differences between these three subgroups was a surprising outcome of the study, considering all principal subjects come under the same school system influences and all are regarded as effective men. Their differences are manifest in their response sets, in their judgment-boundedness, and in their perceptual patterns.

Response Variations

Raw mean discriminating values of the perceptions used typically by system-centered men were much higher than for the individual-centereds; young prospects (who, of course, have not yet sorted themselves into "System" or "Individual" groups) fell in between. The possible range of discriminating values runs from 0 to 9; System types averaged 5.74 and Individual types averaged 3.66. Several inferences are possible: the former may be more absolutistic in their thinking, tending to see persons more in stereotypes, and thus, on the test, check extreme categories (strongly agree or disagree) more often than others; the latter may have less sharply formulated notions of the effective teacher so that their perceptions of the strong and weak teachers tend often to cancel out, leaving a rightly low discriminating value.

Judgment-boundedness

Earlier was suggested the possibility of correlating "Preoccupations" with "Discriminating Values" to study the extent to which a principal was judgment-bound in thought about teachers. A low correlation would indicate little inclination to be judgment-bound, that out of eighteen characteristics, relatively few of them had much to do with effective/ineffective teaching. Here the individual-centered principal and teacher-prospect show low and nonsignificant correlations (.14 and .04) whereas the system-centered principal

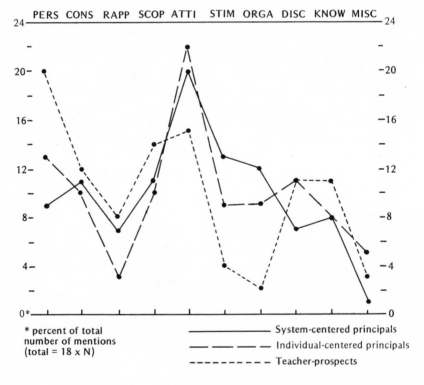

Figure 3-1
Perceptual preoccupations of administrators
asked to consider eighteen combinations of staff members (N = 30)

reveals a definite tendency (r = .55) to have mostly on his mind those thoughts that have most value (to him) in making personnel judgments. As a graphic example, Figures 3-1 and 3-2 chart, respectively, the "Preoccupation" or proportion of times that a comment is made within each category, and the "Discriminating Powers" of these categories. Note, for illustrative purposes, the four adjacent categories: Scope, Attitude, Stimulatingness, and Organization. The system-centered principals' solid line assumes much the same form on both graphs whereas the individual-centered principals' broken lines do not.

Perceptual Profiles

Figure 3-1, or "this is what your principal is probably thinking and talking about," shows profiles that are reasonably similar for all principals. In Figure 3-2, or "but this is what counts," they are not.

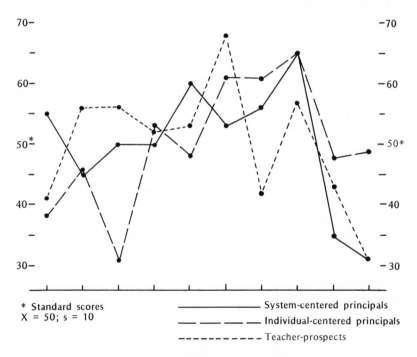

Figure 3-2
Discriminating power
of administrators' perceptions of teachers (N = 30)

(This observation is supported statistically: the Cronbach and Gleser[9] method of assessing similarity between profiles yields a low and nonsignificant D^2 between system-centered and individual-centered profiles of Figure 3-1 but a high and significant D^2 for those of Figure 3-2.) Therein, of course, lies the dilemma for the teacher. In Figure 3-2, personality—when mentioned—counts more with the system (or structure) principal than with the individual-centered (or consideration) one, even though the latter mentions it much more frequently (cf. Figure 3-1). They agree on consideration but diverge sharply with rapport which counts more for the system type possibly for the sake of harmony within the structure. They agree rather well on the importance of a teacher showing a breadth of scope, but job attitude separates the two groups again, it mattering just a little less to the individual-centered principal whether the teacher's attitude toward the institution, to the task, is serious and positive or not. Both had mentioned it with top frequency. The reverse just tends to be true of the teacher's quality of stimulatingness where the individual man—who mentioned it less frequently—regards it in importance on a plane next only to discipline. The same tendency, to a lesser degree, is so of organization. Whatever discipline means matters a lot, thereby confirming the old, but not very helpful, adage that good teaching brings good discipline. Knowledge of the content and method requisite for the job counts a good deal less for the system-centered principals.

There may be something revealing in the finding that relatively more of the individual-centered principals' statements had to be classed "Miscellaneous," and that they had a reasonably high discriminating value.

One can pity the plight of the teacher who is anxious to become successful and to be thought so by his own "significant others." He has two principal-profiles to guide him, either one of which may apply to his own current superior number. But, to confound him even more, the profiles of the young and ambitious teacher-prospects with whom he doubtless identifies and compares notes bear no semblance to either principal group. Here consideration and rapport count a lot, not so attitude; stimulatingness is paramount, but organization is low.

TOWARD TRAINING

Perhaps we contribute something to the wisdom of the species by digging out what is on the administrator's mind, weighing and classifying it according to his predispositions, and accounting for this descent into the interpersonal underworld in terms of leadership styles. But some may be bothered by the "administrationist's" preoccupation with styles and labels. Do we conclude, for example, that certain styles of leadership determine the perceptual patterns uncovered in this paper, and hence, personnel judgments? Possibly, but it is a bleak—even if accurate—prediction.

Try turning it about. Perhaps perceptual patterns determine leadership mode. The author believes we would prefer it that way, at least those of us engaged in administrator-preparation programs. Interpersonal perceptions, being learned, can be unlearned and relearned. Are some of these patterns too deep-rooted in our principal's psychic development? Certainly some—but many are not. Many are suggested and reinforced by existing authority systems only recently in the prospect's career. Interpersonal perceptions are amenable to sharpening and refining, they can be broadened and integrated, they can be understood and developed. And that, as the writer sees it, is the role of the training program.

Notes

This article is based on a paper presented to the National Conference of Professors of Educational Administration at Humboldt State College, California, August 22-28, 1965.

1. T.W. Costello and S.S. Zalkind, *Psychology in Administration* (Englewood Cliffs, N.J.: Prentice-Hall, 1963), p. 3.

2. J.M. Lipham, "Organizational Character of Education: Administrative Behaviour," *Review of Educational Research*, XXXIV (No. 4, October 1964), 435-54.

3. Alan F. Brown, "Conflict and Stress in Administrative Relationships," *Administrator's Notebook*, X (No. 7, March 1962), 1-4.

4. G.A. Kelly, *The Psychology of Personal Constructs*, 2 vols. (New York: Norton, 1955).

5. James Bieri, "Cognitive Complexity—Simplicity and Predictive Behaviour," *Journal of Abnormal and Social Psychology*, LI (No. 2, September 1955), 263-68; *id.* and Albert Trieschman, "Learning as a Function of Perceived Similarity to Self," *Journal of Personality*, XXV (No. 2, December 1956), 213-33.

6. Alan F. Brown, "Exploring Personnel Judgments with Discriminant Perception Analysis," *Proceedings of the Third Canadian Conference on Educational Research* (Ottawa: Canadian Council for Research in Education, 1964), pp. 229-38.

7. Alan F. Brown, "The Self in Interpersonal Theory: Relating Self-Perceptions to Perceptions of Significant Others," *Alberta Journal of Educational Research*, III (No. 3, September 1957), 138-48; Bieri, "Cognitive Behaviour"; Bieri and Trieschman, "Learning as a Function of Self."

8. John H.M. Andrews and Alan F. Brown, "Can Principals Exclude Their Own Personality Characteristics When They Rate Their Teachers?" *Educational Administration and Supervision*, XLV (No. 4, July 1959), 234-43.

9. L.J. Cronbach and G. Gleser, "Assessing Similarity between Profiles," *Psychological Bulletin*, L (1953), 456-73.

COMMENT / Brown's DPRT: A Means of Effectively Evaluating Teachers

Lawrence Grant

Alan Brown has done an excellent job of examining teacher evaluation as it relates to perceptual systems of administrators. His research procedures are sound and somewhat ingenious, his results provide practitioners with data for their work in evaluation, and, what is perhaps most important, he leaves both the teacher and the administrator with a means for improving their interaction in the evaluation situation. Brown's work is of such quality (in an area of critical importance that has seen few pieces of solid research) that any major criticism would be gratuitous. His work is superior, and more like it is needed.

In this analysis three aspects of the paper will be examined. Brown's methodology will be described briefly in order to emphasize the strength of his technique (in an area that seems to defy technique). I will point out some specific findings that seemed significant to me and speculate as to the causes of such findings. Finally, problems found in practice as they relate to Brown's research and possible solutions for such problems as taken from Brown's methodology will be discussed.

METHODOLOGY

Brown has attempted something that from the most modest point of view is difficult, and he has succeeded at it. He has examined perceptual systems within individuals. Educators and others dealing with value systems have avoided research of this nature as they would the plague. The imprecision of research involving the human mind is perhaps the most often quoted reason for such avoidance. Results are debunked as being the product of a priori dispositions toward confirming the hypotheses, meaning that the researcher could make anything of his findings that he wanted to.

There is the further difficulty of rooting out the implicit value systems of the respondents. How does the researcher know that the person being questioned about his value system will respond with what he *really* believes if the value system is by definition an implicit value system? Brown recognizes the problem:

One cannot discover a principal's perception of the effective-rated teacher simply by asking him. He will tell you, of course, but what he will tell you may be as vaporous as the typical set of aims of education, or he will repeat to you the value statements sanctioned by the system though not internalized by himself—probably first enunciated by his superintendent or professional development committee.

The limitations of Brown's instrument, the Discrimination Perception Repertory Test (DPRT), are in proportion to the honesty, intelligence, and creativity of the respondents. Complete spontaneity is desired in taking the DPRT, but it is nearly impossible to obtain. Much of the genius of the DPRT, however, is that it forces respondents to make comparisons between and among individuals. When comparing teachers they know and interact with, administrators will respond with little hesitation. I have known few school administrators who do not have ready opinions on their staff members, and, if not always able to articulate an exact listing of the qualities which make a given person an effective or an ineffective teacher, they respond in seconds to a question asking them to discriminate between two or more staff members.

CONTENT

Brown has commented on the results of his study and speculates about the causes for some of these results. I will do this from my perspective as a high school principal, but I will limit the discussion to a few items, those that appear to hold the most significance for persons involved in the evaluation process.

Tables 3-1 and 3-3 both indicate that administrators and teachers do not "notice" discipline an inordinate amount of the time. It appears, however, that they place considerable emphasis on the importance of this quality in the effective-rated teacher. The discriminating power of 62 is the highest category in Table 3-1. What happens in practice seems consistent with Brown's findings.

The concept of "running a tight ship" is not as ostensibly popular as it once was. Stating that one is a stickler for discipline does not receive the positive sanction of one's colleagues that it once might have. But despite this lessening of outward approval for tight control, most administrators and teachers, whether they state it or not, have a visceral feeling that good apparent order in the school is good for them—and for the institution. I have experienced frustration from superiors in this regard.

For example, an administrator I have worked with talked at length on the virtues of being positive toward students and of accepting them with their many youthful foibles. During periods of community criticism about a lack of standards in student behavior, however, the same administrator was extremely critical of subordinates and teachers for their lack of discipline. I suspect that he always felt strongly about firm discipline, but he did not realize it. Crises brought his true feelings to the surface. Brown's discussion would seem to corroborate this. He says that what people "notice" may not be what they "value." In this instance what was "valued" did not seem to be "noticed" by the administrator.

A finding that surprises some people is that although administrators notice "content and method knowledge" to an expected or predicted extent (or slightly less), they place little value on this quality when it comes to evaluating a teacher. Brown comments lightly and perhaps somewhat remorsefully on this point when he says:

And those in the faculties and schools of education take little solace from the fact that when administrators either commend or dondemn a teacher's knowledge of the job, . . . they are not apt to confuse this notion with their judgment of the teacher's relative worth on the job.

This should not be surprising. Very few teachers fail in their work because they lack knowledge of the subject matter or of teaching methodology. They fail because they cannot relate to students or communicate with them. Teachers teach students to a greater extent than they teach subjects.

Principals tend to "notice" items dealing with job orientation, "broad-narrow scope of the job" and "positive-negative job attitude." This would seem to indicate that administrators are conscious of the teacher's attitude toward his work and the institution. Personal experience bears this out. I attempt to be acutely aware of how much teachers enjoy their work. This can be logically, sensibly, and positively rationalized on the grounds that a happy employee will do a better job. However, speculation as to why there is such a strong desire on the part of administrators to have happy teachers must include the principal's ego: Do I provide well for my staff? Do they like me? Do they respect me?

It is in the area of "personality" that a prototype example of a conflict between what is "valued" and what is "noticed" occurs. Like most people, administrators tend to disavow prejudices based on personal characteristics of people that do not affect their capacity for work success. It appears, however, that, irrespective of what they might say, principals do "notice" personality characteristics much of the time (14% preoccupation on Table 3-1). It is somewhat comforting to see that the discriminating power is relatively low (45 on Table 3-1) indicating that what administrators "notice" is not what they "value" in this area. Apparently teachers will be "noticed" for their idiosyncracies, but not judged on them.

Administrators should not be judged harshly for "noticing" personality characteristics. It seems inescapable that people whose business is other people and who are relatively perceptive could not "notice" these qualities even though social mores would prevent their verbalizing it. The saving grace is that the teacher is judged professionally on other qualities.

I found it surprising that rapport with others was neither highly "noticed" nor "valued." Getting along with students, regardless of the style involved in so doing, seems essential in the top-rated teacher. (Getting along with colleagues is desirable but not essential. I work with teachers who are virtual social isolates with regard to their fellow staff members but who do an excellent job with students.) It is significant that teachers felt (Table 3-2) strongly that "rapport and consideration" are important. This speaks well for teachers and poorly for administrators, who may be too concerned with "running a tight ship."

The data might bear further examination as it seems generalizable to a substantial portion of the population of administrators and teachers. As interesting as specific findings might be, however, the methodology Brown has provided may be the most useful aspect of his research. How this might be used in establishing a system for gathering data on teacher and administrator perceptions in a specific school district in order to improve the evaluation process is discussed in the following section.

THE PROBLEM IN PRACTICE

The following paragraphs detail a problem relating to teacher evaluation. The problem is common enough to assume that it is found in most, if not all, school districts. Brown has pointed out that what administrators "notice" as beliefs concerning teacher evaluation may not be what they "value." Accepting this premise is prerequisite to accepting the ensuing proposals as viable alternatives to present practice.

I work in a school district that uses a conventional teacher evaluation form for all teachers in the district. The form was developed through the efforts of a committee composed of some administrators in the district and some teachers appointed by the local education association. The form is based on a statement of philosophy adopted by the district and related closely in wording to the major points of the statement of philosophy. The final wording of the evaluation form was strongly influenced by one or two administrators who had been prominent in developing the statement of philosophy. The purpose of the evaluation form was simple and positive, to equate pedagogy in the district's schools with its stated philosophy and objectives of education.

A problem in all of this was that few of the teachers or administrators accepted the philosophy in its entirety. Some had difficulty accepting major portions of it. Consequently, the evaluation form mirrored some values that were internalized by neither the persons being evaluated nor the evaluators. Perhaps an even more difficult problem to overcome was the ambiguousness of the criteria by which teachers were evaluated. No one had a clear understanding of what he was being judged by. To illustrate this, the section encompassing discipline will be cited. (Discipline was found by Brown to be of considerable importance to administrators and teachers alike even though they may not have stated, or "noticed," this.)

A. Provides opportunities for dialogue and free expression of ideas among students, staff and resource personnel.
B. Provides the procedure for the development of standards of behavior within which the student is expected to function.
C. Teaches the student to accept responsibility for his actions and their consequences.

Teachers are rated from 1 (poor) to 5 (very strong) on each of these qualities or teacher behaviors. Although each of the three items points toward a desirable goal for teacher behavior, the wording is sufficiently ambiguous to cause varying interpretations to be made for each of the items. Compounding the problem has been an almost total absence of communication for the purpose of refining and clarifying items on the evaluation form.

Teachers and administrators, as they made their own interpretations of the items on the form, found these statements wanting in establishing operational criteria for strong discipline. As a result the credibility of the entire form was placed in question. These deficiencies being recognized, further committees were organized to revise the original evaluation form in hope of making its requirements more congruent with the beliefs and expectations of the administrators and teachers and in hope of clarifying the meaning of the statements on which teachers were being evaluated. The resultant revision was slightly more palatable, but the ambiguous language and lack of clarifying communication remained in most cases, and no attempt was made, or even considered, to ascertain the real values of those doing the evaluating and those being evaluated. If real values are not determined, dissatisfaction with evaluation will remain and committees will meet ad infinitum without reaching the heart of the problem. Brown's work indicates that we will continue to deceive ourselves if we base our evaluations on superficial values, and essentially that is what we are doing. There is now talk of further revising the instrument using the same old methods. We can anticipate the same old problems.

In this situation no one profits. The community and students have teachers in their schools who are evaluated by a process far inferior to what it might be. Administrators are faced with the task of evaluating staff members by criteria that even they do not completely accept, lending an implicit (if not intentional) lessening of integrity to the process of evaluation. But consider the dilemma of the poor teacher. The teacher in our district receives a copy of the evaluation form prior to his formal evaluation to use in completing a self-evaluation. Consequently, he is aware of the ostensible criteria by which he is being evaluated. His confusion begins when he does not understand all of the statements on the evaluation form. He has had the benefit of no explanation of the form by informal discussion, in-service meeting, or written explanation accompanying the form. He must guess what the items mean. His next moment of anxiety comes when he is confronted by an administrator who says, "I don't agree with every item on the form either. But don't worry about it. You know what I'm looking for in a good teacher." That statement might not be so unfortunate if the teacher knows what the administrator wants, but more often than not he does not. So the teacher must play the additional guessing game of trying to figure out what his evaluating superior wants from him.

A final problem is that the evaluation form must, in addition to being understood and accepted by the teaching staff, reflect the needs of the community and be a guide to better teaching. The plight of the teacher who may not understand the administrator's value system is minor compared to the plight of a school system that operates with an inadequate scheme for evaluating staff. It is possible to alleviate the problem for the teacher and yet have an instrument that does not provide the community with what it needs.

A POSSIBLE SOLUTION

The DPRT would be given to all of the administrators in the school district that are directly involved in teacher evaluation. A number of teachers—a selected cross section would be sufficient—would also take the DPRT. (The need for discretion and careful planning is evident as teachers would be placed in the position of judging colleagues. Despite objections that might be raised in light of this undertaking, the task must be accomplished if the desired teacher feedback is to be obtained. It can be done.) Through this process the district would learn what its teachers and administrators "notice" and "value" in quality teachers. It is unlikely that the two groups would agree completely as to what good teaching consists of, but it is likely that, through discussion and obtaining widespread community input, they could arrive at a consensus as to the qualities desired in a top-rated teacher that would be used in composing the new evaluation form. It would be almost akin to the Marxist dialectic, where thesis and antithesis form synthesis; we could hope to perfect the document eventually.

The administrator-evaluator would stand to gain personally and professionally from the experience. He would learn something about his own values—and hang-ups, if you will. He might then be able to refine his perceptions as Brown indicates. This may not be easy. As a body, school administrators seem to have much in common with General Sukhomlinov, Russian Minister of War in 1914, about whom Barbara Tuchman, in *The Guns of August,* said: "Having won the Cross of St. George as a dashing young cavalry officer in the war of 1877 against the Turks, Sukhomlinov believed that knowledge acquired in that campaign was permanent truth." The conservative inertia of many evaluators must be overcome if the process of achieving and reworking evaluation forms and the process of evaluating is to become and remain effective. All of the work by other evaluators and teachers will come to naught if the person working with teachers cannot adapt. How would individual teachers gain in this process? Those who took the DPRT would have the privilege of learning to refine their own perceptions as do the evaluators. Those who do not go through this process will have the benefit of an instrument that can genuinely assist them in becoming better teachers. Also, interaction with an enlightened administrator/ evaluator would be beneficial. The latter benefit may be greater than the former.

I have assumed that a consensus document of what good teaching should be measured by can be obtained. All or most districts have forms or listings of teacher qualities that are used in evaluation. Many of these are obtained by copying the forms of other districts or parroting what the National Education Association or the National Association of Secondary-School Principals says a good teacher should be. More often than not they sound like the Boy Scout Law (reverent, obedient, kind, etc.), and they have been prepared by some individual in the school district—superintendent or personnel director. The lists ask teachers to conform to something that neither they nor evaluators might accept. By using an instrument such as the DPRT to obtain an evaluation form and by communicating this information widely and carefully through in-service meetings and other means so that the teacher and evaluator understand one another, a district might be able to create an evaluation situation in which the teacher has the security of a system he can trust and well-established goals that he can pursue. All this might result in a type of pedagogy that will enhance the educational program of the district.

4 / Some Factors Affecting Teacher Survival in School Districts

W. W. Charters, Jr.

Influenced by the work of British labor statisticians, J. Whitener a few years ago developed an actuarial procedure for investigating staff turnover in school systems,[1] an approach that circumvented the interpretation difficulties of the commonly used crude turnover rate.[2] In an exploratory study, he obtained lists of all teachers entering employment in ten Missouri school districts during the calendar years of 1951, 1952, and 1953—a total of 937 teachers—and recorded their lengths of service at the time they terminated employment in the district, if they did, through a ten-year period. These data were converted into a survival curve, showing the proportions of the cohort still in employment at yearly intervals. Districts involved in the study were located, with one exception, in the St. Louis suburban area and were mostly in the student enrollment range of 1,000-6,000. Most of Whitener's statistical analyses of the factors affecting teacher survival were carried out in a subgroup of 431 teachers between the ages of 22 and 26 at the time of entering employment.

One of the principal questions to which Whitener addressed his investigation was whether survival was affected more strongly by personal attributes of the employed teachers, by characteristics of

Reprinted from *American Educational Research Journal,* VII (No. 1, January 1970), 1-27.

the employing districts, or by some combination of the two. His findings were striking. (1) Two personal attributes—age and sex—each correlated strongly with survival. Males outsurvived females, and older teachers (up to age 50-54) were consistently better risks than their younger colleagues. (2) Survival curves prepared for eight of the districts were virtually identical, even though the districts varied widely in certain seemingly important characteristics.[3] (Two districts could not be compared because of too few entering teachers.) Teacher attributes, not organizational characteristics, would appear to determine survival from his investigation, although it should be noted that his study was designed more to test the methodology than to produce substantive conclusions.

Whitener's data also showed a very steep drop in the survival curves during the early years of employment. Between the beginning of the second and fifth years withdrawals were extremely high in his cohort, but thereafter relatively few teachers left their systems, either numerically or proportionately. In the total cohort, 38 percent survived through five years but over 75 percent of those who survived five years also survived at least ten years in the districts. Whitener viewed this as indicating that, with increased tenure, teachers build up an "investment" in the system, an accumulating force that mitigates against withdrawal.[4]

THE OREGON STUDY

The present study extends Whitener's investigation to a large population of school districts and teachers at a different time and in a different place (the early 1960's in Oregon). Its main purpose was to check the suggestion that survival is governed by career processes of the populations employed by districts rather than by forces residing within the districts themselves. If true, it would challenge most of the thinking and research in the field of teacher personnel. It is generally held that the stability of a school's faculty depends on such school district factors as community conditions, supervisory practices, conditions of work, and, above all, salary levels.[5] Moreover, forty years of turnover research has shown that the crude turnover rate varies inversely with school district size—an organizational attribute.[6] Whether or not survival also varies with size is an interesting question. Whitener's investigation provides no answer since the school systems he compared, while differing in size, did not differ sufficiently to cover the size range in which the relationship is known to operate. In any event, the question of the location of the determinants of the turnover process—in organizations or in individuals—is not an idle one.

Another purpose of the Oregon study was to test the generality of a number of Whitener's findings and to explore relationships he could not pursue. For example, was the steepness he observed in the slope of the survival curve due to the happenstance that his cohort was entering employment in the early 1950's during the unsettling times of the Korean War, or to some peculiarities of suburban districts in Missouri, or is the steep slope a general condition of teacher survival? Are age and sex as powerful determinants of survival as Whitener's study indicated, and how do the two factors interact? In the Oregon study, employment histories were traced only through five years. This time period permitted use of a fairly recent teacher cohort (1962) but prohibited a test of Whitener's interesting finding concerning the effect [of] the length of service on survival.

Formulation of the Survival Process

Survival can be treated as a simple stochastic process with a one-way flow[7] in which a teacher can be in only one of two states—employed or not employed by the district—and during an interval of time can shift from one state to another in only one direction—from employed to not employed. The probability of making such a shift in some small interval of time, say one year, is the separation rate, r, and when specified for the individual teacher is assumed to be an outward manifestation of underlying psychological and social processes inducing withdrawal. The inverse of the separation rate is the survival rate, q, or the probability that the teacher will remain in the same state (i.e., employed) through the time interval.

$$q = 1 - r$$

If the survival rate is constant over a number of time intervals, then the successive application of the rate to a group of teachers reasonably homogeneous with regard to q will lead to a regular decrement in their numbers, a decrement described by the exponential function,

$$p = q^t$$

or

$$ln \ p = (ln \ q) \ t$$

where p_t is the proportion of the cohort surviving after each time interval, t, and ln refers to the natural logarithms. Thus, if a cohort of 100 teachers had a 75 percent chance of surviving into each ensuing year $(q = .75)$ and this rate were invariant through four years, 75 of them could be expected to remain in employment at the end of Year 1, 56 at the end of Year 2, 42 at the end of Year 3, and by the end of Year 4, 32 could be expected to survive. Whether or not the observed survival curve fits the exponential model may be determined by plotting the observed proportions surviving at the end of each time interval on semilog coordinate paper, on which the ordinate is scaled in $ln \, p$. If the data fit the model, the points will fall approximately in a straight line. Its slope when evaluated yields the constant survival rate, q.

The survival rate need not be constant even over as brief a period as four or five years. Among the conditions other than chance that make for annual variations in the value of q are: economic dislocations that require a school system to cut back the teaching staff in certain years; a literal change in the value of q for individual teachers with increasing service in the school system (as implied by Whitener's concept of "investment"); and a selection process such that teachers in the cohort with somewhat lower q values are eliminated faster than their colleagues, thereby raising the average q for the remainder. In any event, it is useful to test the survival curve for its fit with the exponential model and to examine the pattern of nonrandom departures of the empirical data from the model.

METHOD

The Oregon State Department of Education furnished the investigator with a roster of all teachers in the state who were new employees of public school districts at the beginning of the 1962-63 academic year. The roster covered all Oregon districts (except Portland) in which any new appointments had been made. After the list was culled of administrators, nonteaching personnel, and employees of intermediate education districts, a cohort of 2,064 classroom teachers remained. Employment histories were traced by checking county and school district directories for four successive years (culminating with the fall directories of 1966), and when a teacher's name did not appear or when the directory indicated that he had assumed a nonteaching position, he was classified as not having survived into that year. Telephone calls to districts double-checked on females whose names might have changed during the intervening year. This procedure permitted no distinctions to be made between voluntary and involuntary separations, teachers on temporary leave and those who left permanently, or departures due to illness or death. Systematically excluded from this study, in contrast to the procedure used by Whitener, were teachers who entered employment in the course of the first academic year. As a rule, however, relatively few midyear appointments are made in public schools.[8]

Information regarding personal attributes of each teacher at the time of employment was also on the State Department's listing, and data concerning school district characteristics were taken from published reports for the 1962-63 school year or, if unavailable, for an

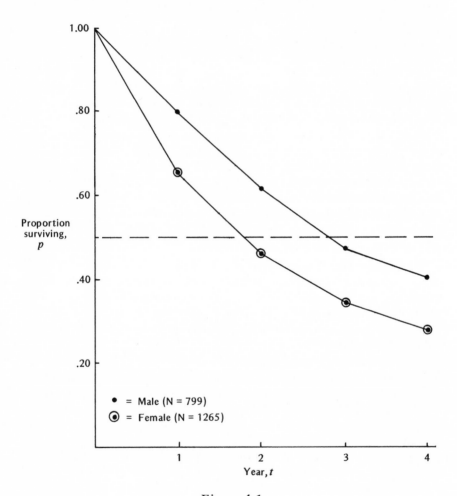

Figure 4-1
Survival curves for male and female Oregon teachers,
1962 cohort

adjacent year. Teachers in districts that consolidated between 1962 and 1966 were regarded as having continued in the same district so long as they remained in the newly formed unit, but in a few cases it was impossible to determine to which of several units teachers should properly be assigned and they were dropped from the study.

A computer program capable of disaggregating the data according to relevant teacher attributes, district characteristics, and combinations of them produced the survival curves that served as the study's main analytical device. It also fitted an exponential function to the survival distributions, applying a standard least-squares solution,[9] and furnished the value of the exponent to describe the slope of the curves. All analyses were carried out for male and female teachers separately.

RESULTS: INDIVIDUAL AND ORGANIZATIONAL DETERMINANTS

Survival curves for 799 male and 1,265 female teachers comprising the Oregon cohort are shown in Figure 4-1. (Values are given in proportions of the groups surviving at each time period.) Two features can be readily noted in the graph, both in accord with Whitener's data: the longer survival of males than of females, and the generally high rate at which either sex leaves the school districts. Only four in ten males and less than three in ten females remained to begin their fifth year of teaching (i.e., survived at Time 4). The proportions are similar to those for the two sexes in Missouri. A precise comparison of the Missouri and Oregon studies, however, must be delayed until some other analyses have been reported.

Also notable in Figure 4-1 is the regularity in the decrement of teacher survival through the time period. The extent of correspondence with the exponential function can be seen better in Figure 4-2 where the data are replotted on semilog coordinates. The points fall approximately on a straight line, whose slope is −.235 for males and −.343 for females. These values correspond to annual survival rates over the period of .79 and .71, respectively. Chi-square tests conducted on the expected and observed frequencies in Table 4-1 indicate that the data for males do, indeed, fit the exponential curve nicely, but not the data for females.

Interactive Effects of Age and Sex on Survival

Whitener studied only the main effects of age and sex on teacher survival and not their interaction;[10] thus an early task of the Oregon study was to examine the relationship between age and survival for

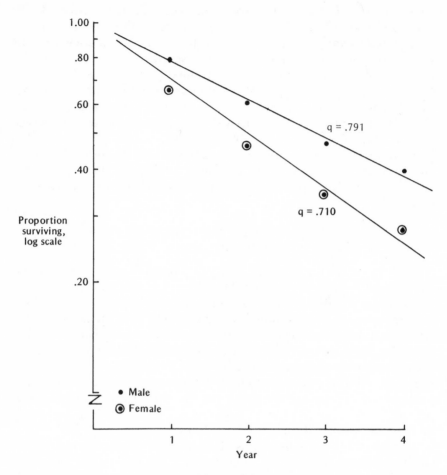

Figure 4-2
Survival data and fitted curves
for male and female Oregon teachers (semilog coordinates)

males and females separately. Table 4-2 reports the survival rates of males and females by age at the time of employment, grouped in five-year intervals, and also the probability level within each age group for accepting the hypothesis of fit between the data and the exponential function, based on the Chi-square test. None of the probabilities are beyond the 5 percent level. Hence, we can assume with some confidence that the survival rates from Years 0-4 are constant and that it is legitimate to use the slope of the exponential curve as an estimate of the rate for each group.

The table reveals the powerful effect of the teacher's age at the time of employment on his chances of survival in the district, but it also shows that the rate for female teachers is considerably more sensitive to the age factor than the rate for males. This finding throws new light on the sex difference in the previous figures. While it is true that male teachers, on the average, survive better than female teachers, the male's advantage holds only up to age 40. Male and female teachers entering employment in the 40-49 range are

TABLE 4-1. Survival data for male and female Oregon teachers, 1962 cohort

Surviving at	Male			Female		
	Number	Propor-tion	Ex-pected[a]	Number	Propor-tion	Ex-pected[b]
Year 0	799	1.000	1.000	1265	1.000	1.000
Year 1	633	.792	.790	829	.655	.710
Year 2	491	.615	.625	584	.462	.504
Year 3	380	.476	.494	433	.342	.358
Year 4	323	.404	.390	354	.280	.254

[a]Least-squares fit, $p = e^{-.235}$. For fit of observed to expected numbers, Chi-square = .9828. Probability 80-90% (3 df).
[b]Least-squares fit, $p = e^{-.343}$. For fit of observed to expected numbers, Chi-square = 14.0211. Probability less than 0.5% (3 df).

nearly alike in their survival rates. The relationship between age and survival rate is shown graphically in Figure 4-3. The points are not altogether regular in these plots, but they do suggest a linear relationship throughout most of the age range. After age 55, in the case of females, the probabilities decline rapidly, reflecting the short survival prospects of teachers employed near retirement age. The plots also make apparent the stronger age effect among females than males. A rough indication of the age-survival relationship was sought by fitting a line (least-squares method) to the points up to age 55, or 50 for males, as shown in the figure. There is substantial variability around the line, so the estimate of the relationship is approximate. The linear equation of survival rate, q, and age, X, (in years) for females is,

$$q = .009 X + .42.$$

For every added year of age at which the female teacher is employed,

TABLE 4-2. Rate of survival by age group, male and female Oregon teachers

Age	Male			Female		
	Rate	Number	Probability[a]	Rate	Number	Probability
			(percent)			(percent)
Less than 25	.729	172	80-90	.592	470	50-70
25-29	.800	264	80-90	.648	221	30-50
30-34	.817	144	90-95	.778	139	30-50
35-39	.810	106	98	.749	80	95-97.5
40-44	.856	47	99	.842	99	80-90
45-49	.801	32	50-70	.798	78	80-90
50-54	___[b]	19		.874	79	95-97.5
55-59	___[b]	9		.775	71	80-90
60 and over	___[b]	6		.523	27	10-20

[a] From Chi-square test.
[b] Too few cases.

to age 55, her survival probability increases nearly .01. Within the 20-50 range for male teachers, the equation is,

$$q = .003 X + .69.$$

Thus, males have a generally higher survival rate than females to begin with, but the rate increases with age only one-third as fast.

Returning to the survival curves within each age group, we inspected the pattern of deviations of the observed values from the exponential function and found much the same thing that Figure 4-2 showed: among females, but not among males, the exponential function tends to overestimate the number who survive to Years 1 and 2 and to underestimate the number who survive to Year 4. Some such curvilinearity would be expected in the female survival curves on the basis of the age data just reported. That is, after each year of survival the teachers are one year older and the annual q values should increase by .009 rather than remain constant through the four years. We checked the possibility that the annual increment in q could account for the systematic departures from the exponential function in both the separate age-group curves and the over-all curve for females shown in Figure 4-2. While "correction" of the observed proportions brought them more closely in line with the assumption of constant survival probabilities, in all cases the pattern of deviations was still discernible. With respect to the Figure 4-2 data, for example, the annual increment in q averages .054, considerably greater than the increment expected from age of .009. It may well be that a curve more elaborate than the exponential function will be required to describe the survival data for females. To repeat, though, the statistical tests run within the age groups provide no grounds for rejecting the exponential curve as a description of survival among either males or females. For the time being at least, we can regard the survival curves as essentially exponential.

Other Individual Attributes

Two other personal attributes were examined for their effects on teacher survival. One of these was teaching level (elementary vs. secondary teachers), a factor that Whitener had found to be unrelated to survival. Table 4-3 displays the survival rates for male and female in elementary and secondary teaching, holding age roughly constant. Marginals in the table suggest that female elementary

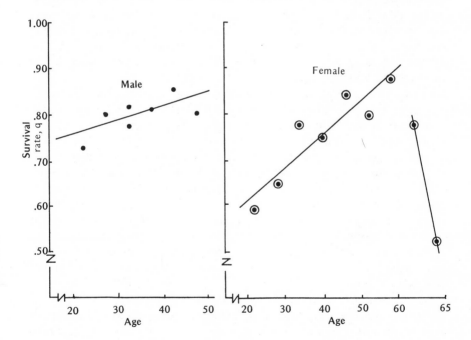

Figure 4-3
Rate of survival by age at employment
of male and female Oregon teachers, 1962 cohort

TABLE 4-3. Rate of survival by teaching level and age group, male and female Oregon teachers

Age group	Male		Female	
	Elementary	Secondary	Elementary	Secondary
Less than 30	.78	.77	.61	.62
30-39	.80	.82	.79	.64[a]
40-49	.79[a]	.87[a]	.83	.78[a]
50 and over	—[b]	—[b]	.82	.73[a]
Teaching level and sex	.78	.80	.72	.67

[a] Fewer than 60 cases.
[b] Fewer than 30 cases.

teachers survive longer than female secondary teachers, although little difference can be noted between elementary and secondary males. A sex-teaching level interaction has been observed occasionally in other studies of teacher mobility.[11] Internal comparisons in the table give some substance to the observation, although the number of cases on which some of the survival rates are based limits the dependability of the data. (Five of them are based on fewer than 60 cases.) In general, the table indicates that teaching level does not have a consistent, independent effect on survival across all age groups and both sexes. The effect is missing altogether in the youngest teachers where, incidentally, the bulk of the cohort lies. Age and sex, in contrast, continue to show the important interdependent relationship described in the preceding section, irrespective of teaching level. (The absence of a clear age relationship among elementary males, however, hints at the uniqueness of this particular category of teacher, a matter that has not escaped the attention of students of teaching personnel.)

The other attribute was the amount of teaching experience the teacher had behind him at the time of his employment in the district. The data at hand, unfortunately, do not allow the detailed analyses that the variable demands. Amount of experience, obviously, is intimately tied to age, and large numbers of cases well distributed over both the age and experience ranges are required in order to separate the effects of the two variables. The Oregon data do not provide these numbers. Suffice it to say that the few comparisons we were able to make after constructing survival curves for three categories of prior experience—none, 1 to 4 years, and 5 years or more—for males and females in four age groups revealed no consistent relationships with survival. Whitener's equally restricted analyses failed, too, to show relationships. The subtle effects of prior teaching experience, if such exist, will have to be teased out with more extensive data and multivariate analysis procedures.[12]

School District Size

To test the effect of size of student enrollment on survival rate, we classified all Oregon districts by average daily membership (ADM) and compiled survival curves within each size group. Table 4-4 reports the rates by group, as estimated from the fitted exponential curves. (Chi-square tests of the eight curves for each sex indicate that all approximate the exponential function and, hence, the values in

TABLE 4-4. Rate of survival by school system size
male and female Oregon teachers

System size (average daily membership)	Male			Female		
	Rate	Number	Proba- bility[a]	Rate	Number	Proba bility
1 to 49	__b	25	*(percent)*	__b	23	*(percent)*
50 to 149	.588	45	30-50	.637	57	10-20
150 to 299	.700	72	20-25	.786	86	95-97.5
300 to 599	.727	65	90-95	.720	77	95-97.5
600 to 1,199	.774	95	99-99.5	.704	145	70-75
2,000 to 2,999	.817	242	70-75	.716	331	30-50
3,000 to 5,999	.810	83	98	.719	171	30-50
6,000 to 11,999	.857	95	90-95	.668	150	10-20
12,000 to 24,999	.857	90	99.5	.706	216	30-50

[a]From Chi-square test.
[b]Too few cases.

Table 4-4 are fair estimations of annual survival rates constant over the four years.) Inspection of the values shows that the survival rate for males increases strongly with school district size, up to about 3,000 ADM, beyond which size makes comparatively little difference in survival. Female survival rates, however, are not consistently related to district size. Only in the smallest size class of district for which rates are reported (50-149 ADM) is the female rate noticeably low; excluding that, female survival is indifferently associated with the size of the system in which they teach. We have graphed the values in Figure 4-4 to facilitate comparisons. The strong, consistent size-survival relationship among males controverts the conclusion Whitener drew from examining the curves of eight districts regarding the absence of organizational determinants of teacher survival.

To check the possibility that the size relationship for males (and the absence of it for females) was not due to the fortuity of differential age distributions in the districts, district size and teacher age were cross-classified as shown in Table 4-5. Here the size classes have been reduced to three: "small" districts with ADM's up to 600, "medium" from 600 to 6,000 ADM, and "large" from 6,000 to 25,000 ADM. Although a number of the cells are vacant in the section of the table for males, the comparative rates show that the size-survival relationship holds within each age group. Thus, with age held roughly constant, male rates increase with district size. By

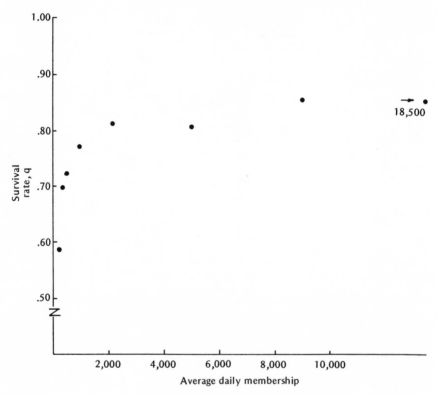

Figure 4-4
Rate of survival by school system size,
male Oregon teachers, 1962 cohort

reading the table the other way, down the columns, we can see that the originally weak age-survival relationship among males persists in the medium and large systems but almost disappears in the small schools. The age factor does not emerge from the table as a consistent, powerful determinant of male survival, but school district size does.

Looking at the section of the table for females, the conclusion is confirmed that school system size has no effect and that age continues to operate as the prime determinant of female survival.

TABLE 4-5. Rate of survival by school system size and age group, male and female Oregon teachers

Age group	Male			Female		
	Small	Medium	Large	Small	Medium	Large
Less than 30	.69	.79	.82	.63	.61	.61
30-39	.71	.81	.90	.76[a]	.78	.77
40-49	__[b]	.86[a]	__[b]	.78[a]	.84	.82[a]
50 and over	__[b]	__[b]	__[b]	.75	.81	__[b]

[a]Fewer than 60 cases.
[b]Fewer than 30 cases.

Other District Characteristics

Several other characteristics of school systems were examined for their relationships with survival. Two of these—wealth of the district and district type (unified, high school, or elementary school district)—proved to be unrelated either to male or female rates.

Several analyses reported elsewhere, including an inspection of regional variations in survival rates in the state, indicated that geographical remoteness of the district could be a factor in the survival of males.[13] Some Oregon districts lie in extremely isolated, sparsely populated areas while others, though located in small towns, are far removed from major metropolitan centers. A classification of districts by geographical remoteness showed that the survival rate for males varied inversely with remoteness. No relationship was observed for females. The more remote districts, of course, tend to be the smaller ones in terms of student enrollment, so remoteness was tested for its ability to account for the relationship between size and survival of male teachers. While the data are not reported here, we can say that remoteness does not explain the relationship. In fact, the effect of remoteness nearly disappears when district size is held roughly constant.

Summary: Individual and Organizational Determinants

The general conclusion derived from the Oregon study regarding the role of organizational factors in teacher survival is that they are, indeed, operative in the case of male teachers. The survival of female teachers, on the other hand, seems to be governed exclusively by their individual attributes. Specifically we found:

1. Age at time of employment was strongly related to the survival rate of females (the older the teacher the better her survival prospects, up to about age 55) but only weakly related to the survival of males.

2. In keeping with the Whitener study, neither teaching level nor amount of teaching experience prior to employment in the district contributed importantly to survival when age and sex were held constant.

3. School district size was directly related to the survival of males but indifferently related to that of females. The size-survival relationship among males diminished as school system size increased; it was strongest in the smaller schools of the state, less strong in the larger districts, and virtually disappeared among systems enrolling over 3,000 students. The relationship could not be explained by differences in age distributions in the districts nor by another factor earlier found to be associated with male survival rates, *viz.*, geographical remoteness.

4. Neither wealth per pupil nor district type were related to survival rates.

Thus, sex, age (for females), and district size (for males) stand out as the prime determinants of the length of time a teacher can be expected to remain in a school district once he is employed. We must postpone for the moment consideration of the nature of the forces underlying these determinants.

COMPARATIVE SURVIVAL DATA

Whitener's survival curves covering a ten-year period for his age-homogeneous cohort (22 to 26 years) have been plotted in Figure 4-5 on semilog coordinates. Recasting his data in this form makes prominent two features of the Missouri curves: the anomolously high rate of teacher retention in the first year as compared with the Oregon data, and a rather abrupt change in survival rate beginning about the fifth year.

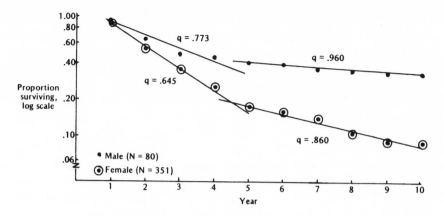

Figure 4-5
Survival curves for male and female Missouri teachers,
22-26 years of age, 1951-1953 cohort (semilog coordinates)

It is difficult to know how to interpret the high rate of teacher retention in the first year—a survival rate of .94 for males and .89 for females. None of the Oregon plots displayed a similarly sharp discrepancy from the exponential function in that year. Moreover, other survival data we obtained for a 1960 cohort in sixteen comparable (and in some instances identical) Missouri school districts failed to show the "overretention" phenomenon. The anomaly could be due to Whitener's data-taking procedures. He calculated survival in terms of elapsed time between the dates of employment and termination, permitting members of his cohort to begin employment at any time during the academic year under observation. In the Oregon study, however, only teachers who entered employment at the beginning of the academic year (fall of 1962) qualified as members of the cohort, and survival was calculated as presence or absence at the beginning of each subsequent year. A similar practice was followed in the 1960 study mentioned above. Or the "overretention" could represent bonafide differences in the circumstances of teachers and school systems. Three of the eight system survival curves Whitener plotted revealed little if any "overretention," while the other five systems displayed it in the extreme. Information is not available in Whitener's report to contrast the districts. Rather than debating the sources of the anomaly, though, we might better await further comparative studies to settle the issue.

The Effect of Service on Survival: Whitener's Study

Whitener sensed that the survival prospects of teachers improved the longer they remained in the district and felt that the fifth year of service marked something of a turning point. The plots in Figure 4-5 make his observations explicit: two distinct exponential functions (for each sex) appear to fit his data reasonably well, one covering Years 1-4 and the other Years 5-10. (The fit in Figure 4-5 is by eye. We could have achieved a closer fit for males by covering Years 1-3 and 4-10, but we chose to keep the time interval consistent between the sexes.) Thus, annual survival probabilities were constant in the second through fourth year, sharply improved in the fifth year, and remained constant at the higher level through the tenth year. It seems that the effects of service on survival were abrupt and discrete rather than gradually incrementing with each year of service, although the latter cannot be ruled out entirely with the data at hand. We have estimated survival rates from slopes of the exponential functions as shown below:

	Male	Female
Years 1-4	.773	.645
Years 5-10	.960	.860
Difference	.187	.215

These figures indicate that the probability of a teacher surviving a year of teaching in the district increases about .20 when he (or she) embarks on his fifth year.

Some of the improvement in survival could have been due to age. By the time Whitener's teachers had served five years in the school district they were, of course, five years older—in the 27-31 age group. To estimate how much of the improvement might be attributable to age, we computed survival rates in Oregon school districts that were equivalent to Whitener's with respect to size and that corresponded precisely to Whitener's age categories: 22-26 and, five years later, 27-31.

	Male	Female
Age 22-26 (Oregon)	.774	.620
Age 27-31 (Oregon)	.845	.698
Difference	.071	.078

According to this computation, a .07 increase in survival rate could be expected from a five-year difference in age at employment in Oregon districts of the size of Whitener's.[14] This improvement due to age alone is considerably less than the rate increase in Whitener's teachers who both were five years older and had five years of accumulated service. Increments due to the various components can be estimated from the values already given.

Increment in q due to:	Male	Female
Age + Service	.187	.215
Age	.071	.078
Service	.116	.137

The exact values of these numbers should not be taken too seriously, but, given comparability of the survival process among Oregon and Missouri teachers, they suggest that the "service effect," or whatever it is that happens around the beginning of the teacher's fifth year, is half again as powerful as age in increasing annual survival probabilities.

Neither Whitener's data nor our reanalyses of them enlighten us with respect to forces underlying the service effect—whether the effect was related to state tenure provisions (three years in Missouri), whether itinerant or poorly committed teachers had finally sifted themselves out of the districts by the fifth year, or whether, as Whitener proposed, the teachers had developed an "investment" in the district with their accumulated years of service—but it is clear that the matter deserves further examination.

Comparison of Survival in Missouri and Oregon

The general impression of the Oregon survival curves (Figures 4-1 or 2) is their essential similarity to the curves reported by Whitener for Missouri teachers ten years earlier, at least on a gross level of comparison. We have already remarked that the Oregon data do not display the high survival probabilities in the first year that were shown in Missouri, but, considering the heterogeneity of Oregon and Missouri school systems with regard to such factors as age distribution and system size that we know make a difference in survival rates, the extent of the similarity is surprising. A more precise comparison, however, can be made between the studies by compiling survival curves for Oregon teachers in the 22-26 age group who are in school systems enrolling between 1,200 and 6,000 students, thereby closely matching the conditions of the Missouri districts. Rate calculations from such curves have just been presented in the preceding paragraphs, but are reassembled below to bring out the comparison.

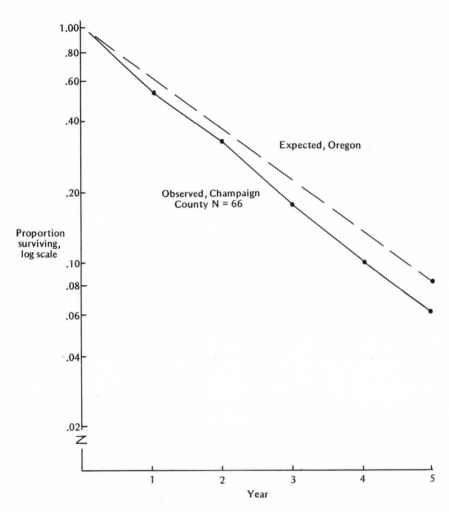

Figure 4-6
Observed survival curve for 1947-48 cohort,
Champaign County, Illinois, and curve expected
for comparable Oregon cohort (semilog coordinates)

	Male	Female
Missouri, 1951-1953 cohort	.773	.645
Oregon, 1962 cohort	.774	.620

The Missouri data, it should be noted, are based on Years 1-4, ignoring the anomalous first year, while the Oregon data are based on Years 0-4, but, within that limitation, the figures demonstrate a virtual identity in survival rates in the two cohorts studied ten years and half a continent apart when care is taken to control for the effects of age and school district size.

Additional Comparative Data

Fragmentary data collected in the course of other investigations add to our confidence in the generality of the survival phenomena with which we are dealing. Earlier we alluded to survival data obtained for a 1960 cohort in sixteen Missouri systems, some of which were the same ones Whitener had used for his 1951-1953 cohort. The data are unsatisfactory in several respects—they cover only three years of survival, "unavoidable" and temporary separations are excluded, and the age-sex distribution of the cohort is unavailable—but they demonstrate that the survival curve was exponential over the brief time period.

Statistics obtained for a 1947-48 cohort (N = 66) in seven very small, rural or small town districts of Champaign County, Illinois, are more adequate. Figure 4-6 indicates that the curve follows a highly regular exponential form through the five years of observation and also that its slope is extremely steep ($q = .572$, fitted by eye). The low survival rate, however, is not substantially discrepant from the rate one would expect in Oregon districts of the same size and sex-age distributions. We have algebraically computed such an "expected" rate by weighting the Oregon rates for males and females (females by age category) in equivalent-sized schools according to the proportional sex-age distribution of the Champaign County cohort. The "expected" rate is .660, somewhat but not markedly higher than the observed rate; its exponential function is plotted in the figure for comparison.

Where all of the survival curves presented to this point, including those from Missouri and Oregon, underscore the similarity in rates through time (in cohorts studied from 1947 to 1962) when age, sex, and system size are controlled, another set of curves illustrates the profound effect on survival of the massive dislocations of World War II. The curves in Figure 4-7 are for University of Illinois graduates who entered teaching in 1937-1939 (Group I) and in 1940-1942

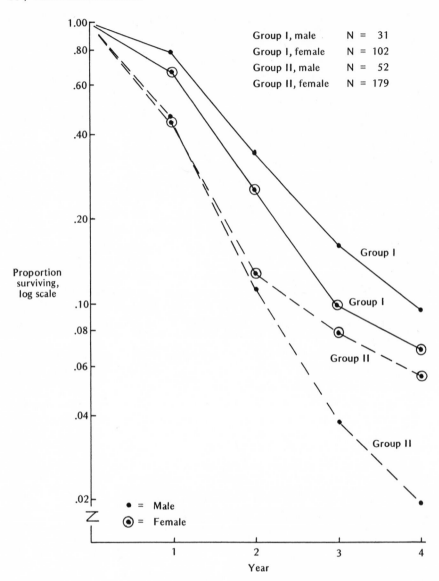

Figure 4-7
Survival curves for male and female
University of Illinois graduates
entering employment in 1937-1939, Group I,
and 1940-1942, Group II (semilog coordinates)

(Group II).[15] The slopes for males were exorbitantly steep, especially the one for males entering employment at the height of the war (Group II); only one member of the 52-man cohort was still teaching in his district at Year 4. While the curves are quite irregular, due in part to the heterogeneity of the cohorts with respect to the timing of events in connection with the war and in part to the small number of cases in the tails of the curves, the fact is that neither male nor female teachers had better than 50-50 odds of surviving into the next year through most of the war period and in some instances the annual rate dropped below .300. We can assume that most of the graduates were in their early 20's at the time of employment and that many of them were entering the smaller school systems of the region, two conditions making for poor survival probabilities under the best of circumstances, but the rates for these wartime teachers were far below those to be expected even from the youngest females in the smallest school districts in normal times. Unquestionably, teacher survival can be influenced by major events in the economy and polity of the nation and constancy in the survival process through time can be overemphasized.

Summary: Comparative Curves

The comparative data assembled in this section indicate that Whitener's finding regarding an initially steeply falling but gradually tapering survival curve is not peculiar to Missouri school districts of the early 1950's. All the curves have the same general conformation. Most of the curves accord reasonably well with an exponential function through the first five years, implying that the probability of surviving into the next year is constant through the period. In Whitener's curves, however, survival through the first year was too great to agree with the exponential function observed in the following three years, an issue that demands further investigation. A sharp improvement in survival rate also can be seen in Whitener's data after Year 4 when his data are examined from the perspective of the exponential model. The improvement is substantially beyond that which would be expected from the fact that the teachers were five years older.

Uncontrolled population differences in age, sex, and system size create wide variations in the slopes of survival curves, but when the differences are controlled, as in the comparison between Whitener's Missouri data (ignoring the anomalous first year) and the Oregon data, or when they are estimated, as in the projection of expectancies from the Oregon data on observed survival in Champaign County, the slopes of the curves are highly similar. Nevertheless, the effect of

World War II on teacher survival is plainly evident, massively depressing the rates of both males and females.

COMMENTARY

The present study has sought to go behind the known fact that school districts vary in the proportion of their faculties that must be replaced each year to identify some of the responsible factors. Whitener's "actuarial approach" has proven to be a useful tool for this purpose. The survival curve carries a large amount of information that normally is lost in conventional studies of the turnover problem, and it draws attention to a feature of the problem rarely considered either at the conceptual or analytical level, the processes of separation occurring through time. We have extended Whitener's approach in this paper by formulating survival as a stochastic process, which renders the survival curve more amenable to formal treatment and which further emphasizes the time dimension of the problem, and by introducing the simplest of all stochastic applications, the exponential model. This model entails only one assumption—that for any given class of teacher, the probability of separation (or, conversely, survival) is constant in all time intervals under observation. It is surely an oversimplified model, but at least it provides a point of departure for discovering where and how elaborations must be added.

The Oregon study, along with Whitener's, allows us to say that the probability of separation from school districts is in large part a function of the teachers' sex, age, length of service already completed, and the system size. These are surface factors, however, in that they offer little in the way of a direct understanding of the fundamental forces affecting teacher separation, so we must turn briefly to a more general level of conceptual analysis. First, we will introduce the concept of "hazards to survival," then examine the meaning of sex, age, and size.

Let us assume that the probability of a teacher separating from his school system in a time interval, earlier symbolized as r, is the sum of the probabilities of a wide variety of withdrawal-inducing events befalling him in the unit of time:

$$r = m_A + m_B + \ldots + m_K.$$

The subscripts $A \ldots K$ indicate the various withdrawal-inducing forces and events, the "hazards" to which he is exposed, and m the probability with which each will occur. Separation rate then is a *resultant* force—the sum of a set of forces acting on a teacher to increase the likelihood of withdrawal from employment in the district.[16] In the absence of hazards ($r = 0$), teachers in a cohort would survive indefinitely, but this is never the case. As mortals, teachers run the usual hazards of accident, illness, and death, as well as many more. Empirically speaking, the value of r always exceeds 0. By definition it can never exceed 1.00. The task of specifying the various hazards in systematic fashion will be avoided here, but an indication of what some of them might be can be gained from lists of "reasons" for turnover commonly found in teacher mobility studies, including such things as maternity, return to school, promotion to administrative or nonteaching position, entrance into another occupation, military draft, as well as the so-called unavoidable hazards of accident, illness, and death. Formulating a reasonable classification scheme of the more important hazards is a high priority problem for the future. Once it is undertaken, it will be possible to begin assembling data to estimate the probability values, m, associated with them.

The significance of the sex factor can now be clearly phrased: males are exposed to a qualitatively different set of hazards than females. Some hazards like illness or death, to be sure, apply with approximately equal force to males and females, but others like the military draft or maternity are sex specific, and still others differ markedly in the probability of affecting the two sexes. Elsewhere we have argued that the forces shaping the occupational behavior of males are so profoundly different from those affecting the behavior of females that they need to be treated as two separate problems. (Our finding that the two factors of age and district size have utterly different consequences for the survival of males and females underscores the point.) We proposed that the forces most strongly implicated in male separations are likely to be economic in nature, while those shaping the mobility of females are mainly related to the culturally defined role of female and the cycle of life events associated with the role.[17] Following this reasoning, the import of the age and school size factors can better be understood.

Many hazards affecting teacher separations are closely associated with age, but age, itself, is not a force acting directly on separations (except in the case of retirement). It merely reflects a number of underlying physiological, cultural, economic, and social forces that happen to impinge on teachers as a function of the number of years since birth. Such hazards as death, illness, maternity, the military draft, and promotion to administrative positions are cases in point; they each operate differentially as a function of the teacher's age.

Findings of the Oregon study suggest that the most potent hazards affecting females are indeed age linked, but perhaps a more useful index than age would be the female teacher's location in the life cycle. The female life cycle might be conceived in terms of the following stages: (a) premarriage, (b) first marriage but prechild-bearing, (c) childbearing, (d) completed family, children between 5 and 17 at home, and (e) emancipated family. Each stage has its unique array of withdrawal-inducing hazards, and we might expect the resultant separation rates to vary accordingly—considerably more closely than with age, given the fact that females pass through the stages of the cycle at different ages. This mode of analysis leads us to expect, too, that females who do not marry, who are widowed, or who otherwise deviate from the conventional life cycle of the female role will be exposed to hazards more similar to those of males than of females.

The Oregon data showed no comparable age effect in the case of male survival, perhaps because the age-linked hazards to survival were overshadowed by more powerful forces. It is also possible, though, that chronological age is an especially insensitive index of with-drawal-inducing forces associated with different periods in the male's life, disguising temporal regularities rather than revealing them. If our assumption about the potency of economic forces in affecting the mobility of male teachers is correct, a more sensitive index would be one that reflected differences in the financial burden he carries. Financial obligations rise as the single man marries and as he begins his family, reaching a peak perhaps when his children start entering college, although the burden may be offset by then if his wife is also working. We believe the press of survival hazards will vary in cor-respondence to financial burden. The probability of returning to school, for example, is certainly greater for an unmarried man than for a man with four young children; the lure of a high-paying job in industry, however, may be greater for the man with a growing family than the single man. How these matters might balance out in the separation rate we do not know, but we feel that an index of financial burden stands a better chance of revealing regularities than the purely fortuitous measure of age.

The significance of school district size as a correlate of male survival is by no means transparent in the Oregon data. Like age, it is an index of many other things and almost certainly does not consti-tute a force in its own right. But it is reasonable to believe that system size is closely associated with salary opportunities and other economic returns to the teacher. One important hazard to the male's survival as a classroom teacher in a school (if it can be called a hazard) is the availability of better-paying jobs in administration, in other school districts, or outside of education altogether, and as a rule the larger school districts pay the more competitive salaries thereby reducing the impact of the hazard. Higher salaries, however, are not necessarily more competitive; salaries depend upon the community in which the school system is located, or more specifically upon what economists call the structure of the labor market. A well-paying position as a social studies teacher may be quite unattractive if the school system is situated in an urban area where demand is high for literate, college-educated young males to fill quasi-professional or junior managerial posts. We suspect that the meaning of school size as a factor in the separation rate of male teachers will be unraveled only through economic approaches to labor market analysis.

Notes

The research reported in this article was conducted as part of the research and development program of the Center for the Advanced Study of Educational Administration at the University of Oregon. CASEA is a national research and development center which was established under provisions of the Cooperative Research Program of the United States Office of Education. Frank Walch and Robert B. Everhart, graduate assistants, aided in the research.

1. Joy E. Whitener, "An Actuarial Approach to Teacher Turnover" (Ph.D. diss., Washington University, St. Louis, Missouri, 1965).

2. K.F. Lane and J.E. Andrew, "A Method of Labour Turnover Analysis," *Journal of the Royal Statistical Society*, Series A, CXVIII (1955), 296-323; H. Silcock, "The Phenomenon of Labour Turnover," *Ibid.*, CXVII (1954), 429-40.

3. Including the crude turnover rate.

4. His observations seem to affirm for teachers a fact well established among industrial laborers: the rate of separation is an inverse function of the employees' years of service with the firm. The nature of the relationship is a subject of discussion later in the article, but we might point out here that the existence of this relationship importantly limits the utility of the crude turnover rate for comparative purposes. (See Lane and Andrew, "Method of Labour Turnover Analysis," and Silcock, "Phenomenon of Labour Turnover. ") The crude turnover rate will be substantially higher in a rapidly growing school district with large numbers of newly employed personnel than in a stable district with proportionally greater numbers of long-service personnel, even though the districts are alike in all other respects affecting turnover.

5. W.W. Charters, Jr., "What Causes Teacher Turnover?" *School Review*, LXIV (1956), 294-99; and "Some 'Obvious' Facts about the Teaching Career," *Education Administration Quarterly*, III (1967), 183-93.

6. W.W. Charters, Jr., "School Size and Rates of Teacher Turnover," unpublished research report, April 1956; Ward S. Mason and Robert K. Bain, *Teacher Turnover in the Public Schools 1957-58*, U.S. Department of Health, Education, and Welfare, Office of Education, Circular No. 608 (Washington, D.C.: U.S. Government Printing Office, 1959).

7. James S. Coleman, *Introduction to Mathematical Sociology* (New York: Free Press of Glencoe, 1964).

8. Mason and Bain, *Teacher Turnover*, p. 1.

9. Where the number of cases in the tail of the survival distribution fell below 30, the least-squares fit was based on numbers at each point in the distribution weighted inversely to their proportion of the total cohort.

10. In a multiple regression analysis involving the effects of age, sex, teaching level, prior experience, and marital status on years of completed service, Whitener found the partial coefficient for age to be .42 and for sex .15, both significant beyond the 1 percent level. Multiple R for the system of variables was .46.

11. W.W. Charters, Jr., "Some Determinants of Teacher Separations from Midwestern School Systems," unpublished research report, September 1967; Mason and Bain, *Teacher Turnover*, p. 10.

12. That this may be important to do is suggested by David J. Bartholomew (*Stochastic Models for Social Processes* [London: Wiley, 1967], pp. 128-30). He comments on the plausibility of a labor turnover model in which length of service is taken as a function of time spent in a previous job.

13. W.W. Charters, Jr., "Teacher Survival in Oregon School Districts: First Results of a State-wide Study," Oregon School Studies Council *Bulletin*, XII (No. 5, January 1969).

14. We might have based the estimate on the age-survival rate relationship presented earlier, which indicated a .003 and .009 increment in survival with each year of age for males and females, respectively. It leads to a lower estimate of the age contribution than shown here—.015 for males and .045 for females.

15. Data were collected in a 1948 follow-up study of graduating classes of teacher trainees by the Office of Teacher Placement, University of Illinois. While coming from the same source, these data should not be confused with data used as the basis for an earlier study of the author's ("Survival in the Profession: A Criterion for Selecting Teacher Trainees," *Journal of Teacher Education*, VII [1956], 253-55) concerned with survival in the occupation, not survival in the school district.

16. It might be more propitious to conceive of r as the resultant of opposing forces in a force field, some acting to increase r and some to depress it, rather than as a simple sum.

17. W.W. Charters, Jr., "Research on Teacher Mobility," *Harvard Studies in Career Development* (No. 27, 1964), mimeo, and "Some 'Obvious' Facts about the Teaching Career."

II / COMPENSATION

INTRODUCTION

Virtually all the articles in the compensation section study teachers' salaries at the expense of other components of the wage package. The emphasis on salary determination has both a normative and an explanatory focus. First, we will examine the design of salary schedules to meet certain specified criteria. Second, we shall investigate the variables that influence the size of teachers' salaries. The disciplines represented in this section are chiefly economics and management science, which probably accounts for the emphasis on formal mathematical and computer models.

The single salary (two-step) schedule, according to which salary increases are based on training and experience only, has been almost universally adopted in public education. Benson[1] has enumerated four basic problems with this plan, which include (1) the absence of rewards for superior classroom performance, (2) the lack of salary differentials for teachers in subject areas in short supply, (3) the emphasis on rewarding experience rather than training, and (4) the failure to distinguish between teachers who want to work full time and those who do not. The first problem has led to the so-called merit-pay controversy. Over the years a number of proposals have come forth for rewarding good teachers which either substitute for or build upon the single salary schedule. Unfortunately, most of these have been unable to meet teachers' desires for an objective determination of salaries. Cohn[2] has a discussion of the advantages and limitations of two such proposals.

Kershaw and McKean's famous work, an excellent example of the application of economic reasoning in educational administration, is addressed to the second problem. Their basic point, that higher pay should be offered to attract individuals with relatively scarce teaching skills, is still applicable today for districts trying to recruit or improve quality in traditionally difficult-to-teach subject areas. Using wage and employment theory they sketch out the advantages at the district and national levels of subject area salary differentials. A great strength of their work is a willingness to deal with some of the complex practical issues involved in the application of their ideas. For example, the suggestion for a three-step salary schedule is a straightforward means of achieving their aims which at the same time represents only an incremental change from existing arrangements. Fortunately or unfortunately, depending upon one's view, the three-step schedule has not met with much acceptance. Perhaps the loudest objections have been raised by teachers concerned with preserving the equality norm in compensation practice. The comment by Benson makes two additional points involving the plan's impact on equality of educational opportunity and its ability to meet the needs of teachers desiring full-time versus part-time employment.

Holtmann suggests a way of estimating the value of teaching resources to a public school system using a linear programming model. See Wagner[3] for an excellent introduction to the topic. Basically, a district's objective, assumed to be the maximization of its graduates' lifetime earnings, is viewed as a linear function of the numbers of students to be educated. Naturally, the extent to which this objective can be achieved is constrained by certain resource limitations such as the number of teachers available in different subject areas. These limitations serve as upper bounds on the amount of resources actually used which are also expressed in the model as linear functions of the students educated. The solution, by known computational techniques, for the highest degree of the objective attainable given the constraints, allows the subsequent calculation of so-called "shadow prices." These are the additional amounts of the objective that can be reached by purchasing one more unit of resources used up to their limits in the solution. (The article's reference to the dual is to a related linear programming problem, formulated from knowledge of the original, the solution of which explicitly yields the shadow prices.) Knowledge of the shadow price for teachers in a certain subject area provides a compensation guideline since the district should be willing to pay up to this amount to attract an extra person. Such information would also be useful in determining the salary differentials in Kershaw and McKean's third step. Once more, they can be used to establish a priority of teaching needs in the various subject areas. Holtmann, however, is not pretentious; he carefully points out the numerous assumptions necessary for the shadow price calculations. A further critique of his work is given by Cohn.[4] Bruno[5] has developed another linear programming model related to compensation.

There are a number of different approaches currently being used to explore the determinants of teachers' salaries. Two economists, Carlsson and Robinson,[6] have worked on a public employment wage theory applicable to teachers by extending the assumptions of the traditional private sector theory. Findings supporting a modified version of their model in a public school context have been reported by Owen.[7] The extensive literature on the determinants of educational expenditures, recently reviewed by Hickrod,[8] constitutes a second approach since teachers' salaries represent so much of a district's budget. And a third approach is to study the actual process by which salary decisions are made, an example of which is Benson's[9] application of James Duesenberry's "demonstration effect."

In his first chapter, Gerwin, in opting for the third approach, utilizes conceptual frameworks borrowed from labor economics and administrative theory. First, he adopts the notion of a wage contour, a group of firms whose wages tend to move together for economic and political reasons. This notion is applied to the study of B.A. minimum salary decisions in a group of six suburban Milwaukee districts over a time period prior to the introduction of collective bargaining. Second, each system's decision, and its impact on all the others, is analyzed in detail from an information-processing viewpoint. Essentially, the researcher looks for policy rules developed on the basis of past experience, which are used to process salary comparison data into a specified choice. These rules, uncovered as the result of interviews with decision makers, are explicitly formulated into a computer model where predictions can be compared to actual choices. The advantage of this approach is that it facilitates the development of highly detailed theory in a rigorous manner; the disadvantage is that focusing on particular districts gives the theory an ad hoc flavor.

In his second offering, Gerwin analyzes the same districts' decisions on the entire salary schedule and fringe benefits under collective bargaining. A formal model is not employed because of the unstructured nature of the problem. Instead, information processing concepts are used as guidelines in a more or less qualitative analysis. For example, an analysis is made of the sources and content of the information used in decision making. Various policy orientations assumed by board members are identified including examples of some of the associated policy rules. A case analysis demonstrates how information and orientations influence compensation outcomes. While this particular application of the analytical guidelines is of most interest to those concerned with the employment relationship, they may also turn out to be helpful in the study of other educational policy issues.

Ulrich's comments provide a new way of looking at the interrelationships among Gerwin's three policy orientations. This new outlook is used in a discussion of some fundamental problems he sees in the ways school boards exercise their functions. His points are illustrated in the context of salary policy formation in the same district from which Gerwin drew his case analysis.

The article by Kasper is perhaps the first to attack in an analytical fashion the effect that collective bargaining has had on teachers' salaries. His tentative answer is based on a simple linear model derived from economic theory and common sense. A state's average teachers' salary is hypothesized to depend upon the extent of teachers' organization and other variables meant to serve as controls. Kasper's formulation also allows him to furnish some clues as to the impact of NEA versus AFT representation and to offer some results on the determinants of the extent of organization. Since the article's publication, the literature on the topic has begun to expand rapidly. It has been argued that his state-wide orientation begets certain methodological problems. For this discussion and a reply, see Baird and Landon[10] and Kasper.[11] Investigations at the individual district level, undertaken by Baird and Landon, and Thornton,[12] have shown somewhat more of an impact than that found by Kasper.

The practitioner's comment in this section is by Slack Ulrich, an executive with Northridge Lakes Development Co. in Milwaukee. His previous work experience includes professional salary administration in the Square D Co. From 1960 through 1969 he served on the school board of the Fox Point-Bayside elementary district. In this capacity, he participated in the development and implementation of a merit plan for teacher compensation, and he represented the board in salary negotiations on a number of occasions.

Notes

1. Charles S. Benson, *The Economics of Public Education*, 2d ed.(Boston: Houghton Mifflin, 1968).

2. Elchanan Cohn, *The Economics of Education* (Lexington, Mass.: Lexington Books, 1972).

3. Harvey M. Wagner, *Principles of Operations Research* (Englewood Cliffs, N.J.: Prentice Hall, 1968).

4. Cohn, *Economics of Education.*

5. James E. Bruno, "Compensation of School District Personnel," *Management Science*, XVII (No. 10, June 1971), B569-87.

6. Robert J. Carlsson and James W. Robinson, "Toward a Public Employment Wage Theory," *Industrial and Labor Relations Review*, XXIII (No. 2, January 1969), 243-48.

7. John D. Owen, "Toward a Public Employment Wage Theory: Some Econometric Evidence on Teacher Quality," *Industrial and Labor Relations Review*, XXV (No. 2, January 1972), 213-22.

8. G. Alan Hickrod, "Local Demand for Education: A Critique of School Finance and Economic Research Circa 1959-1969," *Review of Educational Research*, XL (No. 1, Winter 1971), 35-49.

9. Benson, *Economics of Public Education.*

10. Robert N. Baird and John H. Landon, "The Effects of Collective Bargaining on Public School Teachers' Salaries: Comment," *Industrial and Labor*

Relations Review, XXV (No. 3, April 1972), 410-17.

11. Hirschel Kasper, "The Effects of Collective Bargaining on Public School Teachers' Salaries: Reply," *Industrial and Labor Relations Review,* XXV (No. 3, April 1972), 417-23.

12. Robert J. Thornton, "The Effect of Collective Negotiations on Relative Teachers' Salaries," *Quarterly Review of Economics and Business,* XI (No. 4, Winter 1971), 37-47.

5 / Salary Differences and Salary Reform

Joseph A. Kershaw and *Roland N. McKean*

THE CASE FOR ADDITIONAL SALARY DIFFERENCES

We are troubled by this widespread, almost unquestioning, acceptance of the single salary schedule, especially because the logic of the
case seems to be against the unified schedule and in favor of one that
provides for more salary differences. This is not to suggest, of course,
that salary structure is the only factor shaping the quality of instruction in elementary and secondary education. It is simply to say
that salary structure is *one* of the important influences to be considered. (Similarly, flour is one important ingredient that helps
determine the outcome in baking a cake, though it is not the only
ingredient. Nobody expects a cake to be made of flour alone.) At the
same time, the salary schedule is one influence on the ability to
attract good teachers that the school district can directly control,
unlike such factors as climate, the nature of the community, and
even working conditions.

As we see it, therefore, to have or not to have a new type of salary
schedule with pay differentials according to field of training ought to
be a live issue. Educators, voters, and boards of education ought at
least to consider the pros and cons, not bury them. We are going to
review these pros and cons and present the case that can be made in

Reprinted from Joseph A. Kershaw and Roland N. McKean, *Teacher Shortages
and Salary Schedules* (New York: McGraw-Hill, 1962), chs. 4, 10.

principle for a new kind of schedule. As we go through the argument, questions will no doubt arise about the factual significance of certain points and about the effects of implementing a new salary plan on administrative difficulties and teachers' morale. These matters will be taken up in later chapters, but for the moment we shall simply review the economic and ethical arguments.

The Economic Case

Let us inquire first into the effects of salary structure on economic efficiency—that is, on the use of available resources so as to get the most out of them. Does the single salary schedule cause resources to be misused or wasted?

To say anything about the answer to this question, we must assume that community or school officials know, at least roughly, what they want from the schools. (If no one cares about how things turn out, it makes no difference how resources are used.) But this assumption is surely justified. In elementary and secondary education most people are concerned about outcomes. In some communities they care more about winning football games than teaching algebra to average pupils, but they care, and their concern is transmitted to boards of education, superintendents, principals, and teachers. Moreover, even though there are uncertainties and disagreements, people feel, at least part of the time, that they can distinguish more achievement from less achievement—e.g., football wins from losses, good instruction from bad instruction. Superintendents and principals certainly feel that they can tell a better situation from a worse one. (If they did not feel this way, they would have no business being in school administration, for they would have no basis for choosing among alternative practices or policies.)

In brief, there are ends or objectives in education, and people are able to some extent to distinguish greater from lesser achievement of those objectives. Most of the time, citizens delegate the task of making these judgments to boards of education and school administrators. Some rules and practices can help administrators get more (as they see it) from available resources; other rules and practices can force them to get less from available resources. We do not presume to know exactly what communities and boards of education want from their school systems. Therefore we cannot be sure what degrees of skill they want in the teaching of various classes. Perhaps, for instance, they *want* less able teachers in some fields than in others. For our purposes, however, it is enough to know that school officials are not indifferent to the quality of instruction in the various fields.

Turning now to the design of salary schedules, we wish to ask whether a unified salary schedule helps or hinders efforts to get the most out of resources. For purposes of illustration we shall assume here that administrators are under pressure to get better instruction in academic subjects. The general principles would still apply, however, if the community wanted better coaching or better vocational training. Suppose, as an illustration, that good English teachers are scarcer than good kindergarten teachers in relation to the numbers needed (or that the former are more in demand for nonteaching positions).

Consider the matter first from the viewpoint of an individual school district. To attract and retain the desired number of those relatively scarce English teachers to the district, it may be necessary to offer them relatively high salaries. Paying the higher salaries to teachers in *all* fields would attract competent English teachers and an abundance of first-rate applicants to teach kindergarten—but this policy would force the community to sacrifice other things in order to pay the kindergarten teachers more than was necessary to attract capable persons. Or, more likely, this policy would cost more than taxpayers were willing to spend. Paying a lower salary to teachers in all fields—the policy often chosen by a board of education—would in the assumed circumstances[1] attract competent kindergarten teachers but not enough able and hard-working English teachers. Many English classes would be taught by persons less able than desired or would be watered down so that poorly trained persons could conduct those classes.

Thus, broadly speaking, three choices are open to the district: (1) to have salary differentials, offering higher pay where necessary to attract relatively scarce teaching skills; (2) to have a unified salary schedule, offering sufficiently high salaries to everyone to attract the desired persons in the scarce fields; or (3) to have a unified salary schedule, offering lower salaries than those necessary to attract the desired number and caliber of teachers in the scarce fields. If we neglect for the moment the possible impacts on morale and administrative difficulties (which we shall consider later), the efficient policy from the district's standpoint would appear to be to use salary differentials rather than a unified salary schedule, retaining a capable staff in all departments yet not letting the most acute scarcities determine the salaries that are paid to all.

Pay differences *within* a teaching field may be warranted for essentially the same reasons. If there are differences in the abilities of teachers—and these need not stem solely from different amounts of training or experience—a district may wish to attract and retain some of the unusually able teachers. To draw them from other employment or other school systems, it is necessary to make a position in this district more attractive than the alternative opportunities. One way to do this is to raise the salary offered to such teachers. But the choices open to the district are again the ones mentioned previously—to use differentials, to have a unified salary schedule high enough to attract the best teachers, or to have a unified schedule that offers lower salaries and fails to attract the unusually gifted teachers.

If such differentials were established *within* a teaching field, the result would be similar to some merit-pay schemes. In the present study we are talking about differentials according to the markets for the services of individuals, not according to the merit of individuals in any other sense. Nonetheless, the differentials decided upon in the two cases might be closely correlated, because bonuses for performance would be rather similar to the payments needed to attract and retain the best teachers.

So much for the economics of salary structure from the individual school's point of view. What are the economics of this matter from a national standpoint? Does a unified salary schedule cause the nation's resources to be used inefficiently?

First consider unified schedules that are set too low to attract enough of certain desired teaching skills. In the "short run"—that is, before any effects are felt on the numbers of teachers in the various fields—such salary schedules lead to inefficient use of existing teacher supplies. For one thing these schedules allow teaching skills to be misallocated among regions and schools. Suppose good English teachers are comparatively short in School A, while able science teachers are relatively scarce in School B. In principle, School A should offer relatively high salaries to English teachers, and School B should offer relatively high pay for science instruction. If the two schools have adopted unified schedules, however, school officials lose most of their ability to correct the misallocation. English majors may be teaching some of the science classes in School B, while science majors may be teaching some of the English classes in School A. Recruiting efforts can be directed toward remedying this situation, but recruiters cannot offer monetary inducements. If the entire salary schedule is raised in School A, able English teachers will be drawn there, but the science teachers that are released from teaching English will turn to their next-best opportunity (perhaps teaching social studies), and there is no assurance that School B will get the science instruction that it needs. If both schools raise their schedules, there is again no relative salary differential to help correct the misallocation.

The same train of reasoning would apply to regional misallocation of particular teaching skills. In the preceding paragraph, one could substitute the words "East" and "West" for "School A" and "School B," and the argument would stand. If school districts in both regions had unified salary schedules, the forces operating to correct a misallocation of, say, English teachers would be slight.

So much for the effects of unified schedules on the allocation of teaching skills among regions or schools. Another effect that may be felt is on the utilization of teachers *within* schools. If attracting one skill from its alternative opportunities costs more than attracting another, it is efficient to economize in the use of the more expensive skill. Thus it is efficient, from the standpoints of both a business firm and the whole economy, for an expensive executive to have more secretarial assistance than a less costly executive has. The more costly a service, the more important it becomes to use it carefully. In teacher utilization, the same thing is true. Higher salaries for the relatively scarce skills would almost ensure that schools economized in using the time of teachers possessing those skills while utilizing the relatively abundant skills more freely. At the extreme, the top teaching talent with the comparatively scarce skills might cost $25,000 a year, would certainly not be used to man a single classroom, and would be used only if the teacher's services were made available to thousands of pupils (e.g., by means of television). The comparatively abundant skills and degrees of ability, however, would cost less and could be used more freely.

With unified salary schedules, schools have less of an incentive to behave in this fashion. If a school gets too few teachers with the scarce skills, officials do generally try to use their talents economically (not wasting them in inappropriate assignments), but no extra expense adds to the pressure to use those particular skills frugally. The healthy influence of explicitly recognizing that these are relatively expensive skills is not present. And, if a school gets enough of such teachers, either through good luck or high salaries across the board, it is under no pressure to be more frugal in using the scarce skills than it is in using others. If a particular school does not get *any* of these teachers, of course, it does not use them thriftily or otherwise.

In the long run, a unified salary schedule has more serious impacts on resource use by affecting the new supplies of teachers drawn into the profession and the numbers induced to leave the profession. Let us continue for the present to speak of unified schedules in which salaries are too low to attract the desired number of teachers possessing the relatively scarce types of training. If one assumes that communities want the usual academic subjects taught effectively, the unified schedule is misallocating resources. On the one hand, persons who could teach some of these subjects effectively are not being bid away from less important uses. They are not being induced to enter or remain in teaching. On the other hand, some of the persons who have the relatively abundant teaching skills are being bid away from more important uses. Some individuals are lured into acquiring degrees in the easy but nonscarce majors and entering the teaching profession when they would really make a more valuable contribution in some other occupation. For example, a man might be "worth" $6,000 a year as a teacher (i.e., equally good instruction could be given by persons drawn from positions paying that amount); be worth $7,000 a year as an accountant; yet be drawn into teaching by the $8,000 he can get under the unified salary schedule.

One may ask, "Wouldn't such persons be deterred from becoming teachers by the absence of jobs for teachers with such majors? How can high salaries attract too many of the abundant majors when there are only so many openings for them?" But there *are* more openings, because the unified salary schedule attracts too few of some skills, leaving vacancies to be filled, albeit inadequately, by those having less suitable training. There *are* jobs for physical education majors to teach mathematics and for non-English majors to teach English. And so the process of misallocating these resources can go on indefinitely.

A unified salary schedule can produce further misallocation of resources because of its comparative inflexibility. When the market improves for some skills (for example, as it did for science and mathematics majors in the 1950's), schools have difficulty coping with the new situation. To retain their able teachers in these fields, especially the younger ones who are still mobile, the schools would have to raise these teachers' salaries, but with unified schedules this would mean raising all teachers' salaries. Typically, such action would not be taken promptly, if at all, and some teachers having the now-scarce skills would leave teaching for better opportunities. Some turnover, of course, is inevitable and desirable, but in this situation there would be an abnormal and undesirable rate of turnover. The result would be the waste of part of the training of the departing teachers as well as a loss of their services in education.

There is a close analogy, incidentally, between these effects of unified salary schedules in education and the effects of pay schedules in the armed forces. These effects and possible improvements in pay schedules were studied by the Cordiner Committee, whose activities and report received considerable publicity in 1957.[2] The armed forces had what amounted to a unified salary schedule—with steps and differentials determined by number of years in the service and position in the table of organization. The differentials had little relationship to the markets for various skills—e.g., cooks, truck drivers, jet mechanics, and electronic specialists. Unlike school districts, the military services could draft men for an initial period of service, so that the services' difficulties showed up chiefly in retention rates after the first enlistment.

What happened was that, with the unified salary schedule, the services had plenty of cooks and truck drivers, but too few electronic technicians and highly trained mechanics. After their hitch, the latter found more attractive opportunities in the civilian economy. The services tried exhortation, extra recruiting efforts, pleas to Congress for across-the-board increases in the pay schedule, and cross-training of cooks and bakers to convert them into technicians (where successful, these conversions led to losses among *these* newly trained technicians).

The Cordiner Committee reported:

The military services are not able, at the present time and under the present circumstances, to keep and challenge and develop the kinds of people needed for the period of time necessary for those people to make an effective contribution to the operation of the force.

...We must move forward from a concern with numbers to a deeper concern for quality and for retention of skilled personnel for an extended period of productive service.[3]

The committee argued that the basic trouble was the unified pay schedule and wrote:

Present compensation practices of the armed forces are so clearly out of step with the times, so clearly inadequate to the needs of a technically advanced form of national defense, and so clearly contrary to all that has been learned about human motivations that they can unmistakably be identified as a major impediment to national security.[4]

The report criticized pay increases solely for "protracted service" —for "surviving for a lengthy period of time"—and urged pay differentials that would recognize market realities, attract and retain the skills actually needed, and also provide an incentive for superior effort and performance. By doing this, the armed services could get greater output for their money. As a result of the Cordiner study (and of the thinking and views of persons in the Defense Department and Congress), some pay differentials of the sort recommended were set up, and retention of the scarce skills has improved.

It may be instructive to keep in mind the strong parallel between the personnel situation that existed in the armed forces and the one that now exists in secondary education. We hope that the present study will be in a sense a Cordiner report for education. Like defense, education is becoming increasingly important, and getting the greatest effectiveness from resources devoted to both these activities is urgent.

So far the discussion has pertained to the effects of a unified schedule with salaries too low to attract enough of the relatively scarce skills. One alternative, of course, is simply to have higher salaries across the board. As mentioned earlier, this policy, which could attract the scarce skills as well as the others, would be expensive from the standpoint of the district's taxpayers, too expensive to be accepted by most communities. But would it be a misuse of resources from the nation's standpoint?

The answer is yes. To pay more than enough to attract the relatively abundant skills would do more than merely transfer money from taxpayers to those particular teachers. It would attract persons who were really more valuable in other occupations. As noted before, the schools would be attracting $7,000 men to $6,000 jobs by paying $8,000, but to a greater extent than with the lower salary schedule assumed in the preceding section. In other words, the schools could be very "choosy" in some fields and "hoard" talent that could better be used elsewhere. It is often alleged that a similar situation prevailed during part of the postwar period in the utilization of engineers by defense contractors. With cost-plus contracts and necessarily some control over salaries by contracting officers, something resembling a unified salary schedule began to develop, with salaries higher than those needed to attract draftsmen and certain skills. Firms could attract men more highly trained than they needed *for some positions.* As a consequence, many firms are said to have "hoarded" engineers, using them as draftsmen or for other tasks that did not really require their special skills. In other words, there was a misuse of personnel, because in these circumstances firms were bidding more than was necessary to attract some of the particular skills needed.

In the long run, when we allow time for additional training and for new crops of college students to choose their training and occupations, this effect would be extended further. Not only would persons already trained be misused, but their extension and summer courses would often follow a whimsical pattern instead of providing the types of subject-matter training that are scarce. With pay differentials only for years of experience and numbers of college credits, "retreading" would be aimless rather than the purposeful acquisition of scarce skills. In addition, single salary schedules would induce students entering college to get training that would be partly wasted— to put resources into some forms of education that should have been devoted to other forms. And students who would have been more valuable in other occupations would be drawn into teaching with nonscarce majors and minors.

The economics of pay differentials may become clearer if we consider some extreme examples. What would be the consequences of having a unified pay schedule for everyone? In those circumstances, no differences in pay or prospects would show people where relative shortages existed. No salary differentials would attract people into the occupations where demand was outstripping supply, or into jobs where climate or working conditions were comparatively unattractive. In the longer run, no differences in pay or prospects would induce people to enter courses of training that were especially arduous. Most of us would give little thought to job preparation, choose at random, or want pleasant jobs requiring little preparation and putting us in appealing localities. Most of us would settle for something less, of course, since the pleasant positions would soon be filled, but the forces working toward a sensible allocation of skills would be very weak. Government would have to step in, using crude rules of thumb to decide what allocation was desired and, worst of all, using force as a means of implementing the decision. And the positions requiring relatively scarce skills would be filled by persons not properly trained for them.

This extreme of a unified pay schedule for all is presumably not a serious threat, though Socialist writers used to advocate equal pay for all or "to each according to his need." Nonetheless, the possibilities of unified salary schedules spreading further to cover wider geographical areas or more occupational groups are real enough. The idea of equality has great ethical appeal (though what many people have in mind might more aptly be called "equality of opportunity"). Within education itself, some persons are urging that a unified salary schedule be applied over wider areas and over more occupational groups. According to NEA pamphlets, "Nearly universal adoption of the single salary schedule for classroom teachers has led to discussion of unified schedules for elementary- and secondary-school principals as well,"[5] and "Some have advanced the theory that the time has come when the profession should consider working toward uniform state-wide salary schedules, or even a national schedule."[6]

A unified schedule for a wide area, however, would produce extremely undesirable results. It would put an impossible burden on comparatively poor districts (making Federal control almost inevitable); hamstring other districts so that they could not bid for scarce skills even if they were willing to spend the money; and make for a haphazard allocation of skills among schools and regions.

As an objection to the case for salary differentials, it is often stated or implied that teachers are all alike—that there is no difference between the skills and training desired for these various teaching positions. Many persons who would agree that different salaries for bookkeepers and engineers, or teachers and principals, are appropriate, would deny that salary differentials are in order for teachers in different subject fields. The skills that schools are trying to attract are not really different from each other, they would say. So how can there be any reason for pay differentials?

As an example of explicit statements of this view, consider the following excerpt from an article in *The Nation's Schools*. Although the author argued against a one hundred percent unified salary schedule, he opposed any differentials according to teaching field, urging that the situation in the schools is not like that in business:

> where is the business that has 500 college graduates each doing the same type of work (as do our 500 teachers in Grosse Pointe) and each having the same responsibilities (as our teachers have) that pays these people according to merit. . . . Business pays different rates for different jobs. So do the schools.[7]

None of our earlier arguments about pay differentials would be relevant, of course, if one teacher were perfectly substitutable for another. If teachers were interchangeable without loss of effectiveness (and maybe this is the case for teachers in grades K to 6), there would be no reason for pay differentials. From the school's standpoint, one type would be no harder to attract than the other because one could be used in place of the other.

It is hard to believe, however, that elementary school teachers and high school teachers are interchangeable, or that English teachers, shop instructors, and physical education teachers are close substitutes for each other. What they are supposed to teach differs. Effectiveness in these various fields or situations surely calls for different training, different interests, different degrees of analytical ability, sometimes different physiques and personalities. As a result, the teachers best suited for these several tasks cannot be substituted for each other without loss. Also, the nonteaching opportunities open to these groups of teachers are different. The opportunities open to the writer or editor, the electrician, the expert in physical education, the scientist, and the mathematician are far from being identical (and far from being constant). Similarly, the nonteaching openings for college graduates or teachers with majors in English, vocational training, physical education, science, and mathematics are surely different from each other.

Along these same lines, it may be argued that, even if all teachers are not alike now, they ought to be, because in all classes the schools ought to have teachers who are not narrow specialists, but who have well-rounded general educations. But this is asking the impossible, particularly in this day and age. All teachers should and do have some training in the various basic fields, but they cannot be thoroughly trained in all subjects. It would be nice, to be sure, to have even the physical education classes taught by persons with a full liberal arts and scientific education. Such persons are uncommon, however, and it would be prohibitively expensive to attract such paragons to all teaching positions. The extra gains in instructional effectiveness could scarcely match the extra costs. Some degree of specialization in the secondary schools can produce instruction that is almost as effective as having completely educated generalists in all positions, and such specialization uses far less of the nation's resources.

In summary, it is reasonable to believe that teachers are not all alike, that they are not interchangeable, and that the markets for their services differ. The fact that most educators feel there is a problem of recruiting certain skills indicates the presence of these differences in the economically relevant sense. In later chapters we shall examine the factual evidence that is available regarding these differences to see whether they are of great or little significance— whether they lead to important consequences or not.

Another objection to the argument for pay differentials which is often heard is that people do not choose their occupation or specific position on the basis of salary prospects anyway, so how can a unified salary schedule produce any misallocation of personnel? For example, the National Education Association sometimes argues that salary differentials *within* teaching do not affect persons' choices,[8] though the association does recognize that salary differentials *between teaching and other occupations* do affect individuals' choices. (Thus the NEA's platform states that "The interests of the child require. . . salary schedules adequate to attract and hold men and women of marked ability and thorough preparation.")

The position that salary prospects do not affect occupational choice is often supported by pointing out the numerous other factors that influence one's selection—climate, prestige, working conditions, personalities of administrators, housing in the community, other aspects of the community, and so on. To be sure, these other factors are significant, but their existence does not show that salary is unimportant. Moreover, in deciding what to do about the matter, it should be remembered that salaries can be changed as desired a good deal more easily than the other factors.

A closely related notion is that pay cannot be important since certain occupations or organizations attract *some* people even though they offer lower salaries than similar occupations or organizations. Or at times this notion takes a slightly different form—that pay cannot be important since certain organizations cannot attract enough able persons even though they match the salaries offered elsewhere. Behind these beliefs there seems to be the assumption that if pay is not the *only* factor in one's choice of a job, it cannot be a factor at all. Actually, of course, each occupation—each individual position—is a package of pecuniary and nonpecuniary features, and people weigh all these features in making their choices. Salary is one of these features, and it happens to be one of the few that can be manipulated with some precision.

The claim that salaries do not matter is thought to be supported when surveys show that teachers rank pay rather low as a factor attracting them to teaching. Such a survey was reported several years ago, for example, in *The Phi Delta Kappan*.[9] Two hundred undergraduates who had elected to go into teaching were asked to list their reasons for doing so. Of the forty-nine reasons they mentioned, "teaching is important work" was the one most frequently given, while "teacher pay" ranked seventh. Many persons interpret such data as meaning that salary levels are not important. Yet what the answers indicated was surely that pay was relatively low. Those who entered teaching did so in spite of low salaries—either because they liked teaching very much (or found other nonpecuniary rewards attractive) or because they had rather limited opportunities elsewhere. In these circumstances would salary come to mind frequently as the main attraction? For those few who could be attracted to teaching at $1,200 a year, would salary be the paramount attraction? Hardly. But in such circumstances an *increase* in salaries would certainly be a powerful factor in attracting more and better-trained teachers.

If pay ranked first among the stated reasons for entering a field, it might mean that pay was already attractive, but it would still not show whether an *increase* in salary would have a large or small effect on new entrants. At best, the meaning of these surveys is elusive. Suppose pay ranks first and prestige seventh as stated reasons for entering a field. Does this mean that a $10-a-year pay increase would be more important than a "large" improvement in status? Does it mean that a "little" increase in prestige would mean more than a $3,000-a-year raise? It is virtually impossible to know what such data mean. But they do not demonstrate that manipulating salaries would have little effect on the list of applicants for positions. Sensitivity of behavior to *changes* in various factors may be high or low, whatever the ranking that existing teachers give to those factors as reasons for entering the profession.

Incidentally, there is once more a noticeable parallel with experience in the military services. Confronted with shortages of talent in certain fields, the services wanted to know what to do about it. They contracted for surveys of the reasons for re-enlisting. Pay was seldom high on the list, and many officials drew the remarkable conclusion that pay was therefore an unimportant variable.

On the whole, however, people do realize that salaries are an important factor in occupational choice. As mentioned before, the National Education Association stresses the significance of salaries in attracting good teachers. One NEA study conference reported that "quality teachers come only at quality prices; . . . to expect quality teachers at bargain-basement prices is to destroy the incentive which must keep quality teachers on the market."[10]

Indeed one occasionally hears precisely the opposite objection— namely, that salaries affect occupational choices too much. It is sometimes said that if pay were higher, say, at the secondary level than at the elementary level, *all* teachers would promptly shift to the higher-paying field, leaving nobody to teach in the elementary schools.

This might happen if no variable other than salaries influenced occupational choice so that everyone was always "on the margin." But this condition violates the premise that other variables *are* operative, resulting in relative shortages when teachers in various fields are offered equal pay. In truth, salary changes would alter the decisions of only *part* of the population—that is, of those currently "on the margin" ready to be swayed.

To contend that the slightest salary differentials would cause everyone to rush to the higher-paying occupation is like saying that to tip a pitcher would necessarily cause all the water to flow out. Actually, of course, it is possible to induce some outflow without emptying the pitcher. One might overshoot the mark and have to shift back part of the way to reach the desired situation, but an extra thousand dollars for English or physics teachers would not draw *everyone* to those fields.

Some persons, while conceding that teachers are not all alike and that salaries do affect teachers' choices, may still deny that pay differentials are needed, because they may be willing to accept the pattern of teaching skills attracted under a unified schedule. Suppose it does produce comparatively ineffective teaching in, say, mathematics and English, and superior instruction in, say, home economics and men's physical education. Maybe that is all right with the voters, boards of education, and school administrators.

On this point there is no stand that would be valid for all voters or all boards and administrators. Each voter and school official has to make up his own mind about the relative importance of various fields of learning. Many people, including the authors of this study, would like to see average students receive better instruction in English and mathematics than they receive in many schools. But other persons would feel differently about this. In some communities the prevailing sentiment might be that vocational training should be more thorough. (Unless parents have a fairly wide range of choice about where to send their children to school, it is clear that all voters cannot be pleased.)

It would be a remarkable coincidence, however, if unified salary schedules provided just the pattern of skills and abilities desired in all communities, in all regions, at all times. It might happen here and there, but unless teachers were (nearly) homogeneous, it would not happen often that with unified salary schedules whatever turned up was right. It would be somewhat like offering equal remuneration to all university professors—in law, medicine, classics, engineering, and so on—and expecting to get the applicants desired. (There are pressures, of course, toward unified salary schedules in universities.)

Besides it is clear that educators are *not* happy with the pattern of skills obtained at present. They often deplore the necessity of assigning so many teachers to fields in which they did not major. According to the recent NEA reports on teacher supply and demand, there is cause for concern: *"The distribution of the new prospective candidates among the grade levels and teaching fields is gravely out of balance with the distribution of the demand for teachers."* [11]

Another objection sometimes raised is that merely raising questions about salary differentials is equivalent to asking a forbidden question: Is instruction in some fields of greater worth than instruction in others?

This proposal [to pay higher salaries to teachers of science and mathematics] has very serious implications. It challenges not only the accepted principles of salary scheduling but also the basic philosophy of our whole educational system: "What education is of most worth?"[12]

But salary differentials do not say that one subject is more important than another. Differentials may be necessary to have the same teaching effectiveness in each subject-matter area. It may be necessary to pay more in some fields than in others even to attract comparatively poor additions to the staff in those fields. It depends upon the market conditions for the various skills. As for the relative importance of different subjects—or the relative quality of instruction that is desired in each subject—that issue is not raised by questions about having salary differentials. That issue is with us all the time, and schools reach decisions about this matter, at least implicitly, when they design *any* salary schedule (and set other policies).

The Ethical Case

So far we have considered only the economics of salary differences. But is it "fair" or "just" to pay persons different amounts for giving instruction in different fields? What is a "just" salary structure? If one ponders these questions earnestly, he will surely confess his doubts about the answers. There are no answers that are correct for all persons or for all circumstances. Equal pay for all regardless of effort would have elements of unfairness in the eyes of most persons. Pay differentials according to field would also appear to be inequitable. After all, handling thirty-five fourth-graders or a high school history class is fully as exhausting as teaching ninth-grade (or college) algebra. (Similarly an economist's work may be as tiring as that of a nuclear physicist.)

One essential point to realize is that there is no general agreement on what salary structure would be just. What one person views as fair may seem cruelly unjust to another. Like the equity of many other arrangements, the equity of salary structure is a relative matter— relative to each person's beliefs and tastes—not an ethical absolute based on religion or commanding universal agreement. There is no unique salary structure, therefore, to which we can point and say "That would be fair."

Perhaps most persons would agree to the rather general prescription that, while complete equality would not necessarily be desirable, we would like incomes to be more nearly equal than they are. They might agree, too, that it would be desirable to eliminate windfall increments to income—increments that do not serve the purpose of drawing forth our best efforts or drawing resources into their best uses. (This pertains to windfalls to persons with incomes above some minimum, for obviously most people wish to give windfalls to the poverty-stricken and distressed.) Indeed legislation already works toward leveling incomes—not for persons within one occupational group but for *all* persons—by means of progressive income and inheritance taxes.

Suppose that for ethical reasons we want to go further in that direction. In fact, suppose for the moment that salary equality, or income equality, is taken to be ideal. We cannot have it *now* without drafting people into various jobs. Without the signals and the inducements provided by salary differentials, people would not know where their services were most urgently demanded, nor would they have much incentive to go there anyway. However, we may be able to have a greater degree of equality in the future, and without drafting people into various occupations, by letting pay differentials continue to pull people away from the low-pay occupations and into the high-pay ones.

The market alone would never iron out all pay differences, for some of them are due to differences in physical and mental equipment. But when coupled with equality of opportunity, or at least a high degree of such equality, the market is a powerful force toward the reduction of pay differentials. For as people leave the low-paying activities, the incomes of those who remain gradually rise, and as persons enter the high-paying occupations, salaries there gradually decline. Who can deny that occupational shifts, facilitated by more nearly equal access to education and training, have been great equalizers?[13] For example, the postwar shift of manpower from agriculture to profitable sectors of industry has worked in this direction. Thus a curious paradox exists: The way to reduce pay differentials (without resorting to force in assigning people to jobs) is to have pay differentials, letting them work toward their own abolition.

If we desire to speed up the movement toward greater equality of incomes, the fair and efficient way to do it is surely through the federal tax structure rather than through unified pay schedules for a particular sector of the economy. Employing the progressive income tax for this purpose would be more equitable because it would tend to level incomes (after taxes) in *all* sectors, treating alike those persons who are in similar circumstances. This would also have fewer adverse effects on national income, because a general income tax does not distort the allocation of resources as much as devices, such as unified pay schedules, which apply to particular sectors of the economy.

General Applicability

Does the argument for salary differences apply to various possible situations—that is, to situations where communities choose to pursue different types of education? First, what if communities decide, as many are now deciding, to provide inferior instruction? Of course, if this means that the school board wants *whatever it gets* with a unified salary schedule, the argument for salary differentials does indeed collapse. If it means, however, that the community does not wish to pay for high-quality teaching but still wants to get the best instruction it can for its budget, the case for a 3-step salary schedule applies. If the markets differ for various teaching skills, *both the community and the nation* can get more from the resources expended by using such salary differentials. Even to get second-rate rather than third-rate instruction costs more in some fields than in others. If a community, willing to authorize only a low budget, must offer the same salary steps to teachers in all fields, it will have to accept third-rate teaching in some subjects.

Second, what about communities that wish to provide really high-quality education? Here the argument for a 3-step schedule takes on additional significance. If market conditions for the desired teaching skills are not identical, the community can provide higher-quality instruction for its budget, and the nation can get greater output from its resources, by deviating from the unified salary schedule. To get capable teachers costs a great deal more in some fields than it does in others, and if raising one salary means raising all, the community cannot stretch its budget as far as it otherwise could in obtaining the desired instruction.

Given almost any plausible educational aims, it is urgent that the unified salary schedule, which has been so widely accepted, be re-examined critically. Salary schedules that permit additional steps for scarce kinds of training would appear to be an important component of almost any educational policy to which communities may turn.

METHODS OF SALARY REFORM: OVERCOMING THE PRACTICAL DIFFICULTIES

Thus far we have examined a variety of arguments and evidence, and they make a strong case, it seems to us, for having salary differentials. To attain or maintain excellence in teaching, departures from the unified salary schedule will be needed. What should the school board and school administration do if they decide that these ideas deserve to be tried? There are several practical difficulties that will occur immediately to people in the field of education. How could salary differentials that make sense be introduced into a particular system? What problems would be encountered, and how could these be surmounted?

Coping With the Morale Problem

It is widely believed that any departure from a unified salary schedule would shatter the morale of teaching staffs, thereby reducing their effectiveness and also the schools' ability to recruit good people. We must consider these possibilities seriously, asking whether morale would be worse with salary differentials or with unified schedules.

The answer is not obvious. Those who feel that salary differentials would disrupt morale are often comparing the situation today with that in the 1930's and with the individual bargaining of earlier times. During the depression of the 1930's, nearly everyone's morale was low, at least in the sense that most persons felt insecure and worried. Even these feelings did not necessarily impair effectiveness of teaching or the schools' ability to recruit good people. But in any case that state of unrest can hardly be attributed merely to the lack of unified salary schedules.

As for the period when school boards bargained with each applicant, there were without doubt abuses and occasions for discord. Were they any more serious in the schools than in business firms? They probably were. Business firms are subject to relatively vigorous competition in terms of observable and measurable criteria—sales and profits. It is *comparatively* difficult for favoritism and nepotism to influence decisions. (The more sheltered the firm from competition, the less true this is.) Schools, however, are subject to comparatively little competition in terms of a clear-cut criterion. Boards of education and administrators have money to spend, but no one is breathing down their necks to ensure that they maximize profits or anything that can be measured. They may feel moderate pressure to produce the most desirable education for their budget, but, since nobody can define this sharply or check closely on performance, this pressure is not intense. As a result, administrators have quite a bit of leeway. Unless boards of education set up certain explicit rules, there are few guidelines or checks, and capricious actions can occur too often, producing or aggravating morale difficulties.

We are not going to recommend returning to the depression of the 1930's or to individual bargaining in which neither competition nor guidelines served to restrain capricious behavior. Comparisons of those situations with that of today are not appropriate. They do not demonstrate that salary differentials according to teaching field would destroy the morale of teachers.

Instead of comparing morale in education as of different time periods, it seems to be more pertinent to compare the functioning of different schools and different types of organizations in the same time period. The first thing that occurs to one is a comparison between schools and private business. The fact is that no private profession or industry has a unified salary schedule—these groups do not try to pay the same salaries to persons having different college majors and different skills. Yet these practices have certainly not demolished morale in all private businesses. Other circumstances would seem to determine whether morale is low or high in business firms.

This comparison is of dubious relevance, however, for the reason mentioned earlier. School systems (at least as they are at present organized) cannot compete in terms of profit maximization or any other objective criterion, while much of private industry is fairly competitive. Hence, salary differentials in private firms may not lead to marked favoritism and deterioration of morale, yet in school systems they might do so.

More relevant comparisons would be between morale in schools and in noncompetitive organizations that still have salary differentials. We know of no systematic attempts to make such comparisons, but there are firms that are comparatively sheltered from competition—for example, public utilities, such as telephone and electric companies, nonprofit research organizations, universities, nonprofit foundations, and government agencies—that offer different salaries to college-trained personnel in different fields. We have no measurements, but we suspect that morale is low in some of these organizations, high in others. No one seems to argue that only schools, which are indeed almost the only organizations with fully unified salary schedules, have good morale. As far as ordinary observation can tell, morale and productivity and ability to recruit good people do not appear to be greatly impaired by offering different salaries for training in different fields. The university teacher of Greek will regard it as regrettable, but hardly as degrading, that the professor of medicine has a salary perhaps double his. The civil servant with an M.A. in English working as an editor in the Agriculture Department does not regard it as demoralizing that he makes substantially less than the Physics M.A. in the Bureau of Standards.

In most of these organizations, to be sure, schedules or guidelines exist and tend to prevent purely capricious salary practices. Indeed, departmental rivalry, administrative convenience, and other considerations keep pushing administrators toward a unified salary schedule; but in the meantime the lack of such a schedule does not shatter morale.

For whatever it is worth, introspection suggests the same conclusion to us. As an economist looks around, either in his own organization or in the rest of the economy, he can see that people with about the same ability and education are getting higher salaries than economists in some fields and less than economists in others. Where this situation was anticipated, he is not particularly disturbed, for he chose the "package" (type of work, salary prospects, etc.) knowingly. Where the situation was not anticipated— where the market for, say, construction engineers has improved sharply—he may wish that he had elected to be an engineer and may feel that bad luck has kept him from earning more, but he is unlikely to resent his employers or colleagues. As for occupations for which he had no aptitude—let us say medicine or nuclear physics—they are beside the point, because in these circumstances they were never really open to him.

Perhaps the most relevant comparision of all is between morale in schools that have unified schedules and morale in schools that do not. Two educators, using an attitude inventory to develop an index of morale, studied the relationship between morale and salary policy in five schools having plain unified salary schedules and five schools having merit pay schedules.[14] By making analyses of variance, they tried to test the hypotheses that (1) similar schools do experience morale differences, and (2) school systems with merit schemes have lower morale than the others. The results were consistent with the first hypothesis, but refuted the second one. The authors concluded that morale seems to be a function of many variables and that the type of salary plan (merit or nonmerit) "is not a significant variable in isolation relative to the determination of morale level in a school system"[15]

This one study will not, of course, be the final word on this topic. Moreover, merit pay is not the same as salary differentials according to field. (Actually, many merit schemes seem more likely to lead to favoritism and poor morale than different schedules for scarce skills, since administrators have to pass judgment on the merits of individual teachers rather than on the difficulty of recruiting certain types of teachers.) As far as the study goes, however, it is consistent with the rather common sense view that pay differentials do not necessarily produce poor morale.

Something that is often forgotten in this controversy is that unified schedules themselves can produce morale difficulties. Consider the plight of the able and conscientious teacher who observes, day after day, less capable or less industrious colleagues getting the same salary. Or consider the feelings of the English teacher whose job, if done well, may involve criticizing hundreds of themes each week and working harder than some colleagues who nonetheless face the same salary prospects. These situations can cause a good deal of ill feeling and loss of productivity. (The first situation—inequitable treatment of the more conscientious teachers—could be corrected, however, only by an effective merit scheme—not by differentials according to teaching fields.)

Again it may be instructive to consider the extreme case. If a unified schedule is so beneficial to morale in school systems, would a unified pay schedule for everyone allay ill feelings and spur us all on to greater effectiveness? Would resentments disappear, or would feelings of futility deepen? In all likelihood a scramble for favors, titles, keys to the executive washroom, and other status symbols would take the place of the scramble for salary increases. Man would still be a gamesman, striving to be one up on someone else, still finding himself unhappy when another car passes his, still becoming frustrated when he sees no way of getting ahead. This is not to say that one arrangement has the same effects on morale as any other, but it is by no means clear that a unified pay schedule for everyone would give rise to more constructive effort and a lesser sense of futility than market-determined pay differentials.

Incidentally, to doubt that salary differentials would impair morale does not imply any doubt that they would be resisted. The evidence is clear that a majority of teachers and administrators do support the unified schedule and would resist departures from it. Doubtless many are sincerely worried about possible impacts on morale. Most would oppose salary differentials in any event. A majority of existing teachers probably feel that their best chance of getting salary increases is to work through a unified schedule, and, since such a schedule *does* raise the total salary bill required to hire the existing quality of instruction, they are undoubtedly right. As for administrators, they cannot fail to recognize that salary differentials would augment the burdens of decision making, a problem we will discuss in a moment.

For several reasons, then, any departure from a unified salary schedule would be resisted. When people resist a change, it means they will be disappointed if it is introduced. But it does not follow that they will subsequently be engulfed with frustration and low morale. Removal of tariffs on cloth would be resisted by domestic textile manufacturers. It would require painful adjustment. It would make the producers angry. But it would not permanently ruin their morale. Opposition to an event does not mean that one is permanently depressed if the event occurs.

To sum up the discussion on this point, the evidence does *not* show that any departure from a unified salary schedule would destroy teachers' morale. All things considered, we doubt very much if differentials according to teaching field—if initially set up in a sensible way—would impair for long the morale and productivity of teaching staffs. The evidence to date does not undermine the economic arguments for salary differentials. Schools should not discard all possibilities other than a unified schedule simply because numerous persons assert that only a unified schedule can maintain morale.

It is apparently true, nonetheless, that teachers often have an instinctive reaction against salary differentials because they feel that paying more to one group is attributing more importance to that group. Elementary teachers are particularly prone to have this reaction. For decades they worked for the unified salary schedule on the ground that it would bring their salaries up to those in the high schools, and they have been successful in getting single schedules adopted. They might stand to lose in a relative sense and feel that their prestige was threatened if salary differentials were now accepted. Since they constitute more than half of the teachers, their voice is a loud one. Actually, of course, pay differentials mean that one group is scarcer than another, not that one is more worthy or important. The relatively low price of water does not mean that it is unworthy or unimportant; orange juice costs more simply because it is scarcer in relation to demand.

The existence of these attitudes argues that the ground should be well prepared before introducing a 3-step schedule and the understanding of the teachers should be particularly sought. It would be extremely important for them to understand the allocative function of salaries and to see that the alternative to pay differentials is probably the deterioration of the school's teaching staff. Our belief is that rapid adjustment to the situation would come, although there would undoubtedly be vigorous objections and perhaps some morale problems in the beginning. Even now there are differentials according to *length* of training; authorizing some differentials according to *type* of training goes only a short step further and could surely be accepted before too long.

Making Hard Administrative Choices

Another consideration is the administrative difficulties entailed in the use of a 3-step schedule. Unquestionably the single salary schedule simplifies the problems of the superintendent and, to some extent, of the principals. It simplifies these problems by partially tying their hands—that is, by eliminating certain choices that would otherwise have to be considered.

With the unified schedule, the superintendent and his staff must consider, among other things, the demands of the classroom teachers' association, the competition from other schools in attracting good teachers in general, and the pressures from the taxpayers. In the light of these considerations they draw up a single schedule for the board's consideration. Each year the schedule must be reconsidered, the question usually being whether or not to seek an across-the-board raise and, if so, how much.

These choices are difficult enough. But suppose the unified schedule is to be replaced by a schedule with additional steps applying to different teaching fields. The task becomes more complicated. Many more salary combinations must be considered. Not merely the pressure from one classroom teachers' association must be reckoned with, but conflicting pressures from several groups. Not merely the competition in general from other school systems but the competition for teachers, department by department, must be assessed. Is the school attracting good enough people to the music department? To the sciences? Is the system losing too many of its best English teachers? Should salaries be higher in this field than in that one?

Such questions would have to be faced when the schedules were first prepared. They would have to be faced in succeeding years as enrollment shifted, if the community and the board decided to alter the emphasis on certain fields, or if market conditions for people with different skills changed. Without a doubt, having the option of offering differential salaries would necessitate considering a wider range of alternatives and facing more painful choices than not having that option. The more flexibility one has, the more complex the decision. The more one's hands are tied, the simpler the decision. At the extreme, if there are no options whatever, there is no problem to be faced.

Administrators would welcome flexibility, of course, if communities were constantly pressing to get the best instruction possible with the budget made available. Too often, however, what the community says is, in effect: Take this budget and run a school system with it, seeing mainly that no scandals occur, the quality of instruction does not fall so low as to cause widespread complaint, and the "teenagers" are kept off the streets. Most superintendents want to do a good job, but with the public pressures concentrated on such matters as these, it is natural that school officials should want to simplify decision making somewhat by having single salary schedules

Merit systems, incidentally, call for still more painful decisions than 3-step schedules—they call for the awarding of bonuses to particular individuals *according to merit* rather than according to more objective market forces. In awarding such bonuses, school officials are explicitly saying that teacher A *deserves* this extra compensation more than teacher B. To do this is painful—it is difficult both to make this decision and to announce it. Setting up differentials according to fields of training would presumably be a little less anguishing. In setting up these schedules, officials would be saying not that teacher A is more deserving but rather that the skills acquired by teacher A happen now to be scarcer than those acquired by teacher B relative to the demand for those skills.

Without doubt, then, this new type of salary schedule would put a burden on school administrators, but then operating a school system at all imposes administrative burdens. We can hardly rule out having more than two schools or offering more than two subjects because these complications increase administrative costs. Similarly we should not discard out of hand the use of more than two kinds of salary steps because it would raise administrative costs. These extra costs have to be weighed against the prospective gains.

Deciding Which Skills are Scarcest

One difficulty is to determine what kinds of teachers are relatively difficult to hire and therefore need extra financial inducement to enter the system. Should salary supplements apply to English and mathematics teachers only, to elementary teachers only, to all high school teachers, or what? In this study we have tried to identify some of the principal shortages regionally and nationally. But we did not examine the full range of teaching fields. Our data said nothing about several fields, in some of which good teachers may be especially hard to obtain.

Moreover, as we have stressed, the relative shortages may differ from one school district to the next. Some kinds of skills are rather generally in short supply, such as high school teachers of mathematics, but there may very well be special factors operating in any given locality that create other severe and persistent shortages. For example, a large employer may increase the local demands for certain kinds of professional skills, or local colleges may turn out teachers in some fields with deficient preparation. In some areas today, English teachers are hard to hire, whereas this is not true in others. Some states still find the elementary schools hardest to staff, others find that the shortage has moved to the high school level. The point is that local factors and conditions are always important, and the school board will have to identify these.

Actually, however, school officials *know* which kinds of teachers are hard to hire and hold in their particular district or area. Almost every superintendent or personnel officer can tell offhand what kinds of applicants no longer come knocking at the door—can name the fields where the school board or administration wants better-qualified applicants. Officials can easily get data about recent recruiting experience and the qualifications of their teaching staff—e.g., the percentages of secondary teachers who are teaching in each field without adequate preparation. As in this study, such data would be only clues (although they might be rather easy to read). The informed judgments of the superintendents, principals, personnel officers, and board members would be vital components of the decisions.

To decide precisely where the higher salaries should apply would not be easy or painless. It should be remembered, incidentally, that teachers do not fall neatly into two or three discrete compartments—those that have scarce skills and those whose skills are comparatively easy to obtain. Rather there is a whole spectrum of categories that are scarce in varying degree. In principle we might like to make fine distinctions, offering a variety of salary differentials that would fit each situation. As the number of steps became larger, however, it would promise increasing difficulty and diminishing returns. In any event, one set of supplements for the scarce skills would be an enormous step forward. Let us assume, then, that fine distinctions would not be made. Officials would have to put the teaching skills into a few compartments even though the degrees of scarcity were not homogeneous within each compartment. But they could do this. People make and deal with this sort of rough aggregation every day. School administrators would simply seek to identify the fields in which they have serious trouble in attracting well-qualified applicants. To apply separate salary steps to them would at least be making a finer distinction than no distinction at all. To do that much would make more sense than treating all degrees of scarcity as though they were the same. To repeat, the decision would not be altogether easy or painless, but it could be made, and on defensible grounds, as it is almost everywhere else in our economy.

Determining the Kind and Size of the Pay Differentials

Having identified the scarce fields, the school administrators would next have to decide how to introduce the differentials and how high they should be. Perhaps the simplest way would be to add them on to the general level of the already published schedule. As an illustration, a school district might have the salary schedule that was presented earlier—plus a footnote specifying a new series of steps. Table 5-1 shows an illustrative schedule that does this, providing percentual increments for training in the scarce subject-matter fields. Persons with a minor in mathematics would receive 10 percent more than the schedule would otherwise call for—e.g., $4,950 instead of the $4,500 designated as the first step in the unmodified schedule. Those with a major in mathematics would receive a 15 percent increment. Persons with specified amounts of training in other scarce skills would receive percentual increments as indicated.

The new schedule would really be a rather modest change, making a teacher's place in the schedule depend upon three, rather than two, factors. In the conventional schedule a teacher's salary progresses by means of two kinds of steps:

1. number of years of teaching experience (either in this school district or in the aggregate), and

2. number of courses beyond the bachelor's degree.

All that we propose is a third kind of step:

3. number of courses in certain subjects, including both graduate and undergraduate work.

Note that this would be done without disturbing the present differentials based on experience and training. Thus a new mathematics teacher would enter the schedule at the same point as a new

TABLE 5-1. Example of 3-step salary schedule

Steps in schedule	Group I Bachelor's degree or 124 units[b] or equivalent or temporary vocational credential	Group II Bachelor's degree plus 14 units or equivalent or temporary vocational credential plus 14 units or equivalent	Group III Bachelor's degree plus 28 units or equivalent or vocational credential plus 28 units or equivalent	Group IV Bachelor's degree plus 42 units or master's degree or vocational credential plus 42 units or equivalent	Group V Bachelor's degree plus 56 units or master's degree plus 14 units or vocational credential plus 56 units or equivalent	Group VI Master's degree plus 28 units or vocational credential plus bachelor's degree	Group VII Master's degree plus 42 units or vocational credential plus bachelor's degree plus 14 units	Group VIII[a] Master's degree plus 56 units or vocational credential plus master's degree
1	4,500	4,770	5,040	5,310	5,580	5,850	6,120	6,390
2	4,700	4,970	5,240	5,510	5,780	6,050	6,320	6,590
.	.	.	.	.	.	.	.	.
.	.	.	.	.	.	.	.	.
.	.	.	.	.	.	.	.	.
13	6,900	7,170	7,440	7,710	7,980	8,250	8,520	8,790
14	7,100	7,370	7,640	7,910	8,180	8,450	8,720	8,990

Increment values: steps, $200; groups, $270; subject matter, see below.

[a]Persons who possess the earned doctor's degree, either Ed.D. or Ph.D., will receive $270 more than they would have received on a comparable experience step in Group VIII.

[b]Units applied to group change must be in excess of a minimum of 124. Teachers are to advance one step yearly until they reach the top of their group, and to be assigned to the group for which they qualify by reason of degrees and units.

Persons who have training in the scarce subject-matter fields will receive increments as follows:

Scarce skills	Number of units	Increment (percent)
Mathematics, minor	20	10
Mathematics, major	30	15
Subject X, minor	20	8
Subject X, major	30	12
Subject Y, major	30	10

social studies teacher, with the addition of a published supplement. It might turn out that the supplement would be more effective if it rose as the entering salary rose, so that a mature mathematics teacher would enter the salary schedule with a supplement somewhat higher than the neophyte. These things could be determined as experience showed the need for different sorts of teachers and the reaction of prospective teachers to the salaries offered.

The next question is what the amount of the differential should be. Here again there would be differences from place to place, and indeed from time to time (though not every year). The way to determine the appropriate amount is for district officials to find out what competing jobs are paying. If, for example, the system has determined that mathematicians are short, it is not hard to find out what mathematicians are being paid in each region when they have preparation equivalent to prospective teachers. Officials should also ask the colleges and universities what is happening to the mathematicians that graduate from those institutions, and what salaries they are able to command. This is information that all colleges have on hand and are glad to share with those having legitimate interests. School administrators already keep abreast of salaries offered in nearby school districts and to some extent of nonteaching salaries, but they would need more complete information about the salaries offered for various types of training. . . . It might not be necessary to match those nonteaching salaries because the better working conditions of teachers—hours, vacations, and the like—might make the teaching positions more attractive dollar for dollar. But if certain teaching skills are scarce, the difference that exists between what other employers pay and what the school currently pays needs to be reduced. The supplement should be set to do just that, perhaps closing the gap by two-thirds, or following some other rule of thumb, until it could be determined whether or not this would do the job.

We might pause here to re-emphasize that, while the subject of this chapter is what the individual district can do, our concern about shortages is at two levels. We are of course concerned about the individual district remedying its shortages by attracting already qualified teachers, perhaps new graduates of the schools of education or other schools, perhaps from other occupations. We are also concerned, however, about inducing college students with the right abilities to choose teaching careers and qualify themselves in the right teaching fields. At present the rewards in other occupations are such that too few who have promise in the scarce fields enter the education schools, too few who enter and major in these fields remain in the education schools, and too few of those who graduate with such majors bother to get a certificate or stay in teaching.

For any one school district to offer higher salaries in the relatively scarce fields will alleviate that district's difficulties, but it will hardly make a dent in the problem at the other level. It will not go far in inducing the "right" combination of college sophomores to enter and remain in education. If *numerous* school systems pay higher salaries in the scarce fields, however, larger numbers of good students will be persuaded to choose teaching careers in those fields. It should be noted that unless salaries are adjusted to the shortages, there are no forces operating to correct them, and they may persist indefinitely. In a free society the way to eliminate shortages is through adjustments of prices, in this case salaries. If we could raise the prices of the teaching services in shortest supply enough to encourage more people to enter those fields, the need for salary differentials would diminish in the long run.

The introduction of salary differentials would of course have to be planned carefully and implemented gradually. Since there is no way to determine precisely what differentials are appropriate at the start, trial and error would play a role in determining the size of the salary supplements offered in the scarce fields. The plan for phasing in the differentials would have to provide explicitly for flexibility. How the salary schedules might be modified in various situations would have to be considered in advance and made clear to all.

Flexibility would be needed, for example, in adjusting to transfers of present staff members to the scarce fields. If the 3-step schedule was adopted, some teachers already on the district's staff would set out to acquire the majors that yielded the increments. Up to a point this would be perfectly all right. The school would in this way obtain teachers trained in the scarce fields and could replace them in their original assignments without great difficulty. If too many teachers in a single school tried to acquire majors in the scarce fields, and succeeded in doing so, the salary increments for scarce skills could be diminished in size (although no absolute cuts need be made in the salaries of individuals who have already qualified for the increment).

Incidentally, in arriving at or revising the salary differentials, we would not suggest absolute salary cuts in any teaching field or for any individual. In the first place, we hope the emphasis would be on improving quality at moderate cost, not on getting inferior instruction at minimum cost. In the second place, a proposal to make absolute salary cuts would create all sorts of difficulties that we think must be avoided, and would probably prevent any constructive action being taken. In the third place, there would be no need to achieve appropriate salary differentials by inflicting cuts on any one, because the growth of the economy causes most salaries to rise in real terms, and there seems to be a built-in tendency toward inflation that causes further increases in money terms. Therefore the way to achieve salary differentials would be simply to raise the salaries in some fields more rapidly than salaries in other fields. In the space of a few years, the structure could be quite different from what it was initially, yet all teachers would have larger absolute amounts annually.

Handling Dual Assignments

Another practical difficulty that is frequently mentioned is how to determine salaries wherever dual assignments are, or must be, made. In the secondary schools, for instance, a fair amount of flexibility in the use of teachers is necessary, particularly in the smaller schools. Indeed, it is not at all unusual for a teacher to be teaching more than one subject, and the practice of majoring and minoring during training indicates an intention to prepare for more than one subject. What does one do about the salary of the teacher who has several classes in mathematics and several in physical education? Our answer is that, if mathematics has been found to be a short area, the salary supplement is paid for the *trained mathematics teacher,* not for the teacher trained for something else who is teaching mathematics. Furthermore, the supplement should be paid whether the teacher is teaching in or out of the scarce field he is trained to teach. The supplement is paid because people with a certain training are hard to get, *not* because a certain subject is hard to teach, or is more important. But it will be argued that it does not make sense to pay a supplement and then to use the teacher in a nonshort area. Indeed it does not, and one of the attractive features of this proposal, we think, is that it will put still more pressure on superintendents and principals to use the more expensive skills where they should be used, and not in other assignments. Otherwise it will be all too common to find a good mathematics or physics teacher spending part of his time on the athletic field, or to find everyone teaching a bit of English composition to spread the burden.

A second possibility, which lacks some of the advantages of the method just described, would be a position-type schedule, the salary supplement going to positions or assignments in certain departments. The extra compensation would not be for the scarce training per se, but it would attract more applicants for those positions, and the result would normally be a better-qualified staff in these departments. Dual assignments could be rewarded on a pro rata basis—for example, one-half of the salary supplement if the teacher is assigned to a scarce field one-half the time. Part-time teachers would presumably be paid on a pro rata basis under either plan.

The first plan—extra payments for special training rather than for special teaching assignments—would lead more directly to the employment of teachers with the needed qualifications and more consistently to their efficient utilization. This plan would also eliminate the discretionary power of school officials to reward particular teachers, reducing the teachers' fears of favoritism and administrators' headaches in connection with pressures to give the high-paying assignments to particular individuals. Under either arrangement, of course, school officials *could* still choose inferior personnel. With the ability to offer more for the scarce skills, however, superintendents would have the option of selecting more capable persons, and would usually do so, whereas at present they do not even have this opportunity. Moreover, teachers already employed would have an incentive to acquire the kinds of subject-matter training that are scarce instead of merely piling up credits in extension courses regardless of their usefulness.

There will be some small high schools where it may be impossible to implement pay differentials by field of training because there can be so little specialization. In schools with very small enrollments, however, the gains from employing teachers trained in scarce specialties would be small anyway, the real trouble being the difficulty of having specialization at all. We doubt that high-quality instruction is going to be provided in these schools anyway, and we join Dr. Conant in hoping for an early disappearance of high schools which are so small as to be, inevitably, inadequate.

Determining What Constitutes Sufficient Training

Another problem in adopting supplemental pay for scarce skills would be to determine what is sufficient training. Should the extra pay be offered for either a major or a minor, or only for a major in the scarce field? While we do not claim to know how the question should be answered in all circumstances, we believe firmly that school officials can answer it for themselves. The important thing is for schools to be able to hire high school teachers with good solid training in the subject they teach. In some subjects, no doubt a minor is sufficient to permit effective teaching. In some subjects less than a minor may suffice. In other subjects, a major in the field is quite important.

In general we feel that even a minor in mathematics or physical science contributes significantly to effective teaching of those subjects. These minors should therefore command a modest increment. A major in mathematics or physical science contributes still further and should therefore be "worth" a somewhat larger supplement. In English perhaps a major is usually necessary for effective teaching of that subject, so nothing short of a major should bring an increment. Educators in each district, however, are closer to their own situations than we are; and, in any event, each district must choose for itself. The board of education, with the advice of school officials and classroom teachers' associations, has to determine what the precise salary steps should be. In part the decisions depend upon the kind and quality of education that the community wishes to provide. Whatever the decision, the 3-step salary schedule lends itself conveniently to establishing supplements for either a minor or a major, for both, or a lesser supplement for the minor than for the major. These amounts could be changed, furthermore, as circumstances changed.

Adjusting to Future Market Changes

Another objection sometimes raised is that over time the market for different skills may change, thus rendering the initial differentials obsolete and requiring further changes. Like some of the other "objections," this complaint is really that, since one change will not solve the problem permanently, we should not try to solve the problem at all. Surely the answer is that having some change in the right direction is better than rejecting all change. Besides, the possibility of making further changes is an advantage, not a drawback. What the schools should want is the opportunity to make changes, not every semester or every year to be sure, but whenever they are really needed. Markets do shift over time, and one of the reasons schools have trouble keeping all the skills they want is that the unified salary schedule is simply too unwieldy to keep up with these changes. As a consequence, the salary structure lags badly behind the actualities of the world, and there is no force at work to correct the lack of balance. With the acceptance of more differentials, it is quite possible to make adjustments as the market shifts, and thus to keep the structure approximately up to date. It is done in other parts of the economy and in other professions, and it can be done in the schools.

Administrators would not, of course, try to adjust to every minute shift in supply and demand. Furthermore, the major shifts in the market situation—the shifts that the schools would feel keenly and to which they would need to accommodate—rarely happen overnight or in rapid succession. School officials would adjust the salary differentials only when they experienced serious and persistent difficulty in obtaining certain skills. They would not have to react capriciously or often.

Some Final Comments

It has sometimes been said that going to differential salaries would be a retreat to the nineteenth century, to the rule of the jungle, to the outmoded day of the individual bargain when ruthless school boards pressed the helpless individual teacher into accepting a starvation wage. This is nonsense. There is nothing in our proposal that reduces the importance of the published salary schedule, or denies that there should be one. Nor is there anything in it that would reduce the part played by teachers either individually or through their organizations. Furthermore, there is nothing at variance in our proposal with the merit pay plan. If a school system wants merit pay, it can easily be superimposed on a differential pay plan. This would simply mean that a meritorious teacher in one of the designated scarce fields would receive two supplements rather than one. One supplement would be for merit, and should be recognized for that, the other a simple recognition of special and perhaps temporary circumstances of the market.

Note too that there is no conflict between salary differentials and the unification of school districts. It is entirely possible to have a unified district without having a unified salary schedule. They are independent questions. To be sure, with the single salary schedule taken for granted, the unification of districts meant an extension of that salary schedule and of its defects. In these circumstances, "vertical" unification—the combining of elementary, junior high school, senior high school, and even junior college districts—implied an especially undesirable extension of the single pay schedule. But this is not inherently necessary. Schools can reap whatever advantages unification offers and still have salary steps for type of training or certificate as well as steps for aggregate experience and training.

On balance what are we to say about the practical difficulties? Some of them will turn out to be either very short-lived or even nonexistent if the new system is instituted with care and thought. Others will be real and enduring. A system of differentials will mean more work for the school board and for the staff as well, since it will require up-to-date knowledge of several markets, and the periodic establishment of differentials designed to accommodate to those markets. The board and the staff will have more homework to do, and they will have some decisions to make that will not be popular with some of their teachers. But the fact that there are some difficulties does not foreclose the issue. People that seek the right choice are not noted for choosing the path of least resistance or the course with fewest problems. It is more difficult to build a house than it is to put up a tent, but most of us choose houses. Unless the difficulties are insuperable, the issue is not whether there are difficulties but whether the payoffs outweigh the sacrifices. We think they do. As we see it, a 3-step schedule is the only way, in the coming years, for individual districts and the nation as a whole to provide high-quality instruction and utilize vital skills efficiently.

Notes

1. This is purely an illustration. In later chapters we shall seek factual evidence about the market conditions for selected teaching skills—i.e., about the relative shortages in selected teaching fields.

2. *A Modern Concept of Manpower Management and Compensation for Personnel of the Uniformed Services*, 2 vols., Report of the Defense Advisory Committee on Professional and Technical Compensation (Ralph J. Cordiner, Chairman) (Washington, D.C.: U.S. Government Printing Office, 1957).

3. *Ibid.*, I, 5-6

4. *Ibid.*, p. 12.

5. *Salary Scheduling*, Discussion Pamphlet No. 8, 4th ed. (Washington, D.C.: National Education Association, April 1956).

6. *Classroom Teachers Speak on Professional Salary Schedules*, Report of the Study Conference on Professional Salary Schedules for Classroom Teachers (Washington, D.C.: National Education Association, April 1958), p. 14.

7. James W. Bushong, "Automatic Salary Increases Cannot Be Justified," *The Nation's Schools* (February 1958), 44.

8. *Salary Scheduling*, p. 18.

9. Ellis F. Hartford, "Why Two Hundred Chose Teaching," *The Phi Delta Kappan* (December 1948), 126-27.

10. *Classroom Teachers Speak on Professional Salary Schedules*, p. 12.

11. National Education Association, Research Division, *Teacher Supply and Demand in Public Schools, 1960,* Research Report 1960-R7 (Washington, D.C.: the Association, April 1960), p. 10 [italics in original].

12. *Classroom Teachers Speak on Professional Salary Schedules,* p. 15.

13. For one set of findings and for references to others, see Paul G. Keat, "Long-run Changes in Occupational Wage Structure, 1900-1956," *Journal of Political Economy* (December 1960), 584-600.

14. B. J. Chandler and Claude Mathis, "The Effect of School Salary Policies on Teacher Morale," July, 1957, mimeo; summarized in B. J. Chandler's, "Study Shows That Merit Rating Is Not Detrimental to Morale," *The Nation's Schools* (April 1958), 58-59.

15. *Ibid.,* p. 36.

COMMENT / The Money We Spend
and What Happens to It

Charles S. Benson

We have already noted that in the ten years since 1953-54 expenditures on elementary and secondary schools rose in the amount of $12.2 billion, i.e., from $9.0 billion in the 1953-54 school year to $21.2 billion in 1963-64. During the same period the number of classroom teachers increased from 1,032,000 to 1,575,000, a gain of 543,000, reflecting primarily the rise in number of pupils, not reduction in the size of classes. Also, teachers' salaries went up on the average from $4,000 in 1953-54 to $6,000 in 1963-64. The rise in the vast army of teachers and in their pay accounts for over 40 percent of the increase in school expenditures during the decade.

Of course, salaries and wages generally in our society have gone up since 1953-54, the average annual increase in earnings of persons employed full time being 3.8 percent. If we apply a 3.8 percent rate of increase to the $4,000 average salary of teachers in 1953-54, we get the figure $5,800, not the $6,000 average actually achieved. So, in total, the country can be said to have spent something over a quarter-billion dollars in ten years to improve the relative economic position of teachers. But where does it show? In 1962-63 in California, the state with the highest average pay of teachers, only 4,800 teachers

Reprinted from Charles S. Benson, *The Cheerful Prospect* (Boston: Houghton Mifflin, 1965), pp. 29-38.

out of 131,000 received more than $10,000 in salary. (In Mississippi only 1,800 of 18,000 teachers received above $5,500.) Public school teaching remains a calling with a rather low ceiling of pay relative to other fields that employ college graduates, and the immediate cause is that local school districts are more or less forced by the professional teachers' associations to award increments in pay to all teachers in approximately equal amounts. However administrators may tinker with salary scales to obscure the process, the "across-the-board" raise is the usual thing in American school districts.

Before we consider further the basic cause for this unhappy state of affairs, let us note some effects of egalitarianism in teachers' pay. Since many private and some public employers are not so egalitarian-minded as the professional teachers' associations are, differences in rates of pay are widely characteristic of our society. Accordingly, one would expect the teaching profession—or at least that branch of it which serves the elementary and secondary schools—to have difficulty attracting college graduates in those fields for which demand in the noneducational world is high. An obvious case involves persons who have been trained in mathematics and science. The National Education Association has reported that in twenty-two states and the District of Columbia there were 2,750 persons teaching mathematics for the first time in 1963-64 but that only 2,215 degree candidates in mathematics were graduated in those states in 1962-63. The corresponding figures for chemistry were 283 teachers hired and 264 trained. How was the deficit in numbers of mathematics and chemistry teachers filled? Possibly by importing young graduates from the other twenty-eight states, though this is doubtful. Possibly by attracting trained teachers back to the classroom, but this is even more doubtful because the situation discussed here has existed for many years. In most cases the deficit was met by placing a person in a classroom to teach math who himself had had little schooling in it. After all, the twenty-two states trained 4,582 persons in social studies but had places for only 2,939 of them to work in those subjects in the schools.

In their book, *Teacher Shortages and Salary Schedules* (1962), J. A. Kershaw and R. N. McKean report on a three-state survey of Maryland, New Jersey, and Virginia showing that 40 percent of mathematics teachers had never had a course in calculus in college. For Los Angeles "42 percent of the mathematics teachers in the spring of 1958 had neither a major nor a minor in mathematics in college, and 7 percent had never had a college course in mathematics."[1] Similarly, in Ohio in 1958, only eight out of a hundred physics teachers had majored in physics, and 40 percent had only ten or fewer semester hours of credit in the subject. These are simply indications of the extent to which "conversion" of teachers, i.e., the assigning of classroom responsibilities in areas of study other than those in which one had been prepared to work, can go.

Actually, Kershaw and McKean made a proposal to improve the situation, namely, that an extra award of $2,000 per year be offered to teachers in undermanned fields, such as mathematics, science, and English. The additional pay in scarcity areas would be incorporated as a "third track" in the conventional salary schedules, under which only the two factors of general level of training (bachelor's degree, master's, master's plus 30 semester hours, etc.) and years of experience (or seniority) are used to differentiate the pay of one teacher from that of another. The scheme would allow school districts to recognize market forces in determining pay of teachers. Plainly, something needs to be done, because our survival as a technological nation is dependent on the quality of the future mathematicians and scientists we produce; moreover, the imbalance in teacher preparation makes the achievement of equality of opportunity grossly unattainable. The qualified mathematics teacher, for example, is drawn to the district of good reputation and is likely to work almost exclusively with the students in the college preparatory programs. This allocation of scarce teaching resources to college-bound youth is, I judge, economically necessary. But at the same time, the result is that our future technicians and craftsmen are deprived of high-quality instruction in those fields—math, science, and English—which are the bedrock for their own future careers. It is not necessary to go farther in relating this situation to the distribution of educational resources (in real terms) between the children of privileged and of underprivileged homes.

The Kershaw-McKean proposal did not stir any large favorable response among teachers' groups. In general, teachers prefer to use the shortage of math-science teachers as a lever to raise the salary schedules, monolithic though they are, of the districts of a state, which is to say that they will exploit the problem to prevent the solution of it. If teachers really are keenly committed to egalitarian principles, they should take effective action to reduce geographic differences in pay. They are unwilling to do so because under the present order, they feel, what keeps teachers' salaries moving ahead at a pace in excess of that of the average of salaries and wages in the economy is competition among the large number of local districts. But it is possible that the Kershaw-McKean proposal is a bad one, not because (as the teachers claim) what a person teaches should have no relation to his pay, but because of the fact of decentralization in administration. The introduction of flexibility in our present rigid salary schedules would redound to the benefit of the rich suburban systems first of all, since they have the means to seize the advantage from the cities, always somewhat slow moving in salary policy. The suburban systems would feel themselves free to offer a considerable bonus to an alert math or science teacher who happened to be working in the nearby city, and they would not be morally obliged, as they are now, to raise the pay of all of their present teachers in proportion (which is the meaning of a rigid salary schedule). The city, however, would have to think of several thousand dollars more for each of its several thousand math and science teachers. Further, it would almost surely run into trouble with its teachers' union (and the suburban systems, by and large, do not have unions but only professional associations) if it began to give selective raises to match the competition. Thus, the suburban systems under the Kershaw-McKean plan would raid the large places, luring away their good teachers in scarce fields. But it is the large city that has especially strong needs for math and science teachers, since it has an unduly large proportion of secondary students in technical and vocational programs.

In addition, the Kershaw-McKean proposal does not go to the root of the problem of teachers' pay, as I shall now indicate. The teaching profession includes vast numbers of married persons, both male and female. For both married women and men there is a fundamental conflict between their desires to engage in teaching and their desires to fulfill their role in the family. The conflict between work and family, however, takes a drastically different form for women and for men. With respect to the former, it is a matter of competing demands on time. The woman faces a struggle between the time demands of meeting her classes and preparing for the next day's classes, on the one hand, and the time demands of being a wife and mother, on the other. The man is torn between his inclination to serve society as a conscientious teacher of the young, on the one hand, and his need to make a respectable living and, most particularly, to find the money to pay for the college education of his own children, on the other. Any attempt to resolve the difficulties of one of the parties runs diametrically opposite to the interest of the other. For example, if the working hours expected of teachers are shortened to give women more time in the household (or to allow them to be recruited back to the profession more quickly after childbirth), it becomes that much more difficult to justify high levels of pay in the profession, which the married men need. Or, if the top pay is raised to the $12,000–$14,000 range, which is what education will have to offer if it is to obtain the full-week, full-year services of the competent, well-trained male college graduate, it will be hard for school boards not to demand longer hours of all teachers; but this will drive the married women out of the profession, and the country cannot easily dispense with their services.

We have reached, actually, an uneasy compromise, workable but inefficient. To wit, the teacher's job is simply left in a loose state of definition. This means that those married women who need to can devote considerable amounts of time to their households while appearing to meet the full responsibilities of the teaching position. Those men who need to can supplement their income by moonlighting.[2] Others, who want to devote their full energies to the classroom, are allowed to do that. (Then there is a fourth group: the young men on the way up who use their free time to perform the more menial types of administrative chores in the hope that they will get a chance at some of the extraordinarily high salaries paid to top school administrators in our country.)

It is possible to define a full-time job in teaching, though the precise description will vary from grade level to grade level and from one subject to another. It should be possible, though this is harder, to define a series of part-time positions as well. If both these steps were taken, it would then be feasible to offer people salaries in rough proportion to the contribution they are able to make to the schools. Presumably, most men would opt for the full-time job and would welcome the chance to draw their pay in one check and to give their full energies to what they see (I hope) as their main line of work. Some married women would, I think, find themselves more comfortable working under a part-time arrangement, as long as the more narrowly defined set of responsibilities continued to give them scope to exercise their more important skills. It is not implied, of course, that, to hold a full-time position, a teacher would be expected to have ten classes a day instead of his present four to six (at the secondary level). Rather, to define a full-time position is to state those amounts of study, preparation for class, tutorial responsibilities, in addition to present class loads, that are feasible within a full working week and full working year. On the other hand, to admit persons, particularly women, into part-time assignments in the schools without first defining the full-time position (as is now done in a number of school systems) is not much help, since these persons will simply be undertaking part-time responsibilities in what has come (by default) to be a part-time job.

This general approach—and I shall have a bit more to say about it later—offers, I believe, the best hope for an ultimate solution to the problem of teachers' pay. Unless progress is made in some fashion, districts will continue to pay some teachers more than they should for the services obtained from them but no teacher enough to improve the caliber of basic recruitment to the profession, knowing all the while that these unfortunate things are being done.[3]

By and large, the professional organizations of teachers, such as the National Education Association and its state affiliates, have resisted such redefinition of the teachers' responsibilities and have clung to the loose but unitary concept of teachers' roles. (To my mind, this is the real reason for the failure of schemes of merit pay to receive anything more than lip service.) Women teachers represent a large share of the membership of these organizations. Apparently, they feel that they would suffer a loss of status—and possibly pay—in the formal establishment of a part-time role in education. The expression of the position of the organized teachers is an insistence that local districts pay teachers under a "single-salary schedule," which is to say that for purposes of pay the position of classroom teacher is wholly undifferentiated.

As long as the professional organizations hold to this position, the local district is powerless to redefine roles on its own initiative, since it would face a barrage of resignations on an issue of principle and an outcry from parent-voters who thought that the schooling of their children would be disrupted. And unfortunately, it seems to be always true that a few of the best teachers in a district are those who appear to work the least hours.

But if teachers are so sensitive on the question of job analysis, how do they succeed in getting any raises at all? There are two parts to the answer. First, we note that practically all districts must enter the market each year to hire personnel, partly because of growth in pupil population and partly because of the high rate of wastage in the profession. The only important, visible variable that the local authority can manipulate to improve its competitive position in the market is its hiring salary. (The unitary concept of the teacher's role, for example, rules out the possibility that the district could advertise itself as offering "opportunities for career development.") Indeed, the public activity called education is so ruthlessly and single-mindedly competitive about salaries as to put modern corporate practice to shame. Second, the teachers have won acceptance for the notion that to raise the offer of pay for newly hired teachers without at the same time granting equivalent raises to the present staff is uncouth. Were this to be done, it would place the district in the unhappy position of paying more for experience obtained in other school systems than for experience acquired in its own; no proper school authority could accept such a blow to its esteem.

But though raises continue to be given year after year, they do not amount to much in dollars, and the maximums do not rise very high. The concept of the single-salary schedule, together with the institution of tenure, implies that any teacher can receive the maximum if he lives long enough. In the suburban systems, which, generally speaking, are the leaders with regard to level of pay, many teachers are known to board members individually, and the board members sometimes cannot honestly face the prospect of paying $12,000 to $14,000 to some of the teachers they know. In the cities the problem takes a different form. Here the board members must ask themselves the difficult question of why they should pay a mature teacher $12,000, say, when a much less experienced man can fulfill exactly the same responsibilities in the classroom at a cost of only $6,000. Differentiation of the teacher's role would remove both of these roadblocks to paying high salaries to some teachers, these latter being selected on a basis other than seniority.

Notes

1. Joseph A. Kershaw and Roland N. McKean, *Teacher Shortages and Salary Schedules* (New York: McGraw-Hill Book Company, 1962), pp. 90, 91.

2. It is interesting to note that the number of "multiple job holders" is relatively greater among male elementary and secondary teachers than among all other occupational groups, the next highest group being that of protective service workers, i.e., guards and night watchmen. See U.S. Bureau of Labor Statistics, *Monthly Labor Review* (May 1963), p. 519. The comparison refers to multiple jobs held during the regular school year, not to Christmas vacation and summer work. Of course, many married women teachers can be considered as moonlighting when they carry the responsibility of running a household.

3. Some support for the differential needs of married men and women can be got from practically any survey of why teachers leave the classroom. For example, the Utah Education Association reported in October 1960 that 57 percent of Utah's departing teachers listed "home responsibilities" as the cause for leaving, while 38 percent gave "inadequate salary" as the reason. This is in approximate accord with the proportion of females and males in the profession.

6 / Linear Programming and the Value of an Input to a Local Public School System

A. G. Holtmann

A number of recent studies have been concerned with the economic benefits of formal education to the individual being educated and to the total society.[1] The purpose of this paper is to focus attention on the relationship between the value of education and the value of inputs to a local public school system in the short run. Essentially, the school system is viewed as a profit maximizing institution with a number of fixed inputs. Profits are assumed to be a linear function of the number of students educated, and the input-output relationships are assumed to be linear. This conception of a school system has the advantage of allowing one to determine the value of an additional unit of any input to the school. This could be of use to the school system in its planning. In addition, however, it allows one to compare the value of resources used in the school system with their alternative value elsewhere in the economy. Of course, there is no reason why society should accept the market value of an education as a guide for expenditures on education. Nevertheless, a large proportion of resources are allocated on the basis of the value of their marginal product. It would, therefore, be helpful to have a comparable value for resources used in the school system.

Reprinted from *Public Finance*, XXIII (No. 4, 1968), 429-40.

THE MODEL

As was indicated, it is assumed that the school system is trying to maximize the net additional lifetime income of the graduates. It is also assumed that the school system has four grades, a typical high school. Each grade is specified as so much math, science, English, etc. There is, therefore, no ambiguity about what is meant by a year of school.

The net revenue or profit associated with a graduate is defined as the present value of his net expected future income associated with the completion of a given year of school. The present value of the net expected future income can be written as

$$B_a = \sum_{n=a}^{75} \frac{P^n_{a1} \, P^n_{a2} \, E^n}{(1+r)^{n-a}} \; -C$$

where B_a is the present value of expected net income associated with a given level of education completed at age a; E^n is the additional income for all future periods, n, associated with the additional year of education completed at age a; C is the present variable cost associated with the additional year of schooling completed at age a; P^n_{a1} is the probability that a person age a will live to age n; P^n_{a2} is the probability that an individual age a will have income at age n; and r is the discount rate. From this formula, the net income associated with each of the four levels of schooling can be determined. The total profits from all four levels of schooling can be defined as $P = B_1 X_1 + B_2 X_2 +$ ...... $+ B_8 X_8$ where P is the total profit; $X_1 \ldots X_8$ represent the number of male and female graduates from each of the four levels of school; $B_1 \ldots B_8$ represent the net benefits from a graduate of each grade. This is the function to be maximized.

It is assumed, however, that the school system faces certain limitations or constraints. For example, there are only a given number of teachers in various subjects, a given number of students available, a given number of classrooms. There are mathematics teachers, foreign-language teachers, English teachers, social studies teachers, science teachers, vocational education teachers, and nonvocational education teachers. The total number of each type of teacher is represented by $C_1 \ldots C_7$, respectively. Further, it is assumed that the student to teacher ratio for each subject and the importance of each subject in the curriculum are given. It is also assumed that teachers can teach all grades, but only one subject. The teacher constraints can be written as

$$a_{11}X_1 + a_{12}X_2 + \ldots\ldots + a_{18}X_8 \leqslant C_1$$

$$a_{71}X_1 + a_{72}X_2 + \ldots\ldots + a_{78}X_8 \leqslant C_7$$

The a's, of course, specify the number of teachers of each type needed to produce a unit of output. Similarly, the number of available classrooms is represented by C_8. The classroom constraint is written as a $a_{81}X_1 + a_{82}X_2 + \ldots a_{88}X_8 \leqslant C_8$ where the a's represent the fraction of a classroom needed to produce a graduate from the various grades. It is assumed that classrooms can be used for any course in any grade. Finally, then, the number of students available in each grade is represented by $C_9 \ldots C_{16}$. The fact that the system cannot produce more graduates than students available, and that it cannot produce negative numbers of graduates is given by the following constraints:

$$C_9 \geqslant X_1 \geqslant 0, \ldots\ldots C_{16} \geqslant X_8 \geqslant 0$$

The solution to the above problem, the maximum profit the school system can produce given the input constraints, is not a trivial result in itself. It is the solution of the dual, however, that is of major interest. The solution to the dual will give shadow prices for each of the constraining inputs. These shadow prices are comparable to the value of the marginal product of each input. These values can be compared with the value of these inputs elsewhere in the economy.

There are a number of obvious difficulties that arise with the above model. Some of these difficulties arise from an inability to estimate the benefits from education, or to define education. For example, it is clear that the benefits from educating women exceed the value that is determined in the market.[2] Indeed, it has been suggested that the benefits of all education are greater than the increase in private output associated with education.[3] However, these extra market benefits are difficult to quantify. When these external benefits are quantified, they could easily be integrated into the analysis. In addition, there is the difficulty of determining how much of the increase in the income of educated people is actually attributable to education. While there is no completely satisfactory estimate of the proportion of income that is attributable to education, a study of Werner Hirsch and Elbert Segelhorst suggests that perhaps 12 percent of the variation in income is attributable to education.[4] This adjustment factor has been used in the following example.

Another aspect of the benefits from education is the option value of an education. That is, a year of education allows one to get more education which may have a higher marginal benefit than marginal cost. This idea of an option has been developed by Burton Weisbrod.[5] Of course, in equilibrium the extra benefits from additional education would just equal the extra costs. Therefore, there would be no value to the option. When options do have value, however, this can be added to the benefit estimates presented to determine the "true" benefit from education.

Of course, the assumption of fixed input coefficients in the production function could be questioned. Actually, from a pedagogical viewpoint, little is known about the nature of the production function in education. School administrators, however, behave as if the input coefficients were fixed. Generally, school administrators believe that input-output relationships, such as the teacher to student ratios, should be fixed at some appropriate level. The very small variation found in the student to teacher ratios in various subjects in the Detroit school system reflects this attitude. There is, in fact, very little variation in student to teacher ratios among schools in different sections of the United States. Indeed, the tendency for school administrators to consider input coefficients as fixed seems to be an international phenomenon. Professor Samuel Bowles, for example, found this hypothesis to be supported by the available statistics on schools in northern Nigeria. So the assumptions concerning input constraints seem to be consistent with reality.[6]

Additional adjustments of inputs could have been made to reflect different types of curriculums. Also, different production periods could have been considered. The purpose of this paper, however, is to show that the estimates of the benefits from education that have been made can be used in a programming model to determine the value of an input in a decentralized public school system. The empirical analysis, therefore, serves as an example of this approach and not as a detailed blue print for public school policy decisions.

THE CASE STUDY

The above model, while admittedly a rather simplified representation of the nature of a school system, was applied to the Detroit high school system. The data used in this example were taken from statistics gathered by the Detroit school system near the end of the 1963-64 school year. While the data made available were well suited to the problem, the data were not collected for this purpose, and various adjustments had to be made. These were not so extensive, however, as to distort the conclusions of the study.

At the time of the study, there were approximately 57,000 students registered in the Detroit high schools. There were slightly more girls (29,000) than boys (28,000). The majority of the students were in the tenth, eleventh, and twelfth grades. The ninth grade was grossly underrepresented because most of the students in the Detroit system do not enter the senior high school until they have completed the ninth grade.[7] In this problem, 1,769 teachers were available to provide a high school education to the 57,000 students. There are actually more teachers in the Detroit high school system, but they were excluded from this study for one reason or another.[8]

It was assumed that this system was producing male and female graduates from the ninth, tenth, eleventh, and twelfth grades. In fact, of course, a graduate from any given grade represented the average curriculum that a student received in that particular grade. Actually, no such average graduate exists, but, on the average, a given percentage of time in various courses must be offered to produce a graduate. In all of the grades, the students were assumed to have a curriculum consisting of English, mathematics, foreign language, science, social science, nonvocational training, and vocational training.[9] The relative importance of each subject in the average curriculum, of course, varied from grade to grade. The relative importance of each subject was determined by estimating the percentage of students in a given grade who were taking the subject relative to the number in that grade taking all subjects.[10] The curriculum was assumed to be the same for both boys and girls. While it would have been useful to have separate estimates of subjects taken by boys and girls, these data were not readily available. The products, or graduates of each grade, then were assumed to have had a given amount of education as determined by the estimated average curriculum.

Each boy and girl graduate from a given grade was assumed to contribute to the school system a profit equal to 12 percent of the additional lifetime income that an individual with such an education gains over those individuals who have had one year less education, minus the small variable cost of the education.[11] These lifetime net profits were estimated from cross-section median income figures given by age, sex, and education in the 1960 census.[12] The census income data were adjusted for mortality and the probability of having income at any given age. Since students were assumed to be fixed inputs, rather than variable inputs, forgone earnings for the year the person received the education were not taken into account. Using a 5 percent rate of discount, the estimated profits for girls and boys respectively were: $119 and $440 in the ninth grade, $123 and $455 in the tenth grade, $409 and $494 in the eleventh grade, and $433 and $478 in the twelfth grade.[13]

As was indicated earlier, there were some 1,769 teachers in the school system. They included 366 English teachers, 85 foreign-language teachers, 160 mathematics teachers, 222 science teachers, 212 social science teachers, 515 vocational training teachers, and 209 nonvocational training teachers.[14] The relationship between the production of one graduate from any grade and the fraction of a teacher needed to produce that graduate was determined by weighting the teacher to student ratio in each subject by the relative importance of that subject in the curriculum.[15] The teacher to student ratios in each subject were assumed to be equal to the average for all grades. However, since each subject had a different importance in each grade, the technical input-output relationship between graduates and teachers was different for different grades, as well as for different subjects.

The additional factor limiting the amount of profits the system can produce is classroom space. It was estimated that 1,730 classrooms were available for high school instruction in the Detroit school system. The technical input-output relationship between graduates and classroom space was estimated by summing the teacher to student input-output coefficients for a given grade. This is based on the fact that the total of the teacher to student ratios for any grade is the classroom to student ratio. This is because the typical situation is one classroom and one teacher per class. Classrooms were assumed to be used equally well for all subjects and all grades. Of course, classrooms and teachers are assumed to be divisible.

RESULTS AND CONCLUSIONS

Given the above conditions, it was estimated that the school system could produce a total product worth a maximum of $20,062,004. The $20,062,004 was produced by graduating all the boys available in grades ten through twelve, plus 1,587 boys in grade nine; and by graduating all the girls in grades eleven and twelve, plus 5,400 girls in grade ten. No ninth-grade girls were graduated. Further production of ninth-grade boys and girls in grades nine and ten was impossible because the system had used the available stock of social science teachers and foreign-language teachers.

Returning to the analysis of the dual, the value of all inputs for the Detroit high school system are given in Table 6-1. From this it is seen that one additional foreign-language teacher would allow the system to produce $23,862 worth of additional output. Therefore, it would be profitable to employ another foreign-language teacher at any salary below $23,862. This means that, given the very limited assumptions of the model and the wage rate, the school system is suffering a shortage of language teachers. The definition of a shortage is somewhat clearer than is often the case when individuals discuss the "teacher shortage." If it is assumed that the salaries of those able to teach foreign languages are a measure of their marginal product, and that the rest of the system is in competitive equilibrium, then, there is a shortage of language teachers because the value of total output could be increased by shifting a language teacher to the Detroit school system.

Of course, the same argument could be made for the addition of one more social science teacher. On the other hand, it is also obvious that the school system has a surplus of some teachers. That is, the value of the output would not fall if any one of the inputs with a zero value were to move to some other use in the economy.

TABLE 6-1. Value of one additional unit of various inputs in the Detroit high schools

Inputs	Unit value in dollars
English teachers	0
Foreign-language teachers	23,862
Mathematics teachers	0
Science teachers	0
Social science teachers	62,323
Nonvocational training teachers	0
Vocational training teachers	0
Ninth-grade girls	0
Ninth-grade boys	0
Tenth-grade girls	0
Tenth-grade boys	333
Eleventh-grade girls	10
Eleventh-grade boys	94
Twelfth-grade girls	6
Twelfth-grade boys	52
Classrooms	0

Source: Estimated from data cited in text.

In addition to the value of teachers, there are other implications for school efficiency implicit in Table 6-1. From Table 6-1 it can be seen that the addition of one more male in the tenth, eleventh, and twelfth grades has a positive marginal value. Also, female students in the eleventh and twelfth grades have positive marginal values. These marginal values represent the value of preventing a dropout in each category. Again, this assumes that the school system is attempting to maximize profits and the model is not unreasonably far from reality. Of course, the students with a zero shadow price have no value to the school system. The idea that no effort should be made to prevent a school dropout may seem a bit harsh, but it may be of little value to encourage individuals to return to school when teacher shortages may be so severe that there is truly no education to be obtained.

Even the students that have a positive shadow price may not be worth the cost of preventing their dropping out of school. It has been estimated in one study that the cost of preventing one dropout may be as high as $7,300 per case prevented.[16] This is a rather alarming estimate. It suggests that it would not pay to prevent any type of student from dropping out of the Detroit school system. It should, however, be stressed that all the benefits from education are not included in the estimates presented here. It would, therefore, be a mistake to suggest that programs to prevent dropouts be discontinued. But, the results are, at best, discouraging.

It is not claimed here that the values of the inputs should be the values placed on those particular inputs. Nor is it claimed that the linear programming techniques give a completely accurate estimate of how a high school system actually works. Nevertheless, this technique does provide estimates of the value of a marginal change in any input that is directly comparable to the market value given to comparable inputs. Therefore, it allows crude estimates of the market value of marginal increases in the supply of certain types of teachers and students to given school districts. This, no doubt, will not be sufficient for the social planner who wishes to know how many teachers we need twenty or thirty years from now. However, it may be of incalculable aid to those who would like to make practical marginal changes in the system that would lead to an increase in output. In this regard, this technique provides an internal set of prices for allocating resources among school systems so as to maximize whatever objective function the society cares to specify. In this example, the market value of the input was selected, which is the basis upon which a large amount of the economy's resources are allocated. However, it may be contended that the community has already established the fact that everyone should be educated and that the school system must adjust to this mandate. Of course, if the community also establishes a budget limitation on the school system, it is the quality of the service that must be adjusted. In this problem, the curriculum was taken as given and the analysis continued from there. Although the question of the quality of education is a crucial question, it will not be discussed here. The adjustments that the school system has made to maintain a given curriculum and to educate every child, however, will be considered. In Table 6-2, the number of teachers of each type available in the Detroit high school system, and the number it would take to educate everyone based on the input-output coefficients described earlier in this section are given.

From Table 6-2, it can be seen that the school system does not have enough English teachers, mathematics teachers, foreign-language teachers, or social science teachers to educate everyone in the system. Conversely, the system has a surplus of science teachers, nonvocational training teachers and vocational training teachers. Interestingly, the shortage of teachers numbers eighty-one and the surplus of teachers numbers eighty-six. This provides a great deal of support for the internal consistency of the technical coefficients used in the linear programming model. This is because everyone, in fact, was receiving schooling on some basis. The results may, however, suggest that science, vocational, and nonvocational teachers are teaching the other subjects. While it may not be too alarming that science teachers might teach mathematics, it may be somewhat less satisfying to find that vocational training teachers and nonvocational training teachers are teaching such subjects as foreign languages. Of course, the school may, in fact, be making other types of adjustments which preclude such a facile interpretation.

TABLE 6-2. Number of teachers available and the number of teachers needed in the Detroit high school system

Subject	Number needed	Number available	Surplus or shortage
English	379	366	−13
Foreign language	110	85	−25
Mathematics	180	160	−20
Science	208	222	+14
Social science	235	212	−23
Vocational training	490	515	+25
Nonvocational	162	209	+47

Source: Detroit Board of Education, "Summary of Personnel Changes," pp. 13-15.

The paper has been devoted to applying techniques used in the business sector of the economy to the school system. Some will question the entire concept of profit maximization with respect to the school system. Others, while agreeing in principle with the analytical techniques, will question the estimates of the benefits from education. It is contended here that the profit maximization model is only one type of model that might be used to gain some understanding of the operation of the school system and the demand for inputs. Surely, however, individuals are concerned with the market value of education. If this is an important reason for gaining an education, it should certainly be reflected in the value of teachers' services. As more benefits from education are quantified, they may readily be incorporated into the model. While the previous analysis, then, does not provide even a large number of the answers to the many questions of education policy, hopefully, it provides a meaningful approach for looking at the questions.

Notes

The study was done while the author was a member of the professional staff of the Commission on Human Resources and Higher Education, National Academy of Sciences. He wishes to thank the National Academy for their support, but, of course, the conclusions do not represent the position of the Academy. The author is indebted to Samuel Levy, Thomas Finn, and Michael Rieber for comments on this paper. Gordon McMeekin was helpful with the computer work. They all, of course, receive the usual dispensation.

1. For example, see Werner Z. Hirsch and Elbert W. Segelhorst, "Incremental Income Benefits of Public Education," *The Review of Economics and Statistics* (November 1965), pp. 392-99; H. S. Houthakker, "Education and Income," *Ibid.* (February 1959), pp. 24-28.

2. For some indication of the economic value of a female, see Burton Weisbrod, *The Economics of Public Health* (Philadelphia: University of Pennsylvania Press, 1969), pp. 114-19.

3. See Burton Weisbrod, *External Benefits of Public Education* (Princeton, N.J.: Industrial Relations Section, Princeton University, 1964).

4. Hirsch and Segelhorst, "Incremental Income Benefits," p. 396.

5. Burton Weisbrod, "Education and Investment in Human Capital," *The Journal of Political Economy* (Supplement, October 1962), pp. 109-13.

6. Samuel Bowles, "The Efficient Allocation of Resources in Education," *Quarterly Journal of Economics* (May 1967), p. 198.

7. The number of girls and boys respectively in each grade were 2,359 and 2,315 in the ninth grade, 10,699 and 10,754 in the tenth grade, 9,017 and 8,457 in the eleventh grade, and 7,011 and 6,081 in the twelfth grade.

8. The teachers excluded from the study were either in administrative positions or in special teaching areas such as driver training, training for the deaf, etc.

9. Nonvocational training included art, family living, music, and health. Vocational training included industrial education, business education, retailing,

and home economics. These groupings were not in the school systems, and they are somewhat arbitrary. However, it was the only means of including a large number of "electives" into the model.

10. On the basis of a discussion with a counselor in the school system and a brief study of the plan of study suggested to most students, it was assumed that a student taking nonvocational training should only be given half the weight as those students taking other courses. This is because these courses are often taken for half as many hours as "normal" courses.

11. The variable cost per student amounted to about twenty-five dollars. See City of Detroit Board of Education, *Annual Financial Report*, Fiscal Year Ended June 30, 1964 (Detroit: Board of Education, 1964), p. 27. Through an error, 12 percent of profits was estimated rather than 12 percent of additional income before subtracting costs. However, since the error was trivial and the adjustment factor a crude approximation, the model was not recomputed.

12. United States Bureau of the Census, 1960 Census of Population, Special Report P.C. (2)–3B, *Educational Attainment* (Washington, D.C.: U.S. Government Printing Office, 1963), pp. 88-113. Income figures are only available for one to three years of high school and four years of high school. It was assumed that the one to three years of high school represented the tenth grade, and income estimates for the ninth grade and eleventh grade were estimated by straight line interpolation from the available data. If one assumes that the one to three years of schooling really represents the eleventh grade, it affects the numerical results, but not the conclusions of this paper.

The correct income figure to use in calculating the present value of future income is, of course, the mean for each age and education classification. However, mean income figures for both males and females by age and education are not reported in the census. Because estimating the mean requires some assumption about the open-ended income classification, it was decided to use the median as an approximation of the mean. This is not likely to affect the conclusions reached.

13. There is, of course, the difficulty of determining the proper discount rate for calculating the present value of future income. However, the 5 percent rate is often used, and it was not felt that the results with other rates would add to the value of the paper.

14. Detroit Board of Education, "Summary of Personnel Changes," March 20, 1964 (mimeo), pp. 13-15.

15. Teacher to student ratios were estimated to be 1:31 in English, 1:26 in foreign language, 1:30 in mathematics, 1:31 in science, 1:33 in social studies, 1:28 in nonvocational training, and 1:28 in vocational training. See Detroit Board of Education, "Median Size of Senior High School Classes" (mimeo), p. 8.

16. For a complete analysis of the cost and benefit of preventing dropouts, see Burton Weisbrod, "Preventing High School Dropouts," in Robert Dorfman (ed.), *Measuring Benefits of Government Investments* (Washington, D.C.: The Brookings Institution, 1965), p. 144.

7 / An Information Processing Model of Salary Determination in a Contour of Suburban School Districts

Donald Gerwin

The field of economics has given us a highly developed and well-known theory of wage (and employment) determination due to Hicks, Marshall, and others. Yet many labor economists and students of industrial relations will agree it is most appropriate for analyzing broad aggregates of economic units and long-run trends.[1] If one desires to examine wage movements at the interorganizational level and in the relatively short run, he must study the actual process by which they are set. Here, there is much less agreement as to the contents of a suitable theory.

Nevertheless, it is undoubtedly true that an important set of contributions has been made by Dunlop and Ross.[2] The former envisioned a process in which at the intrafirm level there exist job clusters, fairly stable groups of work assignments with closely related wage movements. A change in the key rate of a cluster, usually the highest paid or that for the largest number of workers, prompts adjustments in other related rates. At the interfirm level, a wage contour consists of a group of key rates of different firms that move together. One of these firms is looked to for the purpose of making the key settlement which sets the pattern for changes in the other rates of the contour. Ross's notion of an orbit of coercive compari-

Enlarged version of a paper that appeared in the *American Educational Research Journal*, X (No. 1, Winter 1973), 5-20.

son, a group of firms which refer to each other's salaries in order to determine equitable pay, is similar to the wage contour. However, he explicitly highlighted the importance of wage comparisons for both the employer and the union.

These and related works have emphasized to empirical researchers the need to study the structure of internal and external wages rather than the single rate predicted by the traditional theory. Much less attention has been paid to the fact that these ideas also describe a process by which wages are set. The purpose of this study is to develop and test a formal model of the wage determination process at the interorganizational level which is based on the Dunlop-Ross framework. In particular, the model analyzes the manner in which the wage decisions of any one unit affect the decisions of all the others. The relatively few process-oriented empirical studies which have utilized aspects of this approach suffer from either one of two problems. Some studies, for example Levinson's case analyses of wage-fringe determination in six Pacific Coast contours,[3] provide considerable detail on actual wage setting at the interfirm level, but at the expense of developing formal models capable of being tested. Other research—that done by Eckstein and Wilson who used regression analysis to indicate the presence of wage spillovers from a key group of industries to other groups[4]—is rigorous enough, but it hardly portrays the process at all, and it is at a highly aggregate level. It is my intention to show that the way to resolve this dilemma is through the use of computer models of actual decision making.

SCOPE OF STUDY

The economic units selected for investigation were public school systems. This choice enables us to examine the applicability of the Dunlop-Ross concepts (originally intended for private sector blue-collar workers) to public sector professionals. It is also possible for the author to build upon some of his previous research which explored the process by which the internal wage structure of a large urban school system was set.[5] Over a twelve-year period the district granted its teachers salary increases four times over and above any raises caused by state regulations. These occurred when and only when no other comparable system had a lower starting salary for teachers with a bachelor's degree. A comparable system was defined to be one with enrollment of at least 50,000, a city as opposed to a county district, and in the same section of the country.

It would have been ideal to build upon this work by investigating the way in which the external wage structure of the comparable systems is determined. However, the infeasibility of conducting lengthy investigations in districts with a wide geographical dispersion ruled out this alternative. Instead the contour of school districts studied was chosen by first considering all eighteen of those in Milwaukee County. Preliminary interviews, as well as the author's above-mentioned research, suggested that the city of Milwaukee is likely to be concerned with other large urban districts rather than with its suburbs, and therefore its salary decisions could be considered as exogenous with respect to the other seventeen. It also appeared as the result of the interviews that the suburbs could be divided roughly into three groups. To claim that the three orbits are completely independent would be unwarranted. Rather, districts in a given orbit tend to be more influenced by each other than systems not in it. My intention in this study is to concentrate on a "north side" group of six districts. The Appendix provides information on their characteristics using 1968-69 figures from various local sources. In short, we are concerned with small, wealthy suburban areas which are willing to support high-cost education, including the highest teachers' salaries in the state. They have had relatively cordial relations with their teachers who are represented in all cases by the N.E.A. Collective bargaining, however, is not a factor in virtually all the years which will be of interest to us.

It seemed prohibitive to try to understand the manner in which all the different types of salary raises in these districts come about. Further, it was not even possible to develop for each district a history of when they occurred and the amount of funds involved. Instead, it was decided to concentrate on increases in one important element of the schedule, the B.A. minimum (Bamin) salary, the starting salary for teachers with a bachelor's degree. Bamin salaries of the six north side districts and Milwaukee were collected for the 1959-60 through 1968-69 school years and are displayed in the Appendix. Administrators find this salary important because of its role in hiring new college graduates. It is important to teachers because, if they can get it raised, all other salaries are also likely to be increased due to equity considerations. As documented in the Appendix, the districts studied have in many instances granted across-the-board raises related to the increase in the B.A. minimum. Hence, to a large extent, understanding the decision process for this one salary leads to an understanding of across-the-board raises. It should be clear, as a result of the above discussion, that the various entries that comprise the teachers' salary schedule represent a job cluster's rates and that the Bamin in many respects fits the definition of a key wage.

The objective of this research may now be stated in better-defined terms. It is the author's purpose to explain B.A. minimum salary increases for the six north side districts in Milwaukee County over the period 1960-61 to 1968-69 using a computer model of the decision process.

METHODOLOGY

The study of the teachers' salary decision will be looked upon as an information-processing problem. Let us consider a school district as the basic unit of analysis. The input to each unit consists of various types of data from within and outside the contour, while a specific salary decision is regarded as the output. The conversion of inputs to outputs, that is each system's policy with regard to the B.A. minimum, is represented by a rudimentary discrimination net. Basically, the net consists of test nodes, operations nodes, terminal nodes, and the pathways between them. At the test nodes questions are asked concerning the content of the data. Depending upon the answer to a question, we are led down one of two paths, each of which leads either to another test node, to an operations node where calculations are made using the data, or to a terminal node where a salary decision is stored. Thus, the net sorts or processes the input data in order to arrive at a particular outcome. This approach is associated with the work of Newell, Simon, and Feigenbaum on individual problem solving and Cyert and March in an organizational context.[6]

Most previous attempts to apply an information-processing framework to organizational decisions have depended primarily upon unstructured interviews and the analysis of written documents, for example, the work of Crecine, Gerwin, and Weber.[7] These methods, while not without merit, are subject to some objections. Respondents, for a variety of reasons, find it difficult to remember accurately what they did in the past (retrospective bias), while written accounts, since prepared for other purposes, do not necessarily provide material on what is of direct concern to the investigator. In order to overcome these objections, a completely different procedure was used to gather data. Essentially, it involves obtaining protocols from respondents while they are making decisions in a simulated situation.

In a preliminary set of unstructured interviews (one with each of the six superintendents) an overall view of the decision process was obtained with special emphasis on learning about the participants, the steps in the process, and the sources and content of information. Then, in-depth sessions were held with each superintendent, and various board and former board members. Individuals in the last two groups were selected on the basis of length of service and their involvement in determining teachers' salary increases. Teachers were not included so concentration could be placed on the large number of individuals who had most to do with the decision over the time period studied.

Prior to his in-depth session, each respondent was asked to identify the information he felt was most crucial in deciding upon the Bamin salary. The most pertinent turned out to be the Bamin salaries of the north side systems and Milwaukee. Other types of data made available included school board composition, cost of living (national and Milwaukee), number of teachers hired, decisions on other parts of the compensation package, and relevant passages from school board minutes. If a particular type of requested information could not be compiled, the respondent, where possible, was asked to make a choice first assuming a high value and then a low value. The data were gathered for each year since 1960-61 that the respondent was with the particular district. When the session began, he was presented with the situation facing the district in the first of these years as represented by the information he had requested. He was then asked to use the data to determine his district's decision in that year, and to think aloud while he was engaged in this process. After the respondent arrived at his answer, any discrepancy between it and the actual magnitude was discussed. The procedure was then repeated for the other years he was with the district, and the information utilized for his previous choices was left available to him. A tape recording of the entire proceeding was made for subsequent analysis.

While the technique led to some useful findings, there were a number of difficulties connected with it. It was hard for many respondents to orally express their thinking. Often they silently perused the data and then blurted out an answer. Some respondents became confused between what they personally would have liked to have seen done and what the board actually did. Occasionally, they remembered the actual outcome and then rationalized the reasons for it, while in other cases they projected imagined trends in the data. Finally, since the Bamin decision is made by a group, the simulated interview should involve the group together instead of its members separately. However, in this particular study, it was infeasible to do so. On the other hand, the technique has advantages which mitigate the effects of retrospective bias. It furnishes information which aids in the recall of circumstances surrounding particular decisions. It allows the collection of data from an actual (although simulated) decision-making situation rather than an interview concerning what happened in the past. Moreover, a number of respondents became highly motivated due to the challenge inherent in finding the right answer, thus increasing their willingness to cooperate.

OUTLINE OF THE MODEL

This section presents an outline of a computer simulation model of the Bamin salary decision. The model consists of a discrimination net for each district and one common to all. The main input to each net is the Bamins which have already been decided upon for the coming year. Some nets also use the initial Bamin request of the local teachers' association. The incorporation of this factor into the model was hampered by the difficulty in gathering an adequate history of requests, and the fact that the data were not available until most of the decision simulation interviews had been held. The model also must be provided with the sequence of settlements in any year, a factor much too complicated to be predicted. For this purpose it is assumed that a district's Bamin becomes available to the others immediately after its decision is made. The settlement date, operationally defined as when the school board votes its approval, is used to indicate when the information is communicated.

The overall structure of the model is depicted in Figure 7-1. Milwaukee is always the first system to make a decision since it is made for a calendar year as opposed to the school year beginning nine months later. As a result, the central city's role in the process takes on aspects of a key settlement. Its Bamin, considered exogenous in the model, is always available to the second district (first suburb) to settle. After the second has come to its decision, there are two Bamins available to the third and so on. Finally, the last system to settle has available the Bamins of all the preceding ones in making its choice.

Two different versions of the model were formulated. Version 1 is in reality a collection of six unrelated ones. A given district's Bamin is predicted using the actual values of all input information. Predictions can be made one year ahead for any suburb but only after the decisions of those neighbors which settled before it are known or predicted exogenously. Version 2 predicts a suburb's Bamin by using its own predictions of the Bamins of those suburbs which settled

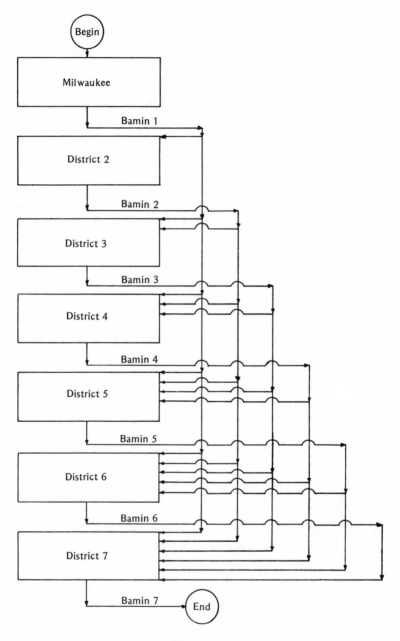

Figure 7-1
Outline of the model

before it for the coming year. All other input information is considered exogenous. It can make predictions one year ahead for all the suburbs provided forecasts of exogenous factors such as the settlement order are made.

Each system's decision process can be viewed as having two stages. First, the school board attempts to structure the situation by determining a range within which the Bamin choice can be made. Second, a particular value is chosen from the range using existing policy. The purpose of the range is to facilitate decision making by narrowing down the alternative salaries from which a choice should be made.

Determining the Range

According to Feigenbaum and Feldman, pattern recognition activity involves the reduction of complex environments to aid in problem solving.[8] It is therefore not surprising that some of the people interviewed mentioned they looked for patterns in the Bamin salaries of those systems that settled previous to theirs. More specifically, they try to develop a range within which the Bamin decision will be made. The most important information for this purpose is the highest and lowest salaries arrived at to date. If just a few other districts have made their choices, the range acts as a hazy guideline so that there may be differences between the values advocated by various board members. As more districts settle, the range set by the previous ones becomes a firmer guide in decision making. In fact, as we shall see, it becomes a rigid boundary which will not be violated.

This phenomenon can be analyzed by referring to Table 7-1a. The data were compiled in the following manner. First, the highest and lowest Bamins of the systems which decided ahead of the kth one (where $k=3,4,5,6,7$ represents the settlement position) were determined for each of the nine years of data. Then the number of times over the entire period that the kth district exceeded the upper limit or failed to reach the lower was calculated. Clearly, there is a tendency for the number of violations to decrease as the settlement position increases whether one considers the upper limit, the lower limit, or both together. In particular, there was only one range violation out of a possible eighteen for districts settling in the sixth or seventh positions.

The balance of Table 7-1a provides for each settlement position the average amount of violation of the upper limit, the lower limit, and both of them. There is a tendency in all three cases for the averages to decrease as the settlement position increases. Moreover,

TABLE 7-1a. Range violations

Settlement position	Number of higher occurrences	Number of lower occurrences	Total	Ave. high violation	Ave. low violation	Ave. violation
3	4	2	6	$62.5	$100.0	$75.0
4	1	2	3	25.0	75.0	58.3
5	2	1	3	25.0	50.0	33.3
6	0	0	0	0.0	0.0	0.0
7	0	1	1	0.0	50.0	50.0
All positions	7	6	13	$46.4	$ 75.0	$59.6

TABLE 7-1b. Range adherences for positions six and seven

Range	Number of adherences for position 6	Number of adherences for position 7
$100	2	1
125	1	1
150	2	2
175	0	0
200	2	2
225	0	0
250	2	2

TABLE 7-1c. Settlement positions

District	Positions					
	2	3	4	5	6	7
FX PT	3	2	1	1	2	0
GLDLE	0	3	2	1	1	2
MPDLE	1	1	2	2	1	2
NCOLT	1	1	2	1	2	2
SHRWD	1	1	2	3	1	1
WF BY	3	1	0	1	2	2

violations of the upper limit are generally smaller than violations of the lower regardless of settlement position.

There exist at least two alternative explanations for these findings which should be considered. Violations early in the sequence must widen the range, making it less likely for violations to occur purely by chance. Some evidence which counters this argument appears in Table 7-1b. Here are tabulated the number of times the sixth or seventh districts adhered to the existing range as a function of the value of the range. There is no tendency for districts facing relatively large values (e.g., $250) to adhere more closely than those facing relatively small values (e.g., $100). It might also be claimed that a suburb tends to settle in the same position each year. Then the observed findings would represent the policies of particular districts rather than a constraint to which they all must adhere. Evidence against this interpretation is presented in Table 7-1c, which shows the number of times each system settled in all the possible positions. Each of them has made its Bamin decision in a large number of different positions.

Policy Breaks

Once some idea of the allowable range for the Bamin has been established, it is necessary to use existing policy to select a particular point. It was not surprising to discover that Bamin policies changed over the years investigated. The model cannot, however, formulate a new policy by modifying the old as is done in human problem-solving simulations. Neither does it predict when a "policy break" occurs. The new policy must be supplied, as well as an instruction to initiate it in the appropriate year. Interviews and the salary data provided clues as to the years in which the breaks occurred. Initiation of major, lasting changes in the type of salary schedule also played a role. There exist five policy breaks in the model, and each one is associated with some type of major schedule change.

Neither the old nor the new policy is a good predictor of the Bamin increase in the policy break year in any of the five districts. However, a common pattern emerged in four of the districts which led to a prediction for them in such a year. The actual Bamin increase was always less than either the old or new strategy would predict. In three of the systems (a determination could not be made for the fourth) this caused all other salaries in the schedule to be lower than would be expected. Since the new type of schedule was always adopted at the request of the teachers' association, it appears that school boards may have gotten a temporary limiting of salary increases in return.

TABLE 7-2. Old policy versus new policy

District	Old for new	Old in all yrs.	No. of yrs. new policy
FX PT	1.20	1.42	1
GLDLE	1.86	2.12	5
MPDLE	1.56	1.86	2
NCOLT[a]	—	—	—
SHRWD	1.80	1.84	6
WF BY	3.37	4.37	6
OVERALL[b]	1.60	1.84	

[a]No policy break
[b]Includes Ncolt

Some empirical justification for the policy break concept, including the special prediction in the policy break year, appears in Table 7-2. The column headed "Old for new" indicates the errors of using the old policy in place of the new policy divided by the errors of Version 1. Here, the model's special prediction is used in the break year. The next column shows the errors of using the old policy in the break year and when the new policy is in effect, as compared to the model's errors. In all cases the errors are computed over the entire nine years of data. Clearly, the model would have performed much less adequately if it had not switched policies.

THE MODEL

The details of each district's part of the model will now be presented. In general the discussion will focus on Bamin policies, the reasons for their existence and the discrimination net. There will also be a separate discussion of constraints common to all the systems including the range phenomenon.

Fox Point—Bayside

Up until 1967-68 there was a de-emphasis on the lower and middle portions of the salary schedule in favor of the upper in order to maintain a hard core of experienced teachers. Each time Fox Point had the lowest Bamin in the cluster, its new salary would be in line with its neighbors' new choices. Otherwise, its new salary would tend to fall short of their selections. A shift in Bamin policy occurred in 1967-68, but its exact nature was not easy to determine. Apparently, comparison pressures have been keeping the district's Bamin more in line than previously.

The discrimination net representing Fox Point's Bamin policy is presented in Figure 7-2a. Initially, it is determined whether the decision is being made for any year before the policy break. If this is true, the old policy is in effect, and the current Fox Point salary (B) is compared to the other areas'. If none are lower, the model's prediction of the Bamin increase (IB) is the average of the earlier settlements for the coming year (AVES) minus the current salary.[9] If B is not at the bottom of the list, then IB is $100 less. If initially it is determined that the decision is being made for 1967-68 or after, IB

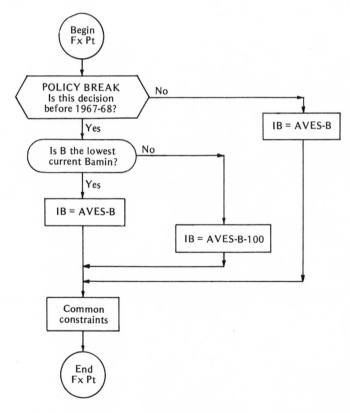

Figure 7-2a
Fox Point–Bayside

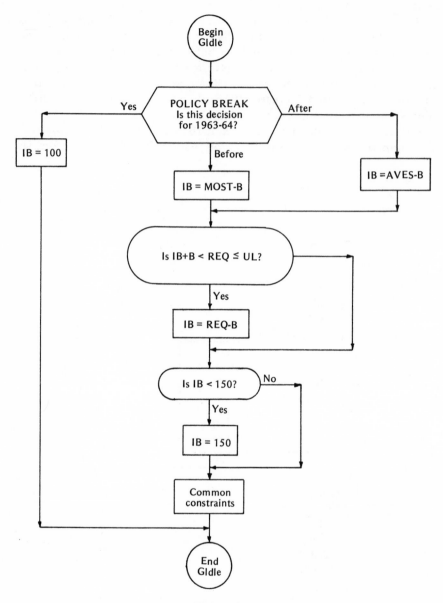

Figure 7-2b
Glendale—River Hills

is set equal to AVES minus B. Finally, the model moves on to consider the effect of constraints common to all districts.

Glendale–River Hills

Glendale's original policy can be succinctly described as desiring to be a Bamin leader in the area. The board felt that, since it was a relatively new system with expanding enrollments, this was needed to attract teachers. The new policy was influenced by a leveling out in enrollment and by the fact that, as more of the teachers progressed upward in the schedule, they began to press for additional financial resources being allocated in that direction. The board was therefore led to shift its emphasis from the lower to the upper parts of the schedule. Under both policies, however, it was willing to alter its Bamin decision by going somewhat higher than it felt was sufficient in order to meet a relatively low teachers' request.

The flowchart for Glendale appears in Figure 7-2b. First, the model inquires whether the decision is being made for the policy break year, 1963-64. If it is being made for a previous year, the Bamin increase (IB) is preliminarily set equal to the largest salary of those districts which have already settled for the coming year (MOST), minus the current Bamin (B). If the decision is being made for after 1963-64, it is preliminarily set equal to the average of the earlier settlements (AVES) minus B.

Next the model considers whether IB should be affected by the teachers' Bamin request (REQ). This involves discovering if REQ is higher than the preliminary decision (IB+B), but lower than some allowable upper limit (UL). If so, it is considered reasonable and accepted. UL was determined by assuming it would be the same as the upper limit of the allowable range within which a district in the kth position will tend to settle. It was therefore necessary to specify a particular value of UL for each value of k even though the range's upper limit may not be precisely determined when k=3,4,5. The expression which was developed is:

$$\text{UL=MOST} + 93.8 - 18.8 \,(k - 1) \qquad k=3,4,5$$
$$=\text{MOST} \qquad\qquad\qquad\qquad =6,7$$

The parameters of the upper equation were determined by calculating the least squares line through the average high violation data of Table 7-1a for k=3,4,5. The lower equation is also based on the results of that table.[10]

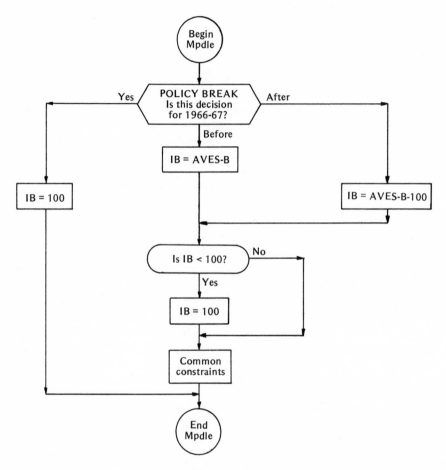

Figure 7-2c
Mapledale—Indian Hills

The model's next step is made to insure that IB is at least $150, and then the common constraints are handled. Provided the decision is being made for the policy break year, the Bamin increase is only $100 reflecting the considerations peculiar to such a year which were discussed earlier. There is no handling of the common constraints if this path is taken.

Mapledale—Indian Hills

Mapledale exhibited two types of policies, the latter being an intensification of the former. Most respondents agreed that the old policy emphasized salaries in the middle and upper part of the schedule in order to add to the few experienced teachers in the system. In 1966-67 this was intensified perhaps due to the larger number of experienced teachers that had been acquired.

The Mapledale decision process is portrayed in Figure 7-2c. If the decision is being made for a year previous to the policy break, the Bamin increase (IB) is the average of the earlier settlements (AVES) minus the current Bamin (B). When the decision is being made for a year after the break, IB is $100 less. Next a check is made to see that IB is at least $100, and then the common constraints are handled. In the policy break year, a $100 increase is used.

Nicolet

Nicolet is the one district for which there was no evidence of a policy break. Its strategy can be summarized as attempting to be neither a leader nor a follower. If the district currently has the highest Bamin, it will give a little bit less than the average increase its neighbors are giving. If it currently has the lowest Bamin, it will provide a little bit more than the average increase. And, if it is at neither of these two extremes, it will tend to give the average increase. It should take only a little reflection to see that this strategy is substantially the same as choosing the average of the coming year's salaries. The policy also involves the use of smoothing constraints, upper and lower limits on the amount of increase in order to reduce year-to-year variation.

Figure 7-2d incorporates the above ideas into a flowchart of the Nicolet decision. Initially, the Bamin increase (IB) is the average of the earlier settlements (AVES) minus the current Bamin (B). However, if the increase is less than $100, it is set equal to $100. If it is greater than $300 but not more than $400, it is set equal to $300. Otherwise, there is no change. The reason that a value of IB greater than $400 is not constrained is to prevent Nicolet from falling too far behind the other systems when they give relatively large raises.

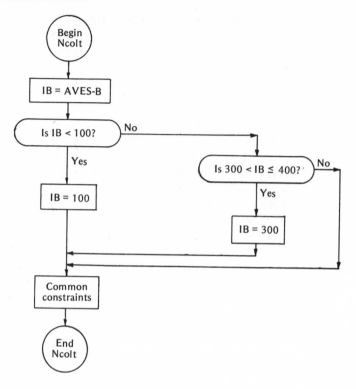

Figure 7-2d
Nicolet

Shorewood

Up until 1962-63 the school board was primarily interested in attracting master's degree teachers. Consequently, the bachelor's column, especially its lower portions, did not receive the emphasis given to the master's column, especially its upper portions. A second factor making for a relatively low Bamin was the existence of a dependency allotment with which it was hoped to attract male teachers. From 1962-63 on, recruiting problems (difficulties in attracting highly qualified teachers) and the reduction in the dependency allotment resulted in greater significance being placed on the lower end. Throughout the entire period, the board was willing to comply with a "reasonable" teachers' request.

The Shorewood discrimination net is shown in Figure 7-2e. It begins by inquiring whether the decision is being made for the policy

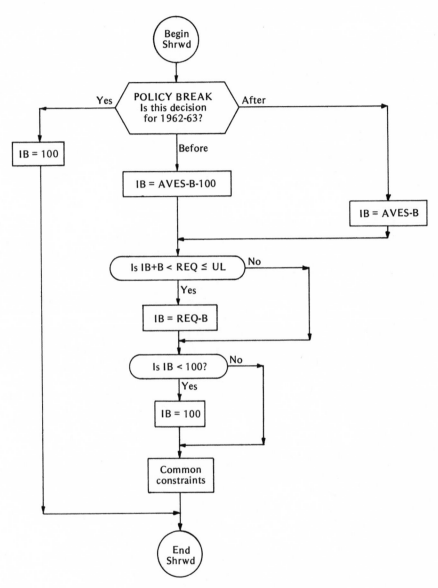

Figure 7-2e
Shorewood

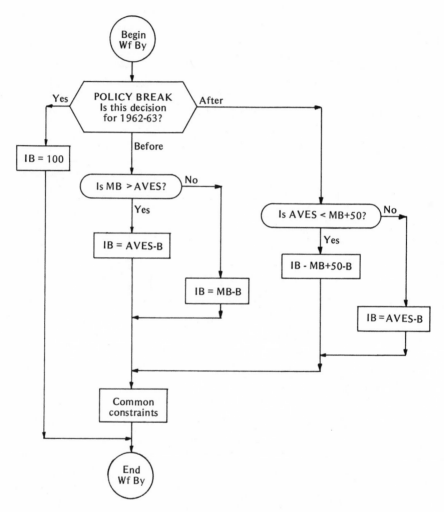

Figure 7-2f
Whitefish Bay

break year. If before, the Bamin increase (IB) is preliminarily set equal to $100 less than the average of the earlier settlements (AVES) minus the current Bamin (B). Provided the decision is being made for a year after 1962-63 IB is preliminarily set equal to AVES minus B. At this point the model examines whether the teachers' Bamin request (REQ) may alter the preliminary decision (IB+B). The procedure is the same as for Glendale. Provided the request is between IB+B and the allowable upper limit (UL) it is accepted.[11] Next a check is made to insure that IB is at least $100, and then the common constraints are handled. If the choice is being made for 1962-63, IB is $100 for reasons already mentioned.

Whitefish Bay

Up until 1962-63 the policy was to stay in the middle of the salaries of the other areas. In fact one respondent's impression was that the board tended to average its neighbors' salaries. The interviews also revealed a feeling that it was unnecessary to go above the Milwaukee Bamin to attract teachers because Whitefish Bay had a well-established reputation. The new strategy, which was to insure that the Bamin was a small amount over Milwaukee's, pushed the district into a position of leadership in the area. There were two primary reasons for the strategy. As in Shorewood, recruiting highly qualified teachers was becoming more difficult. Most of the people interviewed also agreed that status considerations were involved. Since Whitefish Bay was ahead of Milwaukee on so many status characteristics, they felt it incongruent to be behind on the highly visible Bamin dimension.

Whitefish Bay's flowchart appears in Figure 7-2f. First an inquiry is made to see if the year being predicted is subject to a policy break. If the year is before the break, Milwaukee's Bamin (MB) is compared to the average of the earlier settlements, including Milwaukee's (AVES). If MB is larger, the new Bamin is AVES; otherwise, it is MB. The latter path plausibly assumes that MB was never a great deal lower than the suburbs' salaries. If the year being considered occurs after the break, an inquiry is made to see whether AVES is less than MB plus $50. Confirmation allows the new Bamin to be set equal to MB plus $50 which plausibly assumes Milwaukee will not wind up much higher than the suburbs. If AVES is greater than MB plus $50, then AVES is used in order to ensure that the district remains competitive when the other suburbs go above Milwaukee on the average. The common constraints are handled next, and, in the policy break year, the increase is $100.

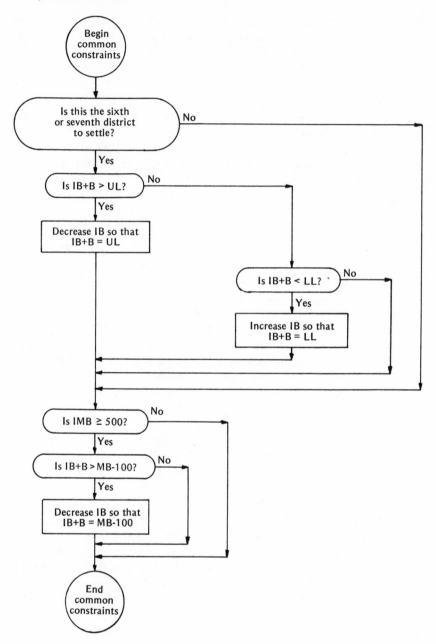

Figure 7-2g
Common constraints

Common Constraints

The final section of the model involves two sets of constraints to which all the districts must adhere. The first set reflects the pattern recognition phenomena. Since the upper and lower limits of the range faced by districts settling in the third, fourth and fifth positions tend to be hazy guidelines, they are not considered as constraints in the model (except when dealing with requests). However, systems deciding in the sixth or seventh positions regard the ranges they face as setting definite limits which are not to be violated. This behavior is incorporated into the model in Figure 7-2g. Initially, it must be determined whether the district being considered has settled sixth or seventh. If true, its new Bamin up to this point in the process (IB+B) is compared to the range's upper limit (UL=the largest salary to date). If IB+B is greater, it must be decreased until it equals UL. Otherwise, a comparison of IB+B to the lower limit (LL=the smallest salary to date) is made. If it is less, it must be increased until it equals LL.

The second set of constraints deals with the effect on the suburbs of Milwaukee's giving an extraordinarily large raise. It is pertinent for the model's treatment of the 1968-69 situation when the city's Bamin of $6,800 represented a $950 increase. In this situation a rule of coming no closer than $100 to the city's Bamin was established. Only one suburb in the county, Shorewood, violated it ($6,750). The rule is built into the model in Figure 7-2g. Milwaukee's Bamin increase (IMB) is checked to see whether it is greater than or equal to $500. This parameter representing an unusually large raise may have a value anywhere from $300 (the city's largest Bamin increase prior to 1968-69) to $950. If IMB is greater than or equal to $500, IB+B is compared to Milwaukee's Bamin (MB) minus $100. If IB+B is greater, it is reduced until it equals MB minus $100.

TESTS OF THE MODEL

Two general procedures were followed in validating the model. First, a comparison between the actual and predicted increases was made, and, second, the predicted increases were compared to those of alternative theories. In all cases tests were conducted on the same data from which parameters were estimated (1960-61 to 1968-69).

The first procedure assumes that the relationship between the jth district's actual increase in school year t (A_{jt}) and its predicted increase (P_{jt}) is given by the linear model:

$$A_{jt} = C_j + B_j P_{jt} + e_{jt}$$

Here, e_{jt} is a random error normally distributed with mean zero and constant variance. Ideally, $C_j{=}0$, $B_j{=}1$, and $e_{jt}{=}0$, for, then:

$$A_{jt} = P_{jt}$$

implying perfect predictions. The extent of agreement between the actual and predicted values is determined by the degree to which this ideal is reached.

The extent of agreement for each district was measured using regression analysis to estimate the parameters of the linear relationship in both versions of the model. Table 7-3 shows the resulting values of c_j (the estimate of C_j), b_j (the estimate of B_j) and r_j (the estimate of the correlation coefficient). Three different statistical hypotheses

TABLE 7-3. Statistics for comparing actual and predicted increases

District	Version 1			Version 2		
	c_j	b_j	r_j	c_j	b_j	r_j
FX PT	31.6	0.99	0.88	36.5	0.93	0.86
GLDLE	27.2	0.85	0.99	47.8	0.82	0.92
MPDLE	−8.3	0.98	0.99	−4.2	0.98	0.94
NCOLT	−6.1	1.01	0.98	4.8	1.00	0.90
SHRWD	−43.4	1.17	0.98	−11.4	1.10	0.95
WF BY	−31.5	1.07	0.99	−20.5	1.08	0.97

were investigated each at the 5 percent level of significance. The usual analysis of variance test indicated a relationship existed between A_{jt} and P_{jt} in all twelve instances. A test of the hypothesis $C_j{=}0$ using the t statistic was not rejected in all cases. A t test of the hypothesis $B_j{=}1$ was not rejected for five of the six districts in Version 1. The exception was Glendale and is due mainly to one observation. The same test involved no rejections in Version 2. Some indication of the magnitude of the random variation about the regression-line relative to that of the dependent variable can be obtained by examining r_j. Version 1's values are all above 0.98 except for Fox Point where relatively high random variation is chiefly due to a single point.

In the second part of the testing procedure, the model's predictions were compared to those of alternative theories. The error measure used for each district was the "standardized absolute error":

$$SAE = \frac{100 \, \Sigma_t \, |A_{jt} - P_{jt}|}{\Sigma_t A_{jt}}$$

A measure of the model's predictive accuracy for all the districts, the "overall standardized absolute error":

$$OSAE = \frac{100 \, \Sigma \, \Sigma_{jt} \, |A_{jt} - P_{jt}|}{\Sigma\Sigma_{jt} A_{jt}}$$

is also used. A value of zero for either measure indicates perfect predictions, while a value of one hundred percent indicates the predictions are no better than assuming the Bamin does not change.

The first alternative theory, which I have termed the "wage leader" hypothesis, is taken from the labor economics literature, specifically Cartter and Marshall.[12] Milwaukee, due to its being such a large employer of teachers in the locality will face an upward sloping labor supply curve. Accordingly, the determination of a Bamin rate will be subject to its discretion instead of the market's. The suburbs, each of which is a very small employer of teachers will adopt the rate set by the central city. Going below means losing teachers while it is not necessary to go above in order to meet recruitment needs. The wage leader theory was operationalized by using Milwaukee's Bamin as the prediction for each of the suburbs.[13] It was also operationalized by predicting each suburb's Bamin from a linear regression model using Milwaukee's salary as the independent variable. In both cases a district's predicted increase in *t* is its predicted salary in *t* minus the actual salary in *t-1*. These formulations assume no institutional barriers to the flow of teachers. In addition, the *ceteris paribus* condition applies to the quality of teachers, fringe benefits, and working conditions among the districts.

A second alternative will be referred to as the institutional theory and is taken from Johnson's explanation of its meaning.[14] Teachers' satisfaction with their raises depends upon whether or not they maintain their relative wage position. An increase in the wages of any one system, which will usually affect its entire schedule, will lead to corresponding raises in the other districts' schedules. This means

TABLE 7-4. Error measure percentages

District	Version 1	Version 2	Linear Hyp.	Milwaukee Bamin	Institu- tional
FX PT	19	21	32	35	40
GLDLE	7	17	28	33	40
MPDLE	10	20	20	28	40
NCOLT	12	20	25	26	44
SHRWD	13	15	25	27	44
WF BY	6	11	28	26	37
Overall	11	17	26	29	41

that Bamin rates will move up together or, in other words, that relative Bamin salaries will exhibit a great deal of inflexibility. Since Milwaukee always makes its decision first, one variation of this theory is to assume that all the suburbs raise their Bamins by the same percentage as the central city.

Due to the manner in which the error measure is constructed, there is implicit consideration of a fourth alternative. A prediction of no change in the Bamin will produce SAE and OSAE values of 100 percent.

A comparison of the values of the error measure appears in Table 7-4. As expected, Version 2's errors are larger than Version 1's in all cases. The most important conclusion is that Version 1's and Version 2's errors are less, overall, and on an individual district basis, than those of the alternative theories. The only exception is that the linear hypothesis is as good as Version 2 for Mapledale. Overall, Version 1 has 11/26=0.42 of the absolute error of its closest competitor, while Version 2 has 17/26=0.65 of the absolute error of its closest competitor. However, the model's favorable performance must be weighed against only one of the alternatives involving any parameters estimated from the data. On the other hand, it is possible that a more rigorous determination of the model's parameters could have reduced errors even further. Due to the paucity of data, Version 1's values were selected in a heuristic manner using the interviews and data as guides. Moreover, no attempt was made to separately estimate parameters for Version 2.

CONCLUSIONS

This research has tried to demonstrate that it is possible to analyze rigorously the actual process by which wages are set at the interorganizational level. The way is thus open to study wage movements at the level of the economic units which make these decisions and avoid the pitfalls many feel are associated with traditional aggregative analysis.[15] Accordingly, the model serves as a prototype for similar studies of more important contours elsewhere in the economy. A caveat must be sounded, however, for little is known about the ways in which collective bargaining will affect the methods and conclusions of this research.

It has also been demonstrated that the Dunlop-Ross framework, originally meant to apply to private sector blue-collar workers, is helpful in exploring salary determination for public school teachers. Such concepts as the job cluster, key wage, wage contour, and key settlement have their counterparts in the public sector, which indicates that wage determination may be studied in terms of concepts common to both areas. Whether we are talking about large city districts or suburban systems, it is meaningful to view the teachers' salary schedule and the wages of other personnel which are tied to it as a job cluster. The starting salary for teachers with a bachelor's degree fits the description of a key wage. My past work has suggested that large urban districts form contours within each of which the Bamin salary decision of any one system affects the others. This chapter indicates that suburbs located in the metropolitan areas of large cities form secondary orbits based on similar geographical and socioeconomic characteristics. Within such an orbit, a given district should be mainly influenced by the salaries of the other suburbs and the central city. There is little evidence that any one of the suburbs in this particular contour has set a pattern with respect to the sequence and amount of settlements. The central city, however, due to the fact that it must always take the first step, does in some sense set an increase pattern although there has been considerable deviation around it. Very recently, the city's decision has become more critical for the suburbs due to its exceptionally large raises.

It has not been possible to determine the effect of market versus institutional forces in the contour's salary comparison process. Due to the fact that we are dealing with one occupation and a limited geographical area, market forces must be influential. Yet, other suburbs in the same metropolitan area have a minor influence in our districts' decision making. The reason is that the north side suburbs' similar socioeconomic characteristics and geographical contiguity lead their citizens, school boards, and teachers to make equity comparisons among themselves. Once more, there does exist a little evidence which indicates that nonmarket factors must be considered. We are dealing with three elementary, one high school (Nicolet), and three K-12 districts including Milwaukee. Market considerations dictate that the high school's salaries will be affected by the last three and not the first three. Yet, the model's overall error for Nicolet was raised in all cases in which increased weighting was given to the K-12 systems' salaries. Some combinations of increased weights for the elementary districts' Bamins reduced the model's overall error for the high school. The tie-in between Nicolet and the elementary systems (which are its feeders) is due to equity factors. Typically, due to the predominance of K-12 districts, high school Bamins are the same as feeder elementary school Bamins. Consequently, Nicolet's school board will not want to go much higher nor its teachers much lower than the Bamins of its feeders.

The Bamin policies uncovered were designed to provide a quasi-unique answer to the salary determination problem. In attempting to solve this problem, a general heuristic of splitting into subproblems was employed; that is, the school boards went through a two-stage decision process. First, structure was obtained by using an allowable range for the Bamin based on the highest and lowest salaries to date. Then a choice was made as to a definite point within the range.

The issue of where to settle, of course, reflects pressures arising from teachers and the superintendent (who is responsible for recruiting) not to go much lower than the other systems, and pressures from citizens and other school boards not to go much higher. The discrimination nets indicate the specific manner in which the boards adapt to these forces. For example, the AVES strategy is similar to a district's giving less than the average raise when it is around the top, more than the average raise when it is near the bottom, and the average when it is around the middle. The use of upper and lower limits on increases is another example. The need to reconcile the pressures mentioned above when the central city gives an unusually large raise has led the suburbs to a rule of selecting Bamins which are at most somewhat lower than Milwaukee's. A final example is the use of a range to impose structure as opposed to other patterns.

Districts which decide early in the sequence consider the range as a hazy guideline; those settling among the last assume it to be an inviolable boundary. Correspondingly, there is some evidence that the amount by which a system will violate the range decreases as its settlement position increases. There is also a tendency for districts to violate the upper end in smaller amounts than the lower irrespective of their settlement position. This suggests that the forces which prevent moving out ahead of one's neighbors are more effective than those which hinder falling behind.

Of course, there exist factors which make for differences among Bamins such as the possibly unique issues facing districts and the personal values of school board members. These are incorporated into the model as detailed heuristics; for example, Whitefish Bay's rule to stay just above Milwaukee. Changes in these factors account for the policy break phenomenon; the adoption of a new set of rules which is typically accompanied by a shift in a district's relative salary position. Some nets incorporated rules designed to keep them on the low side of the Bamin range (Fox Point's old policy, Mapledale's new policy, Shorewood's old policy). In these instances the key issue was seen as maintaining a hard core of experienced teachers. Other districts had rules which led them to the high side of the Bamin range (Glendale's old policy, Whitefish Bay's new policy). Here recruiting was seen as the major issue.

Of all the variables that have been advanced for explaining the short-term movement of wages, this study has focused upon salary comparisons. Other writers, for example, Benson, have testified to the importance of this factor.[16] It is instructive, on the other hand, to consider why other factors were not treated in the model. No relation is developed between fringe benefits and the Bamin. Even though the interviews brought out some instances of trade-offs, it was not possible to compile a history of benefit requests and approvals. Moreover, trade-offs tend to be for relatively small amounts ($50 or less). While we have seen above that supply and demand factors do influence district salary policy, most respondents were of the opinion that the number of new teachers needed for the coming year does not affect the Bamin because it cannot be accurately estimated when salary decisions are made. Cost of living data, although inspected by board members, does not enter into the model. Bamin raises have consistently remained larger than increases in both the national and local indexes so that this constraint has not been tested. Ability to pay (school district wealth) has been found by Pegnetter to be the single most important variable cited by school boards in fact-finding cases.[17] Once more, Hickrod in his review of school finance research finds it to be the most crucial determinant of local spending.[18] It does not enter into the model because the particular systems studied all had uniformly high abilities, the decision rules employed were designed to prevent going to extremes, and citizens were willing to support relatively high-cost education as evidenced by no budget turndowns. Consequently, the study affords an opportunity to examine influences on spending when wealth is more or less controlled. The model exhibits a conspicuous lack of learning in the sense that a system's decisions are not dependent upon its own or others' past salaries (Fox Point being a minor exception). Each year is considered as a separate problem with neighbors' latest salaries being crucial.

Finally, the applicability of the model to future years and other districts must be considered. First of all, it appears that fundamental changes, for example, collective bargaining, joint action by school boards, taxpayers' revolts, are now occurring in the districts studied as well as many others. While Kasper has some evidence that collective bargaining may not raise teachers' salaries by much,[19] it is possible that this and other factors are altering the decision-making process. Second, it is obvious that the discrimination nets of the districts studied are not identical although they do exhibit some common heuristics. Consequently, it should not be expected that the details of each system's policy are necessarily generalizable. Consider, however, the basic findings on the applicability of the Dunlop-Ross framework, the structure of contours, the use of two stages in decision making, behavior with respect to the range, the heuristics used to prevent extreme choice, and so forth. These findings now serve as reasonable hypotheses about the behavior of all suburban districts, which can be tested and refined through subsequent research on more school systems. This can be done by adjusting the existing model in the light of new data as is done in problem-solving simulations, the development of the same type of model elsewhere and subsequent comparison with the present one, or the use of conventional hypothesis-testing techniques.

Notes

The author wishes to acknowledge the helpful comments of George Strauss and Richard Perlman. The work presented herein was performed pursuant to a grant from the U.S. Office of Education, Department of Health, Education, and Welfare. However, the opinions expressed herein do not necessarily reflect the position or policy of the U.S. Office of Education, and no official endorsement by the U.S. Office of Education should be inferred.

1. For example, see Melvin W. Reder, "Wage Determination in Theory and Practice," in Neil W. Chamberlin, *et al.* (eds.), *A Decade of Industrial Relations Research* (New York: Harper, 1958); Arthur M. Ross, "The External Wage Structure," in George W. Taylor and Frank C. Pierson (eds.), *New Concepts in Wage Determination* (New York: McGraw-Hill, 1957).

2. John T. Dunlop, "The Task of Contemporary Wage Theory," in Taylor and Pierson, *New Concepts;* Arthur Ross, *Trade Union Wage Policy* (Berkeley: University of California Press, 1948).

3. Harold M. Levinson, *Determining Forces in Collective Wage Bargaining* (New York: John Wiley, 1966).

4. Otto Eckstein and Thomas A. Wilson, "The Determination of Money Wages in American Industry," *The Quarterly Journal of Economics,* LXXVI (No. 3, August 1962), 379-414.

5. Donald Gerwin, "Compensation Decisions in Public Organizations," *Industrial Relations,* VIII (No. 2, February 1969), 174-183.

6. Allen Newell and H. A. Simon, "GPS, A Program that Simulates Human Thought," in E. A. Feigenbaum and J. Feldman (eds.), *Computers and Thought* (New York: McGraw-Hill, 1963); Edward A. Feigenbaum, "The Simulation of Verbal Learning Behavior," in *ibid.;* R. M. Cyert and J. G. March, *A Behavioral Theory of the Firm* (Englewood Cliffs, N.J.: Prentice-Hall, 1963).

7. J. P. Crecine, *Governmental Problem Solving* (Chicago: Rand-McNally, 1969); Donald Gerwin, *Budgeting Public Funds: The Decision Process in an Urban School District* (Madison: University of Wisconsin Press, 1969); C. E. Weber, "Intraorganizational Decision Processes Influencing the EDP Staff Budget," *Management Science,* XII (No. 4, December 1965), 69-93.

8. Feigenbaum and Feldman, *Computers and Thought.*

9. Note that decision makers think in terms of salary levels which are then used to calculate increases.

10. When k=2, there is no basis for determining a value of UL. However, Glendale never settled second over the time period studied. This issue is therefore not a problem in testing against past data, but must be dealt with when predicting the future.

11. When k=2, there is no way of determining UL. However, the only time Shorewood settled in the second position the teachers' request was unavailable, so it was not necessary to consider the matter.

12. A. M. Cartter and F. R. Marshall, *Labor Economics: Wages, Employment, and Trade Unionism* (Homewood, Ill.: Richard D. Irwin, 1967).

13. The effective Milwaukee Bamin on a school-year basis is higher than the calendar-year figure used since teachers receive a raise four months after they begin work. However, a variation of the wage leader hypothesis which used 0.4 x the current year's Milwaukee Bamin + 0.6 x the following year's Milwaukee Bamin produced much larger errors than the version chosen.

14. G. E. Johnson, "Wage Theory and Inter-regional Variation," *Industrial Relations,* VI (No. 3, May 1967), 321-38.

15. See, for example, G. H. Orcutt, *et al, Microanalysis of Socioeconomic Systems: A Simulation Study* (New York: Harper, 1961); Cyert and March, *Behavioral Theory of the Firm;* O. Eckstein, "Money Wage Determination Revisited," *Review of Economic Studies,* XXXV, 2 (No. 102, April 1968), 133-43.

16. Charles S. Benson, *The Economics of Public Education* (Boston: Houghton Mifflin, 1962).

17. Richard Pegnetter, "Fact Finding and Teacher Salary Disputes: The 1969 Experience in New York State," *Industrial and Labor Relations Review,* XXIV (No. 2, January 1971) 226-42.

18. G. A. Hickrod, "Local Demand for Education: A Critique of School Finance and Economic Research Circa 1959-1969," *Review of Educational Research,* XLI (No. 1, 1971), 35-49.

19. Hirschel Kasper, "The Effects of Collective Bargaining on Public School Teachers' Salaries," *Industrial and Labor Relations Review,* XXIV (No. 1, October 1970), 57-71.

APPENDIX

TABLE 7-5 Characteristics of North Side School Districts[a]

District	Grades	Enrollment	Number of Teachers	Cost per pupil	Coll. barg.[c]
FX PT	K-8	1,528	95	$1,401	1968-69
GLDLE	K-8	2,075	113	1,081	1968-69
MPDLE	K-8	870	47	1,128	—
NCOLT[b]	9-12	2,105	113	1,343	1968-69
SHRWD	K-12	2,828	136	1,015	1965-66
WF BY	K-12	4,181	216	1,076	—
MILW	K-12	130,534	4,906	941	1965

[a]Data sources were each school district; Cooperative Educational Service Agency 19, Milwaukee; Citizen's Governmental Research Bureau, Milwaukee.
[b]Nicolet is a high school district serving the same area as the three elementary systems above it in the table.
[c]Indicates year of first negotiated contract.

TABLE 7-6. Bamin increases and across-the-board increases

District	Direct relation	Partial relation	Indirect relation	No relation
FX PT	5	1	3	0
GLDLE	5	3	0	1
MPDLE	2[a]	2	3	2
NCOLT	3	1	5	0
SHRWD	3	0	5	1
WF BY	5[a]	2	0	2
TOTAL	23	9	16	6

[a]In one of these instances increments in the upper part of the schedule were changed.

The Bamin increase was directly related to the raises in all other elements of the salary schedule in 23 out of a possible 54 instances (6 districts x 9 years). This included using the same amount or percentage of increase throughout in a fixed increment type of schedule or basing all raises on the Bamin change in an index schedule. There were 9 cases in which the Bamin raise was directly related to increases in part of the schedule, but the remainder was changed by a larger amount or percent. In 16 instances either increments or index multiples were extensively changed. Here, the Bamin increase was not the sole determinant of other raises. Finally, there were 6 clear-cut cases in which no relation existed.

TABLE 7-7. B.A. minimum salaries

District	1959-60	1960-61	1961-62	1962-63	1963-64
FX PT	4200	4600	4600	4750	4900
GLDLE	4325	4625	4775	4900	5000
MPDLE	4300	4600	4700	4800	5000
NCOLT	4200	4500	4800	4900	5000
SHRWD	4300	4500	4600	4700	5050
WF BY	4200	4550	4650	4650	5050
MILW	4200	4550	4650	4900	5025

District	1964-65	1965-66	1966-67	1967-68	1968-69
FX PT	5200	5350	5550[a]	6100	6700
GLDLE	5200	5450	5600	6000	6600
MPDLE	5200	5400	5450	5900	6600
NCOLT	5150	5350	5550	6000	6700
SHRWD	5200	5400	5600	6000	6750
WF BY	5300	5450	5600	6000	6700
MILW	5275	5400	5550	5850[b]	6800

[a]A couple of months after all the districts, including Fox Point, made their 1966-67 decisions, the Fox Point school board awarded its teachers an extra across-the-board increase of $100. This situation is handled in the following manner. In order to predict 1966-67 Bamins the original Fox Point decision ($5,550) is used. When predicting 1967-68 Bamins, Fox Point's 1966-67 decision is considered to be $5,650.

[b]The 1967-68 Milwaukee increase was $200 starting in January and $100 starting in September.

8 / Formulating Salary Policy in Suburban School Districts

Donald Gerwin

One of the most timely problems associated with the allocation of financial resources in public education concerns salary increases for teachers. Most of a typical school system's budget is due to this factor. Further, when compared to other occupations, teachers have enjoyed large raises in recent years. From 1960 to 1967, the average yearly earnings of classroom teachers increased 50 percent, as compared to 30 percent for accountants, 33 percent for attorneys, and 40 percent for engineers.[1] Yet, at the same time, tax increases are meeting with more widespread opposition from citizens. It thus seems imperative that we investigate as rigorously as possible the way in which teachers' salaries are determined in local school systems. In order to meet this objective, this paper utilizes a conceptual framework based on a comprehensive analysis of the decision-making process.

There can be no doubt that growing attention is being paid to the study of the determinants of public school expenditures at the local level. Recently, Dye[2] has used a variation of Easton's systems model to study educational outcomes including teachers' salaries in big-city districts. Davis,[3] employing an interpretation of the Downs and Buchanan and Tullock theories, has analyzed teachers' salaries and other expenditure variables in western Pennsylvania school systems. Miner,[4] drawing upon traditional economic analysis, has examined

Reprinted from *Education and Urban Society*, IV (No. 3, May 1972), 313-37.

spending in a sample of over 1,000 districts. Johns and Kimbrough[5] have utilized a community power structure viewpoint to analyze fiscal policy in high- and low-effort school systems. In general, these and other studies, although utilizing diverse theoretical foundations, have been concerned at the empirical level with finding whether or not variables are correlated. There has been little effort devoted to studying the actual process by which hypothesized factors affect spending, an exception being James et al.,[6] who included in their work an examination of the budgetary processes of fourteen large-city systems.

The conceptual framework employed here consists of analyzing the process by which teachers' salary increase decisions are made. It is based on the organizational theories of Cyert, March, and Simon[7] and represents a further exploration of work that I had done earlier.[8] Basically, decisions on teachers' salaries are viewed as made in a process involving three components: information, policy, and outcomes. Information about the environment is either gathered or presented to the decision makers. Existing policy, consisting of more or less standard procedures based on past experience and personal values, is utilized to couple the perceived state of the environment with an appropriate reaction. The result is a specific choice based on applying policy to the available information. This, in turn, has effects on the organization's environment because it acts as an informational input for the making of decisions elsewhere. These provide new inputs to the organization in question (along with its own latest choice), and the cycle is repeated.

The precise nature of the interrelationship between the three components may be made more clear in the following rather abstract example. Let us imagine that school boards make unilateral decisions (no collective bargaining) and that inputs to a particular district consist of its own and neighbors' latest starting salaries. The application of existing policy to the data would involve the use of *operating* rules (average the starting salaries), *testing* rules (is our current starting salary less than the average?), and *decision* rules (if so, set the new starting salary equal to the average; if not, do nothing). A specified outcome is then one of the two possible choices contained in the policy. Its particular value would influence neighbors' starting salaries, which, in turn, become inputs for this district's next choice. Alternatively, where collective bargaining exists, one may desire to consider the school board's proposals as outcomes. These influence counterproposals from teachers, which, along with other information, act as inputs to a process which generates the next board proposal.

In a recent paper the author has used a formalized version of this approach to develop a computer simulation model of teachers' salary increases in a group of suburban districts.[9] They depended heavily on each other for informational inputs such as salary data and thus formed what Ross[10] has termed an "orbit of coercive salary comparison." That study was concerned with the B.A. minimum salary (starting salary for teachers with a bachelor's degree) and primarily with years before the use of collective bargaining. The present study, based on the same districts, is a companion piece concerned with the formulation under collective bargaining of the entire teachers' salary schedule (and, to some extent, fringe benefits). As a result, this analysis is much less formalized than the previous one. It involves three interrelated sections, each of which seeks to throw some light on one of the components of the decision process mentioned above. First, there is an examination of the sources and content of information. Next, there is a discussion of the policy positions likely to be advocated by school board members. Finally, a case analysis of a school board's salary decisions in a particular year is presented.

The districts studied are six "north side" suburban systems in Milwaukee County. Three provide elementary education, one is a high school, and two provide elementary and secondary education. At the time the study was conducted (the 1968-69 school year), the latest available data from local sources indicated that these are small systems with enrollments ranging from 870 to 4,181 and the number of teachers ranging from 47 to 216. The communities they serve are wealthy (a majority of households in the total area have incomes greater than $10,000), and, with one exception, a majority of the land use is devoted to residential development.

All the districts have single salary schedules—matrices whose columns represent academic degree and whose rows represent years of experience. Teachers' salaries are among the highest in the state, as is reflected in per pupil cost ($1,081 to $1,401). Four districts had formal collective bargaining arrangements with their teachers, but three for only one year and one for four years. The remaining two had informal agreements to negotiate. All teachers' groups are affiliated with the National Education Association; the school boards consist of five to seven elected members. Negotiators are selected from the membership of each side. The salary issue is considered from roughly December to March for the coming school year.

The findings of this paper are based on tape-recorded interviews with all six superintendents, from three to five board and ex-board members in each district, and representatives of four of the local teachers' associations. They also depend upon the examination of written documents such as the minutes of school board and negotiations meetings.

SOURCES AND CONTENT OF INFORMATION

According to the paradigm discussed earlier, the inputs to the decision process are in the form of information. The implication is that the first step in understanding a decision is to study the data used in making it. This section has a dual purpose. It is meant to present a systematic procedure for tracing information flows for a wide variety of decisions, including the type of concern here. It also presents the particular sources and content of the data used by the districts studied when they formulate teachers' salary increases.

Information here has two major components: data needed to make reasoned judgments, such as the salaries of other districts, and opinion, as exemplified by citizens' complaints about higher taxes. The ensuing analysis of these two components concentrates on the current situation in a hypothetical unit. It was not possible to inquire whether each district received all the data and from the same sources that are associated with this unit. Rather, the analysis represents my general impressions as to which features are essential and common to most of the systems. Unless otherwise specified, it should be assumed that communications are sent and received during winter and spring, while negotiations are being conducted.

A pictorial representation of the information flow is presented in Figure 8-1. The chart was constructed using three basic dimensions. The first classifies communications according to the eleven general types listed in the key of Figure 8-1. Thus, the different types of data pertaining to recruiting, for example, all belong to the R group. The second classifies the sources according to geographical area. Its five categories, bounded by the inner circle and the three outer ovals, include the negotiations site, the school district, the north side, the metropolitan area, and the rest of the environment. The third classifies sources according to who receives their outputs. The left quadrant is for the school boards, while that on the right is for the teachers. The upper and lower quadrants are for sources which are utilized by both sides, while the inner circle involves communications sent to each other. In the latter case, the board's negotiators are the recipients of proposals from the other side concerning salaries, benefits, and working conditions (P), are informed about settlements in neighboring areas (S), especially those favorable to teachers, and are provided with the results of votes taken by the local association on their proposals (V). The teachers' negotiators likewise receive proposals (P) and are informed about settlements considered favorable to the other side (S).

One channel for sending more or less exclusive information to the board's negotiators involves the members of various school boards. Board members other than negotiators develop their own opinions (O), which are transmitted as influence attempts. Board members in the other north side districts supply on request information on the current state of their own negotiations. The local school board association's members share information about the current state (CS), prepare a report indicating present salary structures (PS), and undoubtedly express their opinions concerning the salary issue (O). The Wisconsin Association of School Boards (WASB) advises districts about any recent settlements (S) and provides data on present salary structures (PS).

The superintendent is asked to make recommendations on the salary structure (O) which are based on opinions he has received from teachers (O), the previous spring's recruiting results (R), and any rough estimate of the number of teachers needed for the coming year (R). He also relays information about the current state (CS).

A district's business manager supplies a great deal of data, including the financial implications of both sides' proposals (F), salaries of other professionals in the metropolitan area (OS), and the cost of living (CL). He also relays the current state of negotiations (CS) and present salary structures (PS) elsewhere by virture of his contacts with the north side business managers and the metropolitan business managers' association (MMBMA).

School board negotiators are also sensitive to the salary increases offered to professionals at their own places of work (OS).

The teachers' negotiators receive most of their information from various teachers' groups. The rest of the salary committee transmit their opinions (O), while the bulk of the teachers express their preferences in polls conducted prior to the negotiations (O) and through votes on various proposals during the negotiations (V). Occasional meetings of the north side teachers' negotiators are designed to share information about the current state (CS), and undoubtedly individuals express their opinion at these times (O). The suburban council of education associations (MSCEA) indicates present salary structures (PS) and discusses the current state (CS). The Wisconsin Education Association establishes policy guidelines (G) which work their way into proposals in one form or another. Its seminars and published re-

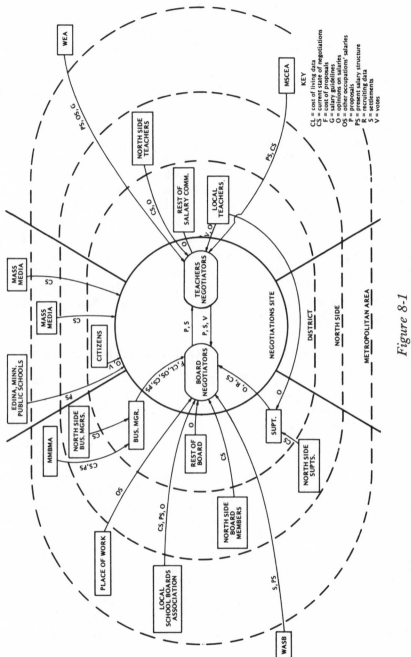

KEY
CL = cost of living data
CS = current state of negotiations
F = cost of proposals
G = salary guidelines
O = opinions on salaries
OS = other occupations' salaries
P = proposals
PS = present salary structure
R = recruiting data
S = settlements
V = votes

Figure 8-1
Sources and content of information

ports cover a wide range of material including present salary structures (PS) and salaries of other occupations (OS).

Certain types of data available to both school boards and teachers must also be considered. Citizens express their opinions about taxes at school board meetings (O), and school board election results (V) may provide significant cues. Local mass media indicate the Milwaukee salary settlement (S), which occurs at the start of the suburbs' negotiations. Both local and national media provide data on the current state (CS) and settlements (S) in large cities and suburbs across the nation. Finally, the Edina, Minnesota, public schools publish a report on the current salaries of suburbs across the nation (PS).

Which types and sources of data are most influential in decision-making? The Milwaukee settlement, obtained from local mass media, fits into this category. Both sides rely heavily upon the settlements and current state of negotiations in the other north side systems. The teachers' main source of these data is their informal contacts, while the school board depends upon its informal contacts and the school board association. Certainly, each side's proposals (including financial implications), which are in part based on the above data, are a final important factor.

POLICY POSITIONS OF SCHOOL BOARD MEMBERS

The next step in our conceptual framework is to discuss the policies which are used to process information as it is gathered. Individual school board members will at least initially have different viewpoints in regard to teachers' salaries. It is intended here to identify three "pure" views in the sense that an individual's and ultimately the school board's actual position is likely to be some combination of them. They have been labeled the professional, fiscal, and competitive orientations and will be examined along five basic dimensions. Of special concern is the identification of the policy rules (alluded to in the introduction) which are associated with each orientation. Some general rules, each of which may apply to a different feature of the decision, are dealt with here. Examples of more detailed operational rules associated with the B.A. minimum salary can be found elsewhere.[11] It is also intended to identify an orientation's rationale, its effect on collective bargaining, the conditions under which it is advocated, and the information that would be considered especially pertinent to it. A summary of the results appears in Table 8-1.

The professional policy orientation views teachers as having an intrinsic value to society at least equal to that of comparable profession-

TABLE 8-1. Policy positions

Characteristic	Professional orientation	Fiscal orientation	Competitive orientation
Rationale	Intrinsic value of teachers	Board must protect citizens	Market determines teachers' value
General policy rules	Achieve parity with other professionals' salaries	Stay within a fixed total allocation	Use salary comparisons with similar districts
Effect on bargaining	No bargaining	Conflict over total cost figure Board seeks public disclosure	Delays
When employed	Teachers and school board share common goals	Community pressure	Teachers dissatisfied with pay Hiring pressure Businessmen on board
Essential information	Other occupations' salaries Teachers' proposals	Community opinions Proposal costs	Current state of negotiations Settlements Recruiting data

al groups (e.g., those with the same number of years of education). Accordingly, teachers' salaries should be raised as fast as possible to the same or greater levels. As a result the district would in all likelihood be pushed into a position of salary schedule leadership in the area. While this may mean attracting high-quality teachers, there must be a willingness to incur the displeasure of neighboring school boards and to run the risk of having citizens turn down the budget.

This orientation may also lead to the desire for a salary schedule with the largest increments[12] in the middle, as is often the case with professional career pay in industry. There will be a reluctance to grant fringe benefits on the grounds that professionals should make such decisions for themselves. A desire for year-round employment of teachers is also a possibility. Collective bargaining will be considered unprofessional, and therefore attempts will be made to avoid it. The initial school board offer to the teachers would be exactly what is intended, and an implicit assumption exists that the teachers would be receptive because of its generosity. A variation would involve both sides in jointly developing a compensation package so that problem-solving, as opposed to bargaining, is stressed.

Aspects of the professional orientation are most likely to be advocated by some or all of the board when they perceive themselves and the teachers sharing common goals. In part, this will be determined by the degree of mutual trust that has developed between the two groups and the extent to which the community is actively concerned about tax increases. The information which holders of this viewpoint should consider most essential will undoubtedly include other occupations' salaries (OS) and the teachers' proposals (P).

The fiscal orientation involves the desire to keep taxes as low as possible. It stems from the belief that a board member's role is to protect the interests of the district's citizens. This may be due to an internalized social norm or the desire to get elected. A more subtle variation is the call for more efficient use of existing financial resources and, in particular, the use of a salary schedule based on merit considerations.

The main policy rule involves starting from a specified increase in the total budget which is acceptable to the community. School systems, however, usually have rather imperfect knowledge of citizens' preferences in part due to unsophisticated information-gathering techniques. Consequently, the amount will be based on the application of naive rules to past experience (e.g., same percentage as last year) and will tend to be underestimated to avoid allocating more than the community actually desires.

The amount to be allowed for teachers' salaries is determined by subtracting large expenses to which the district is more or less committed (e.g., debt service increase). It might be hypothesized that the board will have little interest in the manner in which this sum is divided up. More likely it will be reluctant to yield decision-making authority to the teachers and will be against allocations which imply considerable future cost increases. Once more, it has an interest in allocating the funds in order to increase the chances of obtaining a majority of favorable votes in the teachers' association.

When the school board adopts the fiscal orientation, its goals will be different from those of the teachers, so some form of bargaining will ensue. It may try to form a coalition with the public; an example is the seeking of public disclosure of the negotiations in order to mitigate the teachers' demands. From the teachers' viewpoint, bargaining will focus on the legitimacy of the total cost constraint, due to its being imperfectly rationalized. There is, of course, an increased chance of deadlock and the consequent possibility of an appeal to an outside party for resolution.

The circumstances making for adoption of this type of policy are associated with community pressure to hold the line on taxes. These include a largely residential tax base, educational costs considerably above the average, and a large number of citizens with no children in the public schools. More important in the recent past has been the pressure on personal income caused by inflation and increased taxes. Understandably, the most pertinent information for holders of this orientation will be citizens' opinions (O) and the costs of proposals (F).

The rationale for the competitive orientation stems from the economic argument that the value of teachers is determined by the market test. Thus, the salary schedule in any one district should be heavily influenced by those in "comparable" districts. Comparability for districts of the size dealt with in this paper means propinquity, similar average income levels, and similar land use characteristics, among other factors. A desire to meet the salaries of other systems requires the establishment of an informal communications network, which may be facilitated by the presence of a local school board association.

While both the school board and the teachers may agree on the legitimacy of comparisons as the basis for settlements (although for different reasons), there will still be room for bargaining. One reason is that comparison information provides for any step in the schedule a range within which a particular point must be chosen. Consequently, the board will emphasize the lowest settlements to date, while the teachers will be using the highest ones. Another reason is that decisions may have to be made before an accurate picture of what other systems are doing is available. This should cause a tendency for the board to hold back from committing itself.

The competitive orientation should be more important in developing the lower part of the salary schedule. An institutional barrier—reluctance of new employers to provide full credit for past experience—generally hinders the feasibility of a market test for teachers in the upper part of the schedule. In addition, this orientation should be in evidence where businessmen predominate on the board, when teachers are dissatisfied with their pay and perhaps one or two key staff members have left, or when a relatively large number of new teachers is needed. Essential information will naturally include the current state of negotiations elsewhere (CS), settlement news (S), and recruiting data from the superintendent (R).

A CASE ANALYSIS OF DECISION-MAKING

Now an attempt is made to fit together the three aspects of the decision process: information, policy, outcomes. Emphasis is placed on studying the specific outcomes; in this case, salary proposals. Of interest are the ways in which alternative proposals are developed, the manner of estimating their consequences, the methods used for selecting which one will be proposed, and the criteria employed. However, attention is also paid to the information used and where it enters into the process. Similarly, it is noted which policy orientations appear and where they fit into the total picture.

Attention is focused on one of the six north side districts. Decisions on teachers' salary increases made in the 1968-69 school year (the second year of collective bargaining) for 1969-70 are analyzed in detail. Although it was not possible to attend the teachers' meetings or the negotiations, it was possible to sit in on the school board's executive sessions, which also included the superintendent and the business manager. Consequently, emphasis is placed on the board's decisions with those of the teachers considered as given.

Table 8-2 presents information on the proposals made by each side. It includes proposal dates, the salary increase per teacher, minimum salaries, number of rows, maximum salaries, total costs of salary increases, and total costs of all items. The teachers' initial proposal (T1) involved a 10 percent across-the-board raise made with the knowledge that the city of Milwaukee had settled on varying increases throughout its schedule, including a move from $6,800 to $7,200 at the B.A. minimum level. The teachers also requested raises in summer school salaries, life insurance, and retirement payments; extension of health insurance coverage to diagnostic care; and the inauguration of vacation pay, terminal pay for retirees, and personal leave.

For our purposes, the first important executive meetings of the school board were held in the beginning of February to evaluate the teachers' proposals and to prepare an initial proposal of its own. Evaluation involved the application of a few simple rules due to the uncertainties caused by a lack of information. For example, consequences were measured along only two dimensions: legality and cost. Cost consequences were examined by making comparisons with the initial proposals in neighboring districts and the previous year's initial offer. On these bases, it was found that overall costs were in line with the former and lower than the latter. The legality dimension took on three values: legal, illegal, and uncertain, and it was used in

TABLE 8-2. Board's and teachers' proposals[a]

Date	Proposal	Salary increase per teacher	B.A. column			M.A. column			Total costs	
									Salaries	All items
1968/1969	Settlement	$600	$6,700	15	$11,700	$7,200	20	$13,950	$125,270	$137,070
January 28	T1	10%	7,370	15	12,870	7,920	20	15,345	148,835	221,835
February 13	B1	$600	7,300	15	12,300	7,800	20	14,550	105,821	109,320
February 25	T2	9%	7,300	15	12,763	7,848	20	15,205	139,843	168,883
March 10	B2	$600	7,300	15	12,300	7,800	20	14,550	105,821	114,660
March 22	B3	Varies	7,150	12	11,950	7,700	16	14,600	112,780	119,729
	T3	8%	7,236	15	12,636	7,776	20	15,066	129,080	158,120
March 27	B3L	Varies	7,150	12	11,950	7,700	16	14,600	115,530	122,479
	B4	8%	7,236	12	11,988	7,776	16	14,202	110,290	117,239
	T4	Varies	7,236	15	12,350	7,776	20	15,000	121,014	149,643
March 31	B3L	Varies	7,150	12	11,950	7,700	16	14,600	115,530	122,479
	T5	7½%	7,202	15	12,325	7,740	20	14,996	119,994	128,368
April 16	Settlement	Varies	7,150	12	11,950	7,700	17	14,750	117,330	121,794

[a]There may be some unavoidable discrepancies in the total cost information for T3 or T5 due to incompatibility between the categories desired and those kept for accounting purposes.

studying fringe benefits. In general, benefits which were considered legal and of low cost were looked upon most favorably.

The school board considered two basic proposals of its own. The first, an example of the professional orientation, called for an $800 salary raise (larger than any amount ever given), but no increase in fringe benefits. Its total cost ($125,000) was considerably less than that of the teachers' offer. The second proposal, developed as an alternative to the first, while not specifically an example of the fiscal orientation, had it in mind. It included a $500 raise plus the summer school, life insurance, and diagnostic items. The two salary alternatives set a range within which a decision could be made. The superintendent representing those most concerned with recruiting felt that a B.A. minimum anywhere in the range would be acceptable. Some board members saw being on the high side as heightening the teachers' trust in the school board and lessening their felt need for bargaining. Other board members were concerned that a relatively high offer might be used by the teachers as a base to push for additional amounts and that the community would react unfavorably, especially if no other districts settled lower. The result was a compromise which possessed some aspects of the professional and fiscal orientations. It included a $600 increase, personal leave, diagnostic care, and a provision to finish putting teachers on schedule[13] (promised in the previous year). There was also agreement that, during the negotiations, further benefit increases would lead to salary decreases.

This proposal (B1) was turned down by the teachers' negotiators and by a vote of the association. The reason, a desire for a percentage raise, was due to the large number of teachers in the upper part of the schedule. About 50 percent would be in the upper third of the schedule in the coming year. Accordingly, the teachers proposed a 9 percent raise and dropped some fringe benefit requests (T2). This was supported by information from the first comparable district to settle. It had provided an abundant settlement including a small percentage adjustment as part of each tenured teacher's raise. Once more, the upper part of its new M.A. column was greater than that proposed in T2.

While there was some feeling on the school board that B1 had apparently not been as generous as was originally thought, all agreed not to grant a percentage increase. It would be costly now (about $35,000) and in the future, and it would distort the present rationale of having the largest increments in the middle of the schedule. A decision was made to stand on the original proposal, plus granting summer school raises.

This second proposal (B2) met with exactly the same reaction from the teachers as the first and led the board to develop an entirely new one. The general framework was influenced by at least two other events. At a board meeting, the same citizen who had made motions for budget cuts in the last two annual budget meetings said he would do so again. In addition, settlement information from two comparable districts indicated their B.A. columns were behind that of B2, while their M.A. columns were behind that of B2 from about the middle on up.

The most important overall considerations for the salary schedule of the new proposal were:

1. no percentage increase,
2. a fixed total cost for salary raises (at this point about $110,000 to $115,000),
3. an allocation of funds which would secure the approval of the negotiators and ultimately a majority of the teachers,
4. similarity to the new schedules of comparable districts.

More specific constraints stemming from these included:

1. reduction of the B.A. minimum as compared to B2 to meet 2 and 4 above,
2. condensing the schedule (by eliminating some upper rows) to meet 2 and 4 above but in violation of 3 above because of the large number of teachers in the upper part of the schedule,
3. larger increments near the top to meet 3 above but in partial contrast to the present increment rationale.

The resulting schedule (B3) as compared to B2 had the effect of shifting raises from the uppermost portions of the B.A. column to the upper half of the M.A. column and was roughly in the middle of the recent settlements elsewhere. No additional fringe benefits were considered.

The teachers' negotiators, still pressing for a percentage raise, turned down the board's proposal. They requested an 8 percent raise while making further benefit concessions (T3). As a result, the board saw two general paths to follow: stand firm and go to fact-finding if necessary, or further compromise involving a percentage raise. In electing the latter path, the board gave the teachers a choice between two alternatives. The first was B3 plus a lower limit on any individual's raise (for one year only and therefore not part of the schedule) in order to gain support and achieve equity (B3L). The second involved a percentage raise (with the same lower limit provision) built into the framework of a condensed schedule (B4). The particular amount (8 percent) was chosen so as to make the total salary increase cost less appealing than that of B3L, and due to the feeling that, if the schedule was to be condensed, the teachers would not accept a percentage less than the figure they were currently requesting. This proposal as compared to B3L had the effect of shifting some funds from the M.A. back to the B.A. column.

The teachers' negotiators were more in favor of B4 than B3L, but now the conflict shifted to its compressed nature. Their proposal to add back the eliminated steps at amounts representing somewhat less than an 8 percent raise (T4) was turned down by the board. At this point, its members were beginning to exhibit signs of frustration, which in part contributed to their becoming more interested in the route of standing firm and possible fact-finding. Their thinking was supported by an external authority who recommended making a final offer and then fact-finding if necessary. The salary proposal selected as the final offer was B3L partially because its B.A. minimum and M.A. maximum were the most in line with comparable districts.

Events now moved rapidly toward a resolution of the conflict. The board's final offer was rejected due to its condensed nature, and the teachers' counter of 7.5 percent and less benefits (T5) was rejected in turn. In spite of the board's growing determination to go to fact-finding, it agreed to another meeting. There the teachers agreed to accept B3L if two extra steps were added to each column. The superintendent convinced the board to offer one extra step on the M.A. column, which was accepted.

In concluding the case analysis, let us review the highlights of the board's process. There were at least four criteria utilized in decision-making, and these for the most part were in the form of aspiration levels. One of the most important was the imposition of a total salary increase constraint. It represented the way in which community pressure against tax hikes was translated into board policy. Other criteria included similarity with the salary schedules of neighbors and legality. A more vague goal involved gaining the support of influential teachers and ultimately a majority of them as exemplified by increasing increments at the top, providing lower limits on raises, and shifting funds to the upper half of the M.A. schedule. There was little consideration given to educational benefits because of the difficulty in operationalizing such criteria.

What can be said about alternative generation and selection? In deciding on its initial proposal, the board limited itself to considering just two basic alternatives. The first originated from a belief in the professional orientation, while the second represented more of a concern for fiscal implications. These alternatives set a range within which a compromise could be worked out. In contrast, the board viewed the preparation of its third proposal more as a design problem. It was developed by fashioning an alternative which would meet certain fairly operational specifications. This disparity in approaches was the result of the extent of value consensus in each situation. Initially, the lack of agreement on goals dictated the use of a bargaining strategy. By the time the third proposal was formulated, individuals could agree on fairly operational criteria. These could now function as constraints in a process that had many problem-solving aspects.

The estimation of consequences was superficial throughout but consistent with the board's lack of data. The cost implications of the initial teachers' proposal were evaluated only by using historical and social bench marks. The internal compromise which resulted in the board's first proposal was worked out utilizing rather vague impressions of the implications for various interest groups (recruiting interests, teachers, the community) of being on the high or low side of the range. In view of the difficulties in establishing consequences, decisions were validated by appeal to an external authority and comparison to the decisions of neighboring districts.

CONCLUSIONS

Recent work in educational administration has demonstrated that certain policy issues dealt with by local school systems are routine enough that formal models of the decision-making process can be constructed. For example, I[14] have developed simulation models of the way in which a group of suburban districts decided on B.A. minimum salary raises prior to the introduction of collective negotiations, and of the manner in which a large urban district allocates its budget. There undoubtedly remains a wide and crucial range of policy choices that are too ill-structured to be readily formalized. The issue investigated here, determination of the entire teachers' salary schedule just after the introduction of collective negotiations, fits into this category. The conceptual framework used to analyze this issue represents an attempt to apply the spirit, if not the letter, of the formal simulation approach. Accordingly, a commitment was made to consider the decision the basic unit of analysis and to study the transformation of informational inputs into specified outcomes using existing policy. Let us now consider the implications stemming from our examination of each of these three components.

The procedure for analyzing input information cannot for a number of reasons provide a complete picture. There may be confidential sources and types of data which individuals do not wish to divulge and which would not be readily found by studying written documents. There may be factors which are important in some years but not in others. For example, when a major new piece of legislation affecting the salary decision process is passed, legislators, courts, and lawyers will become important sources. It does not take into consideration the fact that data stored either in a person's or the organization's memory is also used in the process. Thus, board members and teachers have access to the previous values of data and also have knowledge of the pertinent institutional constraints.

The advantage of tracing information flows is that it helps specify the nature of the inputs to the decision-making process. An explicit consideration of information can aid the administrator in the improvement of policy-making by suggesting where sources, types, and channels can be improved. It benefits the researcher by facilitating policy analysis and specifying the inputs to computer simulation models of decision making. Once more, there are benefits for the study of those individuals who are most influential in particular policy decisions. Such persons would be identified as those who either supply or receive the necessary information. Obviously, information is only one source of influence, and those who transmit and receive it are not the only people exerting influence. Hence, the method is more reasonably viewed as a supplement to other approaches or as the main approach only for certain types of decisions.

The identification of policy may be the most vital task in the utilization of the conceptual framework since it mediates between information and outcomes. In contrast to a situation suitable for a formal model, it was not possible to uncover an entire discrimination net of policy rules. Instead, the characteristics of three different policy orientations, including significant decision rules, were identified. The fact that there exists some degree of similarity with other typologies indicates that these orientations are not restricted to the districts studied. For example, Lieberman and Moskow's three approaches to collective negotiations[15] include a marketplace category which has some aspects of the competitive and fiscal orientations, and professional and problem-solving categories somewhat related to the professional orientation.

Nevertheless, the examination of policy has been one-sided in its concentration on the school board. It remains to identify the alternative positions that can be taken by teachers' organizations. It is easiest to see teachers advocating the competitive approach, particularly when salaries in neighboring areas are relatively high, and hardest to see them advocating the fiscal model. Some variant of the professional orientation which includes collective negotiations is feasible. Undoubtedly other approaches exist, such as Frymier's labor model (what's in it for me?).[16] Once these have been uncovered, a fruitful analytical scheme would be to study the implications of the confrontation between various combinations of teacher-board orientations. In the long run, it may be possible to learn whether the orientations are examples of more general strategies used by teachers or school boards in making decisions unrelated to teachers' compensation.

The case analysis was used to demonstrate how specific choices result from policy and information. It highlighted the importance of a school board's internal bargaining processes in determining outcomes. The initial conflict between the fiscal and professional models had to be resolved through some type of compromise which shaped the board's subsequent proposals to the teachers. This seemingly obvious point deserves emphasis here because it has not been sufficiently recognized in the recent literature. Fiscal research, for example, due to its aggregative focus, has with a very few exceptions bypassed it completely. One exception is the work of Rossmiller *et at.*, who found that consensus among school board members as to the role of the district and the board was associated with lower professional salaries.[17] The literature on collective negotiations tends to consider the board's position uniform and concentrates on the confrontation between negotiators. Formal simulations have involved cases in which either the group defers to a single individual or else everyone's rules are more or less the same. If simulations are to handle a wider range of decisions, a way must be found to include in them the process by which individual orientations are reconciled into collective outcomes.

If the trends revealed by the case analysis are applicable to wealthy suburbs in general, then the internal bargaining within school boards is leading them to incorporate more aspects of the fiscal model into policies previously dominated by competitive and professional concerns. This change is occurring through the imposition of a total salary constraint in the generation of proposals to the teachers. Movement in this direction could have some major implications for fiscal policy and collective negotiations. Teachers' groups in wealthy districts, previously used to citizen support or, at worst, apathy, may now start utilizing tactics which directly influence community attitudes. School boards will be seeking to develop coalitions with their publics in order to defend the imperfectly rationalized salary limits. It is to be expected, for example, that we will see a proliferation of board-appointed citizens' committees whose cost-cutting recommendations will be used as evidence in negotiations. More important, the shift toward the fiscal model introduces additional conflict into the negotiation process at an unfortunate time. In many districts, both sides are just beginning to lay the groundwork for bargaining in good faith.

Having considered the implications of the components of the conceptual framework, a brief overall evaluation is in order. The framework's major advantage is the establishment of a systematic means for the investigation of detailed decision process characteristics. It facilitates the study of decision-making criteria, alternative generation and selection, and the estimation of consequences—phenomena not amenable to aggregative analysis. On the other hand, the level of detail precludes the study of a large sample. It is therefore more appropriate as a means of generating new hypotheses rather than as a vehicle for testing existing ones. Nevertheless, our current meager understanding of educational policy formation makes the development of new ideas an important priority. The next step should be an exploration of whether the approach discussed here can be of use in analyzing other types of policy issues.

Notes

The author gratefully acknowledges the help of Professor Wendell Hunt. This research was supported in part by a grant from the U.S. Office of Education.

1. National Education Association, Research Division, *Economic Status of the Teaching Profession, 1967-68* (Washington, D.C.: the Association, 1968).

2. T. R. Dye, "Governmental Structure, Urban Environment and Educational Policy," *Midwest Journal of Political Science*, XI (August 1967), 353-80.

3. O. A. Davis, "Empirical Evidence of Political Influences upon the Expenditure Policies of Public Schools," in J. Margolis (ed.), *The Public Economy of Urban Communities* (Baltimore, Md.: Johns Hopkins Press, 1965), pp. 92-111.

4. J. Miner, *Social and Economic Factors in Spending for Public Education* (Syracuse, N.Y.: Syracuse University Press, 1965).

5. R. L. Johns and R. B. Kimbrough, *The Relationship of Socioeconomic Factors, Educational Leadership Patterns and Elements of Community Power Structure to Local Fiscal Policy* (Washington, D.C.: U.S. Office of Education, 1968).

6. H. T. James, J. A. Kelly, and W. J. Garms, *Determinants of Educational Expenditures in Large Cities of the United States* (Palo Alto, Calif.: Stanford

University School of Education, 1966).

7. R. M. Cyert and J. G. March, *A Behavioral Theory of the Firm* (Englewood Cliffs, N.J.: Prentice-Hall, 1963); J. G. March, "The Business Firm as a Political Coalition," *Journal of Politics*, XXIV (November 1962), 662-78; J. G. March and H. A. Simon, *Organizations* (New York: John Wiley, 1958).

8. D. Gerwin, *Budgeting Public Funds: The Decision Process in an Urban School District* (Madison: University of Wisconsin Press, 1969).

9. D. Gerwin, "An Information Processing Model of Salary Determination in a Contour of Suburban School Districts" *American Educational Research Journal*, X (No. 1, Winter 1973), 5-20.

10. A. M. Ross, *Trade Union Wage Policy* (Berkeley, Calif.: University of California Press, 1948).

11. Gerwin, "An Information Processing Model."

12. An increment is the difference between the salaries in two adjacent rows of the same column.

13. When the district switched from a merit to a single salary schedule, the cost of placing teachers in their appropriate rows was too large to incur in a single year.

14. Gerwin, "An Information Processing Model," and *Budgeting Public Funds.*

15. M. Lieberman and M. H. Moskow, *Collective Negotiations for Teachers* (Chicago: Rand-McNally, 1966).

16. J. R. Frymier, "Teacher Power, Negotiations and the Roads Ahead—an Editorial," *Theory into Practice*, VII (April 1968), 103-104.

17. R. A. Rossmiller, J. M. Lipham, and R. J. Gregg, "Consensus, Conflict, and Expenditures for Education," in *Proceedings of the Eleventh National Conference on School Finance* (Washington, D.C.: National Education Association, 1968), pp. 157-66.

COMMENT / The Fiscal-Professional Conflict: A Professional View

Slack Ulrich

The case analysis presented by Gerwin is an almost perfect example of the frequent outcome of a policy struggle between fiscal and professional orientations within a school board. In early 1969, at the time negotiations leading to the contract for the 1969-70 school year took place, I had been serving on the Fox Point-Bayside suburban school board for nearly ten years. In Gerwin's terms, I was essentially a purist of the professional persuasion; my colleagues included staunch advocates of the fiscal approach as well as defenders of the "competitive" point of view. We did not, of course, think of ourselves and each other in terms of such classifications, but the points of view which we expressed and upheld as individuals were remarkably consistent with one or the other orientation, and the outcome was a clear victory for the fiscal point of view.

Gerwin's account of how our policy formulation proceeded that year brings back strong recollections of a season that was frustrating for everyone concerned. I viewed the conduct of our board as short-sighted and counterproductive. The majority of my colleagues viewed the expectations of our teachers as unreasonable and their conduct as more than somewhat objectionable. In the end I was convinced that we had failed utterly to discharge our primary management responsibility. By concentrating so heavily on our fiscal accountability to the taxpayers, we had ignored our primary responsibility to maintain mutual professional respect. Amity and cooperation gave way to animosity and confrontation.

This comment is presented in hopes of meeting the stated purpose of testifying "whether the actual situation has been understood"; I believe it was. I also endeavor to go beyond evaluation of the specific applicability of Gerwin's conclusions to recap the situation as I encountered it. I vouch for the validity of his dispassionate analysis; mine represents the personal recounting of a disappointing experience.

THE FAILURE OF MANAGEMENT RESPONSIBILITY

There is a generally advantageous tendency in America to place control of public education systems in the hands of laymen (amateurs). Unfortunately, many of these individuals have, at best, only an avocational interest in the "science" of education; more usually they have an avid interest in the practice of economy.

Residents of most suburbs suffer an additional disadvantage in this respect. They frequently constitute an economic elite that considers itself demonstrably superior to employees of their educational systems. The average socioeconomic status of residents is "higher" than that of teachers who, for the most part, commute into the area each day. The residents conceive themselves to be qualified by "noble birth" or nobler acquisition to compete against educators in their specific area of expertise.

In many urban and rural areas opposition to expenditures for education comes from members of the community who recognize that they know very little about education and believe that educators must, therefore, be kept under tight rein. In suburbs the opposite problem is more likely to prevail: suburbanites are much more inclined to oppose on the basis that they "know better" than their educators. The mind which is closed because it is "full" is much harder to penetrate than one that is merely uninformed.

Our board was comprised of three businessmen, a college professor, and a housewife (who was a community leader). We thought of ourselves as being more aware of the educational aspects of a school system than were most school boards. Yet we frequently saw nonexistent parallels to our daily experiences in the worlds of manufacturing material products or providing professional services. We suffered the blindness that produces inapplicable points of view and policy orientations. The more extreme cases of this kind of management failure provoke eminent educational philosophers to suggest "deschooling" the whole mess. Such boards and the communities they represent fully deserve the apathy and the tax opposition that ensure the status quo.

Such management failures occur in other fields as well. The American automobile industry has been strongly criticized for producing cars that are wasteful of resources in manufacture and use and pollute the environment. The manufacturers ignored criticism until circumstances forced them to change. Ecologists now oppose production, foreign competition threatens, and there is strong objection to creating more paved spaces either for traveling or for parking. We are now advised to pool our seating capacity and drive more slowly. Manufacturers advertise the hitherto concealed virtues of smallness, and they promote vehicles they formerly denounced. The facts have not changed; management merely failed either to recognize or to admit the truth.

It should not be surprising that this same mind set, when applied to school system management, similarly fails to comprehend the need to improve the system of public education. While smaller cars will diminish profits to the industry, they also decrease costs born by owners; a greater education effort almost inevitably increases costs across the board. Yet devotion to improved education is the minimum degree of management responsibility that must be demanded from those who seek and acquire positions of direct control in educational systems. In my opinion, performance in this general area has been poor.

Detroit management had a responsibility to promote the conservation aspects of smaller cars; it refused until public demand was generated by foreign competition and domestic outcry. School management has a responsibility to promote the idea that intellectual, social, and economic progress must be achieved through improved education; it continues to wait for public demand. Guilt for the status quo and blame for failure to lead belong to management. Hope lies in the possibility that scholarly investigation and analysis will strengthen professional policy orientation as defined by Gerwin. But factors operant industrially are not yet seen as relevant by managers of public education. We have begun to understand our environmental problem, but priorities in education are still ordered in the wrong direction.

COLLECTIVE BARGAINING

Competent management would have foretold the unionization of American teachers, and it could have forestalled the more deleterious results. The case under study occurred during the period when earlier experimental cultivation of collective bargaining came to full flower in the American public education scene. Thousands of autonomous school districts across the country assumed that the rumblings of unionism in some major city school systems were symptomatic only of those people in those places at that time. What was happening in New York and Philadelphia was simply irrelevant for smaller cities and suburbs where the voters knew the school board and everyone knew the teachers. Complacency characterized the attitudes on both sides of the table, and in the audience as well.

Managements failed across the nation to recognize the threats and react appropriately. Legislatuers and the judiciary had to deal with initial confrontations. Early court decisions produced anxious legislative clarifications with general applicability. New laws and new applications of old laws to employment relations in the teaching field convinced many teachers that only legalistic approaches held any hope for resolutions in areas where frustrations had been developing; they generated negative concerns on both sides where problems did not exist or had not surfaced; they created and fostered points of view (policy orientations) which nurtured distrust and produced trouble-prone environments; they accelerated the transition from latent concern on both sides to overt confrontation.

One factor which seems to defy comprehension by the education managers is the effect of the public nature of the institution. It is generally agreed that teaching is a professional function more akin to medicine, law, and engineering than to mining, truck driving or factory work. A college degree is a nearly universal requirement for employment as a school teacher. Yet the great majority of engineers, lawyers, and doctors are either self-employed or work for private industry while the great majority of teachers are employed by local governments. And "government service" is held in relatively lower esteem by those who work in the private sector.

Public employees are suspected (and accused) of being less ambitious and industrious than industrial employees and at the same time they are expected to be less self-seeking and more devoted to the general welfare of society than their private sector counterparts. In exchange for the security essential to protect them from political reprisal and the evils of the spoils systems, they are expected to relinquish the rights which other workers have painfully gained to use collective force against the economic power which our system of private property allows a few to exercise over the many.

We have learned over the past hundred years to live with labor disruption in the private sector, and even to recognize that rights in this area are justified and must be protected. Yet in the public sector we remain unable to separate the public safety aspects of some public functions from the public convenience aspects of other public functions. The threat of having our children underfoot when they are "supposed to be in school" produces extreme reaction from parents who seem to be willing to awaken, clothe, feed, and dispatch, but not live with, their children.

We accept the possibility that a labor dispute in the private sector may have right on the side of the worker because we are not the management and not directly responsible for his unhappiness. But our theory of democratic government requires that we accept the ultimate responsibility for public management. In the public sector we side with management because we are that management. In the public mind, therefore, the outcome of collective bargaining between teachers and the management which the public has elected (directly or indirectly) is successful to the degree that increases in the costs of operating the education system are minimized.

POLICY ORIENTATIONS

Gerwin's perceptions of underlying factors and influences are important to an improved understanding of school board attitudes. In any field of inquiry it is difficult to derive a common language which can be comprehended by students of varying backgrounds and biases. Gerwin contributes to this development by citing the three-stage process of *information* operated on by *policy* to produce *outcomes*, and particularly by subsequently synthesizing three essential policy orientations from the many item factors observed during his studies. When an acceptable jargon has been developed, it becomes possible to expand the area of study and prediction while maintaining common understandings among students. On the basis of my individual but extensive and involved personal experience, I believe that his policy orientation descriptions are valid, comprehensive, and comprehensible. My reservations are expansions of his conclusions rather than opposition to them.

Gerwin's hierarchy of policy orientations (professional, competitive, and fiscal) may be commonly viewed as a triangular classification in which each element diverges more or less equally from the other two. Each of the three orientations is a distinct entity representing the different sets of conclusions which an individual may develop based on his experience, observation, and background.

I believe a different concept is more valid. In my view the three policy orientations constitute a continuum. The professional and fiscal policy orientations are points of relatively pure philosophy at opposite extremes of the continuum. Simply stated, the professional orientation sees "education" as being of transcendent importance, meriting the highest priority among human endeavors and deserving support at nearly any expense to other societal needs. The fiscal orientation sees "education" as a probably worthwhile busy-ness for the young with practical value in the acquisition of essential basic skills of computation and communication. The fiscal view also sees education as historically subject to unnecessary proliferation. This view holds that public systems are usually guilty of actual subversion whenever they invade the private sanctuaries of ethics, morals, religion, and other areas where we have an inalienable right to be wrong. Although these two policy positions are held by only a few people, their influence is disproportionately significant. They are frequently held by individuals who aspire to control.

A much larger population comprises Gerwin's third orientation (competitive), and this majority group is the main body of the parade. The professional group wants to lead the parade, speed it up, get others to join, occasionally explore other avenues. The fiscal group wants to slow the parade down, keep it controllable, and stay on Main Street. The competitive group wants to be in the parade, or maybe just watch it.

This third orientation may not even be an orientation in one sense. It is characteristic of the area where most of us reside— between the extremes of the professional (generally positive about education) and the fiscal (generally negative about education). It is the area of noninvolvement. Those "competitively" oriented can defend their position with some justification on the grounds that the general public has tacitly approved the status quo, but must be expected to rebel should we propose any sudden or extensive movement in any new direction. Because it is held by so many of us, this orientation possesses the power to promote or frustrate progress. And because it accepts the present status of our infant human institution (public education) as satisfactory, it is unwilling to seek improvement or promote change. Thus it exercises its power in a negative way; by noninvolvement it effectively reinforces the fiscal approach. The term *competitive* is an unfortunate one to use with respect to American education in any sense. The word connotes a principle of the American way of life that is preached more than practiced. Most Americans refuse to compete; instead, they seek uniformity and security.

Education should be progressive—continuous rather than cyclic. Past experience and the history of others should be assimilated while we are young. But when that part of the process is completed we should be educated to proceed ahead. This involves encountering and coping with the unknown (which takes courage), and requires that freedom be allowed by those in power (which takes understanding). The terms professional and fiscal have consistent meanings applicable to the entire field of public education including our consideration of salary administration policies and practices. The term competitive seems applicable only to the restricted subject of salary administration and even here must be understood to mean keeping up but not getting ahead.

MERIT PAY: FISCAL OR PROFESSIONAL?

In terms of the policy orientations described by Gerwin, I identify my position with that categorized as professional. My stand with respect to most aspects which he surveyed hewed strictly to that point of view. With regard to merit pay for teachers, however, I have supported a view which Gerwin attributes to the fiscal orientation.

For several years prior to the inception of collective bargaining in 1967 the general subject of merit pay was discussed intensively—often hotly argued—within our board. Holders of strong opinions both pro and con were nominally of the professional orientation. One of my colleagues (on the School of Education faculty at a local university) persistently upheld the teacher's traditional opposition to the concept of merit pay. Other board members seemed to agree in general that teachers' opposition demonstrated unwillingness to be evaluated by their peers or judged by their institutional superiors. Our faculty were rarely afforded a chance to express their opinions because both sides were so regularly aired within the board. The district administration, however, which consistently refused to support merit pay, was criticized for lack of courage and self-confidence.

It seemed to me that there were two opposite philosophies which could support a "merit pay" concept. The fiscal approach to the subject was by far the most common. Many schemes had been proposed (several were actually inaugurated) for the apparent purpose of holding down overall salary costs for an entire faculty rather than increasing the compensation of a superior few. The fiscal mind seems to be convinced that for every master teacher deserving higher compensation there is at least one inept teacher deserving lower compensation. Since teachers are difficult to fire because their productivity is unmeasurable, they are rarely insubordinate, and moral turpitude can only be defined in terms of sex, a different measure is needed. A penalizing system of salary administration can be effective in reducing costs even though it may not effectively "counsel out" the deadwood.

But there was also a professional approach; prior to the 1967-68 school year we had developed a merit pay scheme which met my requirements for professionalism. Our concept minimized faculty resistance by providing merit without demerit. The basic (minimum) schedule was established on a competitive par with higher paying districts within our generally high paying area. The merit schedule consisted of an advanced series of pay steps starting after the achievement of tenure. At this time, or in succeeding years, a teacher could be recognized for excellence by being placed on the advanced schedule. A third "superior" teacher classification was established for the few outstanding teachers who deserved even higher compensation—recognition that could be granted after ten years in the district.

Development and improvement of the concept had been underway for about four years, and many objections and reservations had been resolved. Confidence grew among the faculty as they better understood the goals and the anticipated demerit aspects failed to materialize. Implementation of the system was the responsibility of the administrators, who remained unenthusiastic. Their concerns were frequently expounded by my educator colleague who opposed the entire idea. Nonetheless, it began to appear that, in our district at least, all teachers could be competitively compensated while perhaps 25 percent or so would be placed on the advanced schedule and the top few would achieve the maximum schedule. Remuneration for the superior teacher with a long career in our district could exceed that of his administrative superior. This was intended to avert the temptation to recognize outstanding teaching ability by a possibly unsuccessful promotion to an administrative position in our (or some other) district.

We were never to learn how well or how poorly the system might have worked. During the spring of 1967 our discussions with the faculty regarding salary schedule revisions for the 1967-68 school year proceeded smoothly until the board decided (over my strong objections) to abandon the merit pay program. This action was ostensibly in accord with faculty opposition to the basic concept, but the result was withdrawal of a salary advantage which our senior faculty had enjoyed in comparison to other districts. The senior faculty perceived the start of a new era of formalized relationships in which the conventional rules of labor negotiations would prevail. They saw our action as abandonment of our previous stand in favor of professionalism and an invitation to them to organize. Since we were adopting a policy of uniform depersonalized salary administration, they saw no recourse other than solidarity on their part. We had destroyed the senior faculty's argument that they did not need a union to protect their interests, and they acceded to the younger faculty demands for organization. They petitioned the Wisconsin Employment Relations Board for recognition of the Teachers Association as the sole bargaining agent in future negotiations with the school board.

In a mood of disillusionment I issued a unilateral personal statement to the faculty expressing both dismay and understanding of their dilemma. My colleagues on the board predicted that the course of events could not be diverted, that the faculty could not be dissuaded. They were right: both sides continued steadfastly along the path to unionism. Gerwin strikes another nail squarely on the head when he cites, under the professional orientation, a strong antipathy toward collective bargaining on the grounds that it defeats professional attitudes on both sides of the table. Basic problems of mistrust and noncooperation seem inherent in the adversary postures characteristic of collective bargaining. It is, of course, incumbent on both sides to keep abreast of what is going on in the world around us. It is extremely unfortunate, however, when the level of mutual confidence sinks so low that we expect with certainty that those we know and have respected on the other side will adopt the undesirable practices we see developing in other areas where, for all we know, they may be completely justified.

During the fall of 1967 and the spring of 1968 I saw the trust and respect that had developed over nearly forty years under earlier boards and administrations disappear. In my view a major contribution to this disastrous course was made by our "professional" group, the Wisconsin Association of School Boards. Their sponsorship of workshops (at the University of Wisconsin in Madison) on how to prepare for the inevitable onslaught of teacher unionism was perceived by the teachers' associations as incontrovertible evidence that the boards held out little hope for continued amity on an informal basis. My pleas, both public and private, that our board not participate in this hysteria went unheeded. We sent representatives to learn the technicalities of bargaining practices, legal avenues open to both sides, and what to do until the mediator comes. We received our manuals of preparedness. We appeared to be "joining up" with all the other boards to go to war while proclaiming the good faith with which we would approach the bargaining table.

For the school year 1967-68 we had returned to a single salary schedule comprised of fifteen B.A. steps and twenty M.A. steps. Placing all teachers on their proper chronological step in this schedule resulted in a budget increase for the 1968-69 school year which everyone, including the teachers, agreed would produce a taxpayers' revolt. The teachers accepted our proposed deferral of full placement on schedule until the following year. The postponed realizations fell almost entirely on the upper-middle-range teachers who comprised the stars of our team. They, nonetheless, received ample raises and were being well compensated on a competitive basis.

In the fall of 1968 at the outset of negotiations for the 1969-70 school year there was no hint in the first board proposal that we might renege on the promise made the previous year. This was the negotiating season that Gerwin studied in depth. The aura of general mistrust increased early in the sessions. A small number of loud voter expressions produced extreme apprehension among other board members that to honor our commitment would be unacceptable to the public. I felt we should take two simultaneous actions: first, to conduct our negotiations with the teachers in public, in a school auditorium if the hoped-for public interest developed; second, to conduct an intensive unilateral education campaign to present and discuss in public forum the board's views on teacher compensation and the larger question of the value to society of public education and its purveyors. I questioned the convictions expressed by other board members regarding the level of public resistance to increased teacher salaries. I believed that public discussion of our varying assessment of the public mood would certainly improve our understanding and probably generate support for a more generous approach. I was also convinced that the same benefits would accrue from conducting the actual negotiations in public.

By February 1969 very little progress had been achieved in our private discussions with the teachers' representatives. I formalized my proposals in a written statement directed to the other members of the board. This private communication to my colleagues included my specific recommendations regarding salary portions of the contract. A short time later I requested approval from the other board members to publish for the district at large a personal statement expressing my stand on the issue of public disclosure. They remained opposed to the basic idea of a public effort and unanimously objected to any individual statements on my part. I felt obligated to honor their wishes. I still believe that it was most unfortunate that we had neither the courage and energy, nor enough confidence in teachers, the public, and ourselves to undertake the public effort.

Meanwhile the negotiations continued, but little progress was made. During the month of March, after confirming our decision to conclude the matter without public involvement, the board considered many alternative suggestions. The majority finally agreed to offer as an alternative a compressed schedule which eliminated the top three B.A. steps and the top four M.A. steps. This effectively overcame the problem of last year's promise to put everyone "on schedule." The new rules implied a new game for all teachers and particularly for those in the upper range of the schedule that was being eliminated. At this point both the teachers and I accepted defeat.

It is impossible to know what the final outcome might have been had we not undertaken the salary schedule compression. It is noteworthy, however, that the final actual settlement was made at lower minimum and maximum B.A. salaries and a lower minimum M.A. salary than had been offered in the initial board proposal, but at an 11 percent increase in overall salary costs. We had manipulated a reduction of salary ranges to produce a greater budget increase. Unquestionable results of these negotiations were 1) solidification of the adversary approach, 2) conviction on the part of the teachers that they had been deceived, 3) doubt in the minds of some board members regarding the ethics of our conduct, and 4) for me, personally, an effective coup de grace to lingering hopes that the inexorable trends of recent years might be reversed.

CONCLUSION

Based on my acquaintance with members of other boards and their practices, I believe that our behavior was no worse than typical in confronting organized teachers. Our "typical" lack of success was more disappointing, however, because of our prior excellent relationships with our staff. On that foundation we could have built successfully if we had demonstrated continued professional respect for our faculty and taken a positive approach with the public.

It is unfortunate that we cannot achieve equal illumination on the teachers' side of the scene. Gerwin recognizes that available avenues of study emphasize boards' functioning more than that of teachers' groups. I believe that this emphasis would be appropriate even if equal access were easily available. There is inherently less internal conflict among teachers regarding goals. They should naturally be expected to agree with the professional orientation, and their behavior is more predictable and consistent.

School boards display a greater tendency to engage in variable action and reaction. It is their management responsibility to coordinate teachers' aspirations with taxpayers' concerns in the interests of optimum public education. Studies and analyses such as Gerwin's will contribute to the enlightenment of all board members, especially those competitively oriented so that they can achieve either the professional or fiscal orientation. I prefer the former because I believe that a positive professional approach holds much greater hope for the improvement of society.

The competitive (do-nothing) orientation is as regressive as the fiscal in its reluctance to innovate. The greatest disservice to society comes from those in the majority who inhabit that competitive vacuum—which nature may abhor but society seems to love.

Although those who read this volume will be too much comprised of teachers, administrators and scholars in the field, which is to say that too few board members will read it, the occasion appears appropriate for this board member practitioner to make another plea for greater responsibility, wisdom, and understanding on the management side. School managements usually profess to be responsible for the success or failure of the "enterprise" as do spokesmen for most managements; all too frequently, however, they practice in a manner calculated to win elections rather than to promote improved education.

9 / The Effects of Collective Bargaining on Public School Teachers' Salaries

Hirschel Kasper

The research reported here was the natural starting point for a project to analyze the economic effects of representation and collective bargaining by public school teachers. The eventual object is to determine the "incidence" or "ultimate burden" of bargaining on matters such as average class size, quality of education, and community tax rates. Estimates of the incidence necessarily require prior estimates of the effect of bargaining on teachers' salaries, which constitute about 60 to 75 percent of local school budgets. Thus, this article reports estimates of the impact of teacher representation and bargaining on salary levels for 1967-68.

The first part of the article presents a synopsis of the recent nature and extent of organization of teachers, while the second provides alternative estimates of the effect of representation and bargaining on salaries. The cross-section estimates of the impact of bargaining are very tentative, but all the alternative models tested suggest that bargaining had little, if any, effect on average state salary levels that year.

Reprinted from *Industrial and Labor Relations Review*, XXIV (No. 1, October 1970), 57-72.

EXTENT AND NATURE OF COLLECTIVE BARGAINING

In spite of the rapid acceleration of teacher representation by the National Education Association (NEA) and American Federation of Teachers (AFT) and the bold headlines about the impasses resulting from school board negotiations, arms-length collective bargaining still is not the prevailing method for determining the wages, hours, and working conditions of the nearly two million public school teachers in the United States. In the academic year 1967-68 fewer than one out of eight school districts engaged in *any* kind of employment negotiations with teacher representatives. Such negotiations as there were ranged from merely allowing a committee of teachers to submit proposals to assist the school board in writing its unilateral policy to more traditional collective bargaining complete with a mutually satisfactory and signed contract covering wages, hours, grievances, and other conditions of employment. In a 1967 survey of 7,157 school systems with enrollment of at least 1,000 students, the NEA Research Division located less than 200 (2.8 percent) agreements which specifically mentioned days or hours of teaching responsibility.[1] Even this, however, reflected an increase since Wildman reported that in his 1963-64 survey of the 6,000 largest school systems (enrollment 1,200 or more) he found only 17 contracts from nearly 1,700 respondents which contained "detailed provisions regarding salaries, hours, or other conditions of employment."[2]

Collective bargaining by public school teachers, as with employees in the private sector, is more likely to occur in the large urban centers of the East and Midwest. Consequently, where there is collective bargaining, it usually involves a larger than average school district. The statewide proportion of teachers and school districts. . .covered by any type of collective agreement in 1967 was 40 percent and 12 percent, respectively.[3] (Both estimates exclude teachers working in the numerous districts of less than 1,000 students and, therefore, overstate the extent of representation and understate its geographic concentration.)

An organizational map of the membership of the NEA and AFT would indicate that the one million members of the NEA are spread across the entire face of the United States and that the NEA holds unchallenged position as teacher representative in the smaller cities and towns, while the AFT strength is in and around the largest cities. The AFT has exclusive representational rights in Boston, Chicago, Cleveland, Detroit, New York, Philadelphia, Providence, Toledo, and Washington, D.C. Its map of organization suggests many hubs of

AFT representation surrounded by spokes of further organization into the nearby suburbs.

Current representation of teachers by the NEA and AFT reflects both the tradition of individual professionals in the industry and the recent emergence of collective bargaining. Representation in public school education is far different from contemporary collective bargaining in the private sector although, perhaps, not too dissimilar from the coincident varieties of individual, collective, and labor union representation during the 1920's. The NEA classifies representation status in five groups:[4]

a. *Nonrecognition:* Is generally a policy of statements which provide for the establishment and election of a committee of teachers to represent the staff. This committee may submit proposals and meet and confer with the board.

b. *Level I agreements: Recognize* local teachers organization as the representative of the professional staff. The teachers organization is the spokesman for the teachers and may submit proposals, negotiate, or meet and confer with the board on matters of mutual concern.

c. *Level II agreements:* Include a *recognition* statement and outline the procedures to be followed in the negotiation process. They establish the specific conditions under which the board and the teachers organization meet to discuss matters of common concern.

d. *Level III agreements:* Contain a *recognition* statement, a negotiation procedure, and a method for obtaining impartial third-party assistance in resolving disagreement or *impasse.*

e. *Level IV agreements:* May or may not contain the elements of Levels I, II, or III, but will contain specific *items negotiated and agreed upon* by the parties. The substantive agreement is the most formal in its structure and usually will contain a statement of parties to the agreement, and effective and expiration dates.

The results of a 1967 NEA survey, summarized in Table 9-1, indicate the relative scarcity of comprehensive quid pro quo collective bargaining by teachers and a very sharp contrast in the nature of representation between the NEA and AFT. Only 27.1 percent (603) of the "agreements" are Level IV agreements, which specify items agreed upon by the parties. All but four of the Level IV agreements were in districts east of the Mississippi and only two in the South (one each in Maryland and Virginia), reflecting, if we view Level IV agreements as the minimal standard for collective bargaining, both community attitudes and state laws on organization and the tendency for NEA-AFT competition to bring about more formal relations. The modal (43.4 percent) NEA agreements (Level II) involve only "procedural" negotiations: how the teachers are to communicate their interests. On the other hand, nearly 90 percent of the reported

TABLE 9-1. Estimated number of agreements with school districts[a] by organization and nature of representation, 1967

Nature of representation	National Education Association		American Federation of Teachers		Other[b]		Total	
	Number	Percent	Number	Percent	Number	Percent	Number	Percent
Level I agreements	83	4.0	3	4.0	1	1.3	87	3.9
Level II agreements	899	43.4	5	6.7	67	85.9	971	43.6
Level III agreements	558	26.9	0	0.0	6	7.7	564	25.3
Level IV agreements	532	25.7	67	89.0	4	5.1	603	27.1
Total	2,072	100.0	75	100.0	78	100.0	2,225	100.0

[a]Total number of school districts was 20,388.
[b]Includes 55 "teacher committees" in Oregon.
Sources: "Negotiation Agreements, 1967-68," in *Negotiation Research Digest* (Washington, D.C.: National Education Association, Research Division, March 1969), Table A-1; U.S. Department of Health, Education, and Welfare, Office of Education, *Digest of Educational Statistics: 1968 Edition* (Washington, D.C.: U.S. Government Printing Office, 1968), Table 55.

AFT agreements are substantive (Level IV) agreements which spell out the specific terms mutually agreed on by the parties.

Although the NEA reported that the number of Level IV agreements in its file increased by 205 from 1966-67 to 1967-68, no hard data are available to check this author's strong impression that the proportion of such agreements also has risen. Based on the history of collective bargaining in the private sector, it seems certain that public school agreements will become more substantive over time as new legislation is developed and as the parties try to define their respective rights and obligations.

In the past two years, a number of states have enacted legislation respecting collective bargaining by public employees, including teachers. The effect undoubtedly has been to encourage teacher representation and negotiation and to increase the proportion of Level III and Level IV agreements. Unfortunately, data on numbers and types of agreements covering the current academic year, 1970-71, are not yet available.

Information presently at hand suggests, however, that no more than 6 percent to 8 percent(=603/7157) and perhaps as few as 3 percent of the school systems bargain as equals with teacher representatives. Perhaps, therefore, it is still too early to try to measure the general effect of collective bargaining on teachers' salaries and the quality of education. Such speculation will not pacify the Cassandras who worry about the harmful effects of collective bargaining on the quality and availability of public education, but they are the ones who should have to bear the burden of quantitative evidence for now.

MODELS AND DETERMINANTS OF TEACHERS' SALARIES

Although collective bargaining by public employees commonly is assumed to raise salaries, there are many reasons why, in fact, bargaining by public school teachers may have little or no effect on their salaries relative to those of either private or other public employees. First, it may be much more difficult for public officials to raise the prices of their "products" than for private firms, since the former may have to go to the taxpayers for an all-or-nothing tax levy or bond issue to pay for higher employee costs. Second, depending on the product, it may be more difficult for public than private managers to reduce the quantity or lower the quality of services. Third, if a community accepts historical occupational differentials among public employees, an increase in the salaries of one group could be expected to lead to large budgetary outlays for all groups combined, i.e., wage "spillover" may be at least as important in the public as private sector.[5] Fourth, unionization may be viewed as an unnecessary attack from unappreciative teachers on the amateur policy-making school board members and on the community at large. Fifth, the traditions of "professionalization" and "community interest" may still mitigate against the full and effective use of bargaining power by teachers.[6]

As partial offsets, we would mention two: collective bargaining may raise wages faster in the public sector, because (1) the absence of a direct (or indirect) profit motive may make the management negotiators more generous and (2) the direct (and indirect) political power of the employees may threaten the (political?) jobs of the management team.

In order to estimate the net effect of collective representation on public school teachers' salaries, alternative models were constructed of interstate variation in 1967-68 salary levels. Our main interest is to learn whether there was a positive relation between the extent of teacher organization, measured by representation by the AFT, NEA, and other teacher organizations, in the academic year 1967-68 and statewide teachers' salaries. Although the models explicitly allow for the effects of other variables, this discussion of the estimated parameters will concentrate almost exclusively on the relation between organization and salaries.

The basic model is of a form where the state's average salary for teachers (S) is a function of state per capita income (I); the extent of urbanization (U); proportion of total educational revenue provided by local (R_l), state (R_s), and federal (R_f) sources; total current expenditures per pupil (E); the relative mix of elementary and secondary teachers (P); a regional dummy for the western states (W); and the extent of teacher organization (O).[7] Our general model is of the form:

$$S = S(I,U,R_l,R_s,R_f,E,P,W,O)$$

On the basis of economic theory and the results of earlier studies of state expenditures,[8] we hypothesized that salaries would be positively related to (a) income, (b) urbanization, (c) the relative support from state revenues, (d) expenditures per pupil (quality?), and (e) the strength of teacher organization. Since elementary teachers generally receive less money than secondary teachers, P was expected to have a negative effect on average salaries. Region was included in the model after preliminary estimates indicated that our model underpredicted for most of the western states.

Alternative measures of both variables of prime interest, teachers' salaries and organizational strength, were used to test the sensitivity of statistical results. Salaries were measured alternatively as the average statewide teacher salary for 1967-68 (S), the arithmetic mean of teacher salaries for 1966-67 and 1967-68 $(\bar{S})$, and the ratio of the 1967-68 teacher salary to the 1967 average police entrance salary (S_p). $\bar{S}$ was felt to be a useful alternative, since, as a two-year average, it reduces the random variation in salary levels which results from the fact that state and local governments ordinarily revise salaries at irregular intervals.[9] On the other hand, the purpose of the S_p alternative is to enable us to examine the impact of bargaining on the salaries of teachers relative to those of another public sector occupation, in this case policemen.[10] Teacher organization was measured by either the proportion of teachers represented by an organization (O_t), proportion of school districts which had representation (O_d), or the proportion of state teachers covered by "formal collective bargaining agreements," defined as Level III and IV agreements (O_b).

The extent of organization in a state was measured by summing the number of instructional personnel, including (unfortunately) principals, supervisors, librarians, etc., as well as classroom teachers, who are represented in local school negotiations and dividing that sum by the total number of classroom teachers in each state. The use of all instructional staff rather than just classroom teachers in the numerator gives our subsequent parameter estimates a small but unknown bias, since the ratio of total instructional staff to classroom teachers varies among states.

SUPPLEMENTARY DATA

The published data used in this study were supplemented by unpublished reports of the NEA and AFT, although some data on the extent of representation came from a personal mail survey in an attempt to fill in noticeable gaps. The survey counted nearly 5,000 more teachers, represented by various organizations in some thirteen school districts (945 from four districts in Rhode Island alone), who apparently had escaped the accounting of both the NEA and AFT. A very elementary check of the basic data on representation persuades us that it still contains nonnegligible amounts of positive and negative miscalculation; therefore, our estimates of the effect of organization must be viewed with caution. Since there is no complete source of data on representation, the reader may be interested in the results of our calculations, reported in column 1 of the Appendix.

The regression analysis may be easier to understand if some simple statistics are presented first. The mean teacher salary (S) across the fifty-one states (including Washington, D.C.) in 1967-68 was $6,920; the standard deviation was $985. The mean understates the average salary of all teachers to the extent that there is a positive relation between the number of teachers and the average salary among states. The average proportion of teachers represented by organizations was 38 percent (with a standard deviation of 32 percent) reflecting the known substantial skewness in the geographic distribution of teacher representation.

The statistical analyses below include both single-equation and two-stage least-squares estimates. All the estimated parameters of teacher organization in the alternative models suggest that representation had little, if any, effect on the average salary of teachers. (N equals the proportion of teachers holding "substandard" certificates, 1967.) Consider the following two estimates:

$$(1) \quad S = 2166.64 - 24.9110R_s{}^* + 0.9161I\ddagger$$
$$ (14.2185) \quad (0.2204)$$
$$+ 81.4988U\dagger - 52.2211U^2{}^*$$
$$(32.9936) \quad (26.7211)$$
$$- 35.6906R_l\ddagger + 3.2522E\ddagger$$
$$(13.1177) \quad (0.7762)$$
$$+ 382.7505W\dagger - 6.6177N$$
$$(149.0276) \quad (10.6392)$$
$$+ 0.99690_t.$$
$$(2.2977)$$

$\bar{R}^2 = .8749$ Standard error = 348.37

$$(2) \quad \bar{S} = 2443.63 - 24.5591R_s{}^* + 0.9835I\ddagger$$
$$\phantom{(2) \quad \bar{S} = 2443.63 - } (12.2033) \quad (0.1858)$$
$$+ 65.1451U\dagger - 38.7790U^2$$
$$(29.3666) \quad (23.7810)$$
$$- 35.6939R_l\ddagger + 2.8914E\ddagger$$
$$(11.2363) \quad (0.6568)$$
$$+ 373.0476W\ddagger - 6.2173N$$
$$(126.7412) \quad (12.3024)$$
$$+ 0.34560_t.$$
$$(1.9353)$$

$(N=50)$ $\bar{R}^2 = .9049$
Standard error = 293.40

   * Significant at .10 level, on 2-sided t test.
   † Significant at .05 level, on 2-sided t test.
   ‡ Significant at .01 level, on 2-sided t test.

    The estimates in equations (1) and (2) indicate that teacher salaries, (S) and ($\bar{S}$), seem to be significantly related to income (positively), proportions of state and local expenditures (negatively), and expenditures per pupil (positively). Salaries and urbanization are positively related, but at a declining rate, perhaps reflecting the fact that school districts in rural states may enjoy monopsony power in hiring and retaining their teachers because there may be no nearby school districts to stimulate competition. The eventual urbanization "turnaround," which others[11] have found too, may be explained on the ground that substantial urbanization is often associated with sharply increased spending for other public services, such as welfare, transportation, and sanitation, which may cut into the educational budget.[12]

There is no statistically significant positive effect of teacher organization on salaries, once other variables such as income and urbanization are taken into account. The simple correlation from equation (1) between salaries and teacher organization is +.558, but the partial correlation falls to +.068 after the effects of income, urbanization, and the other variables are removed. $\overline{S}$ is slightly easier to predict than S since it is a two-year average, thereby eliminating a certain amount of year-to-year random fluctuation.

However, the reader need not dismiss the possibility that representation raises salaries. The standard errors may be too large, because, as Table 9-2 suggests, multicollinearity seems apparent, especially among the representation, income, and urbanization measures. Yet, if the estimated parameter in equation (1) is accepted at face value, it implies that representation has raised average teachers' salaries by only \$38 or 0.5 percent [=(0.9969) (38.22)/6920]. Thus, the tentative conclusion that representation has had very little effect on salaries stems from both the lack of statistical significance of the coefficient and the minor impact which might exist. The adjusted coefficient of determination, $\overline{R}^2$, in equation (1) is .8749, as large as that for many of the earlier studies on the determinants of various state expenditures, including those on education.[13]

Alternative estimates of the effect of organization are reported in Table 9-3, including measures of the extent of organization by school districts (3.4) as well as teachers (3.1–3.3, 3.5–3.6) and the proportion of teachers represented by the NEA (3.7) and AFT (3.8).[14] In no instance is the estimated parameter for representation significant

TABLE 9-2. Simple correlations among the variables estimated in equation (1)

Variables	S	R_s	I	U	R_l	O_t	E	U^2	W	N
S	1.0	.065	.842	.658	.028	.558	.807	.653	.422	.147
R_s		1.0	−.181	−.007	−.960	−.159	−.145	−.011	−.082	−.006
I			1.0	.704	.319	.645	.799	.718	.253	.323
U				1.0	.171	.676	.445	.991	.098	.323
R_l					1.0	.278	.214	.170	.061	.067
O_t						1.0	.472	.688	.145	.222
E							1.0	.473	.311	.259
U^2								1.0	.088	.401
W									1.0	−.154
N										1.0

at the .05 level. This does not imply that NEA or AFT did not affect the cost of education or its quality, nor does it imply that the effects of both organizations on those variables were identical.[15]

MORE APPROPRIATE MODELS

Two alternative models were estimated to try to take into fuller account demand and supply variables: (1) a model which used the ratio of teachers' salaries to police entrance salaries (S_p) as the dependent variable and (2) a two-stage least-squares model where the first stage was a "supply" function which estimated the extent of collective representation.

The salary levels of employees in another local public sector promised to serve as a useful deflator to capture many of the elements in the demand for teachers, including resource availability and "tastes" for public expenditures. Although salaries for an occupation with identical personal and labor-force characteristics to public school teachers would best accomplish the purpose, none were readily available or complete. The most appropriate for our purposes was the entrance salary of policemen, which was available for forty-nine states (excluding Alaska and Vermont) for 1967.

The same basic model was estimated, but there were not as strong a priori expectations about the signs of the variables, with the exception, of course, of teacher organization. The alternative parameter estimates of the effect of representation are consistent with our earlier estimates, although the coefficients of determination are less than half as large. The most satisfactory model, exemplified by equation (3) below, carries the interesting suggestion that bargaining of the Levels III and IV variety may, in fact, raise teacher salaries, even though representation in general is ineffective.

$$(3) \quad S_p = 0.9181 - .003412R_8$$
$$(.005982)$$
$$-.000079I + .01904U^*$$
$$(.000068) \quad (.01016)$$
$$-.0119U^2 - .00543R_l$$
$$(.0081) \quad (.00570)$$
$$+ .0004627E^* + .00212N$$
$$(.0002466) \quad (.00333)$$
$$+ .004369O_b{}^* - .00545O_b{}^2{}^*$$
$$(.002386) \quad (.00321)$$
$$\overline{R}^2 = .4520 \qquad R^2 = .3255$$

* Significant at the .10 level.

TABLE 9-3. Regression coefficients (and standard errors) for alternative models of determinants of teachers' salaries

Model	Dependent variable	Constant	R_s	I	U	U^2	R_l	E	N	W
3.1	S	1950.56	-25.7522^c (14.3076)	0.8941^e (0.2228)	91.2858^d (35.1340)	-0.6003^d (0.2841)	-35.6232^e (13.1671)	3.4136^e (0.8029)	-6.6937 (10.6795)	365.3292^d (151.0421)
3.2	S	1976.51	-22.7512 (14.0911)	1.0069^e (0.2259)	74.1684^d (32.5249)	-0.4480^c (0.2610)	-33.6041^d (12.9544)	3.2050^e (0.7676)	-6.1852 (10.4110)	356.9065^d (149.1221)
3.3	S	1812.07	-24.4414^c (14.2634)	1.0137^e (0.2266)	81.7033^d (33.7381)	-0.5020^c (0.2689)	-34.4270^d (13.0253)	3.3213^e (0.7812)	-10.7281 (11.6626)	328.3300^d (153.0824)
3.4	S	2040.96	-21.5684 (13.9243)	0.8570^e (0.2171)	81.3144^d (31.7456)	-0.5357^d (0.2548)	-32.4224^d (12.8091)	3.2543^e (0.7552)	-2.4182 (10.6767)	416.7554^e (146.3631)
3.5	$\bar{S}$	2443.63	-24.5591^c (12.2033)	0.9835^e (0.1858)	65.1451^d (29.3666)	-0.3878 (0.2378)	-35.6943^e (11.2361)	2.8914 (0.6567)	-6.2173 (12.3025)	373.0476^e (126.7412)
3.6	$\bar{S}$	2225.95	-23.2767^c (11.8982)	1.0708^e (0.1879)	61.8906^d (28.4062)	-0.3510 (0.2278)	-34.5151^e (10.9230)	2.8582^e (0.6406)	-7.9872 (11.9341)	337.0510^d (127.0422)
3.7	$\bar{S}$	2439.48	-24.5258^c (12.2102)	0.9844^e (0.1864)	64.8460^d (29.2833)	-0.3843 (0.2364)	-35.6370^e (11.2392)	2.9035^e (0.6625)	-6.2903 (12.3110)	369.5007^e (130.6777)
3.8	$\bar{S}$	2439.70	-24.4301^c (12.1902)	0.9891^e (0.1852)	64.1879^d (29.7983)	-0.3769 (0.2417)	-35.5004^e (11.1883)	2.8965^e (0.6682)	-6.5526 (12.2834)	371.4180^d (142.2600)

Model	Dependent variable	Constant	O_t	O_t^2	O_b	O_b^2	O_d	O_a^a	O_f^b	R^2
3.1	S	1950.56	−4.1045 (6.5442)	5.3621 (6.4373)						8992
3.2	S	1976.51			−3.6938 (3.2941)					.9259
3.3	S	1812.07			−10.7184 (8.6874)	0.1016 (0.1162)				.9019
3.4	S	2040.96					6.9441 (4.3818)			.9029
3.5	$\bar{S}$	2443.63	0.3456 (1.9353)							.9220
3.6	$\bar{S}$	2225.95			−4.1010 (2.8149)					.9225
3.7	$\bar{S}$	2439.48						0.2887 (2.2290)		.9220
3.8	$\bar{S}$	2439.70							−0.2045 (5.9713)	.9220

[a] O_a = proportion of teachers represented by the NEA.
[b] O_f = proportion of teachers represented by the AFT.
[c] significant at the .10 level, on a 2-sided t test.
[d] significant at the .05 level, on a 2-sided t test.
[e] significant at the .01 level, on a 2 sided t test.

The coefficients for formal negotiations are significant at the .10 level and imply a positive elasticity with regard to relative salary of about 0.0032. (The mean of S_p is 1.268.) This estimated elasticity, though somewhat small, may have significant implications for the future, since it is not unreasonable to expect a very large rise in the proportion of teachers covered by formal agreements during the next decade. Since a doubling or even tripling from the 1967-68 mean O_b of 15 percent is possible, it will be interesting to watch whether the diminishing returns to wide-scale bargaining predicted by the model in fact occur. Indeed, the reader may be interested to learn that the coefficient for O_b was insignificant until O_b^2 was added to the regression. Alternative estimates, none of which indicate that mere representation had a substantial impact on salaries, are reported in Table 9-4.

The above inferences are based on single-equation models. It seemed that a two-stage least-squares model might be more appropriate to understand the relationship between the extent of organization and teachers' salaries and also might lessen the statistical problems caused by multicollinearity. Therefore, we constructed a model for the proportion of teacher organization in states and then used the predicted values of organization, together with other variables, to estimate salaries. Generally, teacher organization was made a function of urbanization (and its square), proportion of teachers with substandard teaching certificates, proportion of total expenditures financed by local government, proportion of teachers who taught in elementary schools (P), and proportion of the nonagricultural labor force who were union members (M). The salary level was generally a function of the extent of teacher organization estimated from the previous equation, $\hat{O}_t$, together with many of the variables used earlier.

VARIABLES OF TEACHER ORGANIZATION

It was hypothesized that teacher organization was positively related to urbanization and labor-force unionization[16] because those variables are associated with knowledge and experience with collective action. It was further felt that teacher organization was negatively related to the proportion of classroom teachers who taught at the elementary level on the grounds that such teachers tended to be women who traditionally have not been attracted to unions and did not have as strong a lifetime commitment to classroom teaching because they expected either to leave the labor force in a few years (women) or to become school administrators (men). It

TABLE 9-4. Alternative parameter estimates (and standard errors) of the determinants of teachers' salaries relative to those of entering policemen

Estimates	Dependent variable	Constant	R_s	I	U	U^2	R_l	E	W	O_t	O_t^2	O_b	R^2
4.1	S_p	0.8311	-0.00434 (0.00586)	-0.00006 (0.00007)	0.02225[a] (0.00773)	-0.014[b] (0.006)	-0.00596 (0.00561)	0.00053[b] (0.00025)	-0.0160 (0.0425)	0.00021 (0.00065)			.4083
4.2	S_p	0.8728	-0.00441 (0.00592)	-0.00006 (0.00007)	0.02091[b] (0.00850)	-0.013[c] (0.007)	-0.00616 (0.00569)	0.00051 (0.00026)	-0.0134 (0.0435)	0.00092 (0.00189)	-0.00075 (0.00187)		.4107
4.3	S_p	0.8384	-0.00459 (0.00585)	-0.00007 (0.00007)	-0.02336[a] (0.00797)	-0.015[b] (0.006)	-0.00613 (0.00559)	0.00054[b] (0.00025)	-0.0104 (0.0430)			0.00059 (0.00095)	.4124
4.4	S_p	0.7095		-0.000077 (0.000058)	0.01537[c] (0.00851)	-0.00873 (0.00677)	-0.00187[b] (0.00078)	0.000413[c] (0.000219)				0.000680 (0.000868)	.4469

[a] significant at the .01 level; two-tailed test.
[b] significant at the .05 level.
[c] significant at the .10 level.

seemed that the proportions of both local financial support and of noncertified teachers were related to teacher organization, but, because of conflicting tendencies, we were unsure of their net effects. For example, on the one hand a high level of local support may reflect the fact that individual school districts are efficient and effective in producing education, while, on the other hand, such support may indicate that the districts have been unable to tap the more affluent higher levels of government. Similarly, the number of noncertified teachers may indicate a continuing shortage of experienced teachers (a positive salary effect) or the substitution of temporary for permanent teachers (a negative effect).

Similarly, we hypothesized that salaries would be positively related to income and expenditures per pupil, since those variables are associated with the demand for education (and, therefore, for teachers). Although none of our single-equation models indicated state support had a positive effect on teacher salaries, it was likely that a more appropriately specified model might bear out Miner's suggestion that the main effect of state funds was to raise teachers' salaries.[17]

The results using this approach are more promising with regard to the effect of organization—and again, even more promising with regard to coverage under formal agreements. Two sets of estimates are reported below: the first uses the percent of teachers represented; the second uses the percent of teachers covered by Level III and IV agreements.

$$(4a) \quad O_t = 137.62\dagger + 0.2916M$$
$$ (62.65) \quad (0.3457)$$
$$-3.3928U* + 3.6619U^2\dagger$$
$$(1.8652) \quad (1.5081)$$
$$+ 0.3627R_I\dagger - 1.1244P\ddagger$$
$$(0.1640) \quad\quad (0.3358)$$
$$-0.7068N$$
$$(0.8284)$$
$$\bar{R}^2 = .5570$$

$$(4) \quad \bar{S} = 218.68 + 18.3458\bar{R}_s\ddagger$$
$$\phantom{(4) \quad \bar{S} = } (520.61) \quad (3.1488)$$
$$+ 1.0339I\ddagger + 2.3854E\ddagger$$

$$(0.1981) \quad (0.7019)$$
$$+ 18.3342P\ddagger + 521.7904W\ddagger$$
$$(6.6118) \quad (136.8784)$$
$$+ 7.4517\hat{O}_t\dagger$$
$$(3.5584)$$

$\overline{R}^2 = .8819$ Standard error = 326.68

(5a) $O_b = 59.96 + 0.4631M*$
$$(45.36) \ (0.2503)$$
$$-1.3690U + 1.4770U^2$$
$$(1.3505) \quad (1.0919)$$
$$+ 0.1192R_l - 0.6956P\ddagger$$
$$(0.1187) \qquad (0.2431)$$
$$-0.0184N$$
$$(0.0600)$$
$$\overline{R}^2 = .3918$$

(5) $\overline{S} = 159.53 + 18.0058R_s\ddagger$
$$(514.02) \ (3.0268)$$
$$+ 0.9832I\ddagger + 2.2790E\ddagger$$
$$(0.1979) \quad (0.6842)$$
$$+ 23.9375P\ddagger + 530.5073W\ddagger$$
$$(7.6671) \qquad (134.7074)$$
$$+ 18.4195\hat{O}_b\dagger$$
$$(7.5137)$$

$\overline{R}^2 = .8859$ Standard error = 321.10

* significant at the .10 level.
† significant at the .05 level.
‡ significant at the .01 level.

It may be useful to digress to discuss the parameter estimates of the models explaining teacher organization (4a) and (5a). Both models corroborate the belief that there is an inverse correlation between the proportions of teacher organization and elementary classroom teachers. Secondary school teachers, who are apt to be the primary breadwinners in their families, are more likely to seek professional representation. The interpretation of the urbanization estimates is that representation increases with urbanization and at a faster rate. Teacher representation increases with the relative importance of local expenditures, suggesting, perhaps, that school districts which must rely heavily on local funds tend to have salaries and working conditions which cause teachers to seek representation. Finally, it is interesting to note that general unionization does not seem to be a determinant of teacher representation in the abstract but is positively related to the proportion of teachers who are covered under the more formal agreements. Familiarity with unionization in the private sector seems to encourage workers in the public sector to seek collective bargaining.

Although the two-stage regression models have not solved all the estimation problems, we believe as matters of both theory and econometrics that they are preferred estimates to those in the single-equation models for S and $\bar{S}$. The estimated parameters in (4) and (5) generally are more consistent with our expectations, less confused because of multicollinearity, and produce slightly larger $\bar{R}^2$'s. As a result, these results are discussed at some length.

VARIABLES OF TEACHERS' SALARIES

Teachers' salaries are positively associated with all the variables—state support, income, educational expenditures, region, classroom teacher "mix," and even estimated teacher representation. We are unsure of the correct interpretation of the effect of the teacher mix on salaries, but the signs of all the other variables are consistent with our earlier hypotheses.

Although both regression coefficients for teacher organization, $\hat{O}_t$ and $\hat{O}_b$, are statistically significant, indicating that organization does raise teachers' salaries, they in no way change our earlier conclusion that the effect on teachers' salaries is small. One estimate of the elasticity of salaries with respect to organization can be gleaned from equation (4). Multiplying the regression coefficient (7.4517) by the ratio of the mean proportion of teacher representation to mean salary (38/6692) gives an estimated elasticity of +.04. We infer that the extent of organization in 1967-68 tended to raise salaries by no more than 4 percent (or nearly \$275) across the board—which may seem like much hard work for little financial return.

One other interesting speculation arises from a comparison of these models. Since both estimated elasticities for organization are .04, the impacts on salaries of both formal agreements and *any* kind of representation appear to be identical. However, unless the mere acknowledgement of organizational interest (Level I and II agreements) is as effective as formal bargaining, it may be that representation which leads to less than Level III agreements has no effect on salaries at all. Classroom teachers well may be skeptical of the financial benefits of "formal representation with informal negotiation."

It is interesting to examine the residuals of equation (5) to learn which states paid more, less, or the same as the model predicted. Table 9-5 lists those states which are farthest from and nearest to the regression surface.

TABLE 9-5. Residuals from equation (5) for selected states

Highly positive		Highly negative		Nearly zero	
Alaska	($602)	S. Dakota	(−$609)	Alabama	($ 0)
Indiana	(588)	Wyoming	(− 486)	Tennessee	(− 15)
New Mexico	(470)	New York	(− 473)	Ohio	(− 15)

The interpretation of Table 9-5 is that Alaska, for example, paid its teachers $602 more than equation (5) predicted, while South Dakota paid its teachers $609 less than was expected. On the other hand, the model came within $0.27 of correctly predicting the average salary in Alabama, and within $15 (an "error" of 0.2 percent) in Ohio.

Finally, we want to make clear that none of the above estimates suggest that organization and representation have little effect at the immediate school district level. We have not yet posed the question with regard to school districts. Conceivably, teachers in a particular city could organize and win substantial salary increases as a result of their bargaining and yet leave the average salary in their state largely unchanged. This caveat cannot be carried very far, since if many school districts bargain and grant large salary increases, the state average must rise.

The calculated and estimated data on salaries and representation appear in the Appendix.

HYPOTHETICAL CASES YIELD 4 PERCENT INCREASE

Table 9-6 illustrates some hypothetical cases where various combinations of salary increases and the proportion of teachers involved yield an average statewide increase of 4 percent, our estimate of the effect of organization in 1967.

TABLE 9-6. Alternative combinations of salary increases and teachers covered yielding an increase in average state salaries of 4 percent[a]

Percent of salary increase	Percent of teachers receiving salary increase
5	80
10	40
20	20
40	10
80	5

[a]Assumes constant number of teachers

For example, consider the possible effect in Ohio, where the model fit fairly well. We calculated that 59.4 percent of the Ohio classroom teachers were covered by some level of agreement in 1967-68 and that this had the effect of raising the average salary in the entire state by 4 percent. This implies that the covered teachers may have raised their own salaries by as much as 6.7 percent relative to the nonrepresented teachers, or $432 that year (assuming no "spill-over").[18] Teachers covered by Level III or IV agreements may have received more but surely not three times as much.

Although these are our best estimates, there should be no reason to warn the reader how many important assumptions have been made to reach this point. These calculations should be viewed more with curiosity than with confidence.

We also examined the effect of organization on total expenditures per pupil for the possibility that organization may tend to raise the nonsalary costs of education. Although the simple correlation between E and O_t was +.47, organization had no independent effect on expenditures once income, urbanization, and the sources of financial support were taken into account.

An additional concern worthy of mention is whether the parameter estimates are adequate measures of the effect of representation on salaries, since one independent variable, E, is in part determined by S:

$$E = \frac{(S)(T) + X}{K},$$

where E = expenditures per pupil in average daily attendance, S = salary, T = number of teachers, X = all other current educational expenses, and K = number of students in average daily attendance.

A rearrangement of the terms in an equation such as (4), so that S appears only on the left-hand side, yields the following expression for the effect of organization on salaries

$$\frac{\partial S}{\partial O} = \left(\frac{K}{K-bT}\right) c,$$

where b is the parameter estimate of E, and c the parameter estimate of O. Thus, the estimated coefficient for O must be multiplied by $K/K\text{-}bT$ to get the effect of O on S.

The median average daily attendance was about 600,000 in fall 1967, and the median number of classroom teachers about 30,000. Thus the estimated parameter for organization in (4) must be "corrected" by

$$\frac{600,000}{600,000 - 2.3854 \,(30,000)} = 1.16$$

This correction raises slightly the estimate of the effect of O_t on S to 8.6658 from 7.4517 and the estimated elasticity to .049.

CONCLUSIONS

It is appropriate to offer some additional warnings about the estimates before we draw our conclusions. The model still is not specified correctly because it tends to somewhat overestimate salaries in the very lowest paying states, and the attribute of being a western state was arbitrarily assigned, with consequent large negative residuals for the "mountain" states such as Wyoming.

The estimated parameters may understate the effect of collective bargaining on salaries, because the appropriate labor market for teachers is probably a metropolitan area or network of towns, ordinarily within a state but occasionally crossing state boundaries, certainly not the state per se. Nor do our models recognize that teacher organization may have a cumulative effect over time on salaries of both organized and unorganized teachers. These objections are even more critical, since the extent of teacher organization varies so much among states: in some states there is no representation; in others nearly all the teachers are represented by some organization.

It is equally important to recognize that bargaining may affect the distribution, as well as the level, of salaries. Thus, our findings that average salaries have not been much affected by bargaining does not preclude the possibility that the salary structure may have been twisted.

Further research at the school district level is necessary to improve estimates of the effect of collective bargaining and representation on teachers' salaries. Such research requires extensive data on classroom teachers rather than on instructional personnel in general, as well as detailed information on school finances, and the economic and social characteristics of school districts.

Thus, for the time being, all that may be said is (1) collective representation does not seem to have had much, if any, effect on teachers' salaries; (2) if there has been a positive effect, it is probably less than $400 (assuming no wage spillover) and could even be as little as $40; (3) given these small estimates, it seems unlikely that bargaining has produced a significant or widespread reallocation of educational resources; but (4) as the AFT and NEA grow stronger in the next decade, it is entirely possible the effects of bargaining may increase. These surprising, if not entirely convincing, conclusions are based on analyses which examined three alternative measures of teachers' salaries and as many measures of the economic power of their organizations.

Notes

Hirschel Kasper would like to express his appreciation to Robert W. Tufts who sparked his interest in the incidence of bargaining in the public sector and to Dixie Sommers and Eileen Howell who aided as undergraduate research assistants. He would also like to express appreciation to the American Federation of Teachers (AFT) which granted an award for financial support of the project. The interpretations and conclusions in this paper are those of the author and do not purport to represent the views and opinions of the AFT or any of its staff.

1. Estimated from Research Division, National Education Association, *Negotiation Agreement Provisions, 1966-67 Edition* (Washington, D.C.: National Education Association, October 1967), pp. 223-25.

2. Wesley A. Wildman, "Representing the Teachers' Interests," from *Collective Bargaining in the Public Service, Proceedings of the 1966 Annual Spring Meeting of the Industrial Relations Research Association, May 6-7, 1966*, pp. 113-123 [reprinted in Richard L. Rowan and Herbert R. Northrup, eds., *Readings in Labor Economics and Labor Relations* (Homewood, Ill.: Irwin, 1968), pp. 278-84].

3. Estimated from National Education Association, *Negotiation Research Digest* (Washington, D.C.: National Education Association, June 1968).

4. *Negotiation Agreement Provisions, 1966-67 Edition.*

5. In some cities there is a traditional relationship between the pay of policemen and firemen. Sometimes salaries of professional school administrators are fixed multiples of salaries of teachers.

6. A more extensive discussion of bargaining power in the public sector appears in John F. Burton, Jr., and Charles Krider, "The Role and Consequence of

Strikes by Public Employees," *Yale Law Journal*, LXXIX (No. 3, January 1970), 418-40.

7. Information on sources of all data is available from the author on request.

8. For example, Glenn W. Fisher, "Interstate Variations in State and Local Government Expenditures," *National Tax Journal*, XVII (No. 1, March 1964), 57-74; Roy W. Bahl and Robert J. Saunders, "Factors Associated with Variations in State and Local Spending," *Journal of Finance*, XXI (No. 3, September 1966), 523-34; Jerry Miner, "The Determinants of School Expenditures" in Jesse Burkhead (ed.), *Public School Finance: Economics and Politics* (Syracuse, N.Y.: Syracuse University Press, 1964), pp. 50-75.

9. For a discussion of the timing of salary increases, see Donald Gerwin, "Compensation Decisions in Public Organizations," *Industrial Relations*, VIII (No. 2, February 1969), 174-84.

10. It was hoped the inclusion of salaries of other public employees would enable us to capture many of the "taste" variables for public employment and services. Deflating teachers' salaries by policemen's salaries will not strongly bias our estimated bargaining effect unless the ratio of the percent of organized teachers to organized policemen varies widely among states, and there is no reason to think it does.

11. Walter Hettich, "Equalization Grants, Minimum Standards, and Unit Cost Differences in Education," *Yale Economic Essays*, VIII (No. 2, Fall 1968), 3-55.

12. For example, see Teh-wei Hu *et al.*, "An Econometric Study of Demand for and Supply of Public Expenditures on Education," *Business and Economics Section, Proceedings of the American Statistical Association, 1968*, pp. 397-402.

13. Miner, "The Determinants of School Expenditures."

14. We have not explored the possibility that the inference of equation (3.8) is that relatively low salaries cause teachers to seek AFT representation.

15. From equations (3.7) and (3.8) the simple correlation between O_a and E is + .33 and between O_f and E is + .43.

16. Data on the proportion of unionization in Washington, D.C., was inseparable from that for Maryland, so both were dropped from the analysis. Thus, models (4) and (5) have only 49 observations.

17. Miner, "The Determinants of School Expenditures," p. 69, reports that one important effect of state aid is to raise teachers' salaries rather than to simply enable the local district to purchase more of all market inputs. He also finds that salaries are not a statistically significant determinant of expenditures per pupil, thus providing some support for the hypothesis that the causal relation is as described in equations (4) and (5).

18. The possible salary increase may have come partly at the expense of teachers in unorganized districts, if financial support from the state is a fixed sum *and* the state pays a guaranteed proportion of the instructional costs of each district. We have not tried to learn whether any state uses these formulas which produce negative spillover. For a discussion on measuring "spillover," see T. W. McGuire and L. A. Rapping, "Interindustry Wage Change Dispersion and the 'Spillover' Hypothesis," *American Economic Review*, LVI (No. 3, June 1966), 493-501.

APPENDIX

TABLE 9-7. Selected data on teacher representation and average salaries

State	Teacher representation		Mean Salary, 1966-1968	
	Calculated by author	Estimated from equation (4a)	Reported	Estimated from equation (4)
Alabama	0.0%	16.3%	$5602	$5572
Alaska	19.5	7.8	9183	8587
Arizona	41.7	22.8	7420	7116
Arkansas	6.3	17.5	5304	5270
California	100.0	79.2	8675	8339
Colorado	69.8	60.7	6762	7069
Connecticut	83.1	53.8	7680	7896
Delaware	26.9	24.8	7537	7999
Florida	56.0	47.0	6815	6481
Georgia	0.0	6.2	6245	6206
Hawaii	0.0	36.9	7871	7974
Idaho	43.8	18.0	5960	5840
Illinois	31.7	70.8	7651	7446
Indiana	34.2	35.5	7601	6957
Iowa	25.4	29.0	6802	6410
Kansas	47.2	32.8	6078	6439
Kentucky	29.7	7.5	5750	5815
Louisiana	0.0	17.2	6813	6401
Maine	22.5	7.5	5987	5904
Massachusetts	92.8	75.5	7425	7266
Michigan	98.7	55.8	7525	7373
Minnesota	75.4	42.3	7187	6896
Mississippi	1.9	10.2	4630	4957
Missouri	20.5	33.3	6436	6570
Montana	10.6	15.7	6187	6441
Nebraska	16.8	37.1	5843	5736
Nevada	25.3	46.1	7607	8024
New Hampshire	21.7	31.8	6187	6061
New Jersey	68.3	81.4	7600	7944
New Mexico	44.7	29.0	6805	6361
New York	67.4	77.6	8100	8570
North Carolina	0.7	(−)10.4	5911	6111
North Dakota	26.3	24.1	5430	5765
Ohio	59.6	44.9	6917	6834
Oklahoma	18.8	40.0	5958	5714
Oregon	0.0	35.7	7275	7157
Pennsylvania	38.8	52.9	7020	7054
Rhode Island	96.3	76.9	7012	7043
South Carolina	2.7	7.8	5486	5656
South Dakota	16.6	13.0	4950	5613
Tennessee	30.0	9.6	5812	5810
Texas	8.9	41.8	6262	6319
Utah	55.5	50.8	6565	6381
Vermont	10.7	25.9	5825	6314
Virginia	17.0	23.8	6500	6201
Washington	94.3	95.4	7540	7640
West Virginia	3.7	20.4	5625	5583
Wisconsin	56.6	45.4	6987	6694
Wyoming	40.0	33.2	6712	7241

III / ORGANIZATIONAL BEHAVIOR

INTRODUCTION

Now we are concerned with the ways individuals and groups involved in the employment relationship behave within educational organizations. What then distinguishes this section from the others? The conceptual frameworks, methodologies, and problems are mainly taken from the behavioral sciences, psychology and sociology in particular. Using a sociological viewpoint, we will examine how the structural and contextual properties of organizations affect behavior. From a psychological frame of reference we will be interested in the impact of needs and attitudes on behavior. Once more, there will be investigations of the structural, contextual, motivational, and attitudinal characteristics themselves. To make matters more specific, the behavior we shall be concerned with includes staff conflict, decision making, and leadership.

Another of the section's characteristics is that the conceptual frameworks are less developed than elsewhere in the volume, reflecting no doubt the recent development of the organizational behavior field and its even more recent application to educational administration. Further, there exists an emphasis on explanation and prediction as opposed to explicit suggestions for redesign. As will be pointed out, however, there are numerous implications in the articles for changing leadership styles. Finally, some educational researchers have cautioned that most behavioral science concepts, developed in other areas, may not be directly applicable to educational problems. There are at least two ways to handle this situation, both of which are reflected in these studies. One is to test the appropriateness of the theory in question in an educational setting; and approach utilized here by Sergiovanni. The other alternative is to contribute toward the building of theory in and for the educational context. The paper by Alutto and Belasco illustrates this approach.

Pondy[1] has discerned three conceptual frameworks developing out of the research on organizational conflict: a bargaining model suitable for interest groups competing for scarce resources, a bureaucratic model concerned with superior-subordinate friction, and a systems model appropriate for lateral relationships. Corwin's article, a more comprehensive account of which appears in his *Militant Professionalism*,[2] contributes toward the development of the second and third type of models. His concern is with a number of different aspects of small-scale, repetitive conflict involving teachers or teachers and administrators. His main point is that conflict is associated with structure, but the relationship is mediated by context. Thus, various conflict indexes are found to be correlated with measures of structural differentiation, regulatory procedures, and other factors, but in a number of cases the associations depend upon the extent of the professional and bureaucratic orientations in the schools studied. In this way Corwin is able to identify variables that should be incorporated into the bureaucratic and systems models mentioned above. Once more, some of his findings such as the "defusing" potential of participation in decision making, have policy implications for administrators concerned with managing conflict. Lytle comments on some of the practical difficulties research on conflict in educational organizations must contend with. He also discusses coping mechanisms used by his large urban school system, some of which turn out to be examples of Corwin's structural variables.

Luttbeg and Zeigler deal with a classical problem of interest groups such as teacher associations; the relationship between leaders' actions and members' desires. As Blau and Scott[3] have pointed out, leaders in their drive to get things done and to extend their power set into motion forces which may sacrifice democratic participation and perhaps lead to their replacement by the membership. The authors conduct survey research on the degree of attitude similarity between leaders and followers in the Oregon Education Association. Their work involves a comparison of members' attitudes, leaders' attitudes, and leaders' perceptions of members' attitudes with regard to organizational policy and related questions. Interestingly enough, the findings bear a certain similarity with the results of attitude research on supervisors and subordinates in business firms as reported by Likert,[4] for example. Although their work is largely descriptive in nature the authors provide some informative reasons for these findings. We also learn why certain policies are emphasized by the leaders, about the adequacy of the organization's communication system, and where potential sources of conflict exist. The comments by Wegmann and Vantine, which appear later in the volume, cast some additional light on the issues raised here.

The "two-factor" theory of Frederick Herzberg[5] and his associates is considered one of the most influential conceptual frameworks for researchers studying human motivation in organizations. It remains rather controversial, however, particularly the methodological aspects, as critiques by Vroom[6] and others indicate. Briefly, Herzberg's position is that intrinsic job characteristics contribute mainly to employee satisfaction while extrinsic factors in the job environment contribute mainly to dissatisfaction. Further, motivation to work results from fulfilling needs for satisfiers and not from eliminating dissatisfiers. Sergiovanni's contribution is to explore the applicability of the two-factor theory to the teaching profession by looking for the types of job factors related to teacher satisfaction and dissatisfaction. His findings indicate that practicing administrators may be misdirecting their motivational efforts by appealing too much to desire for extrinsic rewards. Recent work by Miskel[7] however implies the necessity for a careful matching of job characteristics and individual teachers' needs. He found that young educators want their work to be high on both intrinsic and extrinsic factors, and that in some schools extrinsic, not intrinsic, motivation prevails in teachers. What seems to be needed are investigations of whether augmenting job satisfiers will stimulate teachers' productivity and under what conditions. Hopefully, Sergiovanni's efforts will stimulate the needed research which might be conducted using Herzberg's[8] job enrichment experiments as a guide.

To some leaders in the field, such as Likert,[9] participative styles of management seem to have universal application. One of the trends in organizational behavior research, however, has been an inquiry into this assumption. Researchers are finding that personality, cultural, and technological factors may significantly constrain its effectiveness. The paper by Alutto and Belasco offers a new way of learning about the limits of participation specifically designed for an educational setting. Teachers are classified according to whether they want more participation (decisional deprivation), want less (decisional saturation), or are satisfied (decisional equilibrium). The implication, of course, is that the conflict defusing and productivity increasing benefits associated with more decision-making responsibility by Corwin and Sergiovanni may only apply to the first group. Researchers can, therefore, benefit from the authors' initial exploration of the variables associated with each of the three decisional situations. Practitioners will be interested in their simple operational method for identifying individuals in an organization who desire to be moved toward equilibrium.

Alutto and Belasco's findings are based on a study of a small urban and a medium-sized rural district. Wegmann in his comments discusses the forces associated with deprivation, saturation, and equilibrium in a large urban system, thereby contributing to the expansion of the new framework.

The comments in this section are by James H. Lytle and Robert G. Wegmann. After completing a doctoral program oriented toward organizational behavior and social psychology in the School of Education at Stanford University, Dr. Lytle took a central office administrative position in the School District of Philadelphia. His responsibilities included staff work for the Decentralization Commission, implementing a Student Bill of Rights and Responsibilities in the city's senior high schools, and budget preparation for the instructional arm of the school system. In July 1972 he became director of two experimental schools in the system, the Pennsylvania Advancement School and the Intensive Learning Center. At the 1973 American Educational Research Association meeting he presented a paper which examined the role of the district superintendent in managing conflict in large urban school systems. Dr. Wegmann is assistant professor of sociology, University of Wisconsin-Milwaukee, and he has a special interest in the sociology of education. Since 1971 he has been a member of the Milwaukee Board of School Directors and has taught at the public school level. He is currently editing a book on the future of education.

Notes

1. Louis R. Pondy, "Organizational Conflict: Concepts and Models," *Administrative Science Quarterly,* XII (No. 2, September 1967), 296-320.

2. Ronald G. Corwin, *Militant Professionalism; a Study of Organizational Conflict in High Schools* (New York: Appleton Century Crofts, 1970).

3. Peter M. Blau and W. Richard Scott, *Formal Organizations* (San Francisco: Chandler Publishing Co., 1962).

4. Rensis Likert, *New Patterns of Management* (New York: McGraw-Hill, 1961).

5. Frederick Herzberg, *Work and the Nature of Man* (Cleveland, Ohio: World Publishing Co., 1966).

6. Victor H. Vroom, *Work and Motivation* (New York: John Wiley, 1964).

7. Cecil Miskel, "The Motivation of Educators to Work," *Educational Administration Quarterly,* IX (No. 1, Winter 1972), 42-53.

8. Frederick Herzberg, "One More Time: How Do You Motivate Employees?" *Harvard Business Review,* XLVI (January-February 1968), 53-62.

9. Likert, *New Patterns.*

10 / Patterns of Organizational Conflict

Ronald G. Corwin

Writers have called attention to the compelling need for models of organization that take conflict into account.[1] Such a model would include many types of variables, but at least some conflict might be expected to be related to the organizational structure itself.[2] This paper deals with structural differentiation and structural integration, focusing on some patterns of relationship between selected characteristics of high schools as organizations and rates of staff conflict among teachers. This should help to identify variables that deserve priority in the model and point the way to more fruitful research.

Several types of structure that seem to be related to conflict have been identified. A few of these have been selected for analysis here: structural differentiation, participation in the authority system, regulating procedures, heterogeneity and stability of personnel, and interpersonal structure. Relationships between one or more indexes of each of these five variables and several indexes of organizational conflict are then described, controlling for other relevant variables.

The data were taken from a larger study of routine staff conflicts in 28 public schools.[3] Because the study was exploratory and the emphasis was on discerning general patterns among various dimensions of organizations, the initial field work was confined to a relatively small number of organizations, which could be analyzed in

---

Reprinted from *Administrative Science Quarterly*, XIV (No. 4, December 1969), 507-20.

detail along various dimensions. In addition to the small sample size, the crude measures necessarily limit generalization from these data, and make the propositions advanced here tentative. It is hoped, however, that they may lead to a more secure foundation with more precise measures.

VARIABLES

Structural Differentiation

The degree of differentiation within an organization is reflected in the number of administratively distinct but functionally inter-dependent subunits. It can be assumed that problems of defining the boundaries and responsibilities of subunits typically arise at the linkage points.[4] Accordingly, the division of labor has been identi-fied as one of the major sources of conflict.[5] Some subunits of an organization develop a degree of autonomy from the others. Having distinct functions, they develop their own objectives and norms and compete with other units, even though they must also cooperate.[6] The amount of tension is likely to vary with the proximity of departments, with the relationships among the key members of each department, and with the need for joint decision making.[7] White[8] found that both the drive for departmental autonomy and inter-departmental hostility was greatest where the interrelation of tasks was highest.

This instability is aggravated by the fact that departments within an organization seldom have control over outsiders (even though subject to criticism from them) and by the inconsistent practices and role conceptions among the members of the separate subunits.[9] Complex linkage systems tend to contribute to a general sense of uncertainty, which some authors[10] believe is a major source of conflict. However, the anomie may result from structural character-istics rather than the affective state of the members.

In short, a differentiated structure requires a delicate system of linkages, which becomes a source of strain and accommodation. The greater the number of interrelations, the greater is the likelihood that the organization will break down at some point.[11] It is proposed that *conflict will increase with the degree of differentiation in an organization.* Here the level of specialization of personnel, the num-ber of levels in the hierarchy of authority, and a total measure of organizational complexity are considered in addition to size. Size alone is not a sufficient condition for differentiation.

Specialization. Specialization has the effect of accentuating differ-ences among employees and delineating group boundaries. It seems reasonable to assume that specialists are more likely than nonspecialists to develop vested interests and monopolistic claims over certain spheres of work, which they are then ready to defend from encroachment. Specializations supported by the authority of distinctive competences are particularly identifiable as targets for hostility.[12] It therefore might be expected that *specialization will be positively associated with the incidence of conflict.*

Levels of authority. The number of echelons also contributes to the complexity of the organization. It is often difficult to achieve adequate communication between socially isolated levels of authority, and each echelon in turn presses on its incumbents distinct role conceptions, problems, objectives, and vested interests. It can be expected then that members of the more hierarchical organizations will not identify closely with persons in different echelons, nor share their perceptions and attitudes,[13] and that persons in different echelons frequently compete as special-interest groups for more favorable allocations of rewards, i.e., status, prestige, and monetary returns.[14] Also new levels of authority may be instituted as a means of mediating existing conflicts between subordinate levels, which would have the effect of intensifying the relationship between this characteristic and conflict.[15]

Both supervisors and professional employees are subject to special forms of tension because of anomalies inherent in their positions.[16] Pressures from superiors for efficiency and technical competence may be inconsistent with the professional's value for technical procedure, and executives in complex organizations typically are less qualified than some of their own subordinates to judge the specialists below them.[17] It is expected that *organizational tension and conflict will increase with the number of levels of authority in an organization.*

Organizational complexity. The overall complexity of an organization, then, is a product of the horizontal division of labor as well as the hierarchical division of authority. Interdependent units develop distinctive role conceptions and objectives, and compete for resources and rewards.[18] The differences of interest between functionally differentiated groups may be largely responsible for organizational conflict.[19] It can be hypothesized that *organizational tension and conflict will be positively associated with organizational complexity.*

Participation in the Authority System

Several writers have noted problems that authority systems create for employed professionals.[20] A study of an electrical factory, for example, indicated that a small group of design engineers felt that managers sometimes made arbitrary decisions.[21] Becker[22] reported a conflict between school principals and teachers because of teachers' desires for autonomy.

Coleman[23] argued that conflict was encouraged when channels of legitimate political expression were closed, but this seems to assume that discontent accumulates in reservoirs. Gamson[24] questions this; he maintains that open channels can simply encourage the expression of any existing tensions, so that if there is strain, participation in the decision-making process provides employees who are already discontented with the channel and the opportunity to communicate grievances that otherwise might remain hidden.

In addition to giving subordinates influence against administrators, making routine decisions can promote disagreement among subordinates themselves. Since decisions represent compromises between contending groups and must be implemented under pressure, conflict is likely to accompany the responsibility to make decisions, wherever that responsibility resides. For these reasons, members of an organization will have more opportunity and more reasons to disagree among themselves when the decision-making process is decentralized than when it is centralized. The more frequently subordinates participate in decision making, the greater the likelihood for disagreement; therefore, *organizational tension and conflict will be positively associated with the participation of subordinates in the authority system.*

Regulating Procedures

The existence of tension and conflict probably encourages more organizational control. The precise balance between the divisive conditions and efforts to control divisiveness will fluctuate as power shifts. This makes it very difficult to anticipate how effective particular control procedures will be in regulating conflict.

Since standardization and supervision generally are intended to narrow the discretion of subordinates, to clarify situations, and to protect spheres of authority, it might be expected that they would serve to minimize conflict, especially conflict arising from misunderstanding. Kahn,[25] for example, found that role conflict was highest where there was low emphasis on rules and less close supervision. Close supervision, in particular, could serve as a channel for resolving differences informally before they develop into major problems.

But there are also compelling reasons to expect that controls will be positively associated with conflict. First, the very rules that limit the discretion of some groups can protect other groups and provide them with support and a sense of independence.[26] This protective function gives rules a strategic role in conflict. Each group in conflict, said Crozier,[27] supports the rules and presses the other group to follow the rules, while at the same time preserving its own area of freedom. A study of teachers' sense of power supports the conclusion that certain bureaucratic characteristics of school systems provide teachers with a sense of power.[28] A predictable organization helps individuals to anticipate and influence possible consequences of their actions.

Secondly, if a group subscribes to a professional ideology, in which self-determination of work is central, regulations which specifically restrict their freedom will be resisted. Subordinates may react to rules not only by withdrawing their loyalty,[29] but also by rebelling. For example, the professionally oriented employees of a public welfare agency, in comparison to those oriented to the bureaucracy, more frequently agreed that agency rules and procedures sometimes interfered with professional performance, and they were more likely to deviate from agency rules.[30] Gouldner[31] reported that professionally oriented faculty members were less willing to rely on formal rules as a means of controlling students.

Finally, control procedures are likely to be introduced into situations that are already troubled and where the control of interdependent and semiautonomous units is already difficult. Threatened groups will place more emphasis on rules during periods of conflict than during periods of harmony.[32] Schools must perform many nonroutine tasks, which are likely to cause disagreement,[33] and teachers have become increasingly militant in their drive to increase their authority. Attempts on the part of administrators to exercise more control under these circumstances might only provoke further conflict. For these reasons, it is proposed that *organizational tension and conflict are positively associated with emphasis on procedures for regulating organizational conflict.* Three major types of regulating procedures are examined: standardization of procedures, emphasis on rules, and close supervision.

Heterogeneity and Stability

Recruitment of members from outside the organization makes the organization more or less vulnerable to unofficial influences. Because "people take culture with them,"[34] latent roles arise from differences in training, age, religion, sex, and ethnic backgrounds. Such roles were identified by Thompson[35] as one of three major sources of organizational conflict and adaptability.

Heterogeneity. It seems reasonable to assume that when divergent cultural backgrounds are represented among the members of an organization, they will hold different cultural values and have divergent perspectives toward common organizational problems. Moreover, their backgrounds may be systematically related to their status and authority within the organization. On the other hand, conflict can be expected to diminish when personnel are drawn from the same backgrounds—a preferred teacher's college, a specific regional background, a specific sex, religion, ethnic, or social-economic background. Therefore, heterogeneity of personnel backgrounds should be positively associated with organizational tension and conflict. Becker and Geer[36] propose, however, that latent culture operates in those areas that are less critical for an organization and that are not covered by the formal and informal structural roles. Consequently, *the association between heterogeneity and conflict will be lower in more standardized organizations than in less standardized ones.*

Staff additions. Adding new staff members can be a tension-producing process, irrespective of their backgrounds. The influx of new members can disrupt both informal and formal procedures, and the recruitment of new members may reflect the existence of other problems, particularly turnover among the leadership.[37] It is expected that *the number of staff members added to an organization will be positively associated with organizational tension and conflict.*

Past experience. March and Simon[38] hypothesized that the greater the past experience that members have had with a situation, the less likely is intraindividual conflict. Older and more stable faculties and administrations may have solved many problems that new faculties confront, and they may have expelled nonconforming members. Therefore, *the length of time that members are part of an organization will be inversely associated with organizational tension and conflict.*

Interpersonal Structure

Regardless of the tension-producing conditions, overt incidents are not likely to develop, unless the members of an organization have the means, as well as the desire, to participate in the official system. Informal channels of communication can function in the same way as official channels to provide occasions for expressing problems. Interaction among peers is more conducive to the expression of discontent than is social distance.[39]

It can be hypothesized that the more frequently faculty members associate with one another on social occasions, the greater the likelihood that discontent will be expressed as overt incidents. More generally, it is proposed that *the rate of informal interaction among a faculty, the rate of interaction between a faculty and its administration, and the degree of participation in employee associations are positively associated with organizational tension and conflict.* Two facilitating channels of interaction are considered: the proportion of faculty who lunch together and the proportion of faculty who see each other socially.

PROCEDURES

Data on 28 high schools in Pennsylvania, Ohio, Michigan, and Indiana were collected between 1962 and 1965. Over 1,500 teachers and administrators, representing a stratified sample of more than three-fourths of the faculty, returned lengthy questionnaires. Over 700 of these respondents, stratified by position and subject matter taught, were randomly selected for tape-recorded interviews lasting from 30 to 60 minutes. The people involved are reasonably representative of Ohio and national norms for teachers' ages, years of experience, years of education, marital status, and activity in professional organizations; however, the proportion of males and the salary levels of the sampled teachers are a little higher than the national averages. The sample proportion of teachers with master's degrees is underrepresentative for Ohio, but it is representative for the nation as a whole. The schools represent all size categories, but were chosen to overrepresent the larger schools in the region because it was felt that it was more important to maximize the variability of organizational characteristics than to have a representative sample. The various indexes are only briefly summarized here; further details of their construction are reported elsewhere.[40]

Structural Differentiation

Specialization. Specialization not only depends upon the amount of specialized training required of personnel, but upon the match betweeen their training and the jobs to which they are assigned. Whether teachers were used as specialists was inferred from the proportion of teachers reporting that they were teaching courses in which they had not majored or minored in college.

Levels of authority. As an index of the authority hierarchy, teachers and principals were asked to estimate the number of levels of authority in the school and in the school system, and the mean response was computed for each school.

Organizational complexity. The complexity of an organization is a function of the number of separate work units, without requiring specialized training of its personnel; in fact, refinements in the division of labor often reduce the level of skill and authority needed by an employee.

A quasi-Guttman scale was developed from seventeen variables related to the number of distinct organizational parts in a school system. The scale items, all but one of which were answered by principals, included: the estimated number of weeks it would normally take to effect a curriculum change, the number of staff members in the school and in the system, the percentage of part-time teachers, clerical personnel, and administrators in the system, the number of classes in the school with ability grouping, and the number of separate programs and classes in the school. The coefficient of reproducibility was .85 and the minimal-marginal reproducibility was .65. These are below the desired .90 but this "quasi" scale is used for ordinal measurement.

Participation in the Authority System

Teachers were asked to estimate the extent of their authority to make day-to-day decisions on problems that arose routinely in the course of teaching. The measure consisted of responses to three global statements, which satisfied the scale-value-difference method of scale construction: (1) At my school, teachers are allowed to make their own decisions about the problems that come up in the classroom. (2) At my school, small matters need not be referred higher up for final answer. (3) At my school, the ultimate authority over the major educational decisions is exercised by professional teachers. Possible responses ranged from "strongly agree" to "strongly disagree"; these were weighted from one to five and were averaged for each school. Schools were ranked according to the means of the teachers' responses.

Regulating Procedures

Standardization of work. A quasi-Guttman scale was developed from fifteen questions answered by the principal and teachers of each school. The questions pertained to the amount of discretion permitted in lesson plans, the teachers' role in lesson preparation, teachers' authority to choose textbooks, and their options over the use of textbooks. The scale had a coefficient of reproducibility of .84 and a marginal reproducibility of .74, and is used only for ordinal measurement.

Emphasis on rules. The emphasis a school places on rules was measured by five Likert-scale statements concerning teachers' familiarity with rules and procedures, the existence of an enforced manual of rules, enforced rules stating when teachers should arrive and depart, rules specifying topics not appropriate to classroom discussion, and the willingness of teachers to take risks in interpreting the rules. Teachers were asked how accurately each statement described their schools, and the schools were ranked on the mean of the teachers' responses. The items met the test of the scale-value-difference method.

Close supervision. Surveillance of teachers by principals and central office administrators was measured by a quasi-Guttman scale consisting of fourteen questions answered by principals and teachers. The questions dealt with the number of classroom observations normally made by administrators and the nature of consultations afterwards; whether permission had to be obtained to discuss controversial issues; the amount of supervision by the central office, including the frequency of the superintendent's visits to the school; the number of reports required by the central office; and the fairness and accuracy reported by teachers of their administrators' evaluations of them. The scale had a coefficient of reproducibility of .85 and its minimal-marginal reproducibility was .71; it is used only for ordinal measurement.

Heterogeneity and Stability

A simple profile of faculty backgrounds was constructed for each school by dichotomizing thirteen background characteristics and computing ratios for each characteristic; e.g., the sex ratio of young to old teachers, the ratio of married to unmarried, and the urban-rural ratio. A school's score was the sum of these ratios. Staff stability was measured by the number of staff additions during the past five years and by the average age of the faculty.

Interpersonal Structure

Respondents reported the frequency with which they normally lunched with every other faculty of the school; they also reported the frequency with which they saw each other socially outside of school. Responses were weighted from 1 to 5 and then averaged across all respondents from a school.

Two Moderating Variables

Professional orientation of the school. A Likert-type scale measured the professional orientation of each faculty member. It consisted of sixteen items pertaining to four norms: (*1*) orientation to students, (*2*) emphasis on teachers' authority to make decisions, (*3*) belief that knowledge is the appropriate basis of authority in teaching, and (*4*) responsiveness to colleagues and colleagues' opinions. The items were selected on the basis of the critical ratio scale-value-difference tests of internal consistency and the scale was tested for internal consistency and reliability. For some of the analyses reported here, the 28 schools were dichotomized on the basis of this measure.

Total bureaucratization. Several organizational variables were combined as an index of total bureaucratization. For each school, the ranks on each of the following variables were summed: close supervision, emphasis on rules, the extent to which professional and nonprofessional policy decisions were centralized, and the participation of teachers in routine decisions about classroom work. For some analyses the schools were dichotomized on this distribution and classified as either more or less bureaucratic.

Indexes of Conflict

Several indexes of organizational tension and conflict were developed from questionnaire data and the interviews. On the questionnaire each respondent indicated the faculty members and administrators in his school with whom he had severe and moderate disagreements. He also estimated the degree of *tension* (severe, moderate, slight, or none) in his school for twelve roles. Schools were ranked on the mean rate of conflict per person and on their mean tension score.

During the interviews, descriptions of specific conflict incidents were recorded on tape. Teachers and administrators were asked to describe any difficulties, problems, friction, incidents, or disputes, that they or other members of the faculty had been involved in during the recent past. An *incident* was defined as a concrete episode involving criticism of a teacher, group of teachers, or the school as a whole. An episode was counted as one incident, regardless of the number of teachers involved in it or the number of times the same episode was mentioned by different teachers. Each incident was classified as a complaint, an overt incident, or an instance of impersonal competition. Complaints included general complaints, e.g., "I don't like the way things are run here"; complaints against a specific group or individual; and complaints about policy. Overt incidents included (a) open *disputes* between two people or disputes among three or more people, usually involving an administrator; (b) two or more *heated discussions;* and (c) *major incidents* involving others in addition to the initial parties, usually a substantial segment of the organization and members of the community. *Impersonal competition* included incidents not involving face-to-face confrontation, but involving known tension between two or more parties because of their opposing positions or ideas.

The general content of each incident was classified on the basis of

TABLE 10-1. Rank-order correlations between organizational characteristics and indexes of tension and conflict

| | Indexes of organizational tension and conflict | | | | | | | | | |
| | Degree of tension averaged across all roles and all respondents | Rates of disagreement | | Number of incidents reported per interview | | | | | | |
Organizational characteristics		Total disagreements per faculty member	Severe disagreements per faculty member	All incidents	Disputes	Heated discussions	Major incidents	Teachers vs. administrators	Teachers vs. teachers	Incidents involving authority problems
Organizational size	.22[a]	.16	.35[b]	.38[b]	.27[a]	.37[b]	.04	.41[b]	-.07	.26[a]
Structural differentiation										
1. Specialization										
Did not major in course	.08	.02	-.18	-.03	-.01	-.06	-.22[a]	-.05	-.04	.07
Did not major or minor in course	-.07	-.23[a]	-.12	-.04	-.24[a]	-.12	.05	-.08	-.10	-.03
2. Levels of authority	.30[a]	.18	.37[b]	.48[b]	.32[a]	.39[a]	.18	.40[b]	.08	.26[a]
3. Organizational complexity	.19	.16	.32[b]	.33[b]	.27[a]	.33[a]	.10	.23[a]	.02	.13
Participation in the authority system	.14[a]	.17	.17	.17	.39[b]	.03	-.38[b]	.07	.12	.05
Regulating procedures										
1. Standardization of work	.28[a]	.20	.26[a]	.31[a]	.31[a]	.17	.21	.53[b]	.03	.32[a]
2. Emphasis on rules	.10	.24[a]	.06	.22[a]	.21[a]	.27[a]	.13	.11	.12	-.10
3. Close supervision	-.04	.13	.12	.13	.28[a]	.02	-.14	.03	.15	-.11
Heterogeneity and stability										
1. Heterogeneity of staff	.03	-.08	.10	.18	.16	.08	-.21[a]	.03	.36[b]	.14
2. Staff additions during the past 5 years	.34[b]	.30[a]	.37[b]	.58[b]	.41[b]	.39[b]	-.13	.47[b]	.09	.31[a]
3. Average age of faculty	-.26[a]	-.06	-.40[b]	-.24[a]	-.23[a]	.26[a]	.12	-.19	-.21[a]	-.25[a]
Interpersonal structure										
1. Lunching patterns	.09	-.03	.15	.11	.21[a]	.02	-.13	.12	.00	.10
2. Social contact outside of school	.26[a]	.15	.29[a]	.43[b]	.21[a]	.47[b]	.16	.30[a]	.32[b]	.42[b]

[a] Rank-order correlation significant at $p < .05$.
[b] Rank-order correlation significant at $p < .01$.

the roles involved and further divided into one of six general categories: authority problems, distribution and scheduling problems, communication problems, interpersonal problems, value conflicts, and differences in educational philosophy. Organizational conflict is measured by the frequency with which each type of incident was reported during the interviews. Nearly half of the incidents were either corroborated or reported by reliable respondents; i.e., those mentioning a corroborated incident. The frequencies with which validated, reliable and nonvalidated, nonreliable incidents were mentioned were not significantly different, according to a chi-square test. There also was consistency within each school on the frequency with which types of incidents were mentioned. Using a stratified random sample of 172 incidents, two coders agreed with 87 percent of the incident classifications.

FINDINGS

Rank-order correlations were computed between ten indexes of conflict and each structural variable. Each correlation was recomputed several times to control for variables found in previous analyses to be associated with the dependent or independent variables under consideration. In addition, many of the correlations were computed separately for schools which were above and below the median indexes for professional orientation of the faculty and for total bureaucratization. The results of these more detailed analyses are discussed only when they influence the conclusions. Table 10-1 shows the results of the analyses.

Size

Authority structures appear to be less stable in larger schools. Both the number of conflicts reported involving authority and the rate of conflict between teachers and administrators increase with the size of school; however, conflicts among teachers do not appear to be influenced by size of school.

Controlling for the emphasis that schools place on rules (by using a partial correlation) did not appreciably alter the conclusions; but, when the number of staff additions during the past five years was controlled, reductions occurred in the correlations with total tension and the rate of severe disagreement. This latter finding indicates that conflict is not the result of size in itself; it is probably heavily influenced by factors that are associated with size.

Structural Differentiation

Specialization. Most of the correlations between conflict and specialization indicate a positive relationship. However, only a few of these are statistically significant. The lack of specialization (as reflected in the proportion of a faculty assigned to courses in which they had neither majored nor minored) is inversely associated with total rate of disagreement and with the ratio of disputes, and the rate of major incidents declines with the proportion of teachers assigned to courses outside of their majors. These correlations remain after school size has been controlled for.

But if specialization is associated with the incidence of certain types of conflict, it does not appear to have a bearing on the members who become involved. It is not associated with the volume of conflict occurring either among teachers or between teachers and administrators, and it is not associated with the incidence of authority problems.

The 28 schools were dichotomized on two different variables: total bureaucratization and mean professional orientation. With one exception, the positive relationships between specialization and certain types of conflict were accentuated in the fourteen more bureaucratic schools and in the fourteen more professional schools. However, there was an inverse, but not statistically significant, relationship with major incidents in the fourteen less professional schools (τ = −.28) and the fourteen less bureaucratic schools (τ = −.30), suggesting that conflict among specialists was likely to become uncontrolled in settings where neither bureaucracy nor professionalism dominated.

Levels of authority. Ten of the twelve school systems having six or seven levels of authority reported high rates of severe disagreement, in comparison to only one of the seven systems with three or fewer levels of authority (χ^2 significant at $p < .05$). The more hierarchical organizations appear to have relatively unstable authority structures; both the rate of authority problems and rate of conflict between teachers and administrators increase with the number of authority levels. When schools were divided on the basis of their total bureaucratization schores however, only in the fourteen less bureaucratized schools were authority problems associated with length of the hierarchy. The rate of conflict among teachers themselves does not appear to be associated with the hierarchy.

Departmentalization. The number of officially recognized departments in a school, one aspect of organizational complexity, was associated with the number of moderate and severe disagreements among the faculty (χ^2 significant at $p \leqslant .01$). Seven of the eight schools with more than six departments reported high rates of moderate disagreement in comparison to only three of fifteen schools without department heads. There was a similar pattern for severe disagreements.

Organizational complexity. Indicators of conflict that increase significantly with the index of organizational complexity are: rates of severe disagreement, total incidents, and conflicts between teachers and administrators. In the fourteen more professionally oriented schools, complexity was particularly associated with conflict between teachers and administrators.

When the mean age of the faculty was controlled, the relationships held for all age levels, which perhaps indicates that experience in itself does not necessarily compensate for the problems associated with complexity. Since organizational complexity was associated with school size, controlling for size lowered the correlation, but it did not eliminate it.

Participation in Authority System

Teachers' participation in decisions about their classrooms is positively associated with the rate of disputes, but it is inversely associated with the number of major incidents. The fact that the number of major incidents in a school decreases with faculty authority, even as the rate of other forms of dispute increases, suggests that the contentions of Gamson[41] and Coleman[42] may both be correct in certain respects. The authority to make routine decisions permits more opportunity for the expression of existing disputes and provides more occasions for disputes to arise; however, this opportunity to participate in the decision-making process, by providing occasions for expressing minor forms of conflict, might prevent minor irritations from developing into major incidents.

Regulating Procedures

Standardization. Although it is assumed that standardized procedures are introduced in order to clarify the structure and minimize conflict, standardization is positively associated with the rate of conflict between teachers and administrators, incidents involving authority issues, the total tension within the school, rates of severe disagreement, the number of total incidents, and the rate of disputes.

The correlation between standardization and conflicts between teachers and administrators over authority issues, apparently is confined to the fourteen more professionally oriented schools and to the fourteen less bureaucratized ones; standardization is not associated with conflict over authority in either the less professional or more bureaucratic organizations. Also, although conflicts among teachers themselves do not increase with standardization in the sample as a whole, among the fourteen more professional schools there is a positive association (τ = .41), whereas among the less professional schools the relationship is negative (τ = −.41). Standardization tends to reduce conflict among subordinates in less professional schools, and to increase it in the more professional schools. But since most of these correlations drop below statistical significance when school size is controlled, factors other than standardization are probably contributing to these relationships.

Emphasis on rules. As with standardization, the rates of severe disagreement, disputes, heated discussions, and total incidents increase with the emphasis on rules. Since these variables are related to the number of new staff members added over the preceding five years, they drop appreciably when that factor has been controlled for (except for heated discussions). Also, neither conflict over authority issues nor teacher-administration conflict is prevalent in schools where rules are emphasized.

As with standardization, the rate of total disagreement correlates with emphasis on rules only in the fourteen more professionally oriented schools (τ = .32); the correlation between emphasis on rules and major incidents also approaches statistical significance in the more professionally oriented schools (τ = .30). The correlation between the emphasis on rules and rate of total disagreement, on the other hand, holds only in the fourteen less bureaucratic schools (τ = .33). Among the more bureaucratic schools, emphasis on rules is correlated with a decrease in authority problems.

Close supervision. The evidence here provides only limited support for Gamson's contention that rules are more likely than close supervision to be used in conflict-laden situations, because interpersonal relations tend to be aggravated in difficult situations. Although correlations between close supervision and several of the conflict measures are in the positive direction, only the number of disputes is statistically significant and remains so after school size has been controlled.

There is a very low negative association between close supervision and the ratio of major incidents, which apparently pertains primarily in less professional schools (τ = −.42). Disputes are directly associated with close supervision in the more professional (τ = .38) and in the less bureaucratic schools (τ = .34).

Heterogeneity and Stability

Age of the faculty. Faculties seem to become more peaceful as they grow older. As the mean age of a faculty increases, the incidence of conflict declines on nine of the ten measures examined. Most of these relationships remain after controlling for complexity and the number of staff additions, although the latter control lowers the correlations with total incidents and disputes.

Staff additions. Most of the conflict measures (except for conflict among teachers and major incidents) are positively associated with the number of staff members added during the preceding five years. As staff additions increase, so do open disputes, heated discussions, total tension, total disagreements, and severe disagreements. The rate of conflict involving authority issues also increases. Both total incidents and incidents between teachers and administrators show relatively high correlations, and these measures remain significant after organizational size has been controlled for. The correlations with conflicts over authority and between teachers and administrators are higher in the less bureaucratic schools than the more bureaucratic ones. These findings suggest that it might be more difficult to integrate new members into the administrative system than into the peer group system.

When organizational size was controlled, the correlation between staff additions and major incidents was negative and statistically significant ($\tau_p = -.21$). Insofar as additions of staff replace members who have left, the more discontented faculty members may be replaced before conflicts develop into major incidents. This correlation is probably strengthened by the association of staff additions with other variables (i.e., routine decision-making and close supervision), which are also negatively related to major incidents.

Heterogeneity. Heterogeneity is positively associated with conflict among teachers; and when organizational size is controlled, the positive association with incidents reaches significance ($\tau_p = .25$), as does the association with disputes ($\tau_p = .21$). The association with major incidents, however, is negative ($\tau = -.21$).

It is not immediately clear why there are fewer major incidents in heterogeneous schools. Perhaps one answer is that heterogeneity tends to be associated with close supervision and also with the proportion of faculty seeing each other socially, both of which are inversely related to the occurrence of major incidents.

Interpersonal Structure

Lunching patterns. The proportion of a faculty who lunch together "very frequently" is significantly associated only with the number of disputes. Controlling for school size, the correlation with heated discussions is also significant, but then the correlation with disputes decreases. The positive relationship with the dispute ratio holds up only in the less professional schools. Major incidents occur less often in more sociable schools, the relationship being stronger in less professional ($\tau = -.35$) and in less bureaucratic schools ($\tau = -.25$) than in the more professional and more bureaucratic schools. Apparently the situation that provides an opportunity for open discussion—in the absence of other tension-producing factors, such as those associated with the more professional and more bureaucratic organizations—also helps to counteract the development of major incidents.

The schools were divided into high and low groups on the proportion of their faculty who had been in the school more than four years. The positive correlations between lunching frequency and each measure of conflict (except major incidents) apply only to the more experienced faculties; in less experienced faculties, the relationships are all negative. It is in more experienced faculties, therefore, that frequent lunching is associated with conflict. In less experienced faculties, most conflict (again except for major incidents) tends to decrease with interaction.

Social occasions. The facilitating effects of interaction can be seen even more clearly when the proportion of faculty who "very frequently" see one another socially is used as an index of the informal interaction system. That measure is positively associated with total tensions, severe disagreement, total incidents, disputes, heated discussions, conflicts between teachers and administrators, conflicts among teachers, and conflicts involving authority issues. The association with major incidents reaches statistical significance when professional orientation of the faculty is controlled ($\tau_p = .25$). However, this association is found primarily in less bureaucratic organizations ($\tau = .36$), compared to $\tau = -.12$ in more bureaucratic organizations. Controlling for professional orientation reduces some of the other associations, notably the correlation with disputes ($\tau_p = .14$).

Since both social interaction and conflict were associated with organizational size, this variable was taken into account. It was expected that personnel in smaller, undifferentiated schools would be more likely to face similar problems than personnel in larger schools, where social life tends to form around cliques rather than to reflect school-wide cohesiveness. Controlling for size reduces the correlation of sociability with disputes ($\tau_p = .14$) and with conflicts between teachers and administrators ($\tau_p = .17$). The positive direction of the correlation remains, however, and in four of the correlations, the correlation remains statistically significant. The correlation between sociability and heated discussions is not affected by size (τ_p = .38). Sociability, therefore, seems to be connected with conflict independently of organization size.

DISCUSSION

The results reported here are necessarily tentative and exploratory; but descriptive studies which consider a large number of variables are needed to identify variables that deserve priority in a conflict model. Such studies reveal complexities that must be incorporated in the model. At the very least, further consideration needs to be given to developing (1) a typology of organizational variables based on their relation to conflict, (2) a catalogue of contextual properties that influence the relationship of each variable with conflict, and (3) a typology of organizational conflict.

Typologies of Variables

This paper has concentrated on internal structural variables, rather than social-psychological or contextual variables. Clearly, future studies should compare the relative significance of these different classes of variables in explaining conflict, but the data reported here indicate that structural variables are relevant to organizational conflict.

Gamson[43] proposed that three types of structural variables are relevant in explaining community conflict:

1. *Conductive variables* which permit or facilitate conflict.
2. *Variables associated with organizational strain:* i.e., structural variables that generate conflict.
3. *Integrative variables:* i.e., structural variables that inhibit or prevent conflict.

A correlational analysis using a small number of cases cannot demonstrate whether a particular variable is a cause or a consequence of conflict. However, based on the consistency between these data and other interpretations in the literature, a tentative first approximation can be attempted.

For example, organizational size, specialization, hierarchy, complexity, staff additions, and heterogeneity seem to contribute to organizational *strain;* participation in decision making and cohesive peer relations seem to *facilitate* conflict if it is present. Close supervision also might be included in this category, except for major incidents. Experience and close supervision (to the extent that the latter is associated with reductions in major incidents) are *integrative* variables. Standardization and rules logically might be integrative as well, but under some conditions they appear to be more closely associated with strain than with integration.

Contextual Properties

The indeterminateness of some of the variables in the preceding classification highlights the fact that the same variable may be a source of strain in one context and integrative in another. For example, in both the less professional and the more bureaucratic schools, as bureaucratization increased most forms of conflict diminished; while in the more professional and the less bureaucratic schools, the bureaucratization was positively associated with conflict.

Standardization, emphasis on rules, and close supervision all seem to be associated with tension under conditions where they are least compatible with an organization's tradition and with the belief of employees in their right of self-direction, that is, in the less bureaucratic and in the more professional schools. It is possible that rules are created where a high level of tension already exists, and that attempts to impose rules in professionally oriented, relatively bureaucratic settings may be further provocations. On the other hand, attempts to control conflict seem to be more effective in the more bureaucratic settings, where rules are likely to reinforce other control measures, and in the less professional schools.

Gamson[44] argued that rules are more likely to be used in conflictful situations, because close supervision aggravates intrapersonal problems in difficult situations. However, the data reported here indicate that a supervisory practice that is effective in reducing major incidents in the less professional and less bureaucratic schools fails to contain conflict—and perhaps may aggravate it—in more professional and more bureaucratic schools. While supervision may reduce major incidents in the more bureaucratic and less professional schools, it will be less effective in the opposite types of schools. Moreover, close supervision was positively associated with both standardization ($\tau = .26$) and emphasis on rules ($\tau = .26$).

The extent of hierarchy and staff expansion was more closely associated with conflict in less bureaucratic schools than in more bureaucratic ones. An organization becoming bureaucratized may be more vulnerable than one already bureaucratized to changes in personnel and in its hierarchical structure. Furthermore, both specialization and complexity were more closely associated with conflict in the more professional schools than in the less professional ones; and in the case of complexity, the correlation was higher in the more bureaucratized than in the less bureaucratized organizations.

Finally, the conflict-facilitating effects of peer-group interaction appeared to be limited to the less professional schools and to schools with older faculties; in the younger and professionally oriented faculties, peer-group interaction is associated with less conflict.

Types of Conflict

The various structural variables were associated with conflict in different ways, depending on the type of conflict, i.e., the members involved, and the form and intensity of conflict. Minor disagreements tended to differ from overt disputes; more important, major incidents formed a pattern which tended to be in a direction opposite from that of most other forms of conflict. Since this study considered only routine staff conflicts arising during the normal course of work, it is possible that teacher strikes might show still a different pattern.

Moreover, the data repeatedly indicated that a given organizational characteristic affected relationships among teachers in very different ways from the way it affected relationships between teachers and administrators. For example, although organizational size, staff additions, standardization, and complexity were all positively associated with conflict between teachers and administrators, none of these variables were associated with conflict among teachers themselves. On the other hand, the effect of the heterogeneity of faculty backgrounds was more evident in the increased rate of conflict among teachers than between teachers and administrators.

Conditions such as these complicate the relationship between organizational characteristics and conflict, but their identification illustrates one way in which exploratory descriptive research can contribute to the development of a model that can explain organizational conflict. It is very probable that an accumulation of such empirical evidence must precede the development of an adequate model.

Notes

1. Eugene Litwak, "Models of Bureaucracy Which Permit Conflict," *American Journal of Sociology*, LXVII (1961), 177-85; Ralf Dahrendorf, "Out of Utopia: Toward a Reorientation of Sociological Analysis," *ibid.*, LXIV (1958), 115-27; Lewis Coser, "Social Conflict and the Theory of Social Change," *The British Journal of Sociology*, VII (1957), 197-207; Jessie Barnard, "Where Is the Modern Sociology of Conflict?" *American Journal of Sociology*, LVI (1950), 11-16.

2. Ralf Dahrendorf, *Class and Class Conflict in Industrial Society* (Stanford, Calif.: Stanford University Press, 1958).

3. Ronald G. Corwin, *Militant Professionalism; A Study of Organizational Conflict in High Schools* (New York: Appleton-Century-Crofts, 1970).

4. Robert Dubin, "Stability of Human Organization," in Mason Haire (ed.), *Modern Organizational Theory* (New York: Wiley, 1959).

5. James D. Thompson, "Organizational Management of Conflict," *Administrative Science Quarterly*, IV (1960), 389-409.

6. Fred E. Katz, "The School as a Complex Organization," *Harvard Educational Review*, XXXIV (1964), 428-55.

7. James March and Herbert Simon, *Organizations* (New York: Wiley, 1958).

8. Harrison White, "Management Conflict and Sociometric Structure," *American Journal of Sociology*, LXVII (1961), 185-99.

9. Robert L. Kahn, "Field Studies of Power in Organizations," in Robert L. Kahn and Elise Boulding (eds.), *Power and Conflict in Organizations* (New York: Basic Books, 1964), pp. 52-66.

10. White, "Management Conflict."; Michel Crozier, *The Bureaucratic Phenomenon* (Chicago: University of Chicago Press, 1964); March and Simon, *Organizations*.

11. Chris Argyris, "Human Relations in a Bank," *Harvard Business Review*, XXXII (1954), 63-72.

12. William A. Gamson, "Rancorous Conflict in Community Politics," *American Sociological Review*, XXXI (1966), 71-81.

13. Clagget Smith and Aguz N. Ari, "Organizational Control Structure and Member Consensus," *American Journal of Sociology*, LXIX (1964), 623-38; Victor Thompson, "Hierarchy, Specialization and Organizational Conflict," *Administrative Science Quarterly*, V (1961), 485-521.

14. James Thompson, "Organizational Management"; Katz, "School as Complex Organization."

15. Kenneth Boulding, "A Pure Theory of Conflict Applied to Organizations," in Kahn and Boulding, *Power and Conflict*, pp. 136-45.

16. Kahn, "Field Studies of Power."

17. Alvin Gouldner, "Organizational Tensions," in Robert Merton (ed.), *Sociology Today* (New York: Basic Books, 1959), pp. 400-28.

18. James Q. Wilson, "Innovation in Organization: Notes toward a Theory," in James D. Thompson (ed.), *Approaches to Organizational Design* (Pittsburgh, Pa.: University of Pittsburgh Press, 1966), pp. 193-216.

19. Henry A. Landsberger, "The Horizontal Dimension in Bureaucracy," *Administrative Science Quarterly*, VI (1961), 299-332.

20. Joseph Ben-David, "Professional Role of the Physician in Bureaucratized Medicine: A Study in Role Conflict," *Human Relations*, XI (1958), 255-74; Ronald G. Corwin, "The Professional Employee: Study of Conflict in Nursing Roles," *American Journal of Sociology*, LXVII (1961), 604-15; Roy G. Francis and Robert C. Stone, *Service and Procedure in Bureaucracy* (Minneapolis: University of Minnesota Press, 1956); Mary E. Goss, "Influence and Authority among Physicians," *American Sociological Review*, XXVI (1961), 39-50; Leonard Reissman, "A Study of Role Conception in a Bureaucracy," *Social Forces*, XXVII (1949), 305-10.

21. C.M. Arensberg and R. Macgregor, "Determination of Morale in an Industrial Company," *Applied Anthropology*, I(1942), 12-34.

22. H.S. Becker, "The Teacher in the Authority System of the Public School," *Journal of Educational Sociology*, XXVII (1953), 128-41.

23. James S. Coleman, *Community Conflict* (Glencoe, Ill.: Free Press, 1957).

24. Gamson, "Rancorous Conflict."

25. Kahn, "Field Studies of Power."

26. Alvin Gouldner, "Cosmopolitans and Locals: Toward an Analysis of Latent Social Roles—I." *Aministrative Science Quarterly*, II (1957), 281-306.

27. Crozier, *Bureaucratic Phenomenon.*

28. Gerald H. Moeller and W.W. Charters, "Relation of Bureaucratization to Sense of Power among Teachers," *Administrative Science Quarterly*, X (1966), 444-65.

29. Gouldner, "Organizational Tensions."

30. Peter Blau and W. Richard Scott, *Formal Organizations* (San Francisco: Chandler, 1962), p. 73.

31. Gouldner, "Cosmopolitans and Locals."

32. William A. Rushing, "Organizational Rules and Surveillance: Propositions in Comparative Organizational Analysis," *Administrative Science Quarterly*, X (1966), 423-43.

33. Ronald G. Corwin, "Militant Professionalism, Initiative and Compliance in Public Education," *Sociology of Education*, XXXVIII (1965), 310-31.

34. Howard Becker and Blanche Geer, "Latent Culture: A Research Note," *Administrative Science Quarterly*, V (1960), 304-13.

35. James Thompson, "Organizational Management."

36. Becker and Geer, "Latent Culture."

37. Bernard Levenson, "Bureaucratic Succession," in Amitai Etzioni (ed.), *Complex Organizations: A Sociological Reader* (New York: Holt, Rinehart and Winston, 1961), pp. 262-75; Richard O. Carlson, *Executive Succession and Organizational Change: Place-Bound and Career-Bound Superintendents of Schools* (Chicago: Midwest Administration Center, The University of Chicago, 1961), pp. 30-35.

38. March and Simon, *Organizations.*

39. Gamson, "Rancorous Conflict."

40. Corwin, *Staff Conflict.*

41. Gamson, "Rancorous Conflict."

42. Coleman, *Community Conflict.*

43. Gamson, "Rancorous Conflict."

44. *Ibid.*

COMMENT / The Role of Organizational Conflict in a Large Urban School System

James H. Lytle

I should like to respond to the Corwin study in two ways: first as a piece of research, and then in relation to conflict within the school system and the school where I work.

THE CORWIN STUDY

The question to which the Corwin study is addressed is whether certain organizational characteristics predict the amount of conflict within an organization. For example, Corwin expects and finds a relationship between the "number of levels in the hierarchy of authority" in an organization and the amount of conflict in it. His study is appropriate to this text because it was conducted in 28 high schools in Pennsylvania, Ohio, Michigan, and Indiana. The intent of the research is to test a set of constructs and, with them, elaborate theories of organizational behavior.

Corwin never makes clear whether his intent is to study conflict in an objective, nonpejorative way, or whether he considers conflict as an undesirable element in organizational life that might be eliminated by careful organizational design. The result is that his study gives the impression, because the word *conflict* itself has pejorative connotations, that conflict is undesirable and can be reduced through careful planning. My own view is that a school without conflict between staff members would be a sterile place and a poor model of real-world organizational life for its students. If one were to use the findings of the Corwin study to provide the rationale for designing a low-conflict high school, it would have the following characteristics: small size, few authority levels, no department heads, minimal division of labor, less standardization and more latitude for the use of teacher discretion, an older, experienced, homogeneous, and stable faculty, no lunch period (since these provide a forum for conflict), and a prohibition of social interaction among staff outside the school. That suggests a one-room school house with a sixty-year-old teetotaling spinster as principal-teacher-custodian. As a matter of fact, anyone who has had experience working with secondary alternative programs would recognize several of these characteristics as ones considered desirable for alternative programs. On the other hand, anyone who has worked in secondary alternatives is likely to be very familiar with staff conflict and hard pressed to accept the notion that such characteristics reduce conflict.

A second problem is that Corwin's study does not attend to several major sources of conflict in schools. He focuses on teachers and administrators, but there is no recognition of teacher organizations, particularly unions, in the discussion of "organizational complexity" or "emphasis on rules." To conclude that there is "neither conflict over authority issues nor teacher-administration conflict in schools where rules are emphasized" is to neglect strong-union school systems. In addition, he does not examine conflict between students and staff, between parents and staff, and between community and school. In failing to do so, he overlooks the possibility that many of his hypotheses may have alternate explanations. I do not deny that his findings might be replicated in a city like Philadelphia, but I would be very reluctant to say that they were substantiated because of a relationship between organizational characteristics and teacher-administrator conflict. It is possible that the reason conflict between teachers and administrators increases as the size of a school increases is increased parental or community pressure on the school staff. Similarly, one 4,000-student Philadelphia high school may be in turmoil because of racial conflicts between groups of students and staff, while another high school of the same size with a racially homogeneous student population may be calm. Many factors explain conflict in schools—social class; ethnic, political, or philosophic differences between staff or students; community or parental expectations for a school; pressures from the mayor or city council that the schools be used for patronage; and a jurisdictional dispute between rival unions, among others.

As Corwin indicates, the organization characteristics he examines might even be considered as having been developed in response to various sorts of conflict and as having served to reduce, not increase, conflict. A union contract which mandates civil service hiring procedures controls the patronage powers of school and government administrators and reduces conflict over selection and placement of staff. A college guidance office may be established in a high school to provide a buffer between parents and school staff. So "emphasis on rules" and "specialization" may have reduced conflict, not increased it. Corwin's study is a one-shot design that gives no indication whether conflict has increased or decreased in schools in relation to changes in organizational characteristics over periods of time.

CONFLICT WITHIN THE SCHOOL DISTRICT OF PHILADELPHIA

For my part, I would like to consider conflict in its dictionary-defined context—clash or collision, being at opposition or variance, discord or antagonism. My contention would be that conflict is unavoidable in a large urban school district, that it is recognized as a necessary and perhaps not wholly undesirable fact of life, and that many of the discernible characteristics of the school system reflect an acceptance of the omnipresence of conflict. Further, the "system" has developed mechanisms that allow it to cope with conflict, to survive, and occasionally to change in ways that will reduce conflict and perhaps, although not necessarily, improve its effectiveness. Examples of such mechanisms at several levels of the organization demonstrate my point.

The Board

Starting from the top, the school board in Philadelphia has the authority to enter into contracts and obligate expenses, but it does not have the power to raise revenue through taxation (it is fiscally dependent). The city council and state legislature have the authority to provide funds for the schools, but not to manage the activities of the schools. One result of this situation is a politically convenient mechanism for conflict management. Say, as is indeed the fact, that the State Human Relations Commission orders the school district to desegregate through an extensive cross-bussing plan. The board can express sympathy with the commission, but contend that it does not have the money to implement such a plan. The city council and state legislature can contend that each is already providing more than it can afford to the school district for general operations and refuse to provide funding for the added cost of bussing. The result is a stalemate. Blame is diffused across several agencies, and a politically unpalatable program is avoided. Which is to say that the fiscally dependent status of the board of education might be viewed as an expedient for conflict management.

Similarly, in teacher contract negotiations, the board can legitimately bargain with the teachers, but it does not have the authority to provide funds for increased costs in a new contract. The result is a contract negotiating process that ultimately involves the board, the city council, the mayor, the state legislature, and the governor. And again blame and responsibility can be diffused over several agencies.

Central Administration

In his study, Corwin found a relationship between the number of departments in a school and the amount of conflict. The relationship seems to apply to the central office in Philadelphia. There, changes in the organization chart give a clue to a common central office mechanism for dealing with conflict. In the late 1960's, for example, a large Office of Community Affairs existed to deal with militant black political groups and their counterparts in white neighborhoods. In 1972 that office was phased out, a sign that the schools and district offices were once again capable of dealing with most community pressures. On the other hand, an Office of Labor Relations has emerged in the central office in response to the increasing power of the teachers' union and other unions. Yet over that period the core of the central administrative organization has remained stable.

The District Superintendent

The School District of Philadelphia, like many urban school systems, is a three-tiered organization which in itself reflects a system for conflict management. Central administration is primarily responsible for the allocation of resources (money and personnel). Schools are responsible for the utilization of these resources in a way that provides the best possible program for students. Intermediate between central office and the schools is the district office which has jurisdiction over thirty to forty schools. But the district office has virtually no control over either budget or personnel. Instead it functions to implement, mitigate, and interpolate the decisions of the central office affecting schools, and to reduce the "noise" from schools toward central office. Thus the district superintendent spends the majority of his time mediating—between schools and central office, between principals and teachers, between parents and schools, between community groups with conflicting purposes, and so forth.

For example, a group of parents at a neighborhood elementary school were upset because students from a nearby junior high school were waiting outside the elementary school at dismissal time each day and harassing the younger children. The parents complained to the district superintendent, and he changed the dismissal times at both schools to end the problem.

Schools

At the school level the basic mechanism for conflict management has become the "building committee," a representative group of teachers and nonprofessional staff who *must* be consulted by the principal, according to the terms of their contract, on any matters which affect their working conditions. A competent and cooperative building committee paired with a strong principal can provide a very effective agent for conflict resolution. On the other hand, an antagonistic building committee, especially when paired with an unskilled principal, can create tremendous conflict and even force a principal out of a school. The first but not the second situation is congruent with Corwin's finding that, "Teachers' participation in decisions about their classrooms . . . is inversely associated with the number of major incidents."

The Teacher Contract

The teacher contract provides a mirror for the major areas of past dispute with the administration. For example, there are lengthy sections on duty assignments, rostering (or scheduling), salaries, transfer policies, and meetings. A carefully delineated grievance procedure guarantees several levels of appeal in resolving disputes with the administration. On the other hand, there are almost no provisions regarding method of instruction or selection of curriculum. One could consider the contract as an elaborate set of rules and procedures providing mechanisms for protecting teacher autonomy and for manageing conflicts with administration when they do arise. These considerations seem to illustrate Corwin's finding that emphasis on rules is associated with total incidents, severe disagreements, and other conflict measures.

Secondary Students

Down at the bottom are students. Even they have developed mechanisms for handling conflicts with teachers and administrators. Each high school has a student council. These councils and all high school students are represented by a Union of Student Governments, and the Union of Student Governments has succeeded in having a Bill of Rights for students approved by the board. The most salient feature of the bill is that it provides a grievance procedure, modeled on the teacher contract, for resolving disputes between students and teachers or administrators; the appeal process goes ultimately to the superintendent.

The problem with the grievance procedure is that it does not provide for independent arbitration in case of an impasse. So when students recently lodged a formal complaint against a principal for suppressing an underground newspaper, the hearing officer for the grievance was a high-level administrator who was virtually compelled to support the principal rather than deal with the case on its merits. The students were not pleased by the decision, but the case had dragged on so long that they gave up.

High school students have developed another effective mechanism for reducing conflict—they simply cut class or drop out. Dropping out and cutting can be construed as indications that students have very little power to negotiate their grievances; in conflict situations with teachers or administrators they almost always lose.

CONFLICT MANAGEMENT IN AN ALTERNATIVE SCHOOL

I'd also like to consider briefly the role of conflict within the school I administer—an alternative elementary and middle school for inner-city students. The school is ungraded, with open space instructional areas and team teaching. The program emphasizes skill development and experiential learning, with an end to helping students become autonomous learners and responsible individuals. Teachers on our staff are required to participate in training groups led by the administrative staff. These groups encourage conflict between teachers and administrators (on the nondirective model developed by Herbert Thelen) on the premise that real teacher autonomy can only be achieved through dealing with the issue, "How do I *feel* when the leader doesn't lead." Only when this question has been worked through can teachers understand authority issues as they relate to inquiry teaching, open education, the helping relationship, and other matters.

Further, we assume that the best decisions are made when conflicting interests are represented in a decision-making group. (By "best decision" I mean generating and considering alternatives before reaching a decision which a majority of the parties accept.) For example, during the past year we formed a Space Utilization Committee of teachers whose charge was to develop a plan for using the available space in our building as effectively as possible. In addition, they were to develop a mechanism for allocating instructional spaces to teachers. Although there were many conflicts within the committee during its work, its ultimate solution was more imaginative and realistic, and more acceptable to the rest of the staff, than an administratively derived solution would have been. Similarly, another staff committee has been able to develop a flexible schedule which gives teachers (and to a degree students) a great deal of control over the use of their time.

Another of our concerns is that our teachers come to accept conflict with students as inevitable. Since schools (fortunately) do not control such things as students' home lives, behavior on the way to school, and genetic composition, it is only reasonable to expect conflicts between students, and between students and teachers. These conflicts ought to be resolved in the classroom, not referred to others. This requires that teachers be able to depersonalize high-affect situations and to manage conflict in ways that reflect rational, levelheaded problem solving. We view these abilities as among the most important things we can teach our students.

CONCLUSION

To review my argument, I assume that conflict is a part of life in the School District of Philadelphia. At every level, mechanisms and rules and procedures, both formal and informal, have evolved to allow the resolution of discord. I view these as evidence of the system's adaptiveness—its ability to maintain itself despite continuing pressures and conflicts. I suspect that these same characteristics apply to some degree in any large organization, and, that being so, I see the real challenge not in developing organizational structures that minimize conflict, but rather in learning to deal with conflict in productive ways.

My concern is not the fact of conflict but rather the way conflict is handled when it occurs. As an educator my interest is not in human engineering through organizational designs; instead, it is in modeling and teaching conflict resolution in ways that preserve the dignity of all the individuals involved, whether they be students, teachers, or administrators. To accomplish this, educators need to be expert in group process techniques, negotiations, and such change strategies as transactional evaluation. Each of these approaches uses the energy inherent in conflict to improve the functioning and output of organizations.

11 / Attitude Consensus and Conflict in an Interest Group: An Assessment of Cohesion

Norman R. Luttbeg and *Harmon Zeigler*

In America, interest groups operate within the democratic frame of reference. Like all political organizations, they are accorded more legitimacy when they can show that they are representative of the attitudes and values of a particular segment of the population. Consequently, the leaders of interest groups frequently spend a great deal of time explaining just how democratic their organizations are. If one examines the testimony of interest group leaders at state and national legislative hearings, he is likely to find that much of it is begun with an introductory statement explaining that the leadership of the testifying group is merely the voice of the membership. The personal values of the interest group leader are played down, and his function as representative (as distinguished from delegate) is exaggerated.

On the other hand, relatively few political interest groups have systematic and formalized means of ascertaining the desires of members. We know that most of the devices used to solicit member opinion are not very effective. Truman has shown that the affairs of most interest groups are run on a day-to-day basis by a fraction of the total membership. The mass of the membership takes a relatively passive role with regard to the formation of public policies by the organization.[1]

Reprinted from *American Political Science Review*, LX (No. 3, September 1966), 655-66.

Communication between leaders and followers is spasmodic and cannot provide efficient guidelines for the actions of leaders. Whether or not leadership of an organization seeks to become a manifestation of Michel's iron law of oligarchy, the realities of communication within an organization suggest that most of the communication undertaken by leaders will be with other members of the leadership clique rather than with the larger body of followers in the group.

This situation is not necessarily dysfunctional for the organization. By many criteria the leader's decision is superior to that of the average member. Leaders have more time to give to matters of special concern to the organization. The information on which they make their decisions is likely to be more extensive than that of the average member, and they are likely to be more cognizant of the long-term impact of a particular decision. Unlike the average member, however, the leader's decision is complicated by his need to consider the extragroup and intragroup impact of his various alternative decisions and actions.

In the area of extragroup considerations, he must estimate the probable responses of other actors in the political process and the effect of these responses upon the chances of achieving a desired goal, assuming that he does not possess all capabilities of realizing this goal himself. Concerning intragroup considerations he must consider how the followers will respond to a decision. Will they be aware of it? Do they care about the alternatives, and, if so, how will they respond to a decision which is contrary to their desires?

Even in the absence of efficient consultative mechanisms, leaders and followers exist in a functional relationship.[2] That is to say, leaders are limited by the followers' expressed or latent values and expectations. Regardless of the efficiency of corrective mechanisms and apart from how extensive the violation of the followers' values must be before the corrective mechanism comes into play, the leader's position is less secure if he fails to satisfy the followers. If another leader is vying with him for the followers' support, the implications of failing to satisfy the followers are even more threatening. In a political interest group, the functional relationship of leaders to followers is keyed to the necessity for cohesion as a weapon in extragroup competition. The actuality or at least the appearance of unity is essential.[3]

Assuming that the leader desires to maintain an extragroup competitive position, he will therefore undertake efforts toward the fostering of intragroup cohesion. In a voluntary organization, one of the prime requisites for this cohesion is the extent to which the membership is satisfied with the performance of leaders.[4] There are three ways in which a leader may satisfy the desires of an organization's membership. First, he may unconsciously act consistently with their desires. For example, he may decide to act on the basis of his evaluation of extragroup factors in such a way that the membership will be entirely satisfied. Second, he may respond entirely in terms of his personal attitudes and beliefs and, because he so accurately reflects the attitudes of his membership, again satisfy their desires. Third, a leader may consciously seek to do what he believes the membership of the organization desires. His success in satisfying the membership by this effort is dependent upon the accuracy of his perceptions of their attitudes and expectations.

RESEARCH DESIGN

In this paper we examine the latter two dynamics by which leaders can satisfy members. Our data were gathered from the membership of the Oregon Education Association. Three sets of information were collected: the beliefs and attitudes of the members of the Association, the beliefs and attitudes of the leaders of the Association, and the perception of the attitudes of the members as held by the leaders. The analysis consists of comparing these three sets of information and noting changes in their interrelationships on different attitudes. The nature of the analysis is illustrated by Figure 11-1.

The sample of group members used in this study is a clustered stratified random sample of 803 high school teachers. This represents 14 percent of the high school teachers in Oregon.[5]

The sample of leaders includes all nine of the OEA's top administrative officials. These are the members of the executive staff, which

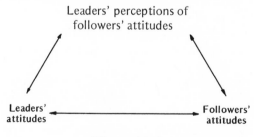

Figure 11-1
Nature of the analysis

is employed by the organization's Board of Trustees. Its official responsibility is to implement the policies of the Representative Council, which consists of 200 representatives elected by local teachers' organizations. The Representative Council is the official policy-making body of the Association. However, both the Representative Council, which meets only once a year, and the Board of Trustees, which is supposed to deal with the specifics of the council's directives, are part-time functions. Thus, the permanent administrative staff is often forced to act in areas in which directives are vague or nonexistent. As is frequently the case in formal organizations, therefore, the permanent administrative staff has great flexibility and is a major delineator of policy.

In interviewing the leaders, we used a majority of the questions included in the teachers' interview schedule. Certain modifications in wording were made to allow for differences in organizational position. Leaders were first asked to answer the questions in terms of their own attitudes. They were then asked to take the point of view of the "average teacher" answering the same questions as they thought the "average teacher" would answer them. Only one of the leaders displayed any difficulty in assuming this attitude perspective; he had difficulty in keeping from answering questions in terms of what the teachers *should* believe rather than what he thought they actually *did* believe. The little difficulty the leaders experienced in answering these questions is evidence that the distinction between personal attitudes and the attitudes of the membership is a meaningful one for them.

These three sets of attitudes (teachers' attitudes, leaders' attitudes, and leaders' perceptions of teachers' attitudes) are studied in four attitudinal contexts. They are:

1. Mandates for organizational action,
2. Expectations and satisfaction with the direction of leadership behavior,
3. Abstract political values, and
4. Norms of teachers' political participation

The mandates for organizational action consist of two parts: expectations of behavior on the part of leaders themselves and expectations of action undertaken by teachers' organizations. In both cases, the satisfaction of the members with a particular action is dependent upon a congruence of the attitudes of the leaders with the actual attitudes of the followers.

Attitudes related to satisfaction with the direction of leadership are concerned with three of the Oregon Education Association's most strenuous activities; efforts toward salary improvement, efforts to raise teacher standards and accreditation, and efforts toward the establishment of a state sales tax with the revenues going to the public schools.

Abstract political values describe a set of attitudes, many of which are clichés often used by persons to persuade others to accept their position. They represent the basic "truths" of both the conservative and liberal points of view. A leader perceiving the membership as adhering to conservative values is ascribing conservatism to the membership and at the same time indicating that he believes an argument for action based upon these values would draw support from the membership.

The attitudes dealing with teachers' political participation concerned a broad set of politically related activities which might be undertaken by teachers in the classroom or during leisure time. The leadership's ability to satisfy members in this regard will be reflected in their efforts or lack of efforts to support teachers in trouble in their local communities for various political activities and in the formal or informal articulation of a professional ethic with respect to these activities.

Although it would be possible to analyze these data using contingency tables, the existence of 50 attitude items and three comparisons for each item would tax the reader's ability to follow the analysis. A single measure which characterizes the relationship on each comparison of attitudes is therefore required. Although numerous measures of association and correlation were considered for this purpose, we settled upon Kendall's tau chi (τ_c).[6] This measure has its faults, the principal one being that its maximum value is dependent upon the marginals of the table. Our tables frequently have marginals of 803 and 9 (the N's of our two samples). Such great differences will yield a correlation of only .044 for a perfect relationship on a 2×2 table. Since we are more interested in finding a measure to characterize the comparison of attitude distributions of leaders and followers than in using the measure as a test of statistical significance, it was decided to rely upon a new measure, τ_c over τ_c maximum.

As we are using this measure in comparing the distributions of attitudes of leaders and followers, a high correlation would indicate a strong relationship between attitudes and the person holding them. That is to say, a high correlation would indicate that leaders hold attitudes different from those of the followers. The sign of the measure will indicate the direction of this difference. Notice that a correlation of .000 indicates that leaders share the attitudes of the followers or that the two sets of attitudes compared have the same distribution.

Some may inquire of the statistical significance of the findings. There are two problems with the application of statistical significance tests to these data. First, one of the samples is not a sample at all but the universe of the administrative leaders of the Oregon Education Association. Thus, with no sampling error contributed by the leadership sample, the comparing of leaders' and followers' attitudes does not necessitate as strong a relationship to achieve statistical significance as would be normally required. In the data comparing leaders' attitudes and their perceptions of followers' attitudes, clearly no statistical significance tests are applicable because the differences are real differences for the universe of leaders. Even if the leaders did constitute a sample, their small number places an unnecessarily strict requirement on the strength of the relationship necessary to achieve statistical significance.[7] In general, therefore, greater reliance is placed upon the consistency of a relationship within an attitude area rather than on the statistical significance of any one item. However, those single-item relationships which are significant are indicated by a small "s" in the tables (the Kruskal-Wallis h test is used to test statistical significance).

FINDINGS

Leaders' perceptions of their roles. Before comparing the three sets of attitudes contained in this study, some discussion should be made of the leaders' perceptions of their roles within the organization. We refer here to the extent to which leaders believe they should act primarily in accordance with their own personal values rather than trying to reflect the desires of those whom they lead. We are asking whether leaders believe they should be delegates or representatives.[8]

Two questions were included in the leaders' interview schedule dealing with the problem of whose attitudes should be acted upon, those of the leaders or those of the followers. In one question the leaders were offered a brief dialogue between two persons, one arguing that a leader must do as the members wish and the other arguing that the leader must do what he personally believes to be correct. The leader was given the opportunity of selecting the argument which he found most satisfactory. Only one leader answered that the membership's desires should rule. Five answered that the leader should do what he personally believes to be right, although they added the comment that they thought the problem would occur very infrequently. Three of the leaders said that, if this problem could not be resolved, the leader should resign.

The second question approached the problem from a slightly different angle and achieved very dissimilar results. The leaders were asked if they felt the organization should do pretty much what the average teacher wants, what the more influential teachers want, what the school administrators want, or what they themselves want. The "pretty much" phrase in the first alternative apparently was easier to accept than the wording in the other question, as five leaders chose this alternative. Two altered the second response to indicate that they believed they should do what the "more informed" teachers wanted while two indicated that they would prefer to do what they themselves thought best.

It would seem, therefore, that the leaders accept the maxim that they should do what the followers want, but they are also jealous of their autonomy to do what they think best. There appears to be a clear internalized conflict between the representatives and delegate roles. Obviously the best of all possible worlds for the leaders would be perfect consensus between them and the members. In the absence of this consensus, they appear unable to reach a clear resolution of the conflict and to find a stable definition of their roles.

The leaders' acute awareness of the problem of communication with followers is indicated by a final question. Leaders were asked what policies of the Oregon Education Association they were most dissatisfied with. Seven volunteered the answer that the greatest problem was the OEA's failure to be true to the desires of its membership. Two of the leaders who gave this response explicitly criticized the administrative structure for not administering impartially the policy decisions of the Representative Council. It appears, therefore, that the representative nature of the organization is not only meaningful to leaders but is also potentially divisive of the leadership.

Expectations concerning organizational activity. The exact nature of this potential conflict within the organization will become clearer as we proceed to the analysis of the four attitude areas. We will first consider the mandates for organizational activity.

Table 11-1 presents the correlations for each of the attitude comparisons for each of the questions. In this, as in the tables which follow, the first column presents the objective attitudes, the "real world," and thus measures the extent of actual conflict. The second column shows the degree to which leaders are accurate in their perceptions of followers' attitudes, while the third column measures the extent of conflict as seen by the leaders. The negative sign of the correlation means that the bottom set of attitudes is more heavily weighted in the direction of believing that leaders of the organization *should* undertake a particular action. For example, in the first column a negative sign means that leaders believe more than the followers that they or the organization should undertake a given activity. In the second column the negative sign means that the leaders perceive the followers as being more in favor of undertaking a particular action than they actually are. The positive sign in the second column means that the followers are more in favor of undertaking a particular activity than the leaders believe them to be. A negative sign in the third column means that the leaders perceive the followers as more supportive of a particular activity than the leaders are. A positive sign in the third column indicates the reverse.

The table indicates that, with the single exception of eliminating from the OEA staff people believed to be politically extreme, the leaders are more inclined to favor the involvement of the organization in each of the actions presented. This is shown by the fact that in seven of the nine cases the signs of the first column are negative. The first three of these items are the more clearly "professional" of the set. They involve the traditional academic values of freedom of expression and the protection of teachers against hostile forces in the community. These are at best *quasi*-political activities. Yet even here the followers are more restrained than the leaders. Note that on the question of eliminating political liberals from the OEA staff the followers are more in favor of such action than are the leaders. However, it is true that the greatest discrepancy between followers' and leaders' attitudes occur on those questions involving the more purely political aspects of the organization, such as endorsing political candidates, taking sides on public issues, and taking part in the electoral activities of school board members.

With regard to these political activities, the followers are much more restrained than they are concerning more purely educational activities. Granted that the distinction between quasi-political and political is arbitrary at best, the followers do appear to make it. Thus, they are much more inclined to support the activities of the OEA if it defends teachers against public attacks than they would be if the teachers' organization endorsed political candidates.

The glaring exception to the general reluctance of the teachers to support the OEA's political activities is on the question of lobbying. Here there is nearly perfect agreement between leaders and followers.

Lobbying is perceived by teachers to be an absolutely legitimate function of the organization. Teachers, therefore, are making a distinction between legislative politics and electoral politics.[9] The association is currently engaged in a vigorous lobbying program at the state legislative level. With regard to lobbying, it is interesting to notice that not only do the attitudes of the leaders and followers converge, but also the leaders perceive that the followers support the lobbying activities. This is indicated by the zero correlation in the second and third columns.

Notice also that with regard to the first three activities (fighting attacks on educational principles and methods, fighting against the dismissal of teachers, and defending teachers from public attacks) the leaders see *more* support among the teachers than actually exists.

TABLE 11-1. Comparison of the three attitude sets in the area of mandate for actions by leaders, teachers' organizations, and the OEA

| Questions | Sets of attitudes compared | | |
	Followers' attitudes vs. leaders' attitudes	Followers' attitudes vs. leaders' perceptions of followers' attitudes	Leaders' attitudes vs. leaders' perceptions of followers' attitudes
Leaders should:			
1. Fight attacks on educational principles and methods.	−.134	−.134	.000
2. Fight against dismissal of teachers.	−.073	−.073	.000
3. Defend teachers from public attacks from getting involved in controversial issues.	−.059	−.059	.000
4. Eliminate from staff political liberals.	+.284	+.061	−.222
5. Give helping hand to school board members coming up for election.	−.317(s)	+.211	+.528
Teachers' organizations should:			
6. Endorse political candidates.	−.419(s)	+.184	+.603
7. Take sides on public issues.	−.404(s)	+.221	+.625
OEA should:			
8. Endorse candidates in school elections.	−.387(s)	+.058	+.444
9. Try to influence legislation.	.000	.000	.000

Since the leaders overestimate the enthusiasm of followers, they see a consensus which does not hold true in the "real world." Hence the perfect correlation in the third column between the leaders' attitudes and their perceptions of teachers' attitudes is based upon faulty perceptions. This is not true with regard to the consensus about lobbying.

It is in the more purely electoral activities of the organization that discrepancies occur. Notice that on questions five, six, seven, and eight, the negative signs of the first column become positive signs in the second column. This means that, whereas leaders are more likely to want to engage in the electoral activities than are followers, the leaders perceive the followers as far more hesitant than the followers actually are. Consequently, these electoral activities can be contrasted with the professional and lobbying activities. In these professional and lobbying activities, the third column indicates that the leaders see little or no discrepancy between their point of view and the point of view of the followers, whereas the correlations on items five, six, seven, and eight in the third column indicate that the leaders see a considerable conflict between their values and those of the followers. With regard to these political activities, the leaders are correct in perceiving conflict although conflict also exists in educational activities but is missed by the leaders.

At this point in its organizational history, the OEA is in fact more likely to engage in professional and lobbying activities than it is in electoral activities. It is these activities in which the leaders see the followers as being entirely supportive of the organization, although they are correct only with regard to lobbying. If the OEA were to increase its electoral activities, therefore, it would be engaging in practices which are less favored by the followers. However, the fact that the teachers are perceived as being more reluctant to support these activities than they actually are might result in the leaders engaging in these activities to a lesser extent than would be tolerated by the followers.

Evaluations of organizational performance. Turning from the extent to which leaders and followers are in agreement as to what the organization should do, we consider now the relationships between sets of attitudes concerning the extent of satisfaction with the actual behavior of the leaders of the organization. In Table 11-2 a negative sign indicates that the bottom set of attitudes is less satisfied with the performance of the teachers' organization. A positive sign indicates that the bottom set is more satisfied.

In the first analysis, we found that the leaders consistently underestimated the followers' activism. In Table 11-2 we find a similar tendency with several notable exceptions. On the question of the importance of the OEA's role in getting improved salaries and benefits in the past, we find a great discrepancy between leaders' and followers' attitudes: the followers are inclined to give the OEA less credit than are the leaders. However, the second column shows that the leaders' perception is accurate. Hence, they perceive followers as exhibiting more dissatisfaction with past performance than the leaders do. Leaders, intimately involved in the successes and failures of

TABLE 11-2. Comparison of the three attitude sets in the areas of expectations and satisfaction with leadership's actions

	Sets of attitudes compared		
Questions	Followers' attitudes vs. leaders' attitudes	Followers' attitudes vs. leaders' perceptions of followers' attitudes	Leaders' attitudes vs. leaders' perceptions of followers' attitudes
1. How important do you think has been the role played by the OEA in getting improved salaries and benefits?	+.556(s)	+.026	−.667
2. How about the Teachers' Union; how important do you think its role was in getting improved salaries and benefits?	−.297	−.098	+.185
3. Do you think the OEA is doing enough to improve teachers' salaries and benefits?	−.332	−.444	−.111
4. How about the Teachers' Union; is it doing enough in improving teachers' salaries and benefits?	−.396	−.396	.000
5. Do you think the OEA is doing enough in its support for higher teacher standards and accreditation to improve professional status?	−.016	−.016	.000
6. Do you think there should be a state sales tax with the revenue going to the schools?	+.253	+.364	+.111

the organization, see their role as more significant than do the more passive followers. Only about one-third of the followers think that the OEA was "very important" in securing past benefits, whereas all the leaders are of this opinion.

With regard to current performance a different situation exists. The leaders are more dissatisfied with the performance of the organization and its constant fight for better salaries. Once again, however, they perceive more dissatisfaction among the followers than actually exists. Although accurate in their perceptions of teacher satisfaction with past performance, leaders fail in their evaluation of current satisfaction. In fact, 56 percent of the followers indicated that they think the OEA is doing enough about salaries. This is not exactly an overwhelming vote of confidence, but it is apparent that more satisfaction exists in reality than is perceived by the OEA leadership.

In view of the current conflict between teachers' unions and professional organizations for the loyalties of teachers, it is interesting to note that the OEA leaders are more likely to denigrate the efforts of the teachers' union than are the teachers themselves. This is indicated by the negative sign of the correlations in column one considering the role of the union in past and present efforts toward salary increases. Again column two tells us that in both of these cases leaders perceive that followers are more dissatisfied with the union than they actually are. This distinction between past and present produces some curious results in the third column, showing the extent of conflict perceived by leaders. While they exaggerate the extent of dissatisfaction on the part of followers, perhaps projecting their own desires more than an objective evaluation would indicate, they recognize that the followers are more impressed with past union performance than they (the leaders) are. Yet they persist in seeing perfect agreement between themselves and teachers concerning current union performance, an agreement which does not exist. These distortions lead the leadership to assume a "what-have-you-done-for-me-lately" attitude somewhat along the lines of old-fashioned bread-and-butter unionism. It seems likely that these perceptions will cause them to channel more of their resources into salary increase efforts at the risk of providing less satisfactory efforts in other areas. On the other hand this risk does not appear to be very great. For example, the leaders are extremely accurate in their perceptions of teacher satisfaction with regard to support for higher professional standards and accreditation. A consensus only slightly weaker than that regarding lobbying exists here.

The final item in the table dealing with the question of state sales tax enables us to return once again to lobbying. We may well ask "Lobbying for what?" The OEA has been strongly lobbying for a state sales tax with revenues going to the public schools, but only a slight majority (53 percent) of the teachers agree that a state sales tax should be enacted, while more than two-thirds of the leadership favor the tax. This is apparently an elite-derived effort enjoying only weak support from the followers. In this case, however, the leaders perceive far more support than actually exists. They actually believe that followers support this effort more than the leaders do, whereas the opposite is the case. Thus, although high consensus is achieved on the legitimacy of lobbying, leaders do not show a great capability of deciding how much effort should be devoted to the pursuit of certain policies by means of lobbying. The leaders want a sales tax, perceive the followers as wanting a sales tax, and pursue this effort vigorously. It is possible that, if the efforts to achieve a sales tax are continued with increased intensity, membership support might be reduced beyond the bare majority it enjoys now, and intragroup conflict may result. If this happens the perceptual errors of the leaders could prove costly.

Abstract political values. Up to this point we have been considering the explicit programs of the Oregon Education Association, and the extent to which there is a congruence between leaders' and followers' values with regard to these programs. Members of organizations, however, may have values which are not directly translatable into explicit programs but which nevertheless color the relationship between leaders and followers. The overall ideological pattern of leaders and followers is, therefore, a component in determining the extent to which leaders represent the followers' values. It is this assumption which leads us to inquire about abstract political values. The items in Table 11-3 are offered as important in the leaders' evaluations as to what programs might appeal to the followers and also what the nature of appeals to the membership for support on a given issue might be. On the basis of their content, the items are separated into those indicating conservatism and those indicating liberalism. The first seven questions are the conservative questions, and the last six are the liberal questions. For each group, a negative sign indicates that the bottom set of attitudes shows greater acceptance of the item.

Looking at the first column, it can readily be seen that the leaders are more likely to disagree with the conservative items and more likely to agree with the liberal items than are the followers. Furthermore, the high correlations in the third column show that the leaders believe that the followers differ greatly from them with regard to

TABLE 11-3. Comparison of the attitude sets in the area of orthodox values

| Questions | Sets of attitudes compared | | |
	Followers' attitudes vs. leaders' attitudes	Followers' attitudes vs. leaders' perceptions of followers' attitudes	Leaders' attitudes vs. leaders' perceptions of followers' attitudes
Conservative			
1. The American form of government may not be perfect, but it's the best type of government yet devised by man.	−.137	+.078	+.222
2. Democracy is considered the ideal form of government by most of the world.	−.160	−.658	−.407
3. Private enterprise could do better most of the things the government is now doing.	+.365	−.171	−.568
4. The participation of the federal government in local affairs leads to undesirable federal controls.	+.564(s)	−.389	−.926
5. Communism is a total evil.	+.142	−.466	−.630
6. People of most underdeveloped countries are by nature incapable of self-government.	+.303	−.226	−.506
7. Private enterprise is the only really workable system in the modern world capable of satisfying our economic needs.	+.257	−.182	−.469
Liberal			
8. Economic and social planning by government does not necessarily lead to dictatorship.	−.326	+.125	+.444
9. Man is the maker of his own society, such events as wars and depressions could be controlled by man.	−.122	+.161	+.259
10. The growth of large corporations make government regulation of business necessary.	−.190	+.088	+.309
11. We could increase spending for many government services without harming the nation's economy.	−.402	+.035	+.432
12. The federal government represents the needs of most people better than local government.	−.030	+.284	+.259
13. The government should increase its activities in matters of health, retirement, wages, and old-age benefits.	−.205	−.034	+.185

these items. Once again, however, the leaders' perceptions of teachers' attitudes tend to exaggerate the differences. In eleven of the thirteen cases, leaders perceive followers to be more conservative and less liberal than they actually are. Thus, although the OEA leaders are a biased section of the teachers with respect to their political and economic values, they tend to perceive their atypical posture as more extreme than it actually is. This discrepancy in perception is likely to influence the leaders to use more conservative appeals to the followers in urging support of particular programs than would be called for by an accurate inventory of their values.

Combined with the bread-and-butter perception described previously, this perceived conservatism of teachers leads the leaders into the path of heavy emphasis on salaries and other basic issues while at the same time forcing them to restrict their activities in the realm of expansion of organizational activities. If the leadership seeks to venture into untried areas which are not specifically related to educational problems, it may be hesitant to begin for fear that the programs are too liberal for the membership.

Of course, as Krech and Crutchfield point out, the degree of association between cognitive attitudes and action-orientated attitudes is not necessarily great.[10] Thus, a person holding conservative beliefs does not automatically favor conservative actions by government. To ascertain the extent to which abstract values are translatable into immediate preferences for governmental action, we administered the items from the Survey Research Center's domestic attitude scale.[11] As in the abstract value index, the leaders proved to be much more liberal than the followers. Also, the leaders saw the followers as not being as liberal as they actually are. In this case, however, the leaders are not so greatly more liberal and they do not see the followers as so greatly more conservative than they actually are. The main thrust of the conservatism scale is identical to that of the abstract political value index, but the discrepancies are not as great. It may be, therefore, that the leaders are less in danger of undercutting the cohesion of the organization should they lend its support to an explicit governmental program outside the realm of education-related issues. The danger to cohesion may be not so much in the undertaking of new programs but in the appeal to followers on the basis of their perceived conservatism.

The political role of the teacher. Teachers, like the holders of any social position, have perceptions of what is permissible behavior by holders of their social position. Others who do not hold this position also have expectations. The interaction of these two expectations constitutes a role. Table 11-4 presents the comparisons between the three sets of attitudes with regard to norms of teachers' political participation. A negative sign indicates that the bottom set of attitudes in the comparison favors teacher participation more than does the top set of attitudes.

Here we see a remarkably consistent pattern. Leaders are, in every case save one, more supportive of actions by teachers in these areas than are the teachers. This is even true of joining a teachers' union, but it is not true of striking to secure higher salaries and other benefits. In this latter case, the teachers are slightly more likely than leaders to be willing to undertake this activity and are much more likely to be willing to strike than leaders perceive them to be. This is the single example of followers being more "activist" than leaders to achieve liberal goals. In every other case, no matter what type of action is involved, leaders are more willing to take a risk, more willing to engage in controversial activity than are followers. When we examine the leaders' perceptions of followers' attitudes, we find once again the consistent pattern of underevaluation of the experimental nature of teachers. Leaders perceive teachers as being unlikely to engage in these activities whereas teachers themselves, although less anxious than leaders to take part in these activities, are more willing to do so than leaders believe them to be. Thus, the teachers are more willing to join teachers' unions, political party organizations, or racial organizations than leaders believe them to be.

CONCLUSIONS

To summarize the findings of this analysis, the following points may be offered. As is true of most organizations, the leaders of the Oregon Education Association are more active than the followers. They are more liberal than the followers, and they are more willing than the followers to expand the activities of the organization, but they consistently exaggerate the atypical nature of their position. They see the followers as being more conservative and restrained than they actually are. These discrepancies, both in perception and in actual attitudes, lead us to speculate as to how they came about. Is the relative activism of leaders a function of their social role, their organizational position, or their personality? It is certainly not feasible to argue that leadership positions somehow recruit more daring people. It is more feasible to seek explanations within the nature of the organization and the teaching profession. Consider, for example, the items dealing with political participation by teachers. Leaders

TABLE 11-4. Comparison of the attitude sets in the area of the norms of teachers' political participation

Questions	Sets of attitudes compared		
	Followers' attitudes vs. leaders' attitudes	Followers' attitudes vs. leaders' perceptions of followers' attitudes	Leaders' attitudes vs. leaders' perceptions of followers' attitudes
Teachers should if they want to:			
1. Join a teachers' union.	−.135	+.532(s)	+.667
2. Go on strike to secure higher salaries and other benefits.	+.067	+.317(s)	+.250
3. Join a political party organization.	−.036	+.186	+.222
4. Serve as party precinct worker in pre-election activities.	−.064	+.269	+.333
5. Publicly criticize local government officials.	−.268	+.510(s)	+.778
6. In a presidential election, outside school time, make speeches or give other services on the behalf of a candidate.	-.110	+.335(s)	+.444
7. Run for political office.	.104	+.451(s)	+.556
8. In a presidential election, explain to class reasons for preferring one candidate.	−.055	+.279	+.333
9. Belong to the NAACP or CORE.	−.129	+.316(s)	+.444
10. Take part in a CORE or NAACP demonstration, such as public picketing.	−.112	+.460(s)	+.571
11. Allow an atheist to address the class.	−.126	+.430(s)	+.556
12. Argue in class against the censoring of literature by people who feel it is pornographic.	−.226	+.039	+.306
13. Speak out in class against the John Birch Society and groups like it.	−.153	+.180	+.333
14. Speak in favor of nationalizing the steel industry and the railroads.	−.249	+.307	+.556
15. Speak in class in favor of the Medicare program.	−.169	+.276	+.444
16. Speak in class in favor of the United Nations.	−.043	+.291	+.333
17. Allow the distribution of anticommunist literature put out by the National Association of Manufacturers.	−.254	+.191	+.444
18. Speak in class favorably about socialism.	−.105	+.229	+.333
19. Argue in class that labor unions should be more regulated or controlled by the government.	-.158	+.176	+.333
20. Allow the distribution of anticommunist literature put out by the John Birch Society.	-.443(s)	+.123	+.556

would be subject to none of the pressures that teachers would feel from their community. Also, while teachers can recall relatively few cases in which the community made demands upon the school system for the dismissal of a teacher for engaging in controversial activity, those who can recall such incidents are of the opinion that the teachers' organization was ineffective in the defense of teachers. It is also true that the teachers look upon the local affiliates of the Oregon Education Association much more favorably than they look upon the state-wide organization which employs the leaders considered in this study. In arguing for organizational position as a fundamental contributor to differential perception, we draw added support from the reaction of the leaders to the competition of the union. Leaders behave in much the same fashion as political party leaders.[12] They are more emotionally committed to the organization than are the rank and file. Hence, they find it difficult to comprehend the problems of teaching and the restrictions traditionally imposed upon teachers by the community.

It might be useful to know something about the leaders' backgrounds. All have at one time been teachers and all have passed through some lower administrative position before achieving their present status. Most have taken graduate work, usually in educational administration. All earn in excess of ten thousand dollars per year. Thus, although they do have a teaching background, they are much more upwardly mobile than the average teacher and make more money. They are also substantially better educated. The upward mobility of the leaders of the OEA can be gleaned from the backgrounds of their fathers. Most of their fathers had less than a high school education and held low-status occupations. Thus holding a position in the OEA marks more of a step up than does teaching. Perhaps, therefore, the leaders consider themselves as more sophisticated and advanced than teachers.

When we consider the fact that serving as an OEA administrator is in a sense moving beyond a teaching position, the explanation offered above becomes more plausible. Combine this with the fact that leaders have interaction with a more heterogeneous environment and their perception of teachers becomes even more understandable. Unlike the teachers, who interact mostly with teachers, students, principals, and parents, the OEA administrative staff interacts with lobbyists, legislators, state officials, and national educational officials.

As a final alternative to the explanation offered above, we considered the possibility that, whereas the leaders incorrectly perceive the political values and political role perceptions of teachers, they may base their reactions upon communication with a biased sample. There are, of course, many different shades of opinion among teachers just as there are among the general public. Is it true that the OEA leaders interact with a segment of the teaching population which is more conservative and more restrained? If this is true, then their perceptions of followers' attitudes might not be a function of their social position, but might be the result of an unrepresentative sample of opinion being communicated to them. However, our evidence indicates quite clearly that there is no relationship between political conservatism and participation in organizational affairs. There is no evidence that the conservative teachers have any more interaction with OEA leaders than do the liberal teachers. Also, those teachers who take a restrained view of the political role of the teacher are no more likely to communicate with OEA leaders than are those teachers who take a more expansionist view.[13] Thus, we can say that there is no weighting of communication which comes to the attention of OEA leaders in favor of conservatism and restraint.

Assuming, therefore, that being a leader in an organization contributes to a discrepancy between leaders' and followers' attitudes, we may inquire finally into the possibility of having a democratic interest group without frequent and carefully supervised consultative mechanisms. Can leaders be representative simply because they intuitively comprehend what is required of them? In considering this question, let us note that, with the exception of the last table, the discrepancy between leaders' attitudes and followers' attitudes is generally *greater* than the errors made by leaders in perceiving these attitudes. Thus, OEA leaders operating entirely upon their personal values would not be representative of the values of their followers. On the other hand, if they adopted a purely representative role, they would become more conservative and restrained than the teachers would prefer. Yet, with the exception of the last set of attitudes, the error would be less than would be true if followers' wishes were ignored. That is to say, if they followed their understanding of followers' values, the resulting conservatism and restraint would be closer to the actual desires of teachers than would be true if leaders used their personal values as the sole criteria of judgment. "Virtual" representation in an interest group cannot serve as a substitute for actual representation, because the position of group leader contributes to the development of attitudes which differ from those of the followers.

Notes

The research reported here was made possible by a grant from the Center for the Advanced Study of Educational Administration, University of Oregon.

1. David B. Truman, *The Governmental Process* (New York: Alfred A. Knopf, Inc., 1951), pp. 129-39.

2. William Haythorn *et al.*, "The Effects of Varying Combinations of Authoritarian and Equalitarian Leaders and Followers," *Journal of Abnormal and Social Psychology*, LIII (September 1956), 210-19.

3. Truman, *Governmental Process*, pp. 167-87.

4. Herbert Simon, *Administrative Behavior* (New York: The Macmillan Co., 1957), pp. 110-22.

5. Attitudes were assessed by personal interviews. There were 91 teachers in the original sample with whom interviews were not completed.

6. Our data justify the use of ordinal measures of association, but there are several characteristics of our data and properties of various measures of association which complicate the choice of such a measure. First, on some of the items only two responses are possible while others are seven-point Likert scales. Thus any measure which is sensitive to the shape of the contingency table from which it is computed will decrease the comparability of the data across items. A measure which reached unity when only one cell is zero is also undesirable, as instances in which the leaders are in perfect agreement while the followers differ are common in our data. Such measures would be insensitive to the degree of followers' disagreement with the leaders. The final difficulty is that some measures are sensitive to the marginals of the contingency table. No measure was discovered which did not have at least one of the characteristics. See Hubert Blalock, *Social Statistics* (New York: McGraw-Hill Book Co., 1960), p. 323; and Leo Goodman and William H. Kruskal, "Measures of Association for Cross Classifications," *Journal of the American Statistical Association*, XLIX (December 1954), 750.

7. David Gold, "Some Problems in Generalizing Aggregate Associations," *American Behavioral Scientist*, VIII (December 1964), 18. .

8. The terms "delegate" and "representative" are borrowed from the literature on the legislative process, where they are applied to the role perceptions of legislators. Heinz Eulau presents three legislative role orientations in John C. Wahlke, Heinz Eulau, William Buchanan, and LeRoy C. Ferguson, *The Legislative System* (New York: John Wiley and Sons, Inc., 1962), pp. 267-86. The "trustee" of Eulau's scheme has traditionally been described as a "delegate" while the "delegate" corresponds to "representative." These roles are the extremes, with "politico" falling somewhere between them.

9. Cf. Gabriel Almond and Sidney Verba, *The Civic Culture* (Boston: Little, Brown, and Co., 1965), pp. 250-51.

10. David Krech and Richard Crutchfield, *Theory and Problems of Social Psychology* (New York: McGraw-Hill Book Co., 1948), p. 251.

11. See Angus Campbell *et al.*, *The American Voter* (New York: John Wiley

and Sons, 1960), pp. 194-98. V. O. Key gives the items used in this scale. See V. O. Key, Jr., *Public Opinion and American Democracy* (New York: Alfred A. Knopf, 1961), p. 561.

12. Herbert McClosky, "Consensus and Ideology in American Politics," *American Political Science Review*, LVIII (June 1964), 361-82.

13. It is true, however, that there is more interaction between leaders and small-town teachers; these teachers are considerably more conservative and restrained than their big-city counterparts.

12 / Factors Which Affect Satisfaction and Dissatisfaction of Teachers

Thomas Sergiovanni

Satisfaction and dissatisfaction of teachers has long been an area of intense interest to researchers in school personnel management. In a recent review of industrial and education job satisfaction research, Robinson[1] notes that over 40 percent of the studies reviewed relate to teachers and their satisfaction or morale. However, the voluminous research in the field to date appears to be lacking in conceptual perspective and may, in fact, be misleading.

An assumption basic to the literature in this area is that factors which account for job satisfaction of teachers and factors which account for job dissatisfaction of teachers are arranged on a conceptual continuum (Figure 12-1). Thus, a factor identified as a source of dissatisfaction is also likely to be a potential satisfier. The administrative prescription based on this assumption is that, if a factor accounting for dissatisfaction is altered or eliminated, job satisfaction will result. Or, failure to maintain a satisfaction condition will result in teacher dissatisfaction.

The Herzberg Study

The impetus for the research reported here comes from the work of Frederick Herzberg, Bernard Mausner, and Barbara Snyderman.[2] In a review of industrial motivation studies, Herzberg observed that a

Reprinted from *The Journal of Educational Administration*, V (No. 1, May 1967), 66-82.

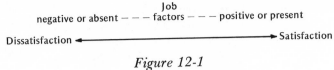

Figure 12-1
The continuum assumption

difference in the primacy of work factors appeared depending upon whether the investigator was searching for factors which led to job satisfaction or factors which led to job dissatisfaction.[3] This observation led to the concept that some factors in the work situation were "satisfiers" and other factors were "dissatisfiers." Herzberg hypothesized that some factors were satisfiers when present but not dissatisfiers when absent; other factors were dissatisfiers, but when eliminated as dissatisfiers did not result in positive motivation (Figure 12-2).

Herzberg's research with accountants and engineers[4] tends to confirm the existence of the satisfier and dissatisfier phenomenon. Herzberg found that five factors (achievement, recognition, work itself, responsibility, and advancement) tended to affect job attitudes in only a positive direction. The absence of these factors did not necessarily result in job dissatisfaction. The eleven remaining factors, if not present, led to employee dissatisfaction. The absence of these factors tended not to lead to employee satisfaction. Herzberg

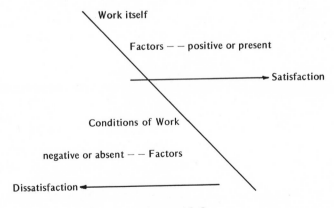

Figure 12-2
Herzberg hypothesis: Satisfaction factors
and Dissatisfaction factors are mutually exclusive

observed that job factors which resulted in satisfaction were directly related to the work itself. Job factors which resulted in dissatisfaction tended to be related to the environment of work. The factors in their two subcategories are as follows.

Satisfiers	Dissatisfiers
(found in work itself)	(found in the environment of work)
1. Achievement	1. Salary
2. Recognition	2. Possibility of growth
3. Work itself	3. Interpersonal relations (subordinates)
4. Responsibility	4. Status
5. Advancement	5. Interpersonal relations (superiors)
	6. Interpersonal relations (peers)
	7. Supervision—technical
	8. Company policy and administration
	9. Working conditions
	10. Personal life
	11. Job security

Though arrived at empirically, the Herzberg findings appear to be consistent with the motivational theory proposed by Maslow.[5] Maslow hypothesized a hierarchy into which needs arranged themselves in order of their appearance. The Maslow hierarchy of needs, from lowest order (most prepotent) to highest order (least basic or prepotent), is as follows: physiological needs, security needs, social needs, esteem needs, and the need for self-actualization. Needs that are at or near the top of the hierarchy, assuming that lower order needs are met, will tend to be the focus of an individual's attention. As long as lower order needs are satisfied, they cease to motivate the individual; in our society the physiological and security needs are well met for most people, thus they seldom motivate behavior. Herzberg identified two levels of needs for his subjects; "hygienic" needs (which tend to focus on the dissatisfaction factors identified in his study) and satisfaction needs (which tend to focus on the satisfaction factors identified). According to Herzberg, if "hygienic" needs are not met, the individual is unhappy. Provision for "hygienic" needs, however, does not ensure increased motivation. The satisfaction needs have motivational potential, but depend upon reasonable satiation of "hygienic" needs before they become operative.[6]

Herzberg's findings have important implications for educational administration and supervision. They suggest that much of present practice in personnel administration may be directed at controlling the hygienic conditions which have, at best, limited motivating power for professional teachers.

THE PROBLEM

The writer undertook a study to determine whether or not the factors reported by teachers would distribute themselves into mutually exclusive satisfaction and dissatisfaction categories. Further, if the satisfaction-dissatisfaction phenomenon existed for teachers, would the factors resulting in satisfaction be concerned with the work itself, and would the factors resulting in dissatisfaction be concerned with the environment of work?

The following questions were raised:

1. Is there one set of factors which tends to satisfy teachers and another set which tends to dissatisfy teachers? Or are these factors better described as being arranged on a continuum with each being a potential satisfier and dissatisfier?
2. Will the distribution of factors vary for subpopulations of teachers? (Subgroups included: (1) male teachers v. female teachers, (2) tenure teachers v. nontenure teachers, (3) elementary school teachers v. secondary school teachers.)

METHODOLOGY

The overall design of this study followed, with some additions and modifications, the design developed and used by Herzberg. Respondents were asked to report incidents judged by them to be representative of their job feelings. Each incident or sequence consisted of three phases: (1) the respondent's attitudes expressed in terms of high job feelings and low job feelings, (2) the first-level and second-level factors[7] which accounted for these attitudes, (3) the effects of these attitudes and factors as reported by respondents. Through content analysis the factors which accounted for the expressed attitudes were sorted into the categories developed, defined, and used by Herzberg in the original study. The effects were sorted and categorized in the same manner.

The Population and Sample

The population for this study consisted of teachers in school districts in Monroe County, New York (the City of Rochester was not included in the sample population). The districts ranged from semi-rural to suburban in orientation and in size from a teaching staff of 36 to a teaching staff of 528. The total sample population consisted of 3,682 teachers.

One hundred and twenty-seven respondents were selected at random from the 3,682 teachers who comprised the study population.

The sample was drawn from lists furnished by each of the participating school districts. Administrators, guidance counselors, department chairmen not involved in actual teaching, librarians, supervisors, and other nonteaching personnel were not included in the sample. Seventy-one of the 127 teachers agreed to participate.

The sample included 30 male teachers and 41 female teachers. Elementary school positions were held by 37 respondents and junior high or senior high school positions were held by 34 respondents. Thirty-seven of the 71 respondents held tenure appointments. Respondents ranged in age from 21 years to 64 years with the average age being 37 and the median age being 32. Years of teaching experience ranged from three months to 36 years with the average experience being nine years and the median experience being seven years.

The Interview

The interview outline and interviewing procedure used in this study were a direct adoption of the Herzberg format. Respondents were told that they could start with either a time when they had felt unusually high or good about their job or a time when they had felt unusually low or bad about their job. After the first unusual sequence, each respondent was asked to give another. If he had previously given a high story, he was then asked for a low. The same procedure was followed for most recent high feelings and most recent low feelings.

The objective events, the actual stories, which were reported by respondents as being the source of high or low feelings about their jobs were coded as first-level factors. The second-level factors were categories which constituted respondents' feelings as a result of the objective stories they had related and the attitudes they had identified. The analysis of second-level factors came primarily from respondents' answers to two questions: "Can you tell me more precisely why you felt the way you did?" and "What did these events mean to you?" One respondent related a story involving a merit salary increase as a source of good feelings about his job. When asked why he felt the way he did, he replied, "It meant that the administration or whoever was responsible for the increase felt that I was doing a good job." The first-level factor in this sequence was coded as salary. This was the objective occurrence. The second-level factor in this sequence, however, was coded as recognition. The respondent perceived the merit increase as a source of recognition.

Respondents were limited to four specific sequences: an unusual high attitude sequence, an unusual low attitude sequence, a most recent high attitude sequence, and a most recent low attitude sequence. Two hundred and eighty-four sequences were collected for the study. The statistical analysis was based on the number of sequences rather than the number of respondents. Focusing on sequences was consistent with the method used by Herzberg.

Analysis of the Interviews

The technique of content analysis was used in coding each sequence. Herzberg suggests two basic approaches to content analysis. The first is an a priori approach in which the analysis is based upon a predetermined categorical scheme. The second approach extracts the categories from the raw data itself. Herzberg chose the a posteriori approach which produced categories specifically related to the data collected in his study. Herzberg noted, however, that the resulting categorical scheme developed through the a posteriori approach was not very different from that which could have been derived from an analysis of the literature.[8]

The scheme used for content analysis in this study was a direct adoption of the categories developed and used by Herzberg, and so represents an a priori approach, but one based on empirical evidence.

Coding Procedure

The next step in the analysis of the interviews required that the factors contained in the high and low attitude stories of respondents be identified and coded into the categorical scheme. Further, since several factors could appear in a given story, the factor which contributed most to the expressed feeling was to be isolated for subsequent analysis. Each sequence was coded in terms of expressed attitude (high or low), sequence type (unusual or recent), and level (first and second).

Sequences were coded, independently, by three of five judges. A total of 284 sequences were coded for the study. Coding decisions were classified as unanimous choice, majority choice, or consensus choice. First-level coding choices of judges for each of the first 160 sequences included 87 unanimous decisions, 69 majority decisions, and 4 consensus decisions. For the second-level factors there were 96 unanimous decisions and 64 majority decisions. Three-way disagreements did not occur for the second-level factors. Figure 12-3 summarizes the basic features of the content analysis.

THE ANALYSIS OF RESULTS

The results of the study are presented in two sections. The first reports the results relating to the mutual exclusiveness of factors for the total sample. This section includes an analysis of the first-level

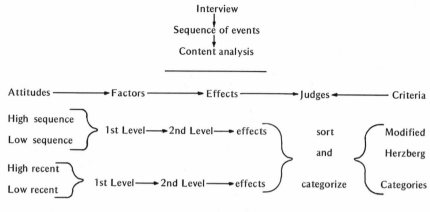

Figure 12-3
Basic design features of the content analysis

and second-level factors which appeared in high attitude sequences and an analysis of the first-level and second-level factors which appeared in low attitude sequences.

The second section includes a summary of the difference in responses for male teachers as compared with female teachers, tenure teachers as compared with nontenure teachers, and for elementary as compared with secondary teachers.

HIGH ATTITUDE SEQUENCES
CONTRASTED WITH LOW ATTITUDE SEQUENCES

Table 12-1 includes the percentages and values of chi-square for the frequency with which first-level factors appeared in high attitude sequences as compared with low attitude sequences for the total group.

Sixty-nine percent of the sequences which accounted for high job attitudes included the first-level factors achievement, recognition, and work itself. Responsibility appeared in 7 percent of the high attitude stories. Advancement did not appear in the 142 high attitude stories.

First-level factors six through sixteen (the environment of work factors) appeared in 24 percent of the high attitude sequences. The major contributors to the 24 percent were possibility of growth (6 percent), and interpersonal relations with subordinates (7 percent). Personal life, status, and security did not appear in the high attitude sequences.

Interpersonal relations (subordinates), interpersonal relations

TABLE 12-1. Percentages[a] and values of chi-square for
the frequency with which each first-level factor
appeared in high attitude sequences as contrasted
with low attitude sequences for the total group

Factor	High	Low	Chi-square	P
	NS[b] = 142	NS[b] = 142		
1. Achievement	30[c]	9	10.500	.01
2. Recognition	28[c]	2	30.139	.001
3. Work itself	11	8	.346	
4. Responsibility	7[c]	1	5.818	.05
5. Advancement	0	1		
6. Salary	2	3		
7. Possibility of growth	6	2	1.454	
8. Interpersonal relations (subordinates)	7	20[c]	7.605	.01
9. Interpersonal relations (superiors)	3	4	.900	
10. Interpersonal relations (peers)	1	15[c]	14.086	.001
11. Supervision—technical	1	10[c]	8.470	.01
12. School policy and administration	2	13[c]	10.227	.01
13. Working conditions	2	6	2.083	
14. Personal life	0	5[c]	5.142	.05
15. Status	0	0		
16. Security	0	1		

[a]Percentages are approximate, but do not vary more than .0075.

[b]NS refers to number of sequences.

[c]Difference between highs and lows is significant. Chi-squared value required for significance at the .05 level is 3.841.

(peers), supervision—technical, and school policy and administration appeared in 58 percent of the low attitude sequences. Achievement, recognition, work itself, responsibility, and advancement accounted for 21 percent of the incidence of factors which appeared in the lows. Status did not appear as a first-level factor in low attitude sequences.

The first-level factors which appeared more often in high attitude sequences were achievement,* recognition,* work itself, responsibility,* and possibility of growth. The first-level factors which appeared

*Differences between highs and lows is significant. Minimum P = .05

more often in low attitude sequences were advancement, salary, interpersonal relations (subordinates),* interpersonal relations (superiors), interpersonal relations (peers),* supervision—technical,* school policy and administration,* working conditions, personal life,* and security.

The percentages and values of chi-square for the frequency with which second-level factors appeared in high attitude and low attitude sequences are reported in Table 12-2.

Achievement, which appeared in 50 percent of the sequences, was the dominant second-level factor for the highs. Recognition appeared in 21 percent of the sequences involving high job feelings. The remaining factors appeared in 29 percent of the high attitude sequences. The major contributors to the 29 percent were work itself (6 percent) and possible growth (6 percent). The second-level factors —advancement, status, salary, and fairness—did not appear in high attitude sequences.

For second-level low attitude sequences, feelings of unfairness, with 32 percent, was the dominant factor. Feelings of guilt and inadequacy, security, and work itself appeared in 31 percent of the low sequences. Recognition with 7 percent and lack of achievement with 13 percent were other contributors to low job feelings. The remaining six factors appeared in 15 percent of the low sequences. The factor advancement did not appear in the lows.

The second-level factors which appeared more often in high attitude sequences were recognition,* achievement,* and possible growth. The second-level factors which appeared more often in low attitude sequences were work itself, status,* security, feelings of unfairness,* feelings of guilt and inadequacy, and salary.

Summary

The results presented in the first section demonstrate that many of the factors which accounted for high job feelings of teachers and many of the factors which accounted for low job feelings of teachers were mutually exclusive.

The first-level factors which appeared significantly as highs (as contrasted with lows) were recognition, achievement, and responsibility. The first-level factors which appeared significantly as lows (as contrasted with highs) were interpersonal relations (subordinates), interpersonal relations (peers), supervision—technical, school policy and administration, and personal life.

Achievement and recognition were the second-level factors which appeared significantly as highs. Feelings of unfairness and low status

*Differences between highs and lows is significant. Minimum P = .05

TABLE 12-2. Percentages[a] and values of chi-square for the frequency with which each second-level factor appeared in high attitude sequences as contrasted with low attitude sequences for the total group

Factor	High	Low	Chi-square	P
	$NS^b = 142$	$NS^b = 142$		
1. Recognition	21[c]	7	9.025	.01
2. Achievement	50[c]	13	26.677	.001
3. Work itself	6	9	.190	
4. Advancement	0	0		
5. Responsibility	4	4		
6. Group feelings	3	3		
7. Possible growth	6	3	1.230	
8. Status	0	5[c]	5.1428	.05
9. Security	5	11	1.565	
10. Fairness-unfairness	0	32[c]	43.002	.001
11. Pride, guilt, inadequacy	5	11	2.782	
12. Salary	0	2		

[a]Percentages are approximate, but do not vary more than .0075.
[b]NS refers to number of sequences.
[c]Difference between highs and lows is significant. Chi-square value required for significance at the .05 level is 3.841.

were the only second-level factors which appeared significantly as lows.

SUBGROUP DIFFERENCES

The analysis of results relating to the second question raised in this study strongly suggests that subgroups of teachers tend not to differ in their responses to sources of high and low job feelings. Significant differences were found in only 3 of 168 possibilities.

Men teachers tended *not* to respond differently from women teachers to sources of high and low job attitudes. No significant exception to this tendency was found.

Tenure teachers and nontenure teachers tended *not* to differ in their responses to sources of high and low job feelings. Three significant exceptions to this tendency were found:

1. The first-level factor interpersonal relations (superiors) appeared as a source of low job feelings for tenure teachers in 4 percent of the 142 low attitude sequences. This factor did not appear as a source of low job feelings for nontenure teachers.

2. Eleven percent of the low attitude sequences involved nontenure teachers citing the first-level factor interpersonal relations (peers) as a source of low job attitudes. This was in contrast to 4 percent for tenure teachers.

3. Security, a second-level factor, appeared in 11 percent of the low attitude sequences. Nine of the 11 percent were cited by nontenure teachers.

Elementary school teachers and secondary school teachers tended *not* to differ in their responses to sources of high job attitudes and low job attitudes. No significant exception to this tendency was found.

DISCUSSION

The Polarity of Factors

The results of this study indicated that achievement, recognition, and responsibility were factors which contributed predominantly to teacher job satisfaction. Interpersonal relations (subordinates), interpersonal relations (peers), supervision—technical, school policy and administration, personal life, and fairness-unfairness were factors which contributed predominantly to teacher job dissatisfaction. The remaining factors appeared to be bipolar, possessing the potential to contribute to both satisfaction and dissatisfaction (many of the factors did not appear with sufficient frequency to test adequately for polarity).

The Satisfaction Factors

The three dominant factors which appeared in high attitude sequences were achievement, recognition, and responsibility. Achievement accounted for nearly one out of three first-level high attitude sequences and for one out of two second-level high attitude sequences. In view of the predominance of the factor achievement, it is interesting to note that most of the teacher achievement-centered stories involved less concrete evidence of actual success and more sensing and feeling by teachers that students had been reached and were presumably affected in some positive way.

This noticeable lack of concrete success reinforces Lortie's notion of psychic gratification as a reward base for teachers. Lortie[9] argues that societal rewards (salary, prestige, and power) are, in general, not perceived by teachers as being in abundance. Thus, teachers tend to focus on psychic gratification as a primary source of reward in their work. One of the major sources of psychic gratification, according to Lortie, is the interaction that the teacher has with individual students and classes where the teacher perceives that something has happened. The teacher senses or believes that, as a result of his activity, a change has taken place in the student or class. Lortie cites the terms "I reached them," "It went today," as being common expressions used by teachers to describe this phenomenon.

This psychic gratification, which is characterized by a task-oriented interaction with some perceived measurable result, was most typical of many of the success stories related by teachers.

Recognition appeared three times as often in high sequences as in low sequences. Sources of recognition for teachers varied. Teachers talked about feedback from principals, supervisors, parents, students, and fellow teachers. Recognition took the form of letters, oral statements, gifts, incentives, and committee appointments.

The need for recognition, the overt bolstering of self-esteem, appears to be important to teachers. The absence of recognition tends not to affect low job attitudes of teachers.

Responsibility, although significantly found to be a high, appeared in only 7 percent of the high attitude sequences. This percentage is small when one considers that teachers do assume a considerable amount of responsibility. As the classroom door closes behind the teacher, it is implied that she assumes responsibility for her own work. This responsibility is limited, however, and falls within the framework of the rules and regulations of the school, school district, and school board. Further limits are imposed by the state legislature and our society at large. Whatever responsibility a teacher assumes, in terms of what to teach, falls within the framework of the prescribed curriculum.

Perhaps even more interesting than the appearance of achievement, recognition, and responsibility as positive polar factors was the absence of advancement and work itself. These factors did appear as satisfiers in Herzberg's study.

The factor advancement was not mentioned by teachers in high attitude stories. Teaching offers little opportunity for concrete advancement (change in status or position) and in fact any particular teaching assignment could be considered as a terminal position. Whatever potential the factor advancement has as a satisfier appears to be lost for teachers under our present system. Capitalizing on this factor, as a potential source of satisfaction, implies providing overt opportunities for advancement within the ranks of teachers.[10]

Work itself appeared as a bipolar factor in the study. Although the factor appeared more frequently in teacher high attitude stories, it also appeared as a frequent source of low job feelings. It appears that the job of teacher (although potentially able to provide unlimited opportunity for creative and varied work) requires considerable attention to maintenance-type activity. Routine or maintenance tasks range from attendance and scheduling details, daily health checks, study hall assignments, and lunch duty to blowing noses and pouring young scholars into snowsuits. The work itself factor, although found to be rich in satisfaction potential, was frequently cited as a source of dissatisfaction for teachers.

The Dissatisfaction Factors

Perhaps of greatest interest among the dissatisfiers was the factor interpersonal relations (subordinates), which appeared in 20 percent of the low attitude sequences and in 7 percent of the high attitude sequences.

It seems appropriate to assume that, since students are the very crux of a teacher's work, they should account for many of the successes and good feelings that teachers have. Indeed, this is so. The students were the raw material for the achievement successes and acts of recognition which teachers perceived as sources of great satisfaction. Establishing an appropriate relationship with students appears to be critical. Once established, the teacher can capitalize on this relationship in pursuit of work-centered or job itself satisfaction. It appears that a happy relationship with students is not in itself potent enough to be a source of job satisfaction. A poor relationship with students, however, can be a source of considerable teacher dissatisfaction.

Responses of Subgroups Tend Not to Differ

A most interesting finding of the study was that subgroups of teachers—tenure and nontenure, male and female, elementary and secondary—tended not to differ in their responses to sources of job satisfaction and dissatisfaction. There were only three exceptions, out of 168 possibilities, to this tendency. All three involved tenure and nontenure teachers.

One interpretation of this finding is that the satisfaction and dissatisfaction factors identified in this study apply to teachers irrespective of their sex, teaching level, or tenure status.

CONCLUSION

This study provides support for the hypothesis that satisfiers and dissatisfiers tend to be mutually exclusive. Further, it was found that factors which accounted for high attitudes of teachers were related to the work itself and factors which accounted for low attitudes of teachers were related to the conditions or environment of work.

Relative to other activities, teachers derive the most satisfaction from work-centered activity. This finding was reflected in the predominance of achievement, recognition, and responsibility as sources of teacher job satisfaction. The low attitude sequences, however, revealed factors which were not in themselves work-centered; rather, they focused on the conditions and people which surround the actual work.

Can we conclude that as long as a teacher experiences personal success, and is recognized for this success, the conditions of work need not be considered? It may be possible (although unlikely) for a teacher, who is immersed in an unsatisfactory work environment, to experience personal success and thus achieve considerable job satisfaction. An environment relatively free from sources of dissatisfaction, however, will tend to increase or enhance the appearance of factors which are direct contributors to job satisfaction.

Herzberg refers to the dissatisfaction factors as "hygienic." In describing these factors, Herzberg states: "They act in a manner analagous to the principles of medical hygiene. Hygiene operates to remove health hazards from the environment of man. It is not a curative; it is, rather, a preventive."[11]

The "hygienic" factors, according to Herzberg, are essential in preventing dissatisfaction, in making work tolerable. Herzberg describes the satisfaction factors as motivators. These are the job-centered, the task-oriented factors which permit the individual to satisfy his need for self-actualization in his work.

The dissatisfaction factors identified for teachers tend to focus on conditions and circumstances which teachers expect to be maintained at acceptable levels. It seems reasonable that teachers should expect fair and adequate supervision, supportive school policies and administrative directives, friendly interpersonal relationships, and pleasant working conditions. However, the satisfaction factors focus directly on conditions and circumstances that are not givens, which do not come with the job. These factors constitute rewards that must be earned through performance of the job. The reinforcement potential of the satisfiers is dependent upon a teacher's individual performance.

What then are the implications of the study for administrative behavior? The findings suggest that the present emphasis on "teacher-centered" behavior (supportive supervision, interpersonal relations, effective communications, and group effectiveness) is an important prescription for effective administrative behavior. The "teacher-centered" approach, however, is limited in that it tends to concentrate on the elimination of dissatisfaction factors and thus does not contribute directly to teacher job satisfaction.

"Task-oriented" behavior (organizing and planning work, implementing goal achievement) emerges as an important and direct contributor to teacher job satisfaction. Such behavior, on the part of the administrator, would include increasing the opportunities for teachers to experience personal and professional success. Basic to this undertaking is the proposition that administrators will permit and encourage teachers to (1) exercise more autonomy in making decisions (intensifying collaborative efforts and consultative management would be a good start), (2) increase individual responsibility in developing and implementing teaching programs, and (3) develop professional skills. These variables will serve to increase individual identification with the task.[12] Task identification appears to be a prerequisite for focusing on achievement as a means to personal and professional success and subsequent job satisfaction.

A corollary to personal success is recognition for such success. Although recognition was not found to be as potent as actual success, it was perceived by teachers as a measure of success. Capitalizing on recognition as a satisfier for teachers implies that dispensing of recognition should be as closely associated with successful teacher task-oriented behavior as possible.

Finally, effective administrative behavior would not exclude or ignore the sources of job dissatisfaction. Supervisory behavior, interpersonal relationships, and other factors relating to the conditions of work are necessary components in promoting an environment which will enhance job itself satisfaction for teachers. Teachers whose energies are taxed in coping with sources of job dissatisfaction will tend not to be vigorous and dynamic pursuers of work-centered satisfaction.

An inherent assumption, in the discussion above, has been that job satisfiers are reinforcers of behavior and motivators of performance. Considerable evidence has been accumulated which disputes the claim that a satisfied worker is more productive than a dissatisfied one. However, when satisfaction is dependent upon performance in work, satisfaction and productivity are related.[13]

The satisfaction factors identified for teachers cannot be separated from performance and, in fact, are dependent upon performance. It was successful performance which accounted for the high attitudes expressed in achievement-centered stories. Performance was also the basis for recognition-centered sequences. If performance is rewarded in terms of intrinsic personal success and extrinsic recognition for success, it will tend to be repeated.

SUMMARY

The assumption that factors which tend to satisfy teachers and factors which tend to dissatisfy teachers are arranged on a conceptual continuum tends *not* to be supported by this study. Factors which appeared as sources of high job feelings for teachers tended to differ from factors which appeared as sources of low job feelings. Further, the satisfaction factors tended to focus on the work itself, and the dissatisfaction factors tended to focus on the conditions of work.

It was concluded that the elimination of the dissatisfiers would tend not to result in job satisfaction. However, it does not appear likely that one can experience work satisfaction *without* the elimination or tempering of the dissatisfiers. Deriving satisfaction from work-centered activity assumes that one's energies and efforts are not taxed or depleted by unsatisfactory conditions of work. The point is not whether satisfiers are more crucial than dissatisfiers, or vice versa, but rather the dependence of the satisfiers on the elimination or tempering of the dissatisfiers.

Notes

The research here reported was performed pursuant to a contract with the U.S. Department of Health, Education and Welfare, Office of Education. The author is indebted to Dean Robert B. Howsam of the University of Houston in the preparation of this paper.

1. Alan Robinson, Ralph Conners, and Ann Robinson, "Job Satisfaction Researches of 1963," *Personnel and Guidance Journal*, XLIII (1964), 361.

2. Frederick Herzberg, Bernard Mausner, and Barbara Snyderman, *The Motivation to Work* (New York: John Wiley and Sons, 1959).

3. Frederick Herzberg, Bernard Mausner, Richard Peterson, and Dora Capewell, *Job Attitudes: Review of Research and Opinion* (Pittsburgh: Psychological Service of Pittsburgh, 1957).

4. Herzberg, Mausner, and Snyderman, *Motivation to Work*.

5. A. H. Maslow, *Motivation and Personality* (New York: Harper & Brothers, 1954).

6. Herzberg, Mausner, and Snyderman, *Motivation to Work*, pp. 113-19.

7. Herzberg differentiated between the objective events, the actual stories reported by respondents, and the subsequent perceptions of respondents of what the objective events meant to them. The actual stories were the basis for the first-level factors, and the "interpretation" of the stories by respondents comprised the second-level factors. First-level factors are listed in Table 12-1 and second-level factors are listed in Table 12-2.

8. Herzberg, Mausner, and Snyderman, *Motivation to Work*, p. 38.

9. Dan Lortie, "The Changing Role of Teachers as a Result of Such Innovations as Television, Programmed Instruction, and Team Teaching," in Richard

Lonsdale and Carl Steinhoff (eds.), *The Administrative Analysis of Selected Educational Innovations.* (Report of the First Interuniversity Conference for School Administrators, Syracuse University, 1964).

10. Schools frequently contain an informal promotion system for teachers. Advancement within the informal promotion system may include movement to another grade level, being assigned "quality" students, receiving equipment and facility priorities, and moving to a better school within the district. This informal promotion system was not described in teacher high attitude sequences, but did appear in low attitude sequences. Judges coded these low attitude sequences into the factor categories working conditions or school policy and administration.

11. Herzberg, Mausner, and Snyderman, *Motivation to Work*, p. 113.

12. James March and Herbert Simon, *Organizations* (New York: John Wiley and Sons, 1958), p. 77.

13. Bernard Bass, *Organizational Psychology* (Boston: Allyn and Bacon, Inc., 1965), p. 38.

13 / A Typology for Participation in Organizational Decision Making

Joseph A. Alutto and James A. Belasco

Organizational theorists from Weber, Barnard, and Taylor to March and Simon[1] have been concerned with aspects of individual participation in organizational decision making. This study examines the utility of a definition of decisional participation which is based on the discrepancy between a system member's actual and desired rates of participation rather than simply on the absolute current rate of decisional participation. This concept is then utilized to re-examine certain propositions concerning organizational correlates of participation suggested by previous authors.

PAST RESEARCH

In reviewing the literature on individual participation, at least three distinct themes emerge. The first concerns the importance of decisional participation by employees in determining the acceptance of organizational change. Following the original work of Coch and French,[2] most investigators have concluded that, by encouraging participation in decision making, organizations can increase both the probability that change will be accepted and the overall effectiveness of that change. It has also been suggested that allowing participation in decisions over which participants exercise no control may be just as damaging as no participation at all.[3]

Reprinted from *Administrative Science Quarterly*, XVII (No. 1, March 1972), 117-25.

The second major area of research concentrates on interactions between the decisional participation rates of subordinates and the perceived relative influence of administrative superiors. Gouldner,[4] Tannenbaum and his colleagues,[5] and Mulder[6] have argued that by allowing subordinates to participate in decision making, superiors gain influence over the actions of individual role performers. As a participation franchise is extended and superiors relinquish complete control over decisions, they gain both increased certainty concerning the actions of their subordinates (encouraging commitment through involvement) and increased influence over a widespread set of decisional issues (gaining in the legitimate exercise of authority). It is suggested that one clear consequence of shared decision making is increased administrative control.

Finally, several organizational analysts have focused on the more generalized positive effects of employee participation in decision making. For example, Patchen[7] has studied the relationships between decisional participation and job satisfaction on the one hand and job achievement and organizational integration on the other. His research among TVA employees suggests that, along with other consequences, increased participation in institutional decision making leads to greater job satisfaction and work achievement, as well as greater individual integration into the organization.

Many researchers and practitioners assume a somewhat simple linear relationship between increased participation in organizational decision making and such valued system outcomes as willingness to adopt change, increased administrative control, and greater individual integration into the organization.[8] Yet, distinguishing pure decisional participation is a complex task. Participation can range from the mere presentation of an opinion, where the locus of final authority rests elsewhere, to membership in the group which exercises final authority over an issue.[9] Given varying shades of participation, not all forms of participation will produce identical or even similar organizational outcomes.

Researchers too often maintain that the desire for increased participation is equally and widely distributed throughout an organization. Other evidence indicates that organizational populations are far from homogeneous in attitudes, sentiments, and expectations concerning a wide range of organizational issues.[10] It is more reasonable to assume that not all segments of the population are equally desirous of additional participation in organizational life. If this is correct, then the crucial variable is the discrepancy between current and desired rates of participation rather than a system member's absolute rate of participation.

In this article it is argued that one can deal effectively with decisional participation by considering a continuum of participation typified by the following three conditions: (1) decisional deprivation—actual participation in fewer decisions than desired, (2) decisional equilibrium—actual participation in as many decisions as desired; and (3) decisional saturation—actual participation in a greater number of decisions than desired. It is recognized that, in addition to the absolute discrepancy between current and preferred participation rates, the nature of the specific issue with which the individual is confronted constitutes an important dimension. It is possible, for instance, that certain individuals may be, at one and the same time, decisionally deprived, in that they wish to participate in some decisions from which they are currently excluded, and decisionally saturated, in that they do not wish to participate in some of the decisions in which they are currently involved.

This study is concerned with typifying overall conditions of decisional participation. In essence, it seeks to establish that one can effectively characterize organizations and organizational members in terms of an all-encompassing discrepancy participation concept, much as it is useful to determine and describe such global system variables as organizational climate,[11] morale,[12] or control.[13] If the three participation conditions are differentially distributed throughout organizational populations, and if these conditions are related to differing organizational outcomes, then this discrepancy concept of participation has both research and theoretical value.

Finally, this article is also concerned with the extent to which the degree or level of involvement in decision making affects correlates of decisional participation. For example, do those individuals experiencing high deprivation differ from those experiencing low levels of decisional deprivation; do those characterized by high levels of saturation differ from those characterized by low levels; or, do those who participate in few decisions and want to participate in only a few decisions differ from those who achieve decisional equilibrium through participation in a large number of decisions? The answers to these questions will determine whether the extent of decisional involvement is important when considering varying types of decisional participation.

METHODOLOGY

Data for this study were collected through use of questionnaire survey techniques. Subjects receiving the questionnaires were teachers employed in two school districts located in Western New York State. Research site I was a small (population 50,000) urban school district and site II, a medium-sized rural district. Complete usable responses from teachers in each district resulted in return rates of 60 percent in system I and 75 percent in district II. An analysis of the demographic characteristics of respondents and nonrespondents in each district revealed no significant differences when considering population and survey sample distributions of attributes such as age, sex, marital status, and teaching level.

Information about the age, sex, seniority in district, teaching level, and employing district of each subject was taken directly from completed questionnaires. Use of the following characteristics as variables for analytical purposes required the computation of specific indexes for each subject.

TABLE 13-1. Decisional situations

1. Hiring new faculty members
2. Selecting specific instructional texts
3. Resolving learning problems of individual students
4. Determining appropriate instructional methods and techniques
5. Establishing general instructional policies
6. Establishing classroom disciplinary policies
7. Planning school budgets
8. Determining specific faculty assignments
9. Resolving faculty member grievances
10. Planning new buildings and facilities
11. Resolving problems with community groups
12. Determining faculty salaries

Deprivation, equilibrium, and saturation. Subjects responded to a series of twelve decisions (listed in Table 13-1). For each decisional situation, subjects indicated (a) whether they currently participated in that decision, and (b) whether they wished to participate. Each subject's condition of decisional participation was derived by summing over the number of decisions in which he wished to participate, and then computing the absolute difference between these two figures. For analysis purposes, subjects were placed in groups characterized by (a) decisional deprivation (current participation less than preferred, n = 260), (b) decisional equilibrium (current participation equal to desired participation, n = 107), and (c) decisional saturation (current participation greater than desired, n = 87). The distributions of subjects based on each of the three decisional conditions are presented in Table 13-2. Individuals categorized as

decisionally deprived evidenced a clear preference for greater participation. Although no subjects in this group currently participated in
nine or more decisions, 30 percent expressed a desire to participate
in nine or more decisions. Subjects characterized as having achieved
decisional equilibrium were well distributed throughout the range of
decisional situations, although none of these individuals participated
in more than nine different decisions. Although 23 percent of this
group failed to participate in any of the decisional situations, they
appeared to be satisfied with this condition. Decisionally saturated
subjects evidenced a clear preference for reduction in decisional
participation rates. While 70 percent of these individuals currently
participated in more than five decisional situations, 74 percent preferred participation in fewer than five decisions.

Organizational commitment. Patchen[14] has postulated that personal integration is related to a subject's decisional participation.
Organizational commitment would be one indicator of this integration. For example, following Patchen it would be expected that
those either decisionally deprived or saturated would have lower
degrees of organizational commitment than individuals who had
achieved a degree of decisional equilibrium. Consequently, an index

TABLE 13-2. Distribution of subjects by decisional condition

| | Modes of decisional participation | | | | |
| | Deprived | | | Saturated | |
Number of decisions	Current	Preferred	Equilibrium[a]	Current	Preferred
0	16	0	25	0	16
1	29	4	9	0	10
2	41	3	19	2	12
3	51	12	6	5	13
4	44	24	11	9	13
5	31	30	9	10	13
6	22	31	11	13	7
7	12	42	8	13	3
8	14	36	5	14	0
9	0	27	4	9	0
10	0	26	0	6	0
11	0	13	0	6	0
12	0	12	0	0	0
Total	260	260	107	87	87

[a]By definition, current participation rate is equal to that preferred for those
subjects experiencing decisional equilibrium.

of organizational commitment was constructed for each subject based on responses to whether or not the subject would leave his current school system for employment in another district if offered such inducements as a slight increase in pay, a slight increase in status, a position allowing slightly greater creativity, or a position in which colleagues were slightly friendlier.

Perceptions and preferences of administrative influence. In an effort to re-examine Tannenbaum's postulates, subjects were asked to rank order a series of role performers, including school principals and superintendents, in terms of their currently perceived influence and the relative influence they believed should exist. Thus, for each subject an indication was received of perceived current influence for principals and superintendents, as well as of levels of preferred relative influence for these same administrative officials.

Authoritarianism. It was anticipated that, given the characteristics of the authoritarian personality,[15] the degree of authoritarianism exhibited by subjects would be related to respective states of decisional participation. A shortened version of the F-Scale was employed for this purpose.

Role conflict. Examples of various types of role conflict abound in empirical research conducted in a host of organizational settings. [16] In most instances data have been provided as evidence that professionals dislike administrative obstruction of, or interference with, activities regarded by this group as constituting an integral part of their professional role behavior. As professionals experience greater role conflict, their organizational commitments and involvements tend to decrease, with consequent effects on their rates of participation in decision making.

The index of conflict utilized in the present analysis focuses on perceptions of current role conflicts. Subjects were asked to respond to a list of ten activities by stating the percentage of work time they believed should be devoted to the performance of each activity. The index was comprised of the sum or absolute magnitude of the differences between desired and prescribed time allotments, that is, between professional ideals and perceived reality.

Interpersonal trust. It was believed that the degree to which individuals find their interpersonal environments supportive and predictable would be an important correlate of decisional participation. Consequently, a six-item scale was employed. As the scores for subjects increase, interpersonal trust is said to become greater.

Attitudes toward militancy. It has been demonstrated that one correlate of increased desire to participate in decision making among teaching personnel is greater attitudinal militancy.[17] In an attempt to discover whether or not conditions of decisional participation served to differentiate among attitudinal predispositions, subject evaluations of strikes, unions, and collective bargaining were measured through semantic differential techniques. For interpretation purposes, the greater each subject's attitudinal score, the more positive his evaluation of each object. Based on previous research, it would be expected that those teachers characterized by decisional deprivation would be the most militant (most favorably disposed toward strikes, unions, and collective bargaining).

FINDINGS

Comparisons of subjects characterized by conditions of decisional deprivation, equilibrium, and saturation are presented in Table 13-3. In terms of personality characteristics, it is surprising that degrees of interpersonal trust, authoritarianism, and organizational commitment are not differentially distributed among individuals with varying decisional attributes. Contrary to Patchen's prediction, although decisionally deprived subjects are somewhat less organizationally committed than others ($\overline{X}$= 9.8 versus 10.1 and 10.4), they are not significantly different. For teaching personnel, decisional deprivation does not lead to significantly lower organizational commitment than decisional equilibrium or saturation.

Of the remaining personality characteristics, seniority provides a weak, though effective, basis for differentiation. The longer subjects were employed in given school districts, the greater the probability that they would be decisionally saturated ($\overline{X}$ seniority for deprivation = 6.8, equilibrium = 7.1, saturation = 9.1).

Sex and age proved to be the most effective bases for distinguishing between the personality characteristics of individuals in various decisional participation states. Consistent with data concerning seniority, decisionally deprived subjects tended to be young males ($\overline{X}$ age = 33.4) and those decisionally saturated primarily older females ($\overline{X}$ age = 39.1). The data also suggest that teachers characterized as having achieved equilibrium between decisional participation desires and actions tended to be middle-aged females.

Data concerning the relationship between administrative influence and conditions of decisional participation suggest definite patterns of control perceptions. Teachers experiencing decisional deprivation rank school superintendents as currently more influential than others ($\overline{X}$ ranks, deprivation = 3.4, equilibrium = 3.5, saturation = 4.5). Those decisionally deprived also desire reduced future administrative influence for both building principals ($\overline{X}$ ranks, deprivation = 4.1, equilibrium = 3.5, saturation = 3.4) and district superintendents ($\overline{X}$ ranks,

TABLE 13-3. Analyses of decisional deprivation, equilibrium, and saturation groupings

Variables	Group means			F-Value	Signifi-cance level[a]
	Depri-vation	Equi-librium	Satura-tion		
Personality					
Trust	13.9	14.0	13.3	1.53	NS
Authoritarianism	34.2	34.1	36.4	1.91	NS
Age	33.4	37.5	39.1	6.05	0.01
Seniority	6.8	7.1	9.1	2.96	0.10
Organizational commitment	9.8	10.1	10.4	1.31	NS
Sex (males 1, females 2)	1.6	1.8	1.9	7.71	0.01
Organizational					
Current rank principal[b]	3.3	3.1	3.2	0.39	NS
Current rank superintendent[b]	3.4	3.5	4.5	6.05	0.01
Preferred rank principal[b]	4.1	3.5	3.4	3.02	0.05
Preferred rank superintendent[b]	5.4	4.7	4.9	2.60	0.10
Role conflict	34.4	27.8	28.5	2.63	0.10
Attitude toward:					
Collective bargaining	5.4	4.4	4.7	10.35	0.001
Strikes	3.3	2.2	2.5	15.94	0.001
Unions	4.0	2.7	2.9	19.45	0.001
Teaching level (elementary 1, secondary 2)	1.5	1.2	1.2	10.96	0.001
School district (urban 1, rural 2)	1.5	1.2	1.3	11.42	0.001

[a]Degrees of freedom (2/453).

[b]Due to characteristics of the ranking techniques, the lower the numerical value assigned to a role performer, the more influential subjects believe him to be currently or the more influential they wish him to be.

deprivation = 5.4, equilibrium = 4.7, and saturation = 4.9). Thus, individuals who desire greater decisional participation than currently experienced tend to see top administrative officials as exercising high decisional control. These teachers would like to see a control structure instituted which encourages greater participation by subordinates due to the reduced decisional control of top administrators and immediate superiors.

Although providing a weaker basis for subdivision, various states of decisional participation are characterized by differing levels of role conflict. Maximum role conflict was perceived not by those experiencing decisional saturation ($\overline{X}$ = 28.5) but by individuals character-ized by decisional deprivation ($\overline{X}$ = 34.4). A lack of input into decision-making structures appears to contribute more to the genera-tion of role conflicts than the more obvious situation of excessive decisional participation.

The relationship between attitudinal militancy and decisional par-ticipation is particularly clear. The most militant group of teachers were those experiencing decisional deprivation ($\overline{X}$ scores, collective bargaining = 5.4, strikes = 3.3, unions = 4.0). The least militant subjects were those who achieved equilibrium between participation desires and actions ($\overline{X}$ scores, collective bargaining = 4.4, strikes = 2.2, unions = 2.7). This provides definite support for the hypothesis that unfulfilled desires for participation in decision making provide the basis for much of the current militancy among professionals.[18]

Decisional condition is definitely differentially distributed among subjects teaching at various levels in school systems. Decisional saturation tended to be characteristic of elementary school teachers, and conditions of decisional deprivation were primarily associated with teachers in secondary schools. This is consistent with the previously reported findings that females (predominant at elemen-tary levels) tended to experience decisional saturation and males (predominant at secondary levels) tended to perceive conditions of deprivation.

The two school districts in this study were quite different in respect to decisional participation. District I, the small urban district, was characterized by teachers experiencing decisional equilibrium or saturation. In the rural district teachers tended to feel decisionally deprived. This distinction received verification through interviews which revealed that the rural district had a well-articulated and centralized decision-making structure. District I, on the other hand, exhibited far greater decisional decentralization, with a larger num-ber of administrative subdivisions and with personnel serving as technical specialists.

When comparing within-group differences for those individuals decisionally saturated and at decisional equilibrium, there appeared to exist few differences between those subjects with low, medium, and high involvements. The only statistically significant differences appeared in attitudinal militancy and teaching levels of those teach-ers achieving decisional equilibrium. For this group, involvement in many decisions was associated with teaching in secondary schools and greatest militancy.

The effects of varying degrees of decisional involvement are most clearly observed in the group of teachers previously characterized as decisionally deprived (Table 13-4). The larger the number of decisions in which teachers wish to participate but do not (a) the greater the perceived role conflict, (b) the greater the probability that they are males, (c) the greater the attitudinal militancy, (d) the greater the probability of employment in the rural district, (e) the higher the probability that the top administrative official will be perceived as relatively influential, and (f) the greater the probability of employment in secondary schools.

CONCLUSIONS

As summarized in Table 13-5, the personal and organizational characteristics of individuals experiencing each decisional participa-

TABLE 13-4. Levels of deprivation

Variables	Low	Medium	High	F-Value	Significance level[a]
Personality:					
Trust	14.0	14.1	13.6	0.427	NS
Authoritarianism	34.4	33.3	34.5	0.431	NS
Seniority	6.4	8.0	6.6	1.228	NS
Organizational commitment	10.3	9.7	9.3	2.747	NS
Sex (males 1, females 2)	1.7	1.5	1.3	4.547	0.02
Organizational:					
Current rank principal[b]	3.1	3.3	3.6	1.523	NS
Current rank superintendent[b]	3.8	2.6	3.3	4.801	0.01
Preferred rank principal[b]	3.8	3.9	4.0	0.334	NS
Preferred rank superintendent[b]	5.1	5.3	5.4	0.477	NS
Role conflict	31.9	30.1	41.8	3.869	0.05
Teaching level (elementary 1, secondary 2)	1.3	1.5	1.6	4.075	0.05
Employing district (urban 1, rural 2)	1.4	1.6	1.7	7.241	0.01
Attitude toward:					
Collective bargaining	52.7	52.6	59.5	3.678	0.05
Strikes	29.7	31.2	40.8	8.764	0.01
Unions	38.8	35.6	46.6	5.050	0.01

[a]Degrees of freedom (2/259).

[b]Due to characteristics of the ranking techniques, the lower the numerical value assigned to a role performer, the more influential subjects believe him to be currently or the more influential they wish him to be.

tion state were discovered to be different. Those decisionally deprived tended to be younger males teaching at secondary levels, employed in the rural district, perceiving highest levels of role conflict, and possessing the most favorable attitudes toward collective bargaining, strikes, and unions. In addition, the decisionally deprived perceived decisional control to be residing at top administrative levels and desired that both principals and superintendents be given lower degrees of influence. On the other hand, teachers experiencing decisional saturation tended to be older females teaching at elementary levels in the urban district, perceiving moderate levels of role conflict and possessing moderately unfavorable attitudes toward collective bargaining, strikes, and unions.

TABLE 13-5. Summary of relative and organizational characteristics

	Decisional saturation	Decisional equilibrium	Decisional deprivation
Age	Older	Medium	Younger
Seniority	Senior	Medium	Younger
Sex	Female	Female	Male
Perceived influence superintendent	Lower	Higher	Higher
Preferred influence principal	Higher	Higher	Lower
Preferred influence superintendent	Higher	Higher	Lower
Role conflict	Moderate	Low	High
Attitudinal militancy	Moderate	Low	High
Teaching level	Elementary	Elementary	Secondary
School district	Urban	Urban	Rural

An attempt was made in this article to demonstrate the empirical utility of a somewhat global conceptualization of decisional participation based on the discrepancy between actual and desired participation rates in organizational decision making. While recognizing the importance of ascertaining levels of participation in individual decisions, this study indicates that organizational typologies based on overall conditions of decisional participation are viable.

The research also suggests that the extent of involvement in decision making is particularly important for situations of decisional deprivation. Individuals experiencing high levels of deprivation possess different characteristics than those typified by lower levels of deprivation. Degree of saturation and extent of decisional involvement when at equilibrium do not appear to be crucial variables. It may be that in instances of saturation and equilibrium, organizational members react more to the overall condition than to the specific level of saturation or equilibrium. Thus, in such cases the key question is whether an individual is experiencing decisional saturation or equilibrium and not how much saturation or involvement is involved.

This research also suggests that some assumptions about the consequences of increased participation in decision making should be modified. For example, no evidence was found supporting the assumption that decisional participation leads to increased organizational commitment.[19] Unlike the recommendations of Tannenbaum and others, the study shows that for at least two segments of each organizational population, the introduction of shared decision making is not a viable administrative strategy. For system members currently encountering conditions of decisional equilibrium or saturation, such a tactic for increasing administrative influence may actually prove highly dysfunctional. In the case of those decisionally saturated, a reduction in shared decision making through the centralization of decisional control among superiors may offer the greatest benefits.

The results of this research provide verification for those who have assumed that conditions of decisional deprivation constitute a basis for the increased militancy evidenced among the members of many professional occupations.

Data also suggest at least two future directions for research on participation in organizational decision making. Although all decisions have been treated as though they were of equal importance to all subjects, it is apparent from other research that not all issues are equal.[20] Given the high cost of participation in terms of time and effort, it would be useful to ascertain the differential effects of deprivation or saturation as they vary with the nature of the decisional issue. For example, does denial of the desire to participate in matters which are central to the core task of the profession (as instruction is to the teaching profession) result in greater feelings of deprivation than the denial of the desire to participate in such instrumental matters as the design of building facilities? In the same vein, does participation in decisions concerning the physical plant contribute more toward feelings of saturation than participation in role-defining situations? Are the decisions currently participated in identical to those in which the individual wishes to participate? The research question raised is, what effect does the substantive issue have on conditions of deprivation, saturation, or equilibrium and any associated organizationally relevant results?

While this article has concentrated primarily on rates of decisional participation, the quality of that participation has not been systematically examined. Participation can range from mere consultation to absolute control over final decisions. It is probable that various modes of participation will differentially contribute to situations of decisional deprivation, saturation, or equilibrium. Thus, future research efforts might profitably focus on the relative impact of differing methods of participation in organization decision making, namely, concentration on type of participation in conjunction with overall rates of participation.

Notes

The authors wish to thank George Strauss for constructive and insightful suggestions offered during the preparation of this article.

1. Max Weber, *The Theory of Social and Economic Organization* (Glencoe, Ill.: Free Press, 1947); Chester I. Barnard, *The Functions of the Executive* (Cambridge, Mass.: Harvard University Press, 1938); Frederick W. Taylor, *Scientific Management* (New York: Harper & Row, 1947); James March and Herbert Simon, *Organizations* (New York: John Wiley, 1958).

2. Lester Coch and John R. P. French, "Overcoming Resistance to Change," *Human Relations*, I (1948), 512-32.

3. C. J. Lammers, "Power and Participation in Decision Making in Formal Organizations," *American Journal of Sociology*, LXXIII (1967), 201-16.

4. Alvin W. Gouldner, *Patterns of Industrial Bureaucracy* (New York: Free Press, 1954).

5. Arnold S. Tannenbaum (ed.), *Control in Organizations* (New York: McGraw-Hill, 1968).

6. Mauk Mulder, "Power Equalization through Participation?" *Administrative Science Quarterly*, XVI (1971), 31-39.

7. Martin Patchen, *Participation, Achievement, and Involvement on the Job* (Englewood Cliffs, N.J.: Prentice-Hall, 1970).

8. Julian Feldman and Herschel E. Kanter, "Organizational Decision Making," in James March (ed.), *Handbook of Organizations* (Chicago: Rand-McNally, 1965), pp. 614-49.

9. James A. Belasco and Joseph A. Alutto, "Organizational Impacts of Teacher Negotiations." *Industrial Relations*, IX (1969), 67-79.

10. Robert T. Golembiewski, "Small Groups and Large Organizations," in March, *Handbook of Organizations*, pp. 87-141.

11. Eugene E. Kaczka and Roy Kirk, "Managerial Climate, Work Groups, and Organizational Performance," *Administrative Science Quarterly*, XII (1967), 253-72.

12. Victor Vroom, *Work and Motivation* (New York: John Wiley, 1964).

13. Arnold S. Tannenbaum and Basil S. Georgopolous, "The Distribution of Control in Formal Organizations," *Social Forces*, XXXVI (1957), 44-50.

14. Patchen, *Participation*.

15. Theodor W. Adorno *et al.*, *The Authoritarian Personality* (New York: Harper & Row, 1950).

16. Joseph A. Alutto, "Role Theory in Propositional Form" (Ph.D. diss., Cornell University, 1968).

17. Belasco and Alutto, "Organizational Impacts of Teacher Negotiations, 67-79; James A. Belasco, Joseph A. Alutto, and Frederick Greene, "A Case Analysis of Negotiation Behavior in an Urban School System," *Education and Urban Society*, II (1969), 22-39. 22-39.

18. Belasco and Alutto, "Organizational Impacts."

19. Patchen, *Participation*.

20. Joseph A. Alutto and James A. Belasco, "Decisional Participation among Teaching Personnel and Perceptions of Administrative Influence," paper presented at the 1970 meeting of the American Educational Research Association, Minneapolis; Mulder, "Power Equalization."

COMMENT / Teacher Participation in Educational Decision Making

Robert G. Wegmann

At a time when pressures for educational change are not only building, but are aimed at the very structure of public education (in contrast to the pressures of the 1960's, which focused on less central matters such as curriculum content and academic standards), the issues raised by Alutto and Belasco are relevant indeed. Demands for community control, decentralization, management by objectives and program budgeting (all of which are heard in any large school system) implicitly raise the issue of how great a share teachers are to have in educational decision making. The concepts of decisional deprivation, equilibrium, and saturation may prove to be highly useful in evaluating the actual effect of these proposed reforms on staff morale.

As to the specific findings reported by Alutto and Belasco, however, some caution would seem warranted. The study involved only two school districts, and, although these districts are described as quite different, data from them are often lumped together. A strong argument can be made, however, that the political characteristics of a school district set the most fundamental context within which teacher (or any other) participation in educational decision making takes place. How "teachers" view their present and potential participation in school governance is very much a function of both the external political situation and the internal organizational structure.

This may become particularly important if one attempts to apply Alutto and Belasco's findings to a large city school system. As McCarty and Ramsey[1] have shown in their survey of 51 school districts throughout the Northeast and Midwest, strikingly different patterns of community power structure, board composition, and superintendent behavior can be found in small towns, suburban communities, and large cities. They report (and my own experience confirms) that a big-city superintendent who wishes to obtain maximum teacher involvement faces serious and inherent problems. The pressures from a diverse community, a factionalized board, a heavily bureaucratized central office, and equally bureaucratized teacher and supervisory unions all combine to produce situations quite different from either the small urban or medium-sized rural district surveyed by Alutto and Belasco. Remsberg and Remsberg,[2] for example, detail some excellent examples of what is encountered in the large school district.

Even within school districts of approximately similar size there can be significant differences in the degree of control exerted over the individual school by the central administration, not unlike the differences that Alutto and Belasco discovered, depending on the philosophy of the superintendent and the demands and pressures exerted by the school board and the community. In some school systems, new teachers are selected by the personnel department and then assigned, perhaps at the last minute, to teach at a particular school. Other systems leave the choice of new faculty to the principal, who may involve teachers or department heads in the decision. Similarly, both the general school budget and approval for particular expenditures may be primarily set at either the central office or local school level. In some systems subject matter specialists from the central office exert strong influence on individual teachers, visiting them regularly and keeping in close touch with their classroom activities. In other school systems, subject matter specialists are rarely seen in the schools, and they confine their operations to printed curricular outlines and in-service workshops. Even the high school's master schedule is constructed by the central office computer in some systems, while in others it is done by the local principal. The more decisions that are made at the school itself, the easier it is for the individual teacher to have a voice in those decisions.

A second difficulty with the study as reported is that it fails to identify which of the twelve decisional situations are most important to the teachers being surveyed (or whether there might be some other decisions of greater concern). The fact that Table 13-2 relates the total number of decisions in which a teacher participated to the total number in which a teacher preferred to participate glosses over both (a) whether the decisions in which a teacher participates are the same as those in which he wants to participate, and (b) how strongly a teacher feels about the need to participate in a given decision. Apparently, as Table 13-2 is constructed, a teacher could participate in six decisions about which he cares little, not participate in six others about which he cares a great deal, and be counted as in decisional equilibrium. This fact, combined with the lack of interview data which might give some meaning to the results obtained, would seem to call for some caution in any attempted application of Alutto and Belasco's findings, especially if one wants to extrapolate them to a large city school system.

An issue which particularly needs to be explored when considering the large school district is this: just what is the decisional *process* in which a teacher might become involved? Is it a frustrating, time-consuming, conflict-filled process of trying to bring about major changes in school structure and operation, or is it a simple, effective straightforward process of helping to make the kind of decision that produces a relatively pleasant year in the classroom? A few faculty and the principal putting together a special assembly schedule after lunch is one example of a decisional process; so is service as chairman of the district's mathematics curriculum committee. Depending on the kind of decision to be made, the degree of centralization in the school district, the structural complexity of the school, the number of people involved, the amount of time consumed (and at what hour of the day or time of the week or year), the kind of impact that can be seen as a result of the decision (and the praise or blame that that impact attracts), an invitation to participate in educational decision making can be either an opportunity to exert significant control over one's working environment or an invitation to share in the frustration of long hours spent trying to get a very large number of participants to agree on decisions whose impact seems a long way away from the pressing problems of tomorrow morning. This latter situation is not at all uncommon in Milwaukee and, undoubtedly, in many other large school districts.

There is, in fact, a whole educational art to setting up nonsignificant decisions in which others are to participate. Such situations are not created exclusively for teachers. Principals, for example, are well known for allowing PTA's and student councils to make decisions only in carefully limited areas.[3] Similarly, school board members in cities of any size are routinely inundated with indigestible quantities of information, often about trivial issues, so that they never quite get to the key educational decisions.[4] Whatever one may think of the honesty of this "art of the sham decision," it is not difficult to understand the pressures on the educational administrator to practice it. The fundamental fact is that there are an extraordinary number of individuals and groups who can claim a legitimate voice in any educational decision. The students are the ones most directly affected; the parents have a basic responsibility for what happens to their children; the teachers are the professionals who actually carry on the educational program; the principal is to be responsible for what happens in the school; the central office obviously has supervisory responsibility; the taxpayer has to foot the bill; the superintendent will have to explain to the board if any questions are raised, for the board, after all, has been elected to oversee the entire educational system. Any one of these groups—students, parents, teachers, principals, central office administrators, taxpayers, superintendent or school board—can, if sufficiently aroused, block almost any educational decision. Under such circumstances it is obviously safest to do this year what has been done the year before. This course of action, if challenged, has the force of precedent going for it and is the easiest to justify.

Other issues raised by Alutto and Belasco's findings also deserve further clarification if research of this type is to provide results which are applicable in practice. Thus it is intriguing to report more decisional deprivation among secondary teachers and also among male teachers. But is this because there are more male secondary teachers, or is it that male secondary teachers are also more decisionally deprived than female secondary teachers? Since there is no cross-tabulation provided in the study as reported, this rather important kind of distinction cannot be made.

There are, in my observation, numerous consequences for the individual teacher in the structural differences between elementary and secondary schools. Grade schools are, even in large city systems, typically quite a bit smaller than high schools so that fewer people need ordinarily be involved in any particular decision. The grade school teacher is a generalist; the high school teacher is a subject matter specialist. ("I teach third grade," says the one; "I teach mathematics," says the other.) The grade school teacher deals with the same students all day; the high school teacher instructs class after class in his subject matter specialty. Access to authority in the grade school is much more direct. A teacher with a problem goes directly to the principal. Indeed, in many grade schools the principal and the school secretary run the school between them (sometimes who plays the more important role is not immediately evident!). The high school teacher, on the other hand, is separated from the principal by a more complex hierarchy of assistant principals, guidance specialists, deans of discipline, department heads, and others who share in the organization, scheduling, control-maintenance and curriculum decision-making authority. As a result, the decision-making process in the high school is ordinarily more formal. With so many to be involved, meetings must be scheduled, and an effort must be made to include everyone who has some legitimate interest in what is being decided.

It is, in fact, the much simpler grade school structure and the accompanying informality that can so magnify the effect of a principal's personality on a school. It has often been noted that, from year to year, a school will have the same faculty, the same curriculum, the same building and materials, the same kind of student; yet because of a new principal the place is genuinely a new school. On paper, Milwaukee's elementary schools look quite uniform; yet actually visiting the schools, even in the same part of town, one can hardly believe that they are part of the same system. In contrast, the effect of a principal's educational philosophy and style of leadership on a high school is diluted by the administrative layers between himself and the individual teacher; it does not seem to become apparent as quickly or permeate a school as deeply as is the case in the elementary school.

In this context the "role conflict" reported by Alutto and Belasco in the decisionally deprived male secondary teacher makes sense. Boxed in by a department head, principal, other faculty and central office subject matter specialists, few of whom he may know personally in a large system, it is difficult for the young high school teacher not to feel caught in a situation over which he has little control. The grade school teacher, as already noted, is much more likely to have direct access to the principal; in addition, the decisions and changes which she seeks to influence will more often involve few other adults. Unlike the high school teacher, she normally has the same students under her charge all day long. Thus, even in the first year of teaching, she may be able to exert considerable control over her teaching environment and even, within limits, to introduce important changes into it.[5]

With respect to the relationship between decisional deprivation and teacher militancy suggested by Alutto and Belasco, one must note that there is no objective information given by them on the actual strength of the teachers' association or union in the school districts studied. My own experience would at least suggest as a hypothesis that there may well be a curvilinear relationship between decisional deprivation and the strength of a teacher's association. That is, with a very weak organization teachers may find little leverage in obtaining a significant voice in educational decisions. Then, with increasing organization and strength, they may find in the union a powerful vehicle to affect the educational decisions most important to them. As the union itself, however, grows larger and becomes progressively more entrenched and bureaucratized, it may come to hinder teacher participation in decision-making as much as to facilitate it, a process not confined to teachers' unions.[6]

It is, in fact, a central tenet of collective bargaining that management (the school board and superintendent) *cannot* deal directly on matters of wages, hours, and working conditions with individual teachers or staffs, but must deal with the recognized bargaining agent. And this does not mean the union representative at the local school; it means only the union leadership.

Just what constitutes "wages, hours and working conditions" can be construed quite broadly. On September 11, 1972, the Milwaukee Public School administration dismissed classes early so that principals could discuss goals and objectives for the year with their staffs. The Milwaukee Teachers Education Association responded by filing a grievance with the Wisconsin Employment Relations Commission, instructing their membership not to participate in any such discussions. As TEAM, the MTEA paper, reported in its December issue:

The goals stated by the principals are working conditions. Therefore, the MTEA contended that the administration was engaging in individual negotiations and circumventing the elected bargaining representative, MTEA. This method of simply not bargaining with the exclusive bargaining agent is considered to be a prohibited practice.

Another article in the same issue deals with the role of the MTEA Building Representative (BR), and strikes the same theme:

As a building *leader*, the BR is responsible for the isolation of violations of the teacher contract or of administrative attempts to treat teachers improperly and/or unjustly. A BR must be continually wary of his principal and local administrators. Most contractual evasions or violations are presented by a "nice-guy" principal under the guise of a policy of "friendly cooperation" between local administrators and staff. This "cooperation" can be made to seem logical, necessary and desirable. But a wise BR realizes that cooperation, though necessary within a school, must be based on the contract and upon the guaranteed ability of teachers to work toward improving their schools.[7]

Thus teachers who might wish to interview new faculty coming to their school may find union opposition lest the seniority transfer clauses of the contract be undercut; staffs which believe that a shortened lunch hour in the school would improve discipline and increase instructional time will find union opposition because this is in violation of the contract; attempts to extend the school day to make particular courses available to students who would otherwise not be able to take them may meet similar opposition, since the length of the school day is also set by contract.

Contract administration and enforcement is much easier when curricula, practices, and organizational patterns are uniform throughout a large school district, however little this may serve the diverse student population of the city. When the inherent conservative force of this fact is added to the administrative habit of invoking probable teacher union interference as a reason for not considering any innovation or improvement, the impact on teacher (or any other) participation in bringing about educational change is very considerable.

How all of this can work out in practice is illustrated by the verbatim minutes of exchanges that took place before the Finance Committee of the Milwaukee Board of School Directors the evening of May 1, 1973.

Lincoln Junior-Senior High School, a predominantly black school on Milwaukee's lower east side, developed a program to improve the preparation of their seventh- and eighth-grade students for high school. It involved (a) decreasing the number of courses taken by seventh-grade students from 9 to 6; (b) scheduling the classes in blocks so as to facilitate cooperative planning and interdisciplinary team teaching; (c) greater emphasis on major subject areas; (d) a formal reading program for every seventh- and eighth-grade student; (e) a "core period" for various uses as part of the seventh-grade program; (f) three additional teachers; and, (g) a five-day summer workshop for the faculty involved. The proposal, having been approved by the Committee on Appointment and Instruction, came before the Committee on Finance because it involved an additional expenditure of $20,061 which had to be transferred from the board's Contingent Fund.

A board member friendly to the MTEA moved to hold the matter in committee, which would delay approval for at least a month. A discussion ensued on whether or not there had been sufficient involvement of the Lincoln faculty in developing the proposal. The curriculum coordinator for Lincoln defended the proposal and the involvement process. ("Every single staff member has had a copy of it since January 24th. And this is May. I am in the building every day all day.") The superintendent pointed out that the MTEA had complained of insufficient MTEA involvement at the Appointment and Instruction meeting (held April 17) and that this had been followed up. Mr. Cook,[8] Executive Director of the MTEA, had been contacted by letter a few days after, but had not replied. The MTEA, however, had in the interim constructed a questionnaire on faculty involvement to be sent to the staff at Lincoln.

The Lincoln guidance director spoke up and indicated that holding up the program for a month would throw off programming for the fall. A parent from Lincoln reported that there had been parental involvement, and gave as her opinion that, "The hassle stems from the fact that there are some teachers in Lincoln Junior-Senior High School who do not want to teach seventh and eighth graders. It is beneath them." Shortly thereafter, a teacher from Lincoln asked for the floor.[9]

Miss June A. Wojak: June Wojak, I am a reading teacher at Lincoln High School. As reading teacher at Lincoln High School, I was given one of the surveys by the MTEA. I did hand it in. I wonder, since you have been kind enough to listen to us as long as you have, and since we do have someone here from the MTEA, could I not find out for my own curiosity and maybe for yours what were the results of those surveys that were turned in? Since they were to have been turned in by yesterday for consideration for today's meeting, could we ask for that information?

Director[10] Davis: Is there a representative of the MTEA?

Mr. Michael J. Sullivan: Yes.

Davis: Would you wish to address the committee on behalf of the MTEA?

Sullivan: I would prefer not to at this time. Mike Sullivan, staff representative. I would prefer not to at this time.

Davis: The chair might just ask, have you been aware that this matter was up before this committee?

Sullivan: Yes.

. . . .

Davis: All right. I will make it very blunt. What excuse, if any, have you for not wishing to express the MTEA position before this committee at this very moment?

. . . .

Sullivan: Okay. I am Assistant Executive Director and the Executive Director, Mr. Cook, who did receive Mr. North's [a central office administrator] letter, asked me to come tonight and expressed his wish that I would not speak at this time. I think if you want to get into a lot of debate about the involvement and Mr. Nowak's [the Chief Negotiator] position on the contract and concerns about the state law, we could go into all that. But I would prefer not to speak at this time.

But I would say that things that have been said and some of the things that you have said, Director Davis, concerning what MTEA involvement means, should be considered by the committee. We have been receiving the surveys and we would have to put those together. We don't have the total results tabulated. But there was concern about teacher involvement. There was concern from the teachers whether or not they understood what the program meant. Also, a question related to whether they would volunteer for the program, and very few of those surveyed indicated that they would. And this is the kind of information, I think, that Miss Wojak wants at this time. But it is not totally tabulated.

And I think we do need time, number one, to get the entire concerns of the Lincoln staff, and then, number two, to sit down and see how these things match up with contractual obligations to all 6,000 teachers. We do need that time. And that's all we are asking for.

There is no criticism of the program or its impact. There is nothing in the program itself. But, as the bargaining agent, we would [like to] be appropriately involved.

Wojak: June Wojak again. One of the Directors pointed out before, and I was very glad that he did, that this is in fact an open meeting. Anyone may come; anyone may speak. Mr. Sullivan has come but he has chosen not to speak. No other teachers or no other representatives have chosen to come and speak. The concerned teachers have come. They have spoken.

Since I saw the survey sent, I [know there were] ten simple questions. I do not believe it takes very long to tabulate 10 simple questions sent out to 38 or 42. The cover letter that came with the survey said very clearly that the results had to be in so that the results could be considered at this meeting, May 1st. If they couldn't do it by May 1st, why did they say they could do it?

Here we have asked you this. We are asking for it again. We hear no one speaking specifically against it. I, therefore, urge you to reconsider and perhaps pass this thing tonight. Thank you.

Despite this teacher's plea the committee, made up largely of board members supported by the MTEA in their election campaigns, voted 4-1 to delay the matter a month. Only Director Davis voted against the motion to hold in committee.[11]

Under conditions such as these one may perhaps speak of an individual teacher's decisional deprivation, but the deprivation is caused as much by the teacher's own bargaining agent as by the school administration. It is at least questionable whether such a situation is likely to lead to increased militancy—at least in the sense of increased interest in promoting teacher unionism.

In sum, then, the concepts of decisional deprivation, decisional equilibrium, and decisional saturation are both clever and provocative, and Alutto and Belasco should be given credit for an enterprising first attempt at their use. Findings of real substance, however, seem likely to come only when more attention is paid to the objective constraints of community power structure and board composition, the school district's internal organizational pattern, the specific decisions to be influenced, the size and bureaucratization of the local teacher association, the student population of both school and school district, and the significantly different structures of elementary and secondary schools. Failing this, it is too easy to fall into the fallacy of attributing to psychological characteristics or states the results which are in fact due to the political, organizational, and social structures which act as powerful constraints on the behavior of the individual teacher.

Notes

1. Donald McCarty and Charles Ramsey, *The School Managers* (Westport, Connecticut: Greenwood, 1971).

2. Charles Remsberg and Bonnie Remsberg, "Chicago Voices: Tales Told Out of School," in Raymond Mack (ed.), *Our Children's Burden* (New York: Random House, 1968), pp. 273-386.

3. See Arthur Vidich and Joseph Bensman, "The Clash of Class Interests in School Politics," in Alan Rosenthal (ed.), *Governing Education* (Garden City, N. Y.: Doubleday, 1969), pp. 225-252, for a good example; Susan Jacoby, "What Happened When a High School Tried Self-Government," *Saturday Review*, LV (1972), 49-53, describes a refreshing exception.

4. Joseph Pois, "The Board and the General Superintendent," in Rosenthal, *Governing Education*, pp. 427-54.

5. Herbert Kohl, *The Open Classroom* (New York: Random House, 1969).

6. Martin Glaberman, "Unions vs. Workers in the Seventies: The Rise of Militancy in the Auto Industry," *Society*, X (1972), 85-89.

7. *TEAM* (December 1972), pp. 3, 5.

8. All names of individuals in this account have been changed.

9. The quotations here are from the verbatim transcript of the meeting, with the proper names changed.

10. School board members in Milwaukee are addressed as "Director."

11. The program was finally passed by the board on June 28 in modified form, with provisions that it begin as a pilot program staffed only by volunteer teachers.

IV / COLLECTIVE BARGAINING AND RELATED ISSUES

INTRODUCTION

Much descriptive literature exists in the area of collective negotiations. We know, for example, about the history of teachers' unions, the similarities and differences between unions, and the details of pertinent state laws. On the other hand explanatory work, especially that which is backed up empirically, is only beginning. There is no theoretical base for collective bargaining in public education; we know little about the factors influencing the outcome of negotiations, or the effects of bargaining on organizational structures and processes. Further, as was indicated in the previous section, research into the extent to which bargaining improves the teachers' lot is just being initiated. Certainly one can always point to some spectacular settlement in which this has occurred. However, it will require serious analytical work to discover whether or not these are just spectacular exceptions.

On the normative side, a lot has been said about the ways negotiations should be conducted. For the most part these observations do not rely on a solid empirical foundation, but on the personal viewpoints of their advocates, some of which have been formed on the basis of experience in the private sector. It is little wonder that such prescriptions are often contradictory. What should be the composition of negotiating teams? What is the optimum geographical area for negotiations? What strategies should be employed to lower the chances of an impasse? These and numerous other questions are still waiting to be answered from an analytical viewpoint.

The research presented here will by no means provide the definitive answers for which scholars and practitioners are searching. Yet, collectively, it represents a solid foundation upon which further work is already building. The studies divide into three broad categories including structure of the bargaining relationship, prevention and handling of impasses, and reactions of teachers to collective negotiations. Most of the work has been done by students of industrial relations, but contributions from educational administration and sociology are also included.

With respect to the first issue, the fundamental question is no longer whether we shall have collective bargaining in public education, but what form the bargaining relationship will take. Here, our concern must be not only with formal, institutionalized aspects reflected in state regulations and bargaining agreements, but also with informal behavioral characteristics exhibited in actual practice. At one extreme there may turn out to be a unique negotiating structure designed to meet the specific needs of teachers who regard themselves and are regarded by school boards as public sector professionals. At the other extreme union-type relationships copied from the private sector may evolve. The chapter by Garbarino outlines some verbal models of the bargaining relationship involving professional and union orientations, and it explores the similarities and differences among them. Then he utilizes the models to analyze California's experience under the Winton Act, a law considered to be at the professional end of the continuum. Of particular interest is his discussion of how actual practice departs from the philosophy of the statutes and his predictions of likely trends. Further insight into the impact of the Winton Act can be obtained from an article by Craft[1] who has tested some of these predictions.

It is little wonder that a significant portion of the current literature on negotiations has dealt with impasses. Since strikes still run counter to most prevailing legal norms, it is crucial to (1) design statutory methods for handling impasses and (2) discover strategies which reduce the chances of their occurring. Accordingly, research which inquires into the effectiveness of third-party intervention and the reasons for the occurrence of deadlocks has a high priority. Drotning and Lipsky's article is an exploratory effort which studies these two problems utilizing data from the New York situation under the Taylor Law. In dealing with the first one, they ask some pertinent questions, suggest measures for crucial variables, and develop some meaningful hypotheses. For example, they come to grips with the problem of choosing a criterion to judge the effectiveness of alternative strategies for handling impasses. With respect to the investigation of the causes of deadlocks, they generate a conceptual framework involving economic, institutional, and procedural reasons. Although empirical evidence for the framework is not presented, the necessary research is currently being conducted by the authors.

Sarthory's paper has a dual function. It is one of the first attempts to examine the effectiveness of some of the conflicting normative assertions on bargaining. The criterion employed is whether or not a particular prescription is associated with third-party intervention. His work is consequently an empirically oriented complement to Drotning and Lipsky's efforts. Coincidentally, it is based on data from New York school districts during the first year of operation of the Taylor Law. Sarthory is mainly concerned with the structural reasons for the occurrence of impasses such as negotiating team composition. Many of these would seem to best fit into Drotning and Lipsky's procedural category. However, his particular hypotheses are not considered by them. Additional perspectives on impasse prevention are available from the second Gerwin paper in the compensation section which includes a case analysis of negotiations which almost ended in a deadlock, and a recent article by Vantine[2] which uses conflict resolution theory to understand bargaining tactics during negotiations.

Research into teachers' reactions to collective bargaining gives us deeper understanding into such questions as why teachers join unions, which ones they join, and why strikes are supported. Moreover, there are policy implications for school boards trying to contain militancy and for teachers' organizations attempting to use it as a bargaining tactic. Cole's work is concerned with the sociological as opposed to economic reasons for the support of strikes, a question that is explored by using decision making as the unit of analysis. Suppose a teacher is predisposed one way or the other on the strike issue. What factors from his immediate work environment determine whether or not he actually behaves that way? In providing answers to this question, Cole makes extensive use of the concept of cross pressures, the situation arising when predispositions point one way and environmental factors the other way. A more comprehensive account of his research is to be found in Cole[3].

The article by Hellriegel, French, and Peterson is a logical complement to Cole's work. By studying the reasons for teachers' attitudes toward various dimensions of collective negotiations including the support of strikes, they are in effect analyzing the factors shaping the predispositions Cole took as given. Their original conceptual model has a psychological orientation; the basic constructs are attitudes, aspiration levels, and reinforcements. It is also systems oriented in that allowance is made for feedback loops among certain variables. Further, the system is considered to be open in the sense that uncontrollable environmental factors affect internal system variables. While the authors have made only a start in testing the richness of the model, their findings are in general supportive. Vantine's comments work within the conceptual framework to expand on the impact of at least four of its variables. He is largely concerned with institutional factors such as organizational climate, professionalism as exhibited by the desire for participation in decision making, state regulations, and teachers' power and control. The interested reader may also want to see Moore's[4] critique of the article and the reply by Hellriegel and Peterson[5].

The commenter in this section, Dr. A. William Vantine, is Superintendent of the Abington Heights School District, Clarks Summit, Pennsylvania. In his last position he was Director of Personnel and chief negotiator for the Mt. Lebanon School District, Pittsburgh, and he has worked as a professional negotiator and management consultant for school boards in New York and New England. He served as welfare chairman and president of a large teachers' association in New York State. Dr. Vantine has also written on the subject of collective negotiations for professional journals.

Notes

1. James A. Craft, "Proportional Representation for Teacher Negotiations," *Industrial Relations,* VIII (No. 3, May 1969), 236-46.

2. A. William Vantine, "Toward a Theory of Collective Negotiations," *Educational Administration Quarterly,* VIII (No. 1, Winter 1972), 27-43.

3. Stephen Cole, *The Unionization of Teachers* (New York: Praeger, 1969).

4. William J. Moore, "Collective Negotiations and Teachers: A Behavioral Analysis, Comment," *Industrial and Labor Relations Review,* XXIV (No. 2, January 1971), 249-57.

5. Don Hellriegel and Richard B. Peterson, "Collective Negotiations and Teachers: A Behavioral Analysis, Reply," *Industrial and Labor Relations Review,* XXIV (No. 2, January 1971), 257-64.

14 / Professional Negotiations in Education

Joseph W. Garbarino

In the mid-fifties Daniel Bell pointed out that the American labor movement had grown through an alliterative process of eruption, extension, and enforcement. By eruption he meant unionism's massive penetration of previously unorganized sectors of the economy, a process epitomized by the large-scale organizing drives of the thirties which brought unionism to the mass production industries. One of the first of the prophets of gloom and doom for the unions, Bell saw little evidence in 1954 that any new eruption was likely in the foreseeable future.[1] Although Bell's prophecy displayed impressive durability, a moderately good case can be made that the condition of the labor movement today resembles that of the early thirties and that a new era of expansion of major proportions may be in prospect.

ECHOES OF THE THIRTIES

In the sixties, as in the thirties, the union movement was being accused of a failure to adapt to environmental changes that provided opportunities for growth in membership and influence, its leaders were seen as aging and unimaginative, it was accused of parochialism and of failure to meet the challenge of social reform by espousing the

Reprinted from *Industrial Relations*, VII (No. 2, February 1968), 93-106.

cause of the underprivileged poor and the minorities, and it was charged with a lack of initiative in dealing with the changes in the occupational and industrial structure of the labor force which threatened the traditional blue-collar base of the movement. From a position outside the confines of the labor "establishment," Walter Reuther, a colorful and successful leader, appeared ready to essay the role played by John L. Lewis in the earlier period.

There is no reason why this particular period of "decline" need be followed by a new revival, but there are some signs of life in the patient. Most of these signs are to be found in the public or non-profit sector of the economy. In 1963 President Kennedy promulgated Executive Order 10988, aimed at "providing (federal) employees an opportunity for greater participation in the formation and implementation of policies and procedures affecting the conditions of their employment." In recent years, several states have adopted laws extending collective bargaining rights to public employees, following the lead of municipalities such as New York and Philadelphia which previously had established special procedures for certain of their employees. Unions of government employees, such as the American Federation of State, County, and Municipal Employees, the American Federation of Government Employees, the American Federation of Teachers (which includes some private employees), the National Federation of Post Office Clerks, and the National Association of Letter Carriers, have been among the fastest growing unions. The Teamsters Union, the corporate conglomerate of the union movement, has been growing steadily over a wide range of public and private jurisdictions, and unions in the service industries such as the Retail Clerks and the Building Service workers have been increasing in size.

At least as important, the long and well-established state and municipal employee associations and professional associations, such as the affiliates of the National Education Association (NEA) and the American Nursing Association, have become more aggressive in acting as employee representatives and have taken on many of the characteristics of more traditional unions. As a result, strikes and other forms of "direct action" have appeared among some rather unusual occupational groups, such as social workers, teachers, and nurses, as well as among more traditional groups such as transit workers.

Of these incidents, the most significant almost certainly have been those involving teachers. The massive education "industry" employs nearly two million instructional personnel at the elementary and secondary levels (hereafter referred to for convenience as public education), about 90 percent of them in the public sector. Nearly a half million more teachers work in higher education, with the bulk of them also found in public institutions.

NEA affiliates have approximately one million members currently (not all of them instructional staff) and the American Federation of Teachers (AFT) is reported to have about 130,000 members. No other organization plays a significant role as an employee representative in education, although partisans of the American Association of University Professors (AAUP) might challenge this evaluation in the higher education sector. Both the NEA and the AFT have experienced rapid growth since the crucial "confrontation" in New York City in 1961 involving the United Federation of Teachers (UFT), the local affiliate of the AFT. Since then, the AFT has grown from about 60,000 to its present size, with the UFT alone spurting from some 4,000 members in 1961 to over 35,000 in 1967 to account for about half of the new growth and about one-quarter of the total AFT membership. The NEA appears to have increased by a third over the same period.[2]

The ferment in education resembles in some respects the flurry of organizing that occurred among engineers in the latter half of the fifties. In the earlier instance, a nascent union movement appeared for a few years to be a potential challenger to the professional societies' role as the dominant form of occupational association. Union activity among engineers never reached major proportions and has since receded from its modest level of advance. The engineering societies have expanded their interest in economic matters somewhat, but it appears that in general the flurry of organizational activity had relatively little lasting impact.

In public education, however, the eruption has progressed much further and there is considerable reason to believe that momentum is continuing to build up. No one needs to be convinced that education is in a period of radical change in virtually all its aspects, and the employee relations pattern is being transformed as part of the process. The organizations not only have made major gains in membership, but have drastically changed relationships between the teachers, their organizations, and the school boards in a number of communities and states. Fundamentally, the objective conditions of the teacher's situation are different from those of the engineer in terms of salary, status, working conditions, organizational environment, and many other factors. In spite of these differences, they share an occupational classification on the margin of the professional group. While the rank-and-file engineer or teacher may not exhibit all the attributes of a "true" professional by some sociological standard, they usually regard themselves and are regarded by many of the general public as professional in some meaningful sense. This is an important fact because of its implications for organizational affiliation, employee attitudes, and the range of acceptable tactics. Although many of the self-imposed restrictions traditionally observed by American professionals in advancing their occupational self-interest are disappearing, the ideology and tactics appropriate to "professionalism" are still important issues.

In the next section, a set of models of professional relationships specifically relevant to education will be formulated. Following this general discussion, the analysis will be applied to the current situation in California public education and the developing pattern under the California collective negotiations law, the Winton Act.

ALTERNATIVE APPROACHES TO PROFESSIONAL RELATIONSHIPS

In this section, a number of different concepts or "models" of professional relationships will be identified and analyzed, beginning with the traditional model of the *self-employed professional.* The significance of this example is that most of the behavior that is generally accepted as "professional" and most of the techniques denoted as "professionalism" stem from this model. We shall argue that these traditional techniques are inadequate to deal with the occupational problems of the employed professional and that new forms of professional relationships are evolving to deal with these issues. A generalized version of an *employed professional* model will be outlined, after which a special example of this class, the *ideal academic* model, will be examined. (The adjective "ideal" is attached to this model to emphasize that only a minority of relatively prestigious university and college faculties have actually achieved this level of occupational control.) We will argue that the academic version of the employed professional model is the ideal or goal of virtually all professional groups. The last model to be studied is the *union* model of professional relationships.

PROFESSIONALISM AS A TECHNIQUE OF JOB CONTROL

Considered as a system of occupational control, the key element in professionalism is the concept of the self-governing community of practitioners. Traditional professional groups, such as physicians and lawyers, have long had the dominant role in controlling admission to and expulsion from the ranks of practitioners and in regulating the internal affairs of the occupational community. According to the usual analysis, society has granted the organized profession special privileges of self-government because the layman, and in particular the lay client of the professional, is incapable of informed judgment in identifying a qualified practitioner and in evaluating the quality of the service performed.[3] No one is presumed to be able to make sound judgments about the quality of medical care provided by a physician except another physician. In return for this special occupational status, the profession assumes a group responsibility for the quality, and to some extent availability, of professional service to their clientele.

As long as a large majority of the members of a profession are self-employed, the classic techniques of professionalism can work reasonably well to protect their economic interests. These techniques can be divided into three categories.

Control over supply. Professional control over supply is primarily a matter of control of entry to the profession. It is accomplished by gaining acceptance of a system of certification and by controlling the method by which individuals become certified. Usually this involves control over the educational process by setting educational requirements, by accrediting the institutions providing the required education, or by administering an examination system.

Control over entry is often identified with state licensing, but this is only the most common method of accreditation. Although it is convenient to have state support through a licensing procedure, accreditation can be privately administered quite successfully. An example is the status of the Ph.D. degree as an informal system of accreditation for college teaching. The key requirement is the acceptance by the profession's clients of the claim that the certificate of accreditation represents an important and meaningful differential in the quality of service available to them.

Control over professional behavior. The control of access to professional status is supplemented by techniques to control professional behavior. This is typically handled by the use of codes of ethics. One purpose of such codes is the protection of the client. An effective tradition of explicit recognition of obligations to the clientele, rather than a philosophy of caveat emptor, is probably the most important distinguishing feature of professionalism. Many sections of such codes, however, also operate to regulate competition for business among practitioners. The ban by medical and legal societies on advertising is one example, as are attempts to influence the levels and types of fees charged to clients.

Control over work jurisdiction. Control over entry and professional behavior are of little value to a profession if it loses control over the provision of the service. Physicians attempt to limit the activities of chiropractors and are concerned with the possibility of pharmacists prescribing drugs after a recital of customer symptoms; lawyers and accountants disagree over the status of tax work.

As methods of influencing the earnings, working conditions, and status of the professional, these techniques reflect the economic organization of the traditional professions at the time they were developed. They are concerned with relations among professionals or between professionals and their clients. Few of these tactics are likely to be generally effective against an employer, and this limits the usefulness of the traditional professional society as an employee representative.

THE EMPLOYED PROFESSIONAL MODEL

As a result of large-scale social and technological change, a large proportion of the membership of the traditional professions has been absorbed into organizations as salaried employees. Between 1951 and 1963, for example, the proportion of salaried lawyers almost doubled, from 6.4 to 12.5 percent. In 1964 about one-third of active physicians were not even in private practice, and some of those practicing privately undoubtedly were employed on salary.[4] Of greater importance, however, has been the capacity of modern society to create large numbers of new "professional" occupations (e.g., social workers, systems analysts) and to expand the numbers in the existing employed professional categories, at least in the popular definition of the term. Not only are these new professionals likely to be employees, but they work in large bureaucratic organizations, such as government departments, large corporations, universities, schools, and hospitals.

New professional societies and subgroups of existing associations have been formed to represent the interests of these employed occupations. In substantial measure they adopted the ideology and the patterns of operation of the existing professional societies, but found the control techniques of traditional professionalism inadequate to their problems.

Employers are prone to substitute hierarchical administrative control for professional control based on individual expertise. In contrast to the layman, who feels ignorant in dealing with professionals, institutional employers are likely to take the position that they are informed consumers qualified to select their own suppliers of professional services and to judge the quality of their performance. The problem is only partially alleviated if supervisors are chosen from the professional staff, since they typically are selected by the employer and are integrated into the administrative superstructure under management control. Employers are likely to insist on controlling compensation, the scheduling of work, and the assignment of duties, and may even want to reorganize the performance of the entire range of professional tasks so thoroughly as to deprofessionalize the occupation. Some professional groups have tried with limited success to forestall this process by denying potential employers the use of the corporate form of organization through legislative prohibition or "ethical" practice controls, but, overall, the need for more specific methods of occupational control has been becoming apparent. Large-scale medical and legal service organizations are usually formally organized as partnerships, but this has proved compatible with the use of salaried professionals. The engineer in a design group in a large aerospace firm frequently feels that he needs a representative who can be an effective force in influencing conditions now on *this* job with *this* employer. Even self-employed professionals increasingly find themselves "negotiating" fee schedules with mass buyers of services, such as insurers, unions, and government agencies. It is no longer enough to be able to influence the environment of the occupation as a whole.

In the new circumstances, new techniques of job control began to be developed to help alleviate the problems of the employed professional. Since governments were perhaps the first of the large-scale employers of professionals, political action and lobbying for improved salaries and working conditions were among the first new weapons brought into play. Associations in both the private and public sector also developed the salary survey as a technique for influencing pay levels. Comparative salary information can be an effective pressure tactic, at least when the relevant labor supply is moderately tight. Low relative salaries are a potent source of dissatisfaction among current employees and an embarrassing handicap in the recruitment of new employees. Perhaps at one time division chiefs felt pride in knowing that they had kept salaries in their jurisdiction below those of comparable units; this is no longer a cause for pride today.

Professional societies went on to develop a variety of sanctions that might be applied to individual employers. These can be divided into two classes, direct and indirect, depending on whether they call for positive action by the current employees of the offending employer or rely on actions of the rest of the profession. The best example of the indirect sanction is the tactic known as censure, the blacklist, or the blockade, in which the existence of unsatisfactory conditions is publicized and members of the profession at large are urged to refuse to accept positions with the recalcitrant employer.[5]

A critical turning point is reached when the profession moves on to direct sanctions. It is at this point that doubts set in as to whether a particular action is "professional" or not. (It is common for society representatives to argue that mere membership in a labor union is unprofessional per se, but this is surely because of the union's presumed affinity for direct sanctions.)

The strike, of course, is the classic example of the direct sanction, but many actions short of the strike have been developed. These include slowdowns, "working to rule," organized absences, picketing, demonstration meetings, sit-ins, "sick-outs," refusal to accept special assignments or to work overtime, mass resignations submitted in advance of a deadline, short-term stoppages, and a variety of other actions limited only by the ingenuity of the participants.

As long as the concept of a profession is accepted as a distinctive occupational role, there is a legitimate question as to whether many of the forms of industrial warfare are compatible with "professionalism." We argued earlier that the recognition of a special and direct obligation to a clientele (as distinct from an obligation to an employer) is crucial to the concept of a profession. If this is persuasive, then any action taken to win concessions from an employer that relies on the denial of service to that clientele for its effectiveness might be legitimately regarded as "unprofessional." Increasing numbers of professionals, however, seem to be able to resolve this moral dilemma in their own minds by falling back on the argument that achieving the goal of the strike—for example, higher salaries or more professional autonomy—is really essential to ensure the availability of high-quality professional services to the clientele *in the future*. An uncertain, but not negligible, amount of skepticism may occasionally be appropriate in this situation.

THE IDEAL ACADEMIC MODEL

As noted earlier a substantial number of university and college faculties have developed a system of professional relationships which appears to represent a goal of other professional groups.[6] These faculties seem to have achieved the best of two worlds: a high degree of professional autonomy and self-direction coupled with the regularity and security of the employment relationship.

Organized as a "community of scholars," college and university faculty dominate educational policy matters and, in many instances, exert a major influence in deciding questions of departmental and college organizational structure. These divisions become the basic units of professional self-government. In their own institution, academic faculty control the education and certification of new entrants to the profession as a whole. They also largely control the selection, retention, and promotion of their colleagues. Their educational "supervisors," the deans and department chairmen, are typically chosen from their ranks and the faculty usually has a major voice in their selection. Probably in most instances the occupants of many of these positions not only adhere to the values of the profession, but expect to return to the ranks of its practitioners after a relatively short period.

The faculty largely control the content of the curriculum, the scheduling of work, and the evaluation of performance. In addition to a highly developed tradition of professional courtesy, the independence of the individual faculty member is buttressed by the twin principles of academic freedom and job tenure. Operating within these limits, the administration depends for influence primarily on financial controls and effective personal leadership at all levels; ultimately it must rely on a strong sense of professional self-discipline and professional ethics among the faculty.

Interestingly enough, the strongest current pressures to modify this system may well stem from the clientele rather than the employer, as students argue for expanding the concept of the community of scholars to include themselves. In the context of this analysis, faculty responsiveness to these pressures sometimes has some of the aspects of an occupational death wish, since there are few institutionalized protections from organized client pressures.

For our purposes, the most relevant aspect of the ideal academic model is the assumption of the existence of a community of interest among the various elements of the institution. In general, the institutional employer accepts the goals of the profession as its own. This explains why a professionally oriented lower- and middle-management group, often serving on a part-time or rotational basis, can be successfully utilized.

Structurally, the faculty is usually organized into a campuswide academic "senate," with no ties to an external organization, with universal automatic membership including many academic administrators, with part-time leadership, and with the organizational budget provided by the institution. This description could serve as a classic example of what in industry would be called a company union. That such a body, operating with delegated authority and officially possessing only advisory decision-making powers, can nevertheless function as a major power center is a tribute to the degree of acceptance by all parties of both the tenets of professionalism and the community of interest interpretation of academic relationships (with perhaps also some credit to the current state of the academic labor market).

It is chiefly in institutions which have not fully developed academic senate models of this type that other organizations, such as the American Association of University Professors, the AFT, or other employee representation units, compete for representation rights with the goal of establishing the academic model.

THE UNION MODEL

While the characteristics of the union model are those that are typical of unions in general and unions of professionals in particular, there is no reason why other types of organizations cannot share these attributes and adopt the same patterns of behavior. Indeed, in later sections we will argue that the union model will appear with increasing frequency in a wide variety of situations, but not necessarily under the union label.

In the last section we argued that the assumption of the existence of a community of interest was the most relevant aspect of the academic professional approach. In contrast, the essential element of the union model is the belief that a fundamental and permanent conflict of interest exists between managers and the managed. The classic role of the union as the defender of labor's interest in the conflict between Labor and Capital (significantly, later changed to the lower case, labor and management) is adapted to the professional situation. Professionals who fill positions as first-level supervisors may occasionally be included in the union, but usually administrators are regarded as enlisted in the forces of management. The exclusion of supervisors from an organization may be the best external evidence of the existence of union attitudes.

Unions do not deny the legitimacy of organizational goals nor do they deny that elements of community of interest do exist. They emphasize that the goals of the system as a whole and the terms in which community of interest is defined allow for wide differences of opinion. Conflict arises in the process of translating generalized goals of organizations into operating policy decisions. The role of the union is to make sure that the actions actually taken adequately reflect the interests of the rank-and-file professionals. If employees are to influence these decisions, they must be ready and able, continuously and forcefully, to pressure management to adopt their preferred policies.

Unions, particularly American unions, are notoriously pragmatic, and they are quick to adopt any tactic that promises success. They have cheerfully used lobbying, salary surveys, control of entry, control over jurisdiction, and all of the other paraphernalia of professionalism for decades. Their frank acceptance of the conflict model of relationships has led them to concentrate on conditions in the individual employing unit and to organize the work group for possible conflict, while standing ready to cooperate if the price is right. In time of peace they prepare for at least limited war.

The attraction of the union approach lies in the willingness and ability to regulate and aggressively police the day-to-day working conditions on individual jobs in a way that professional associations are barely beginning to emulate.

The concept of collective bargaining, as developed by American unions, includes the acquisition of exclusive bargaining rights by one organization, with regular formal negotiations carried on by full-time professional negotiators. An explicit and often lengthy agenda of demands is presented, culminating in a written contract covering a wide range of conditions of employment, including formal grievance procedures, usually with third-party arbitration as the final step. Just as the unions and the associations appear to be converging in terms of the pressure tactics regarded as appropriate, they also are converging in terms of the apparatus and the procedures of bargaining. Differences based on the unions' stress on the conflict aspects of the employer-employee relationship rather than the community of interest aspects that remain attractive to the professional, are likely to be more enduring, but not necessarily permanent.

PROFESSIONAL NEGOTIATIONS IN CALIFORNIA EDUCATION

By the summer of 1967, the ferment in teacher-employer relations noted in the opening section of this paper had produced legislative action affecting these relationships in 13 states. Because national labor legislation in the past has been directed primarily to the private, profit-oriented sector of the economy, because of the tradition of local control of education, and because the regulation of the professions is in the province of the states, direct federal influence has been minimal. The result has been the adoption of very different approaches to the problem of educational industrial relations in the various states. The differences existing in state legislation cover most of the models developed in the earlier sections, and eventually some knowledge of how the various approaches work out in practice will be available. As of now, however, only a limited amount of experience has been accumulated, analyzed, and published. In this section, the California approach, embodied in the Winton Act (AB 1474) passed in 1965, will be analyzed with a view toward evaluating its potential impact on the developing employee relations system in education.

If the various state laws were arranged on a continuum running from the pure professional model on one end to the pure union model on the other, California's law almost certainly would be found at the extreme on the professional end. One attempt to array 11 of the state laws—by scoring according to adherence to a set of plausible criteria—ranks them in descending order of conformity to the professional model: California, Florida, Oregon, New Jersey, Washington, Alaska, New Hampshire, Massachusetts, Michigan, and Connecticut-Wisconsin (tie).[7] This characterization of the Winton Act appears to be generally accepted by all parties concerned, specifically the California Teachers Association (the state NEA affiliate) and the AFT. Since the reasons for this judgment and the assessment of the significance of the resulting situation differ, the features of the California system that illustrate the emphasis on professionalism are discussed below.

1. The law recognizes that educational employee relations in the public schools are separate and distinct not only from those of other employees generally, but specifically from those of other public employees. The Act is part of the Education Code, and its first section effects the transfer of educational employee matters from their former location in the Government Code. This transfer will be important if, as is quite likely, there is further legislation dealing with the problems of public employee relations in California. The identification of the elementary and secondary schools with the education "industry," rather than with the overall government "industry," enhances the likelihood of retaining a "professional" approach.

The possibility of a more unified approach to the problems of education at all levels is suggested by the pervasive appeal of the "senate" model to all faculty groups. The University of California is an outstanding example of the ideal academic model described earlier. The state college system is evolving its own "senate" system, clearly with the ideal model as the goal of its faculty. (But at the same time, the colleges are the center of an active struggle for representation rights between the AFT, the California Teachers Association (a branch of the NEA), the AAUP, the California State Employees Association, and an independent Association of State College Professors.) The junior college system is administratively linked to the lower schools, under the State Board of Education, but their faculty has won the right to organize academic senates. The junior colleges represent a connecting link between the colleges and the lower schools. Preliminary discussions have been held on establishing a state-wide organization of all faculty in higher education, public and private. Already in one local unified school district, a large high school unit's faculty has established its own academic senate. Perhaps the academic model may work its way downward from the university level or, on the other hand, the legislative model may work its way up from the public schools. In any event, employee relations problems may provide the base for a new version of "articulation" between the proliferating levels of the entire educational system.

2. The Winton Act permits employee representation rights to be held by groups which include supervisors of all levels among its members. The only distinction made is between "certificated" employees and all others. The cause of professionalism is further advanced by providing that certificated employees have the right to meet and confer with school boards with regard to the definition of educational objectives and all other aspects of the instructional program which are within the discretion of the employer. This suggests, or at least does not preclude, acceptance of the predominance of the community of interest philosophy of the professional approach rather than the conflict of interest approach more characteristic of the union model. The Rhode Island statute in contrast excludes superintendents, assistant superintendents, principals, and assistant principals from coverage. This same statute lists as the scope of bargaining, "hours, salary, working conditions and all other terms and conditions of professional employment."

3. The unique feature of the Winton Act, and a complete departure from traditional American practice in industrial relations,[8] is the provision for negotiations to be carried on through a "negotiating council made up. . . of representatives of those employee organizations who are entitled to representation on the negotiating council."

Briefly, the negotiating council provides for proportional representation of all organizations competing to represent certificated employees in the district. The councils may range in size from five to nine members, with these members distributed among the organizations according to a membership count. The council is the channel through which the employee representatives "meet and confer" with "the public school employer." This unusual institution has been the focus of attention under the California act, with the most important points of discussion being these:

a. The negotiating council system eliminates the possibility of exclusive representation for any group as long as a competing organization of an appropriate minimum size exists. Although this is clearly at variance with the union model (and the AFT's desires), there is no inherent reason why proportional representation should be linked with the professional association approach. In point of fact, however, it was supported by the CTA and, therefore, might be counted as evidence of the underlying philosophy of the act.

b. Although the negotiating council device rejects the concept of exclusive bargaining rights, it has been interpreted to mean that the council itself is recognized virtually as the exclusive bargaining agent for all organized certificated employees in their dealings with the school board. One reasonable interpretation (but not the only one) of the way the council system might work is to view the council as formulating a set of negotiating "demands" or a negotiating position by a process of internal consensus and then pressing for the adoption of these proposals in meetings with the representative (usually the superintendent) of the school board. If minority dissenters from the official council position are not permitted to "meet and confer" with the board as official representatives of the teachers, then the council as a body has become the de facto exclusive bargaining agent. Given the present distribution of organizational membership (the CTA reports a state-wide membership of about 150,000, while AFT membership is surely only a minor fraction of that), this would mean that in the majority of districts, the professional association would dominate the negotiating process. In this sense, the act could be viewed as supporting the professional approach. Note, however, that a shift in membership patterns would change the impact of this arrangement.

c. More important than the provision for proportional representation itself, is the proviso that the proportions will be based on the membership rolls of the competing organizations at the time the council is formed. Although the exact interpretation of this language may still be subject to judicial challenge, at the moment it seems to mean that a membership count rather than a special representation election will be the method of apportioning seats on the council. If this interpretation holds, it represents a major victory for the "professional" point of view. This is true not only because the CTA is the larger and more entrenched organization, but because it implies that the negotiating councils' activities are seen as part of a more comprehensive system of professional relationships. Representation elections with seats on the council at stake would elevate the council and its negotiating role to the status of a dominant feature of the employer-employee relationship. It would stress conflict of interest at the expense of the community of interest.

FROM THEORY TO PRACTICE

After emphasizing the professional rather than the union orientation of the current California legislation in the preceding section, this portion of the paper will argue that the probable objective effects of the legislation are substantially overrated by both the proponents and the opponents of the present arrangements. In other words, the structural features of the system are potentially important in determining the outcome of the competition between the CTA and the AFT, but in practice they are likely to be less crucial in shaping employment conditions than are the underlying facts of employer-employee relations. These underlying facts include the strength and pervasiveness of teacher grievances, the financial situation of the educational system, and the attitudes and skills of the organizational leadership of all parties. This position will be argued by discussing structural features regarded by the parties as of prime importance.

Exclusive versus proportional representation. In my opinion, the failure of the Winton Act to provide for exclusive bargaining rights is likely to be of decreasing importance as the system evolves. The AFT reacted to the Winton procedures by a virtual complete boycott of the negotiating councils. The strategy appears to have been to try to minimize the effectiveness of the councils (indeed to prevent them from claiming legitimacy as representative bodies), while the union would try to deal directly with the administration as an independent de facto bargaining agent. This tactic seems to have had little success to date, and union representatives are appearing on councils with increasing frequency.

While in the United States the basic bargaining laws governing collective bargaining in the private sector call for representation elections, with the winner being awarded exclusive bargaining rights, this is not the typical practice in other industrial countries. In most countries, an informal system of proportional bargaining structures exists in fact. Note also that the private sector laws in the U.S. provide for exclusive representation by the majority union *in a bargaining unit*. The bargaining unit need not be, and in most cases is not, coextensive with all operations of a single employer. Like the determination of political legislative districts, the definition of the bargaining unit becomes a crucial variable affecting the results of representation elections. In the private sector, the National Labor Relations Board determines the scope of the bargaining unit in which exclusive representation applies. As an example of the results, although the International Union of Electrical Workers has been the dominant union in negotiations with General Electric in recent years, G.E. deals with a number of other major unions and with more than twenty unions in total, each of which has exclusive bargaining rights in some segment of its operations. Interestingly enough, in their last negotiations several of the unions in G.E. formed a sort of "negotiating council" to carry on bargaining. Employee organizations in education may come to look upon joint action as advantageous rather than the opposite. In short, we do not know enough about the way the councils will actually function and how they will affect negotiating strategy to assess the significance of proportional representation.

If exclusive representation had been provided for in the act, the diversity of interests found among certificated employees (between nonsupervisory administrative personnel and classroom teachers, or between disciplines or levels of schools) would have to be accommodated within the structure of a single organization or else multiple bargaining units would have to be established. The result might not be much different from the way negotiating councils will work in practice.

Meet and confer versus bargaining in good faith. Much has been made of the failure of the legislation to require that the parties bargain in "good faith," in the National Labor Relations Act pattern. "Meet and confer" is regarded as a pale shadow of a phrase compared to the traditional language. It is doubtful if, in practice, this much-remarked semantic distinction will be of great importance. President Kennedy's Executive Order 10988 is generally regarded as supporting collective bargaining for federal employees. The word "bargain" does not appear in the order, but agencies are required to "meet at reasonable times and confer..." with recognized employee organizations. Although the Taft-Hartley Act makes it an unfair labor practice to refuse to bargain collectively in good faith, it defines collective bargaining as "the mutual obligation of the employer and the representatives of the employees *to meet* at reasonable times and *confer* in good faith. . ." (my emphasis). If administration representatives are able to refuse to "bargain" because the law only requires them "to meet and confer," it suggests that the underlying balance of bargaining power is such that the distinction is not very important.

The import of the preceding discussion is that a static analysis of the negotiation system of the Winton Act bears out the dominance of the professional model, but the real question is a dynamic one: how will the system work in practice? (In the following, I ignore the real possibility that one organization in some jurisdictions may force direct bargaining outside the negotiating council framework, in spite of the provisions of the law.)

It is not likely that a single pattern of development will prevail universally; rather, a variety of patterns will evolve. In some instances, a conflict pattern will develop that will be close to the trade union model, with its stress on conflict of interest. Negotiating council activities will come to dominate the employer-employee relationship. Competing organizations will concentrate on publicizing and pressing their demands in the council. Even without explicit representation elections, the pattern of organizational membership will change to reflect the differential appeal of the negotiating positions of the competitors, and council seats will be distributed (and periodically redistributed) accordingly. De facto leadership on the council will come to be lodged in one organization. The adoption of the conflict of interest stance need not mean that the union will necessarily become the leading organization. Other teacher organizations may be formed to compete for membership with the established groups. The CTA will adopt whatever strategy appears necessary to compete successfully regardless of professional considerations. Some CTA local associations have employed full-time negotiators (e.g., Oakland) and are increasingly militant.

Outside the centers of conflict, the professional model will probably function adequately in most districts. The professional model has a great deal of utility and attractiveness to large numbers, perhaps the majority, of teachers. In the language of industrial relations, the conflict centers will become "pattern setters," while organizations in most districts will become "pattern followers," enjoying the benefits of militancy without the necessity of being militant themselves. As long as the financial and nonfinancial results of this system in the pattern-following districts are satisfactory, organizational conflict will be muted and the organizational status quo will prevail. Financial constraints will cause difficulty in particular school districts, but the increasing role of the state and federal governments in educational finance will lubricate the machinery and keep it in working order. The various employee organizations and the school boards will find it easy to unite in pressing for increased financial aid from the state and federal governments.

In matters of educational policy, the system will move toward the academic professional model. Most districts have already used advisory committees of teachers in making educational policy decisions in an informal way. The role of these committees will be strengthened, and they will be accorded more formal recognition. Large school units or special purpose units within single districts will on occasion develop an all-encompassing form of senate-type organization. These groups will probably supplement rather than replace the existing organizations. Superintendents may feel that the senate approach is preferable to the alternatives and actually encourage its development.

The role of the superintendent will be a difficult one. In the conflict centers he will be forced to choose sides, and he will most likely become identified with the school board. Outside of these centers, he may be able to function in a mediator's role between the board and the council, indicating to the council what he feels the board will accept, and conveying to the board what he interprets the minimum demands of the teachers to be. The superintendent will on occasion form a professional coalition with the teachers in opposition to the interests of the lay board, but, in the general case, the superintendent is more likely to move into an explicit management role.

In short, the dynamics of employer-employee relationships in education will produce a situation in which relationships will become more formal, more structured, more the product of joint action, more subject to review, more responsive to employee demands, and closer to the collective bargaining model.

SUMMARY

I have identified three pure types of employed professional relationships: (1) the general employed professional model, (2) the ideal academic professional model, and (3) the professional union model. Experience with these models, in particular a review of the California approach to professional negotiations in public education, leads to a forecast that organizations of professional employees—both those which call themselves unions and those which do not—will increasingly take their ideology and their rhetoric from the general employed professional model, their goals and status aspirations from the academic model, and their tactics from the union model. In brief, they will do their best to look and sound like professional societies, but, if necessary, will act more like unions.

Notes

The cooperation and assistance of Glen Grant, James Craft, and Peter Thorman is gratefully acknowledged with the usual disclaimer of responsibility.

1. Daniel Bell, in a 1954 paper, in Walter Galenson and Seymour Martin Lipset (eds.), *Labor and Trade Unionism* (New York: Wiley, 1960), p. 90.

2. Membership figures are from Benjamin Solomon, "Analyzing the Growth of the American Federation of Teachers," *Educators Negotiating Service* (May 1, 1967).

3. For a good statement, see T. H. Marshall, "The Recent History of Professionalism in Relation to Social Structure and Social Policy," *Canadian Journal of Economics and Political Science*, V (August 1939), 325-40.

4. U.S. Bureau of the Census, *Statistical Abstract of the U.S., 1966* (Washington, D.C.: U.S. Government Printing Office, 1966), pp. 65, 158.

5. In the current intense competition for new entrants to the profession, reports of poor conditions of employment relayed to university academic departments have been judged effective by embattled employees.

6. Note that this assumes that the "profession" in question is the academic profession, not the discipline of the scholar, e.g., historian, physicist, etc.

7. James Craft, in a large-scale study of the California experience that is currently in preparation.

8. Since the passage of the Wagner Act in 1935.

15 / The Outcome of Impasse Procedures in New York Schools under the Taylor Law

John E. Drotning and *David B. Lipsky*

The search for effective strike substitutes in public employment has led scholars to devote much attention to the study of mediation, arbitration, and fact-finding in the public sector.[1] In September 1967 New York public employees came under the coverage of the Taylor Law, providing impasse procedures for collective negotiations in the public sector. An examination of some aspects of the New York experience may provide some insights about the use and effectiveness of statutory impasse procedures in public employee disputes.

In the first section of this paper we discuss the general effectiveness of public sector settlement procedures in terms of their avowed objectives. Reference is made to the use of impasse procedures under New York's Taylor Law. In the second section of the paper the factors that are probably related to the incidence of fact-finding in public teacher disputes are analyzed. No doubt the analysis in this section can be extended to other categories of public employees. In addition, information is supplied on the composition and experience of the panel of mediators and fact finders employed by New York's Public Employment Relations Board (PERB) and also on the costs of mediation and fact-finding in New York.

Reprinted from *The Arbitration Journal,* XXVI (No. 2, 1971), 87-102.

THE USE OF IMPASSE PROCEDURES
IN ACHIEVING THE LAW'S OBJECTIVES

The effectiveness of any legislation can be evaluated only in light of its professed purposes, which in the case of the Taylor Law are two-fold: (1) "to promote harmonious and cooperative relationships between government and its employees" and (2) "to protect the public by assuring, at all times, the orderly and uninterrupted operations and functions of government."[2] Stated somewhat differently, then, the act seeks to prevent strikes and to encourage the resolution of contract disputes by the parties themselves.

It is exceedingly difficult to judge the impasse procedures according to the absence or presence of strikes. Stoppages in the public service are illegal, and the Taylor Law imposes strict penalties on violators of this proscription.[3] This does not mean, of course, that the strike weapon is never used by public employees. Nevertheless, the possible penalties for striking are probably one factor explaining the relative absence of strikes in New York State education, as well as other public sector jurisdictions.

If the strike criterion is an inadequate measure of effectiveness, another must be framed. One alternative is to ask whether or not the impasse procedures increase the parties' reliance on outside intervention. That is, does the law stimulate the resolution of conflict without a third party? Or does the law induce undue reliance on outside help?

Either alternative could be justified as an a priori hypothesis. For example, one might expect, particularly in the case of teachers unions and school boards with little negotiating experience, that outside experts called in a difficult situation would be able to provide valuable lessons in the art of bargaining. The parties might learn from a mediator how to avoid committing themselves publicly to an untenable position, or from a fact finder how to formulate and defend reasonable and realistic proposals and counterproposals. In short, knowledgeable third parties might serve as instructors to inexperienced participants on both sides.

On the other hand, there is some prior experience to indicate that, whenever free and unlimited outside intervention is available to the parties, they tend to forgo bargaining in anticipation of the third party's arrival and to condition their behavior on the expected impact it will have on the outside agent. The classic example, of course, is the railroad industry, where the parties' insistence on bargaining nationally has, for all intents and purposes, precluded resort to the strike weapon. The recent history of bargaining on the railroads, if it can be called "bargaining" in the conventional sense at all, hardly invites optimism for bargaining in the public service.[4] Furthermore, returning to the point made earlier, few observers of labor relations on the railroads would conclude from the absence of strike activity that the Railway Labor Act is working well.

Therefore it seems that the most promising way to evaluate mediation and fact-finding under the Taylor Law is to measure the extent to which the parties are encouraged to reach their own settlements or, conversely, are led to depend on outsiders to help them. At this juncture, certain conceptual problems present themselves. First, how is a voluntary settlement defined? Clearly, a dichotomous definition would be inappropriate, since there are obviously gradations of third-party intervention. It thus becomes necessary to arrange bargaining outcomes on some scale which measures the extent to which the parties arrived at a settlement on their own. The extremes of this spectrum are fairly clear—bilateral agreement without an intervenor at one end, and perhaps unilateral imposition of terms with complete utilization of the impasse procedures at the other. However, the intermediate steps are somewhat fuzzier. Have the procedures worked "better," for example, if a fact finder's report is accepted without change than if the report merely furnishes the basis for a subsequent settlement on somewhat different terms?

One obvious outcome of the fact-finding process is for both parties to accept the report in its entirety. Another successful outcome is for both sides jointly to modify the report to their mutual satisfaction. On the other hand, both sides may strongly reject the report. But it is outcomes in between which pose some difficulties, that is, near settlements and no settlements. For example, one party may accept while the other modifies in a fashion unacceptable to the other, or both parties may modify, each in a way that is incompatible with the other (near settlements). Another class of outcomes involves combinations of rejection by one party with unmodified or modified acceptances by the other (no settlement). The difficulty, then, is to array these outcomes in a rank order which is a valid measure of voluntarism.

The records of New York State's Public Employment Relations Board permit some flesh to be added to the discussion. Table 15-1 shows the experience under the Taylor Law for the calendar year 1969. Table 15-2 gives the record for the first nine months of 1970.[5] First it should be noted that the bulk of cases closed by PERB involved public school disputes (453 out of 569, about 80 percent in 1969 and 373 out of 481 or 78 percent in 1970). Second, not all

TABLE 15-1. Use of impasse procedures under the Taylor Law, 1969

Stage at which case closed	Total Cases		School Cases		Nonschool Cases	
	Number	Percent	Number	Percent	Number	Percent
Settled without intervention	28	4.9	21	4.6	7	6.0
Settled by mediation	258	45.3	184	40.6	74	63.8
Settled by mediated fact-finding (no report)	53	9.3	46	10.2	7	6.0
Settled by fact-finding; report accepted without modification	93	16.3	83	18.3	10	8.7
Settled by fact-finding; report modified	135	23.7	117	25.8	18	15.5
Closed for other reasons	2	0.5	2	0.5	0	0.0
Superconciliations[a]	(37)	(6.5)	(33)	(7.3)	(4)	(3.4)
Total cases closed	569	100.0	453	100.0	116	100.0

[a]Nonadditive

Source: New York Public Employment Relations Board.

school districts have used the procedures of the Taylor Law. There were about 751 school districts in the state in 1969. A large but unknown number had not yet been organized for collective bargaining; presumably most of the unorganized districts were small and rural. The remainder of the districts were organized, but either settled without any intervention whatsoever or did not carry on authentic collective bargaining (in which case the school board continued to exercise effective unilateral authority).

Of the cases coming to PERB, 45.3 percent in 1969 and 60.1 percent in 1970 were settled by mediation. In 1969, as Table 15-1 shows, a higher percentage of nonschool cases were settled by mediation than were school cases. But in 1970 the picture changes. About 63 percent of nonschool cases were settled by mediation in 1970. Further, although no hard statistics are available, the proportion of nonschool cases reaching impasse is believed to be significantly lower than school cases. Note that a handful of cases coming to PERB were settled *without* mediation. In these cases one or both of the parties declared an impasse, but settlement was achieved before a PERB appointed mediator entered actively into the negotiations.

TABLE 15-2. Use of impasse procedures under the Taylor Law, January to September 1970

Stage at which case closed	Total Cases Number	Total Cases Percent	School Cases Number	School Cases Percent	Nonschool Cases Number	Nonschool Cases Percent
Settled without intervention	9	1.8	9	2.4	0	0.0
Settled by mediation	289	60.1	221	59.2	68	63.0
Settled by mediated fact-finding (no report)	42	8.7	36	9.7	6	5.5
Settled by fact-finding; report accepted without modification	75	15.6	60	16.1	15	13.9
Settled by fact-finding; report modified	56	11.7	42	11.3	14	13.0
Closed for other reasons	10	2.1	5	1.3	5	4.6
Superconciliation[a]	(20)	(4.2)	(15)	(4.0)	(5)	(4.6)
Total cases closed	481	100.0	373	100.0	108	100.0

[a]Nonadditive

Source: New York Public Employment Relations Board.

Exactly 200 fact-finding reports were written in school cases in 1969 compared to 28 in nonschool cases. In 1970, the number of fact-finding reports in school cases dropped to 102, about half of the previous year's total. The total of nonschool cases for 1970 will obviously exceed that of 1969, since many nonschool negotiations begin in September. The contract expiration date for many municipal employees is December 31st.

What comparison of 1969 and 1970 may suggest is that reliance on PERB by school districts and teachers is declining, while more nonschool negotiators are coming to PERB for assistance in negotiations.

However, the evidence covers less than two years. In order to judge whether, abstracting from other influences, the impasse procedures available to the parties are being relied on to a greater or lesser degree over time, one should follow negotiations over as many years as possible. Certainly this should give some indication as to whether or not the act tends to "promote harmonious and cooperative relationships between government and its employees."

FACTORS RELATED TO THE USE OF FACT-FINDING IN SCHOOL NEGOTIATIONS

What are the various factors which influence the method or manner in which settlement is achieved in public sector disputes? Why is it that some school districts are able to reach settlement by themselves, while others require outside help? And why do some districts require only the assistance of a mediator (essentially a behavioral intervenor) while others proceed to the fact-finding state (which is at least partly a juridical process—the third party proposes the terms of settlement)? What factors, if any, distinguish bargaining relationships, which rely to varying degrees on third parties who perform the actual functions of bargaining, that is, who formulate and propose specific resolutions of labor disputes?

The variables which influence the mode of settlement in a given set of circumstances may be conveniently grouped into three categories. These can be designated economic, institutional, and procedural.[6] The discussion rests specifically on the incidence of fact-finding in New York public teacher disputes.

Economic Variables

One factor which may be related to the difficulty or ease of resolving teacher disputes without outside intervention is the district's ability to pay. However, the best measure of ability to pay is not entirely clear. Perhaps the most appropriate standard is that suggested by David B. Ross: "In order to reflect a community's ability to pay, the potential tax base must be considered in light of the community's need for a particular service. Available tax resources thus may be defined as the potential tax base per unit of need."[7] Whatever the measure used, however, the relationship is uncertain.[8] One might argue that a wealthy district can afford to be more generous and satisfy its teachers' demands with little haggling. On the other hand, unions facing wealthy districts are likely to escalate their demands accordingly, and thus make voluntary settlements more difficult. Moreover, in some districts, there may be discrepancies between the political unit's assessed value and income. It must be remembered that taxes are paid out of income, not assessed valuation.

A sophisticated public negotiator might know that ability to pay is a criterion likely to be used by a fact finder. Stern found that it was the second most important criterion, falling right behind wage comparisons as a standard applied in Wisconsin fact-finding cases.[9] If the parties know the fact finder will invoke ability to pay as a basis for his recommendations, school boards in wealthier districts may wish to avoid fact-finding for this reason, while unions in such districts may be encouraged to hold out for a fact finder. But since in New York State either party can invoke the fact-finding procedure, it is likely that in the aggregate a direct relation between ability to pay and the incidence of fact-finding exists.

Another economic factor must be considered. Undoubtedly there are patterns in the negotiation of teacher collective agreements, and discovering the configuration of these patterns may help us to predict the probability of voluntary settlements. Those districts most instrumental in setting the pattern—the "leaders"—may undergo the most difficult negotiations and therefore be more prone to go to fact-finding. But "followers" may require little authentic bargaining, let alone fact-finding, to arrive at a settlement. They merely imitate the key settlement.

The time sequence of sets of negotiations may determine the pattern: early negotiators set the pattern, later ones follow it. The size, composition, and location of the district may also help determine the pattern. But scholars such as Reder and Eckstein and Wilson have demonstrated that, even though patterns may have certain institutional parameters, they are fundamentally related to economic factors.[10] One might then look at clusters of districts, geographically proximate, with similar tax bases, school expenditures, and salary structures, to see if fact-finding is more prevalent among certain districts within a pattern, or alternatively whether leaders (provided they can be identified) are more prone to fact-finding than followers.

It would seem reasonable to argue that, once a pattern has been firmly set for a given region, there should be little need for fact-finding, unless one of the parties has a good reason for trying to break the pattern, and hence becomes a "tough bargainer." Even then, given the disposition of fact finders to use wage comparisons as a principal basis for their recommendations, one must doubt the usefulness of fact-finding to a "pattern-breaker." In fact, in such situations, it may be that the party's latent reason for requesting fact-finding is to get the intervenor's support for the existing pattern.

If a tightening market makes bargaining more difficult, one would expect a greater tendency to rely upon fact-finding in the face of upward shifts in the demand for teachers. This implies a rising starting salary: public employers may resist such market pressures, thus forcing the employees to push to fact-finding. In these cases it is extremely important that the negotiating parties consider relevant measures of teacher demand: the rate of increase of new hires in a district, the rate of increase of pupils in a district, or declines in the teacher-pupil ratio. Moreover, increases in the supply of teachers, a likely picture in the coming years, will exert downward pressure on salaries, especially if demand rises less rapidly than supply. This, compounded with the inflation of the past few years, can only exacerbate problems for the negotiators. It might be safe to say that rapid economic change is likely to increase the probability of fact-finding.

Institutional Variables

The use of fact-finding in a school district must be related partly to the political climate of that district. In judging the "political climate" of a given school district, it is necessary to avoid simplistic epithets like "liberal" and "conservative." It is plausible to hypothesize, however, that districts in which there is political *stability* would find it easier to reach voluntary settlement than those where the situation is more volatile. The school board member who is constantly peering over his shoulder at his constituency might well feel obliged to adopt a "tougher" bargaining stance than his more secure counterpart. And the more adamant bargainer, of course, is in turn more likely to find himself in fact-finding. All this says simply that political instability is the parallel of economic instability. Both are likely to increase the incidence of third-party intervention.

There are a number of possible approaches to measuring political instability. One is to ascertain the tenure of school board members or their relative turnover. Another might be to use the results of recent votes on bond issues or budgets in the district or neighboring districts. Presumably, board members in areas where school expenditures have been the object of voter dismay will be politically sensitive to the demands of teachers. Still another consideration would be whether the school board is fiscally independent, although it is not immediately clear whether independent boards would be more or less likely to reach agreement without intervention.[11]

The political climate of a school district is related to the district's willingness to pay. To some extent this factor is beclouded by the same problems as ability to pay. A district which is more willing to pay may want to settle quickly (and generously), but a union may take advantage of the district's instincts and push them to fact-finding. However—in contrast to ability to pay—a district already straining its resources to meet its educational needs may receive a good deal of sympathy from a fact finder. This would provide a union with a disincentive to call upon outsiders. Therefore, one might expect to find a direct relationship between some relevant measure of willingness to pay and the probability of voluntary settlement.

In this connection David B. Ross speaks of a community's "effort": "An idea of the effort a community has made to supply public services comes from comparing its ability to pay, measured by its taxable resources, and the amount of tax revenues which actually have been collected and spent on services."[12] Thus one useful measure of willingness to pay is the ratio of the wage and salary component of school expenditures to assessed value of real property, which Ross would call the "Resource utilization ratio."[13]

On the question of union strength, McKelvey seems to believe that where "strong and militant labor organizations" exist, fact-finding is likely to be less "effective."[14] That is, it will be heavily relied upon and further, the fact finders' reports will be rejected. Stern adds, "In the future strong unions in the big cities may tend to overuse the procedure and then tire of it."[15]

Independent and unaffiliated local bargaining agents are probably less militant than groups associated with either the National Education Association or the American Federation of Teachers. AFT locals are probably more militant than NEA affiliates. Other measures of union strength may be more useful. The ratio of union membership to the number of teachers in the district gives an indication of union strength. The rate of growth of union membership would be another indicator of union strength.

Further, McKelvey believes fact-finding is less effective, "where both sides have had more experience in collective bargaining, have more sophisticated practitioners, or have a longer history of joint dealings."[16] It should be noted again that McKelvey, in speaking of "effectiveness," is referring principally to the acceptance of the fact finder's report, and not to the incidence of fact-finding itself.

In New York State, the parties have the opportunity to enter into voluntary written agreements providing for procedures to be followed in the event of impasse, rather than relying upon the statutory procedures.[17] McKelvey predicts, "Contractual impasse procedures will become more prevalent and may well replace statutory procedures."[18] If this is so, a longer bargaining history may lead to less reliance upon the statutory procedure of fact-finding. There is no obvious reason why contract impasse procedures should be substantively different from the impasse procedures of the Taylor Law.

Further, Krinsky, in his study of the Wisconsin procedure, discovered that "initial use of fact-finding has improved the bargaining relationships both in terms of educating the parties through the recommendations and making them realize that they should be able to bargain themselves and reach the same point that a fact finder would recommend without going through the cost and delays of the process."[19] This may not be true in New York State where there is no direct cost to the parties of fact-finding. (Nevertheless, there are delays, which have a cost equivalent, and can serve the function of promoting voluntary settlements.)

At this point it is interesting to look at the cost of the procedures to the State of New York. Table 15-3 shows a breakdown of mediation and fact-finding costs for 1969 and 1970. The median cost of mediation was about $350 a case both years. The median cost of fact-finding was about $450 a case in 1969 and about $500 a case in 1970. Whether these costs are excessive or not is a function of the benefits flowing from the settlements or conversely the costs avoided as a consequence of few work stoppages in public employment in New York State since the advent of the Taylor Law. In any event there is not evidence to indicate that the costs of the impasse procedures to the taxpayers of New York have been increasing substantially.

In addition to the opinions of McKelvey and Krinsky, Belasco and and Alutto found that, as a consequence of the high turnover and inexperience of teacher negotiators, "the negotiation process itself was laborious and agreement difficult to reach. In particular, there were

TABLE 15-3. Cost of impasse procedures in New York State, 1969 and 1970[a]

Cost per case	1969				1970			
	Mediation		Fact-Finding		Mediation		Fact-Finding	
	Number	Percent	Number	Percent	Number	Percent	Number	Percent
$ 50-349	161	50.1	105	36.2	177	54.3	84	34.3
350-499	78	24.3	51	17.6	55	16.9	38	15.5
500-649	38	11.8	47	16.2	48	14.7	44	18.0
650-949	27	8.4	45	15.5	22	6.7	37	15.1
950-1099	10	3.2	11	3.8	11	3.4	15	6.1
1,100 and up	7	2.2	31	10.7	13	4.0	27	11.0
Total	321	100.0	290	100.0	326	100.0	245	100.0

[a]Only bills submitted between the months of January and September of each year are shown, permitting direct comparisons between the two years.

innumerable instances in which negotiators for both sides missed crucial 'signals' because they were insensitive to such cues."[20] Hence, one might hypothesize that experienced or professional negotiators would lead to less reliance on fact-finding.

It might be posited, on the other hand, that if fact-finding has an educational function, it is to teach the parties the advantages of its use. The age, or "vintage," of a bargaining relationship can be measured in at least two ways: the number of years the district's teachers have been organized, and the number of contracts negotiated in the district. The "maturity" of the relationship can also be represented in one of several ways, e.g., whether the contract contains a grievance procedure and arbitration provision or whether professional negotiators are employed. Thus, mature relationships may be characterized by a high incidence of fact-finding.

Belasco and Alutto also found that "those teachers most favorably disposed toward both collective bargaining and strikes were either married males, teaching in the secondary schools, and/or between the ages of 31 and 45. These results . . . indicate that while the bulk of teachers are favorably disposed towards collective action, some groups of teachers may be more willing than others to actually engage in collective activities."[21] This finding leads to the hypothesis that there may be a relationship between the composition of the teacher work force and the proclivity to use fact-finding. Districts characterized by a work force predominantly consisting of prime-age, married males may show a higher incidence of fact-finding. Put in other terms, the higher the degree of commitment to bargaining, the likelier the use of all dispute settlement procedures available to the parties.[22]

It can also be postulated that the extent of participation is related to fact-finding. Where many persons—and interests—are a party to bargaining, settlements become more difficult to achieve. The presence of diverse interests may be reflected by the size and nature of the district—voluntary settlements are likelier in small, homogeneous districts.

There seems to be a difference of opinion on the relation between location and fact-finding. McKelvey says, "Fact-finding seems to be more effective in smaller communities and rural areas than in large urban centers . . ."[23] Stern reaches the opposite conclusion: in all cases where fact-finding failed, "the municipal employer was a county or small city in a rural or suburban section of Wisconsin."[24] Once again, however, the measure of effectiveness is whether the report was *accepted,* not whether the procedure was used. Whether, all other things being equal, fact-finding is more frequently used in rural, sub-urban, or urban areas is a question which needs to be explored. To the extent that urban areas are characterized by militant unions (as McKelvey believes), then fact-finding is likely to have a higher incidence in such areas. The real question is what location by itself represents, when it is not serving as a surrogate for something else, e.g., militancy or inexperience.

Procedural Variables

One can put forth the proposition that effective mediation of a dispute will forestall the need for fact-finding, but how is one to measure effective mediation? Obviously mediation is effective if it achieves a settlement, but this tells us little about the characteristics of the process which lead to settlements. Is effective mediation dependent upon the timing of intervention? Some observers recommend early intervention, and it may be that early entrance by a mediator lessens the necessity of fact-finding. However, as Stevens points out, attention must be paid to the "negotiation cycle," i.e., the progression of events or succession of stages common to many collective negotiations.[25] The function of the mediator will vary according to the stage of the cycle at which he enters. Early entrance may result in grandstanding and lessen the chance for settlement.

Another aspect of the timing question is the rapidity of response of PERB and the appointed mediator to the request of the parties. If, for some reason, there should be delays between the parties' call for a mediator and his actual appearance at negotiations, the chances of his playing an effective role would seem to be diminished and the likelihood of fact-finding increased.

The mediation process is one of the most intensely personal facets of labor relations. The effectiveness of mediation depends largely on the skills, experience, and personality of the mediator. A thorough exploration is needed of the extent to which the characteristics of the mediator help lead to settlement rather than fact-finding.

A number of considerations are relevant here—the mediator's primary occupation, his age, the number of PERB cases he has handled, his record of success in the past, and so forth. One would think that younger, inexperienced mediators, with little experience in labor relations, would have less chance of success. However, older, well-known mediators may have developed biases and rigidities which make them less effective. But there is some evidence to suggest that experienced people are partly responsible for PERB's record since

1967. Table 15-4 shows that 45 percent of the PERB's 309 panel members are lawyers and 18 percent have doctorates. Moreover, another 9 percent have Masters' degrees. In addition, when tabulated by primary occupation, nearly 74 percent of the panel are attorneys, educators, or professional arbitrators. Attorneys and educators serving on the PERB panel are likely to have prior experience in collective bargaining.

There are other aspects of mediation which may have an impact on the possibility of settlement. For example, are panels (multiple neutrals) more effective than single intervenors? Small-group psychology suggests that two or three men in groups of ten to twelve can have a significant impact on the direction of the group. Put simply, a panel may be able to generate much more pressure for settlement than a single person. Moreover, how does time affect the process? One might expect that successful negotiations are affected by the amount of time (other things equal) that the mediator spends with negotiating parties. In addition, his own drive to settle the dispute must play a very important role in his efforts. Clearly, there are times when holding on to a case too long hurts rather than helps, but this is not likely to be a frequent problem. Another aspect of time is the relationship of the meeting to the budget deadline. It seems reasonable to think that successful mediation efforts occur in time reasonably close to the budget or contract deadline, simply because of the mounting pressures for settlement felt by both parties.

TABLE 15-4. Education and occupation of PERB fact finders and mediators (N = 309)

Education	Percent	Primary occupation	Percent
High school only	1.9	Consultant	3.2
Some college	3.6	Mediator-arbitrator	9.1
B.S. or B.A.	5.8	Clergy	0.7
Some graduate work	4.2	Attorney	41.4
Master's	9.1	Educator	24.6
Law	45.3	Management (personnel)	8.4
Doctorate	17.8	Labor official	1.9
Combination law &		Student	1.0
adv. degree	11.0	Other	9.7
Others or unknown	1.3		100.0
	100.0		

CONCLUDING OBSERVATIONS

In the discussion above, the factors which cause variation in the use of the impasse procedures were discussed; the question of the effect of those variations on the terms of settlement was not taken up. Does the use in varying degree of third parties differentiate the quality of the final settlement? For example, are mediated settlements significantly different from fact-finding settlements? Do unions which rely on third parties do better than those which reach settlement on their own?

At first glance, the answer may appear self-evident. Since it is exceedingly unlikely that a fact finder would recommend settlement terms inferior to those last proposed by the school board, one might be tempted to conclude that a union will always do at least as well, and sometimes better, than if it eschewed third-party intervention. This assertion is simplistic, for it ignores the bargaining strategy of the school board. If the school were convinced that third-party intervention was inevitable, might it not deliberately refrain from putting its best offer on the table? It then becomes conceivable that a fact finder might recommend terms which are less valuable to the union than those it should have obtained without fact-finding. In this respect, moreover, the maturity of the bargaining relationship becomes crucial, for one might well expect school boards which are relatively inexperienced in bargaining matters to be less likely to adopt this strategy.

Since the terms of settlement will depend on many factors other than the settlement process, it would be necessary somehow to adjust for these other factors. Economic variables, in particular, seem especially important. One possible approach would be to group school districts in terms of some measure of ability to pay and to examine each group separately. Other variables, such as "orbits of coercive comparison," would also require standardization. In this case, school districts might be grouped into a number of geographical units, with each unit analyzed separately.

In conclusion, it is obvious from the analysis in this paper that there are numerous questions in the area of the resolution of teacher bargaining disputes that need to be answered. The authors are now undertaking a systematic examination of the empirical evidence available in New York State, using the framework and hypotheses shaped in this article, in the hope that some of the answers can be provided.[26]

Any thorough, empirical investigation of the hypotheses and questions raised in earlier pages doubtless would involve difficult conceptual and methodological problems. Nevertheless, the authors are convinced that such problems would not be insurmountable. Further, there is little doubt that an administrative agency such as New York State's Public Employment Relations Board ought to use all the relevant information it can get in order to improve its ability to implement the law. Certainly, organized research can be one significant input for the makers of public policy.[27] New information is one necessary ingredient of successful policy formulation, and this research is contemplated in that light.

Notes

The authors express gratitude to Dr. Thomas E. Joyner, Director of Research, and to Mr. Joseph B. Phillips, Assistant Director of Research, New York State Public Employment Relations Board, for their cooperation and suggestions. However, the authors retain full responsibility for the analysis and conclusions in this article.

1. For example, see Richard Pegnetter, "Fact-Finding and Teacher Salary Disputes: The 1969 Experience in New York State," *Industrial and Labor Relations Review*, XXIV (No. 2, January 1971), 226-42; Jean T. McKelvey, "Fact-Finding in Public Employment Disputes: Promise or Illusion," *ibid.*, XXII (No. 4, July 1969), 528-43; James L. Stern, "The Wisconsin Public Employee Fact-Finding Procedure," *ibid.*, XX (No. 1, October 1966), 3-29; David B. Ross, "The Arbitration of Public Employee Wage Disputes," *ibid.*, XXIII (No. 1, October 1969), 3-14; Robert J. Jossen, "Fact-Finding: Is It Adjudication or Adjustment?" *Arbitration Journal*, XXIV (No. 2, 1969). For an excellent bibliography of collective bargaining in the public sector generally, see Michael H. Moskow, J. Joseph Loewenberg, and Edward C. Koziara, *Collective Bargaining in Public Employment* (New York: Random House, 1970), pp. 307-25.

2. Public Employees Fair Employment Law (New York State), Sec. 200.

3. Under the Taylor Law, a striking union may be subject to loss of check off privileges and court-imposed fines. An individual striker may (1) lose two days' pay for each day he is out; (2) be placed on probation for one year during which time he serves without tenure; and (3) suffer other disciplinary action (fine and/or imprisonment) as provided by the Civil Service Law. Many have argued that such penalties encourage employees to manifest their grievances in more subtle ways, which may have equally or even more severe repercussions on the efficient operation of government than a strike itself. The inability to resolve disputes to the satisfaction, let alone delight, of the parties may result in excessive turnover, morale problems, slowdowns, or other minor acts of sabotage (not necessarily in the violent sense) which inhibit progress toward the central function of government, namely, the provision of certain collective services.

4. See Jacob J. Kaufman, "The Railroad Labor Dispute: A Marathon of Maneuver and Improvisation," *Industrial and Labor Relations Review*, XVIII (No. 2, January 1965), 196-212.

5. The record for the final three months of 1970 was not available at the

time of this writing. Almost all school cases are closed by the end of September. On the other hand, many nonschool cases arise between October and December, the usual date of municipal contract expirations.

6. A fourth possible category can be labeled "behavioral." This category is excluded from discussion here, although the authors readily concede the critical influence of behavioral factors (e.g., interpersonal relations and attitudes) on the settlement process. The authors are principally concerned, however, with factors which are more easily observable, more nearly objective and measurable, and, further, which may more readily lend themselves to control by public policy.

7. Ross, "Arbitration," p. 8.

8. Ashenfelter and Johnson have found that, in the private sector, profits have a negligible effect on strike levels. One might regard profits as analogous to ability to pay and strikes analogous to settlement procedures. Orley Ashenfelter and George E. Johnson, "Bargaining Theory, Trade Unions, and Industrial Strike Activity," *American Economic Review,* LIX (No. 1, March 1969), 45.

9. Stern, "Wisconsin Public Employee Fact-Finding Procedure," p. 15. According to Pegnetter, "Ability to pay was the rationale most frequently relied on by school board negotiators." ("Fact-Finding," p. 235.) Fact finders cited the criterion in about one-quarter of their reports. (*Ibid.,* p. 231.)

10. Melvin Reder, "The Theory of Union Wage Policy," *Review of Economics and Statistics,* XXXIV (No. 1, February 1952), 34-45; O. Eckstein and T. A. Wilson, "The Determinants of Money Wage Changes in American Industry," *Quarterly Journal of Economics,* LXXVI (No. 3, August 1962), 379-414.

11. The independent board may be in a better position to agree to union demands because of its control over the budget, but at the same time it would presumably be more vulnerable to political pressures and less able to "pass the buck" to another public authority.

12. Ross, "Arbitration," p. 6.

13. *Ibid.,* p. 7.

14. McKelvey, "Fact-Finding," p. 539.

15. Stern, "Wisconsin Public Employee Fact-Finding Procedure," p. 19.

16. McKelvey, "Fact-Finding," p. 543.

17. Public Employees Fair Employment Law (New York State [the Taylor Law]), Sec. 209.

18. McKelvey, "Fact-Finding," p. 543.

19. Edward B. Krinsky, "An Analysis of Fact-Finding as a Procedure for the Settlement of Labor Disputes Involving Public Employees," (Ph.D. diss., University of Wisconsin, 1969).

20. James A. Belasco and Joseph A. Alutto, "Organizational Impacts of Teacher Negotiations," *Industrial Relations,* IX (No. 1, October 1969), 70.

21. *Ibid.*

22. Stern found that "successful fact-finding," that is, acceptance of the fact finder's report, was likelier in cases where the parties were committed to bargaining. In "unsuccessful" cases, on the other hand, "managements did not look with favor upon any part of the process of collective bargaining." ("Wisconsin Public Employee Fact-Finding Procedure," p. 12.)

23. McKelvey, "Fact-Finding," p. 539.

24. Stern, "Wisconsin Public Employee Fact-Finding Procedure," p. 12.

25. Carl Stevens, "Mediation and the Role of the Neutral," in John T. Dunlop and Neil W. Chamberlain (eds.), *Frontiers of Collective Bargaining* (New York: Harper and Row, 1967), p. 275.

26. The study is being sponsored by PERB under authority of the Taylor Law.

27. See, for example, James A. Gross, "Economics, Politics and the Law: The NLRB's Division of Economic Research, 1935-40," *Cornell Law Review* (February 1970), p. 344.

16 / Structural Characteristics and the Outcome of Collective Negotiations

Joseph A. Sarthory

The growing body of literature on negotiations in education suggests that certain structural characteristics of the negotiating process relate to the outcomes of that process. Lieberman and Moskow indicate that the size of negotiating teams is an important structural factor when they note: "On the other hand, larger negotiating groups find it more difficult to make concessions and are less likely to respect the confidences that are frequently essential to effective negotiations. Furthermore, large negotiating committees make it more difficult for the chief spokesman to control the negotiations."[1]

The role of the board of education in negotiations also receives extensive treatment in the literature. Lieberman and Moskow suggest that practice might logically differ in relation to the size of the district. In large districts, it is perhaps feasible to have personnel experienced in collective negotiations negotiate for the board while in small rural districts, due to the lack of experienced personnel it is more reasonable to expect board members to negotiate.[2] Gilroy *et al.* are somewhat more specific and state that, "Nevertheless, the board should not become involved in negotiations unless the board's confidence in its administrators is shaken. The board's chief role is to

Reprinted from *Educational Administration Quarterly*, VII (No. 3, Autumn 1971), 78-89.

provide policy guidelines to the administrators prior to negotiations in order that the administrator have a reference point to guide him through the sessions."[3] This statement clearly implies that the board negotiating team should be composed of members of the district's administrative staff.

Whether or not the chief school officer should be involved in negotiations and to what extent are subject to much disagreement in the literature. Gilroy *et al.* state flatly that, "For the school system the spokesman should be the superintendent or his designated official."[4] Lieberman and Moskow are in agreement with this position. Others, including the National Education Association and American Association of School Administrators, abhor this approach and suggest that the chief school officer should function both as an advisor to the board and as the leader of the professional staff. Still others suggest that the superintendent should not become involved in negotiations at all.

Most teacher organizations take the position that teacher teams should be composed of members from the various instructional levels in the school district. Thus the elementary, junior high, and senior high levels should be represented along with certified personnel who are clearly not a part of the administrative staff (counselors, curriculum coordinators, etc.). The reasoning is that this will afford the inclusion of varied viewpoints in the teacher package thus ensuring a united front in the give-and-take of negotiations. Gilroy *et al.* put forth this point of view and note that, "The negotiating committee should be comprised of a representative cross section of the teachers in the bargaining unit."[5] The NEA agrees and suggests that, "Without sacrificing quality, team members should represent the diverse interests of the teaching staff. This requires consideration of sex, age, grade level, subject field, race, ethnic minorities, and such special interest groups as coaches and teachers of forensics. It is very helpful if each teacher is able to identify strongly with one or more individuals on the team."[6]

The literature is somewhat diffuse as to whether or not building principals are first line management or instructional personnel and what their status should be in collective negotiations. Many writers suggest that building principals are management, should be represented on board of education negotiating teams, and should thus be excluded from membership in teacher organizations and on teacher negotiating teams. This is essentially the AFT view and is espoused by Doherty,[7] Donovon *et al.*,[8] and others. The NEA, on the other hand, perceives a negotiations umbrella over the entire certificated staff, although it condones separate negotiating units for teacher and administrators if this is the wish of the practitioners.

The degree to which lawyers should be involved in negotiations in education is also subject to differing opinions. There is a great fear on the part of some that as lawyers become more heavily involved the legal precedents with which they are familiar—namely, the labor-management conflict model from the private sphere—will become the education model. It is felt that this model is not appropriate to organizations staffed by professionals which provide essential public services and can only lead to the divisiveness which has characterized employer-employee relations in private industry. On the other hand, there is some feeling that, since teachers have access to negotiations experts through their state and national organizations, boards of education should arm themselves with legal experts to counteract this expertise.[9]

The frequency and length of negotiating sessions are often cited as influencing the outcomes of negotiations. It appears obvious that adequate time must be allowed for negotiations if an agreement is to be reached which is satisfactory to both parties. Poor preparation as well as a shortage of time for compromises to emerge can lead to unsuccessful negotiations. Gilroy *et al.* make this very clear when they say, "Formal talks usually begin two to three months before contract expiration or renewal time. . ."[10] Lieberman and Moskow support this view with the comment, "An organization can devote much or little time to these procedures. If little time is devoted, there will be less membership understanding and support for the proposals, a fact which can be decisive in negotiations."[11]

As negotiations move along, it would seem necessary to maintain accurate records of the progress being made up to any given point in time. To reach final agreement, both sides have to agree on what has been decided upon throughout the course of negotiations. The NEA is very aware of this and makes the point in a bulletin to its members. The NEA says:

Many authorities on negotiation have underlined that it is most important for the negotiation panel to have a written understanding of all points on which the negotiating teams reached agreement during each negotiating session. Not only does agreement on one item speed agreement on other items, but it is just too easy for team members to forget what was agreed upon. A written record is made of the session and permits review.[12]

Finally, educators are enjoined "not to negotiate in the press," that attempts to undermine the other side's positions through the mobilization of public opinion is in the long run counterproductive and makes it much more difficult to reach agreement. This suggests that press releases concerning the progress of negotiations should not be made unilaterally but rather should be in the form of a joint statement agreed upon by both sides. Gilroy *et al.* imply this when, in describing what "should be," they note, "A joint release was issued to the press reporting the successful proceedings, including the pre-school workshop programs."[13]

METHOD

This study is an attempt to discover the direction and strength of relationships between the factors (variables) noted above and the outcome of negotiations defined as reaching agreement internally versus the development of an impasse situation wherein outsiders must be brought in to promote agreement through fact-finding or mediation. In essence, the author hoped to discover if certain of these factors, singly or in clusters, tend to promote agreement or impasse.

To this end, in the spring of 1969, nineteen school districts were identified in western New York in which negotiations had occurred during the 1967-68 school year (the Taylor Law which allows public employees the right to negotiate with their employers took effect in New York on September 1, 1967). Ten of these districts had gone to impasse while nine had been successful in reaching agreement internally. The districts were matched as closely as possible on the following dimensions: average daily attendance, per pupil expenditure, assessed valuation per pupil in resident attendance, property tax per pupil in resident attendance, and the nature of the districts on an urban-rural continuum.

A questionnaire was developed by the author designed to differentiate among the school districts on the structural characteristics of negotiations noted above. The initial instrument was submitted to other professors of education and was amended in line with their recommendations. It was then administered to graduate students in the author's classes and further amended in light of their remarks. The final form of the instrument was mailed to a classroom teacher in each of the districts, the teacher having been designated by teachers and administrators in the area as very knowledgeable about the 1967-68 negotiations which had occurred in their districts. In all cases, the respondents were either members of the teacher negotiating team or officers of their local teacher organizations. It was felt that teachers would be more likely to provide information about negotiations than would be board members or administrators who have been somewhat "closed" about the subject. Evidently this was the case since the response rate was 100 percent. Respondents were guaranteed anonymity as were their school districts.

The instrument gathered data concerning the following structural aspects of the negotiating process. The data were largely factual and were not subject to interpretations of the respondent. Something was or was not the case; hopefully perceptual bias was reduced to a minimum in this way.

I. Composition of negotiating teams
    A.   Board of education team
        1. Occupational category
        2. Membership on the board (yes or no)
        3. If yes, years on the board
    B.   The teacher team
        1. Organizational role (teacher, principal, supervisor, etc.)
        2. Employment level (elementary, high school, central office, etc.)
II. Role of the chief school officer in negotiations
III. Status of building principals in negotiations
IV. Extent to which legal assistance was used in the negotiating process
V. Time allotted for negotiations
VI. Method of recording progress of negotiations
VII. Method of releasing information concerning negotiations to the press

Data were analyzed through the use of the chi-square test of independence for contingency tables. A contingency table was constructed for each of the items noted above in which the row variable classified the nineteen school districts into impasse and nonimpasse districts and the column variable reflected the frequency distribution for each of the possible response categories for each item.

Roscoe notes that the chi-square test for independence may be used to determine whether two or more populations are distributed in the same fashion with respect to the criterion, and he adds that there is no restriction as to the number of categories when the chi-square statistic is used in this manner.[14] The use of the chi-square statistic has historically been restricted by sample size considerations but forthcoming research by Roscoe and Byars suggests that sample size is not the limiting factor it was formerly assumed to be.[15]

TABLE 16-1. Factors distinguishing between impasse and non-impasse districts

Factor	N	DF	Chi-square
Teacher team composition—Factor A	19	1	4.54[a]
Teacher team composition—Factor B	19	1	2.89[b]
Tenure of teacher team members	19	2	5.87[b]
Utilization of legal assistance	19	4	7.24[c]
Frequency of negotiating sessions	19	2	5.22[b]

[a]Significant at the .05 level.
[b]Significant at the .10 level.
[c]Approaches significance at the .10 level.

RESULTS

The chi-square statistic reached or approached significance at the .10 level or above in 5 of the contingency tables which were constructed. This suggests that there are significant differences between impasse and nonimpasse districts on the structural characteristics included in these tables. These factors and the results of the chi-square analysis are shown in Table 16-1.

The factor which appears to be most strongly related to the occurrence of impasse is the composition of the teacher-negotiating team. In nine of the ten impasse districts, the teacher team was composed of members from all grade levels: elementary school, junior high school, and senior high school. This was the case in only four of the nine districts which did not go to impasse. The chi-square of 4.54 is significant at the .05 level.

Within teacher teams, a preponderance of secondary teachers on the teams seems to be related to successful negotiations without the occurrence of an impasse. In four of the nine nonimpasse districts, the teacher team was composed primarily of secondary teachers, while this was the case in only one of the ten districts which went to impasse. The chi-square of 2.89 is significant at the .10 level.

The number of years teaching experience of members of the teacher team also relates to the outcome of negotiations. In the 10 impasse districts, 55 percent of teacher team members had 11+ years of experience while only 37 percent of teacher team members in nonimpasse districts had this much experience. The chi-square of 5.87 is significant at the .10 level and approaches significance at the .05 level of probability.

Also associated with the occurrence of impasse is the use of legal assistance by at least one of the teams during the course of negotiations. Legal assistance other than for the final writing of the contract was utilized in five of the ten districts which went to impasse while in only one of the nine nonimpasse districts did at least one of the teams solicit legal help. The chi-square in this instance of 7.24 approaches significance at the .10 level of probability.

Finally, the frequency of negotiating sessions appears to be related to agreement or the occurrence of impasse. The more frequent the sessions, the more likely is the possibility of reaching agreement internally. Conversely, less frequent sessions tend to be associated with the occurrence of impasse. In only three of the ten impasse districts did teams meet at least weekly while weekly sessions were the rule in seven of the nine nonimpasse districts. On the other hand, none of the nonimpasse districts met less frequently than every two weeks, while this was the case in three of the ten impasse districts. The chi-square of 5.22 is significant at the .10 level and approaches significance at the .05 level of probability.

DISCUSSION

The results noted above suggest that the composition of the teacher negotiating team is a crucial factor in the conduct of negotiations in education. It is perhaps desirable to have input from teachers at all levels to the teacher team, but it appears dysfunctional to have all levels represented on the team. Evidently such a situation makes it more difficult for the teacher team to reach agreement internally, thus complicating the process of reaching agreement with the board team.

Somewhat surprisingly, perhaps, the findings suggest that teacher negotiating teams should be primarily composed of secondary teachers. Such teams appear more likely to reach agreement with the board team than are teams wherein secondary teachers are in the minority. This finding contradicts the author's expectation that secondary teachers are more likely male, more militant, and thus more difficult to deal with in negotiations. It is true, however, that there are few women on teacher negotiating teams, and perhaps the increasing number of male elementary teachers is a more militant breed than their secondary brethren.

Perhaps also surprisingly, the findings of this study suggest that it is more difficult to reach agreement with teacher teams composed of teachers with more than ten years of experience than it is to reach agreement with teacher teams composed primarily of teachers with less than ten years experience. This contradicts the vision of the young turk, newly entered into the profession, demanding teacher power and leading the charge at the negotiating table. A more accurate vision seems to be that of the teacher who, as he starts his second decade of teaching, perhaps with a master's degree, begins to experience the pressures of increasing family expenditures, more poignantly feels the discrepancy between his level of income and his degree of professional preparation, and decides that negotiation affords him the opportunity to redress economic grievances and is thus very militant in negotiations, particularly with respect to salary and fringe benefit items.

Interestingly, the composition of the board team seems not to be significantly related to the outcome of negotiations. In this study, the size of the board team, its composition (whether composed solely of board members, administrators, or both), and the tenure of board members on board negotiating teams failed to discriminate between impasse and nonimpasse districts. Additionally, the composition of board teams as to occupation (professional versus non-professional) also failed to differentiate. This finding is fascinating and strongly supports the conclusion that the composition of the teacher team is a more crucial factor in the conduct of negotiations in education than is the composition of its board counterpart.

Although lawyers are becoming more widely involved in the conduct of negotiations in education, this study suggests that such a practice is more likely to lead to impasse than to internal agreement. Perhaps this is partially due to the fact that lawyers, although they may be experts in labor law, are not trained negotiators and yet are often used in this role. Additionally, the labor law with which they are familiar derives overwhelmingly from the private sphere and reflects the conflict model of labor-management relations so common in private industry. Also, it is conceivable that lawyers tend to see things as "either-or" in terms of legal and statutory precedents and that such an orientation makes compromise and problem-solving extremely difficult. It is also true that lawyers tend not to have to live with the contract once it has been negotiated. Usually their service is then terminated, and it is up to organizational members to operate within a new framework which is only partially of their own doing. An interesting sidelight on this point is that many lawyers are forming organizations to deal exclusively with negotiations in education. This has been true on Long Island, New York, which has had a high incidence of impasse situations.

Finally, frequent negotiating sessions appear to contribute more to successful negotiations than do infrequent ones. Short, weekly sessions of two hours or less duration are more desirable than less frequent sessions of longer duration. In this study, the average duration of negotiating sessions in nonimpasse districts was two hours, while the impasse districts reported sessions of from three to four hours. It may be that more frequent, shorter sessions insure more continuity than do less frequent, longer ones. Also, longer sessions likely tire people to the extent that tempers can become frayed and stances assumed which become hardened as the session progresses.

In closing this section, it is perhaps important to note those factors measured in this study which do not differentiate between impasse and nonimpasse districts. As was mentioned above, characteristics of the board team—indeed, who negotiates for the board—fail to discriminate between impasse and nonimpasse districts. Chi-squares in this dimension do not approach significance at the .25 level of probability. Nor is the role played by the chief school officer significantly related to the outcomes of negotiations. Equal proportions of superintendents served as a member of the board team, a consultant for both sides, or as a consultant to the board team only in both the impasse and nonimpasse districts. These three roles were the only ones played by the chief school officer and in no case was he a member of the teacher team, a consultant for the teacher team only, or uninvolved in negotiations. Perhaps the controversy in the literature about the superintendent as the board's man or educational leader relates more to role conflict in the superintendency than to the success or failure of negotiations in the district.

The status of building principals in negotiations also fails to discriminate between impasse and nonimpasse situations. It is interesting to note, however, that principals were not involved in negotiations in thirteen of the nineteen districts included in this study. In three instances principals had their own negotiating unit while in only one case were principals represented by the teacher team. In no case were principals represented by the board team. Perhaps as building principals come down on one side of the fence or the other, their role will more significantly relate to the conduct of negotiations.

Perhaps surprisingly, neither methods of recording the progress of negotiations nor releasing information to the press appears to relate to impasse or an internally reached agreement. Educators are admonished to keep accurate records of tentative agreements and not to negotiate in the press. In this study, however, neither factor differentiated between impasse and nonimpasse districts. Conceivably these factors relate to the size of the district and the complexity of issues and the relatively small size of the majority of districts included in this study reduced their significance as predictor variables.

CONCLUDING REMARKS

This study was an attempt to discover if certain structural characteristics of the negotiating process are related to the outcomes of that process. To this end, certain predictor variables mentioned in the literature were measured in nineteen school districts in upstate New York to discern whether or not they could differentiate between districts which had gone to impasse and those which had not. The chi-square test of independence for contingency tables was the method of statistical analysis.

Five of the predictor variables significantly discriminated between impasse and nonimpasse districts. Three of these have to do with the composition of the teacher team while the other two relate to the utilization of legal assistance in negotiations and to the frequency and length of negotiating sessions. Homogeneous teacher teams composed primarily of secondary teachers with less than ten years of experience are more likely to be associated with internal agreement. The use of legal assistance other than in the final writing of the contract appears related to the occurrence of impasse. Shorter, more frequent negotiating sessions appear more likely to facilitate agreement than do longer, less frequent ones.

The findings of this study are initial, exploratory, and derive from a rather small sample. The study needs to be replicated with a larger sample in a variety of situations. The findings can serve as guidelines, however, particularly in those states which have recently arrived or have not yet arrived in the negotiations arena. Hopefully such guidelines can reduce the conflict and tensions which have characterized negotiations in some states and can lead to more fruitful and beneficial relationships for all concerned.

In conclusion, it is important to remember that this study deals only with certain structural characteristics of the negotiations process. Certainly numerous categories of other variables might logically relate to the success or failure of negotiations in any given school district. Among these might be community socioeconomic characteristics, the effectiveness of the school's public relations program, the predisposition of the community power structure and the school's relationship to it, the congruence of teacher demands with community values, the history and degree of unionism in the community, and others. These factors also need to be identified and researched in the hope that ultimately a powerfully predictive regression model can be developed to improve the conduct of negotiations in public education.

Notes

1. Myron Lieberman and M. H. Moskow, *Collective Negotiations for Teachers: An Approach to School Administration* (Chicago: Rand-McNally & Company, 1966), p. 253.

2. *Ibid.*, pp. 249-50.

3. Thomas P. Gilroy, A. V. Sinicropi, F. D.Stone, and T. R. Urich, *Educator's Guide to Collective Negotiations* (Columbus: Charles E. Merrill Publishing Co., 1969), p. 34.

4. *Ibid.*, p. 33.

5. *Ibid.*

6. National Education Association (NEA), *How to Negotiate* (Washington, D.C.: the Association, 1969), p. 3.

7. R. E. Doherty, "Negotiation: Impact of Teacher Organizations upon Setting School Policies," *Clearing House*, XL (1966), 515-24.

8. B. E. Donovon, A. Anderson, C. Cogen, and A. W. Wolpert, "Collective Bargaining versus Professional Negotiations," *School Management*, IX (1965), 68-75.

9. John Blackhall Smith, Supt. of the Birmingham, Michigan, Schools, expressed this view in a panel discussion held at the American Association of School Administrators Convention, Atlantic City, February 17-21, 1968.

10. Gilroy *et al.*, *Educator's Guide*, p. 35.

11. Lieberman and Moskow, *Collective Negotiations*, p. 254.

12. NEA Guidelines No. 11, "Negotiation Pointers," 1965.

13. Gilroy *et al.*, *Educator's Guide*, p. 99.

14. John T. Roscoe, *Fundamental Research Statistics for the Behavioral Sciences* (New York: Holt, Rinehart, and Winston, Inc., 1969), ch. 29.

15. John T. Roscoe and Jackson A. Byars, "An Investigation of the Restraints with Respect to Sample Size Commonly Imposed on the Use of the Chi-Square Statistic," *Journal of the American Statistical Association*, LXVI (No. 336, December 1971), 755-59.

17 / Teacher's Strike: A Study of the Conversion of Predisposition into Action

Stephen Cole

When survey research first became popular, its users employed primarily social-psychological variables characterizing individuals. In recent years sociologists have attempted to make survey research more sociological. In the late 1950's we began to use a mode of analysis called "contextual analysis," in which we examined how the relationship between two variables characterizing individuals was affected by different social contexts.[1] Today, although we disagree over the relative strength of contextual and individual variables,[2] we are nevertheless continuing our development of the survey as a tool for studying sociological processes as opposed to social-psychological phenomena. In this paper we use data on the behavior of teachers during strikes as a research site to study the sociological processes that intervene between an individual's social-psychological predispositions and his actual behavior.

Sociologists have noted that predisposition is not invariably converted into action. For example, men who have characteristics which are ordinarily associated with voting Democratic sometimes vote Republican. In a study of political behavior in the International Typographical Union, Lipset, Trow, and Coleman found that in some circumstances liberal printers supported the more conservative

Reprinted from *American Journal of Sociology*, LXXIV (No. 4, March 1969), 506-20.

party.[3] Knowing an individual's predisposition enables us to predict his behavior in a rough way. If 60 percent of a certain group of teachers supported a strike, we would make a mistake 40 percent of the time in predicting the behavior of teachers in this group. In this paper we attempt to develop a more sophisticated explanation of behavior in a decision-making situation by looking in detail at several processes mediating between an individual's predisposition and his behavior. When predisposition is held constant, how do differences in social environment influence behavior? In answering this question we have examined the influence of the presence or absence of social support, cross-pressures, and structurally determined fear of sanctions. Also, in the last part of the paper we have analyzed the significance of reference groups in explaining the behavior of teachers who were pulled in two different directions. Reference group data will enable us to predict the strength of a contextual variable when context and predisposition do not coincide.

Most of the data presented in this paper were obtained from a survey conducted in New York in June 1962, two months after the United Federation of Teachers had sponsored a highly successful one-day strike on April 11. This strike, in which 22,000 of New York's 40,000 teachers stayed away from school, was perhaps the most crucial event in the subsequent success of the teacher-union movement.[4] The questionnaire was placed in the mailboxes of 900 teachers at three senior high schools, two junior high schools, and seven elementary schools. These schools were located in middle- and lower-class neighborhoods in three of New York's five boroughs. Three hundred and thirty-one questionnaires were returned. Despite the poor response rate the sample statistics were quite close to the known population parameters. Furthermore, we have made no use of marginals but have used only internal correlations.[5] In addition to the survey data some statistics on union membership and the behavior of teachers during the April strike were collected from the records of the Board of Education.[6] Finally, we have presented some data from a survey conducted in Perth Amboy, New Jersey, in January 1966, two months after the Perth Amboy teachers had been involved in a two-week strike. Questionnaires were mailed to the homes of all 261 teachers in the Perth Amboy school system, and 126, or 48 percent, were returned. Here, too, the sample statistics very closely matched known population parameters.[7]

The first step in the analysis was to determine what characteristics of teachers influenced their predisposition to support or oppose the New York City strike. Since the survey data were all collected after the strike was over, there was no way of knowing what a teacher's prestrike predisposition was. Therefore, we have taken the behavior of teachers on the strike as an indicator of their predisposition; for example, we assume that if a higher percentage of Jewish teachers than Christian teachers supported the strike, then being a Jew made a teacher more predisposed to accept the militant program of the union's leadership than being a Christian.[8]

Table 17-1 presents the relationship between five nonteaching characteristics of teachers and support of the April 11 strike. Age, class of origin, political affiliation, religion, and sex are correlated with supporting the strike.[9] But the central point is that not all teachers acted in accord with their predisposition. Some who were predisposed to support the strike crossed the picket line; others who were predisposed to oppose the strike stayed away from school. Here we shall show the conditions under which predispositions created by these nonteaching characteristics were converted into action.

SOCIAL SUPPORT

One variable likely to influence the conversion of a predisposition into action is the amount of social support present for the action. A strike is a divisive event. Some workers put their jobs on the line in a fight which, if successful, will result in benefits for all, even those who actively jeopardize the success of the strike by crossing the picket lines. In this type of situation, behavior is especially influenced by the attitudes and behavior of significant others in the work environment. Sixty-nine percent of those teachers who said that the majority of their school friends favored the strike supported the strike themselves, whereas only 26 percent of those who said that less than half of their friends favored the strike did so.[10] We shall use the teachers' reports of their friends' attitudes toward the strike as a crude measure of the amount of social support for the strike that existed in their schools.[11]

Of all nonteaching statuses, political affiliation was most highly correlated with support of the strike. Seventy-two percent of Democrats and 38 percent of Republicans supported the strike (see Table 17-1). In Table 17-2 we see how political affiliation influenced behavior under different conditions of social support. If Republicans worked in a school where the majority of their friends did not favor the strike, their inclination to oppose the strike was reinforced and only 14 percent respected the picket lines. But if Republicans worked in schools where most of their friends supported the strike, then 69

TABLE 17-1. Percentage supporting the strike by five nonteaching statuses (New York sample)

Status	Percentage supporting the strike	Number of teachers
Age:		
Under 30	74	78
30-40	59	76
41-50	38	54
Over 50	32	69
Class of origin:		
Middle class	60	94
Working class	72	161
Political affiliation:		
Republicans	38	60
Democrats	72	233
Religion:		
Christians	46	98
Jews	78	157
Sex:		
Women	57	159
Men	81	120

Note. The number of teachers does not add up to 331 because not all teachers provided complete information. Class of origin was measured by the information provided by the teachers on the main occupation of their fathers. These occupations were coded using the census categories and split into two groups. Teachers whose fathers had professional, semiprofessional, managerial, clerical, and sales occupations came from "middle-class" families, all others from "lower-class" families. Included with the Democrats were those who said they generally voted for a left-of-center third party. Whether or not teachers supported the strike was determined by answers to the following question: "What did you do on the day of the strike? (a) I punched the time clock that day as usual; (b) I walked on a picket line; (c) I called in sick on that day; (d) I just stayed home." Those giving the last three answers were considered to have supported the strike.

TABLE 17-2. Percentage supporting the strike by political affiliation and social support (New York sample)

School friends favoring the strike	Percentage supporting the strike	
	Republicans	Democrats
50% or less	14 (30)	38 (60)
More than 50%	69 (29)	85 (169)

Note. Figures in parentheses represent the numbers of teachers in each category.

percent acted against their own predisposition and refused to cross picket lines. The data from Table 17-2 can be recomputed to show whether or not the teachers acted in accord with their predispositions depending upon the environment. Where social support, either positive or negative (i.e., in favor of or opposed to the strike), was present, 85 percent acted in accord with their predisposition. When social support was not present, only 37 percent acted in accord with their predisposition.[12]

As a summary measure of predisposition, we constructed an Index of Militant Predisposition (IMP). A teacher's score on this index was simply the number of militant characteristics shown in Table 17-1 that he possessed. Thus, a Jewish, Democratic male, under the age of forty, from a lower-class family, received an IMP score of five. As may be seen in Table 17-3, the IMP was highly correlated with support of the strike. The importance of social support in converting predisposition into action is also clearly illustrated in Table 17-3. Without social support, even those teachers who were highly pre-

TABLE 17-3. Percentage supporting the strike by Index of Militant Predisposition (IMP) and social support (New York sample)

IMP	Percentage supporting strike	School friends favoring the strike	
		50% or less	More than 50%
Low (0, 1, 2)	43 (97)	24 (51)	65 (46)
High (4, 5, 6)	81 (179)	38 (37	93 (142)

disposed to be militant (i.e., had three, four, or five militant characteristics) found it difficult to support the strike. Only 38 percent of those teachers with high IMP scores but little social support acted in accord with their predisposition. Likewise, those teachers who were predisposed to oppose the strike found it difficult to do so if they worked in a school where the majority of their colleagues supported the strike. Sixty-five percent of these teachers supported the strike. When social support was present, 89 percent acted in accord with their predisposition. When social support was not present, only 36 percent acted in accord with their predisposition.[13]

This analysis underscores once again how contextual variables influence the interaction of variables characterizing individuals. Knowing a teacher's IMP score tells us a lot about how he behaved during the strike. But when we know the attitudinal context in which he worked, we can interpret behavior that deviates from the prediction based upon the IMP. These findings confirm the analysis of Lipset, Trow, and Coleman of the effect of attitudinal contexts on whether political predispositions are acted on.[14]

The aggregate data collected from the records of the New York City Board of Education provide additional evidence on how social support influenced the behavior of teachers. We know that there was a higher probability that men would support the strike than women. Therefore, we would predict that women would be more likely to strike in schools where there were many men present. For in schools where there was widespread social support for striking, even teachers with relatively low scores on the IMP would be more likely to support the strike.

For the junior high schools in our aggregate sample, we had information on the number of men in each school and the proportion of each sex that supported the strike. We divided the schools into those in which 40 percent or more of the staff were men and those in which less than 40 percent of the staff were men. We then computed the percentage of women supporting the strike in each of these groups. In those schools which had less than 40 percent male teachers, 51 percent of the women supported the strike. In those schools that had a relatively high proportion of male teachers, 62 percent of the women struck.

These aggregate data provide further corroborative evidence that the social support of men was significant in the activation of militancy among female teachers. The majority of teachers in the girls' high schools are women, and the majority of teachers in the boys' high schools are men. The faculties of the co-ed high schools are about evenly split between men and women.[15] Forty-five percent of the teachers in all girls' high schools struck, as opposed to 68 percent of the teachers in all boys' schools and 69 percent of those in the co-ed schools.[16] Since we can assume that men who taught in co-ed schools were no more likely to support the strike than men who taught in boys' schools, and since the percentage striking in these two types of schools was the same, the data indicate that in the co-ed schools the female teachers supported the strike just as strongly as did their male colleagues. Thus, the difference in militancy of the female teachers in girls' schools and in co-ed schools may possibly be explained by the presence of the militant men in the latter schools. Where men were present to take the lead and give social support, the predisposition of women to oppose the strike was overcome; where men were not present, the predisposition of women to oppose the strike was converted into action, and the women were likely to cross the picket lines and report for work.

Activation of militancy depended upon the sheer number of colleagues who supported the strike and also the presence of effective leadership in the schools. In fact, the presence of effective leadership was likely to be a factor influencing the amount of social support. The quality of union leadership varied from school to school, with some schools having strong chapter chairmen who enlisted a large number of UFT members, and others having weak and ineffective chapter chairmen. There were some schools in which there was no UFT chapter, nor even a single UFT member. For Table 17-4 we have classified the schools in all four divisions by the percentage of teachers in each school who were UFT members in January 1962, three months before the strike of April 11.[17] The percentage of UFT members in a school is taken as an indicator of both the quality of union leadership and the number of teachers who were likely to be active supporters of the strike. Table 17-4 provides the obvious result that there was more support for the strike in those schools where union membership was large than in those where it was small or nonexistent. But what is rather less evident is the further finding in Table 17-4 that the presence of strong leadership made the most difference in that division where support of the strike was weakest, that is, in the elementary schools. In the divisions where support for the strike was strong, the addition of effective leadership as a source of social support had less effect. We might say that effective chapter leadership had a greater impact in preventing the negatively disposed

TABLE 17-4. Percentage supporting the strike by type of school and union membership (aggregate data)

Teachers who were union members prior to the strike (percent)	Teachers supporting the strike			
	Elementary	Junior high	Academic high	Vocational high
0-9	30 (3,929)	65 (1,063)	55 (2,776)	60 (1,656)
10-29	45 (716)	69 (1,960)	73 (3,901)	62 (519)
30 or more	56 (204)	76 (2,021)	76 (1,075)	64 (98)

from crossing picket lines than it did in reinforcing the inclination of those predisposed to support the strike.

We thought it possible that the number of union members in a school might depend upon the conditions within the school. It was possible that those schools in which working conditions were worst would have the most union members and that the data in Table 17-4 would be a result of differential degrees of job dissatisfaction rather than differences in the quality of union leadership. To test this hypothesis we looked at the percentage of teachers belonging to the union in "special-service" schools and in regular schools. The special-service schools are all located in low-income neighborhoods and generally have more difficult working conditions and thus more dissatisfaction. We found that 19 percent of teachers in both special-service schools and regular schools taught in schools where more than 10 percent of the teachers were UFT members. Since union membership prior to the strike was not correlated with difficulty of working conditions, we may conclude that social support provided by effective leadership had an independent effect on the conversion of predisposition into action.

When teachers had to decide what to do about the strike, they were influenced by a set of attitudes they had acquired before becoming teachers. These attitudes or social-psychological characteristics had different consequences depending upon the teacher's social environment. Those teachers who found their predispositions supported by their colleagues' attitudes and behavior tended to act in accord with their predisposition. Those whose predisposition conflicted with their environment were less likely to act in accord with these predispositions. These latter teachers were under cross-pressure. In the next section we analyze the sources and consequences of cross-pressure.

TABLE 17-5. Percentage calling in sick by IMP score and attitudes of friends toward the strike (New York sample)

School friends favoring the strike	Percentage calling in sick	
	Low IMP (0, 1, 2)	High IMP (3, 4, 5)
50% or less	10 (51)	16 (37)
More than 50%	41 (46)	22 (142)

CROSS-PRESSURES AND AVOIDANCE BEHAVIOR

The strike situation was analogous to a voting situation in that there were three alternative courses of action. In an election you may vote for one candidate or another, *or* you may choose not to vote, to avoid making a clear decision. In a strike a teacher could walk on the picket line or cross the picket line and report for work, *or* he could call in sick and thus avoid a firm commitment. Here, we shall show how teachers who experienced cross-pressures were the most likely to engage in avoidance behavior.[18]

We found four types of cross-pressure that led to avoidance behavior:

Type 1: Conflict between a social context and a predisposition created by a status. Cross-pressure occurred when a teacher occupied a status predisposing him to act in one way, while most of his colleagues were taking a contrary position. When a teacher occupying a status (or statuses) predisposing him to support the strike worked in a school where the majority of his friends did not support the strike, he was under cross-pressure. Correlatively, a teacher whose status-set made him predisposed not to support the strike, and who had a majority of friends supporting the strike, was also under cross-pressure (see Table 17-5). Of those teachers who said that more than half of their friends supported the strike, 41 percent of those with low IMP scores, as opposed to 22 percent of those with high IMP scores, called in sick. We found a similar but weaker pattern among teachers who said that 50 percent or fewer of their friends supported the strike. If we recompute the data from Table 17-5, combining the data in cells 1 and 4 with the data in cells 2 and 3, we find that, when the context and the predisposition coincided, 19 percent engaged in avoidance behavior; when the context and the predisposition conflicted, 30 percent engaged in avoidance behavior.

Type 2: Conflict between objective statuses and subjective attitudes. An individual occupies statuses which ordinarily create a predisposition to act in one way. His subjective evaluation of the situation may support or oppose this predisposition. The most common example of such conflict is the blue-collar worker who identifies with the middle class. When objective statuses and subjective evaluations do not coincide, the individual is likely to be under cross-pressure. Teachers who measured low on the IMP and thought the strike justified, as well as those who measured high on IMP and thought the strike unjustified, were under cross-pressure and were more likely to engage in avoidance behavior than their noncross-pressured colleagues. Thirty-two percent of teachers under this type of cross-pressure called in sick, as opposed to 18 percent of those not under this type of cross-pressure.

It was possible that those teachers who had nonteaching statuses predisposing them to support the strike but who viewed the strike as unjustified did not have those typical attitudes associated with their nonteaching statuses. However, if this were true, they should have behaved like their colleagues who had low IMP scores. Since they did not, we can assume that they had conflicting attitudes. This type of cross-pressure would seem to be psychological, that is, internal to the individual. However, we might ask under what conditions individuals will form opinions which conflict with their predisposition. We thought that the opinion of one's friends would be a crucial factor in the genesis of this type of cross-pressure. Indeed, we found that, where one's predisposition and the attitudes of friends were in agreement, only 14 percent were under this type of cross-pressure. But when the individual's predisposition conflicted with the attitude of his friends, 62 percent were under this type of cross-pressure. Thus, internal psychological conflict can be seen partially as a result of social location.

Type 3: Polarization in a social context. In a situation where polarization on an issue occurs, such as in a strike or an election, an individual will be under cross-pressure if some of his friends and associates are on one side and others on the opposite side. The more

TABLE 17-6a. Percentage calling in sick by IMP score (New York sample)

Index of Militant Predisposition					
0	*1*	*2*	*3*	*4*	*5*
0 (11)	24 (34)	31 (58)	28 (78)	20 (80)	10 (39)

evenly split are one's associates, the greater the cross-pressure experienced. The Perth Amboy data provide a good site to test this hypothesis. Perth Amboy teachers were asked when they decided what they would do on the day of the strike. Making up one's mind right before the strike is a type of avoidance behavior. It turned out that the more agreement there was among friends, the more likely a teacher was to make up his mind early. If friends were split, a decision was more likely to be delayed. Sixty-eight percent of those who reported disagreement among friends, as opposed to 81 percent of those who reported unanimity, made up their minds a few days before the Perth Amboy strike.

Type 4: Conflict between two or more statuses. The first three types of cross-pressure were a result of conflict between an individual's predisposition and his school environment or a result of conflict within the school environment itself. Cross-pressure could also have resulted from conflict outside the school. A teacher could have occupied one or more statuses which predisposed him to favor the strike and one or more statuses which, at the same time, predisposed him to disapprove of it. As a result of having such a status-set, an individual would associate with groups of people who had conflicting expectations of how he should behave. The IMP may be used as an indicator of the degree of cross-pressure resulting from the occupation of nonteaching statuses which make for conflicting predispositions. Those teachers who scored 0 or 5 on the Index were under no cross-pressure. All their statuses combined to make them either highly predisposed to favor the strike or highly predisposed to oppose the strike. Those teachers who scored 1 or 4 on the IMP had one status which put them under cross-pressure, whereas those teachers who scored 2 or 3 on the Index were under the most cross-pressure. These teachers had two statuses pulling them in one way and three statuses pushing them in the opposite direction. As may be seen in Table 17-6, those teachers who were under the greatest cross-pressure were the ones most likely to engage in avoidance behavior. In part A of Table 17-6 we show the percentage of teachers in each category of the IMP who called in sick, and in part B we see how the number of cross-pressures

TABLE 17-6b. Percentage calling in sick by number of cross-pressure-producing statuses (New York sample)

0 (IMP 0, 5)	1 (IMP 1, 4)	2 (IMP 2, 3)
8 (50)	21 (114)	29 (136)

influenced this type of behavior.[19] Only 8 percent of the teachers with no cross-pressure-producing status, and 29 percent of the teachers with two cross-pressure-producing statuses, called in sick.

FEAR OF SANCTIONS

Fear of sanctions influenced the decision of teachers about whether to support the strike. Although teachers had struck in the past, such events were rare and on a smaller scale than the New York City strike of April 11, 1962. The striking teachers had to violate the highly punitive Condon-Wadlin Act, which called for dismissal and loss of pay, tenure, and salary increments, among other frightening prospects. It would be incorrect, however, to assume that frightened teachers would be less likely to strike. A teacher who himself did not favor the strike and who did not feel pressured by his colleagues to support the strike had little to be afraid of. Having definitely made up his mind not to strike he would have little reason to fear the penalties of striking. Thus, the teachers least likely to be militant were also least likely to be fearful.[20] Eighty per cent of those teachers who expressed fear thought the strike was justified.[21]

TABLE 17-7. Fear and action on April 11—Only those believing the strike justified (New York sample)

Fear	Action on April 11			
	Punched time clock (percent)	Picketed (percent)	Called in sick (percent)	Number of teachers
Not afraid	8	67	25	152
Afraid	21	46	33	48

Table 17-7 presents the relationship between fear and action among those teachers who believed the strike justified.[22] Teachers who were afraid were more likely to punch the time clock, less likely to picket, and more likely to escape from the anguish of a direct commitment by calling in sick. Calling in sick was clearly less dangerous than picketing. If the strike failed and the Condon-Wadlin Act was invoked, a friendly physician could be found to legitimate the claim to illness. Also, by calling in sick the teacher did not lose a day's pay.

The effect of fear on the conversion of predisposition into action may be seen in Table 17-8. Of those teachers who scored high on the IMP, the ones who expressed fear were more likely to cross the picket line and more likely to call in sick. Fear had only minor influence on the teachers who were not predisposed to favor the union movement.

Fear was not randomly distributed throughout the school system, but was created by both social-psychological and contextual variables. Some individuals had attributes which made them more frightened than their colleagues. We thought that both the oldest and the youngest teachers had most to lose if the strike failed and would, therefore, be more afraid to support the strike even if they believed

TABLE 17-8. Index of militant predisposition, fear, and action on April 11 (New York sample)

| Fear | Action on April 11 | | | |
	Punched time clock (percent)	Picketed (percent)	Called in sick (percent)	Number of teachers
Low IMP (0, 1, 2):				
Not afraid	59	19	22	80
Afraid	55	15	30	20
High IMP (3, 4, 5):				
Not afraid	17	64	19	139
Afraid	28	47	26	43

it to be justified. Indeed, age was curvilinearly related to fear among those who believed the strike to be justified. Teachers under thirty and over fifty were more likely to say they were afraid than those between thirty and fifty.[23] Many of the younger teachers were either "substitutes" or regulars on probation without tenure. These teachers were afraid that participation in the strike would prevent them from getting tenure. The older teachers, in addition to fearing loss of their pension, knew that if they were fired it would be difficult for them to find new jobs. Most school systems prefer to hire young teachers whom they have to pay less and who, if given tenure, will give many years of service.

Fear was influenced by individual characteristics of the teachers and by the context in which the individual worked. In some schools there was more reason to be afraid than in others. The attitudes toward the strike of supervisory personnel having direct authority over the teacher differed from school to school. If supervisors gave indications that they would punish teachers participating in the strike, there was more reason for a teacher to be afraid. If supervisors either ignored the strike, or, as happened in some cases, indicated that they were in sympathy with the strikers, teachers were less likely to be afraid.

The New York survey did not include a question on the teacher's perception of his supervisor's attitudes toward the strike, but in Perth Amboy we asked the teachers such a question.[24] Forty-three percent of those teachers who thought that their principals were opposed to the strike, and 31 percent who thought that their

TABLE 17-9. Index of militant predisposition, type of school, and action on April 11 (New York sample)

School type	Action on April 11			
	Punched time clock (percent)	Picketed (percent)	Called in sick (percent)	Number of teachers
Low IMP (0, 1, 2):				
Elementary	71	8	21	24
Secondary	55	18	26	65
High IMP (3, 4, 5):				
Elementary	41	39	20	54
Secondary	16	63	21	135

principals favored the strike or were neutral, were afraid. The perceived attitude of the principal was also related to action on the first day of the strike. Eighty-three percent who said their principal favored the strike supported it themselves, as opposed to 33 percent of those who said their principal opposed the strike. Although it is possible that there might be other variables explaining these data, they suggest that the visible attitudes of supervisors were probably significant in influencing the conversion of predisposition into action.

In New York another contextual variable influencing fear was type of school. In the elementary schools 30 percent of the teachers were fearful, and in the secondary schools, 20 percent. This finding does not result from differences in the sex composition of the faculties of the two types of schools. Men, in fact, were slightly more afraid than women.[25] Also, if the difference in fear between the two types of schools was dependent upon the sex distribution of the teachers, we would expect female secondary school teachers to be just as frightened as their elementary school counterparts. This was not the case. Thirty-one percent of female elementary school teachers and 15 percent of female secondary school teachers were afraid. We may conclude that the social organization of the elementary schools was a factor contributing to the fear experienced by teachers who taught there.

In the elementary schools there is a more direct relationship between school authorities and the teacher. The elementary schools are relatively small, and contact between the principal and the teachers is frequent, making it difficult to remain anonymous. Therefore, the threat of negative sanctions was closer and more menacing in the elementary schools than in the junior and senior high schools. In the high schools the teacher's immediate supervisor was his departmental chairman, who may also have been a member of the union and, in some cases, may have actively supported the strike. It is probable that, because of the greater amount of fear that existed in the elementary schools, even those teachers who were highly predisposed to support the strike found it difficult to do so (see Table 17-9). Of those teachers who scored high on the IMP, 41 percent of the elementary school teachers and 16 percent of the secondary school teachers crossed the picket line.

Those teachers who were highly predisposed to be militant and yet were afraid of negative sanctions were under a type of cross-pressure. We wanted to specify the conditions under which an individual would conquer fear and act in accord with his militant predisposition. Perhaps the most crucial variable in determining whether fear would prevent the favorably predisposed from striking was social support. Fear could be conquered if the teacher was one of many putting his job on the line. Psychologically, the perceived danger of striking was inversely related to the number of teachers who supported the strike in one's *own* school.

The importance of social support for those who were afraid may be seen in Table 17-10. If teachers who were afraid did not perceive their friends as favoring the strike, 74 percent crossed the picket line. If they did perceive their friends as favoring the strike, only 13 percent crossed the picket line.

Social support was most lacking in the elementary schools. Whereas 74 percent of the secondary school teachers said that three-quarters or more of their school friends favored the strike, only 52

TABLE 17-10. Percentage of friends favoring the strike and action
on April 11—Only those who were afraid (New York
sample)

| | Action on April 11 | | | |
Friends favoring the strike	Punched time clock (percent)	Picketed (percent)	Called in sick (percent)	Number of teachers
50% or less	74	17	9	23
More than 50%	13	49	38	39

percent of the elementary school teachers reported as much support.
If fear was more prevalent in elementary schools because their small
size made it more difficult to remain anonymous and less likely that
there would be social support for striking, we would expect that
the larger the elementary school, the more nearly conditions would
approach those found in high schools. To study the effect of size
of elementary school we must return to the aggregate data. Twenty-
two percent of teachers in schools having staffs of fewer than thirty
supported the strike, as opposed to 31 percent in schools with staffs
of thirty to thirty-nine, and 39 percent in schools with staffs of forty
or more. In large elementary schools the teacher who was highly predisposed to support the strike had a better chance of finding colleagues who felt the same way. In the small elementary schools
there was a high probability that the militant teacher would find
herself isolated.[26] In large elementary schools it was also more likely
that the relationship between teacher and supervisor would be impersonal. It was easier to call in sick and go unnoticed. Large size
created anonymity and provided social support and thus reduced the
effect of fear.

COLLEAGUES AS A REFERENCE GROUP

Throughout this paper we have stressed the significance of interaction in converting predisposition into action. The way in which
such interaction influenced behavior depended in part on whether
colleagues were a significant reference group. The teachers were
asked whether they were afraid that they would lose the respect of
their colleagues if they did not support the strike.[27] We assume that
colleagues were a more important reference group for those who
feared losing their respect than for those who did not fear such a
loss.[28]

In the first section of this paper we used the percentage of friends supporting the strike as an indicator of the amount of social support for striking. It is clear, however, that what was social support to some was social pressure to others. Those teachers who had low scores on the IMP and who taught in schools where more than half their friends favored the strike were under considerable pressure to act contrary to their predisposition. What determined whether they yielded to this pressure? Here we are extending our analysis of how decisions are made when men are under cross-pressure. Those teachers who had low IMP scores and worked in schools where the majority of their friends favored the strike were under cross-pressure. Above we showed how these teachers were likely to avoid a decision by calling in sick. But what of those who could not avoid a decision— what influenced the *direction* of their decision? We hypothesized that those teachers who had colleagues as a reference group would be the most likely to yield to pressure.

The data indicate that social pressure was difficult to ignore even for those teachers who did not fear losing the respect of their colleagues. Only 45 percent acted in accord with their predisposition and crossed the picket line (see Table 17-11). However, when social pressure was exerted by colleagues who were a significant reference group, practically all teachers acted contrary to their predispositions. Only 17 percent of teachers who had low IMP scores and reported that more than 50 percent of their colleagues supported the strike, and who feared losing the respect of these colleagues, acted in accord with their predisposition.[29] Knowing the salience of man's relations with those around him helps us understand the effect that attitudinal

TABLE 17-11. Fear of losing respect of colleagues and action on April 11—For those low on IMP and having more than 50 percent of their friends favor the strike (New York sample)

| Fear | Action on April 11 | | | |
	Punched time clock (percent)	Picketed (percent)	Called in sick (percent)	Number of teachers
Feared loss of respect	17	28	56	18
Did not fear loss of respect	45	21	34	29

context has on the conversion of the individual's predisposition into action.

Whether or not colleagues were a reference group also determined whether teachers who had high IMP scores but feared negative sanctions would act in accord with their predisposition. Although the percentages are based upon a very small number of cases, the data in Table 17-12 suggest that, if colleagues were a reference group, frightened teachers were able to overcome their fear and act in accord with their predisposition. Above (Table 17-10) we showed that social support enabled the frightened teacher to overcome his fear. The data in Table 17-12 suggest that the support of colleagues will be a more effective bolster if these colleagues are a meaningful reference group.[30]

TABLE 17-12. Fear of losing respect of colleagues and action on April 11—For those high on IMP and fearing sanctions from supervisors (New York sample)

	Action on April 11			
Fear	Punched time clock (percent)	Picketed (percent)	Called in sick (percent)	Number of teachers
Feared loss of respect	23	42	35	31
Did not fear loss of respect	42	58	0	12

Fear of loss of respect, like fear of sanctions, served to specify the conditions under which predisposition will be converted into action. Of those teachers who scored low on the IMP, 22 percent fearing loss of respect and 69 percent not fearing such a loss acted in accord with their predisposition. However, fear of loss of respect had little influence on those who scored high on the IMP. The data in Table 17-13 present an informative contrast to those of Table 17-8. Whereas fear of sanctions had little influence on those not predisposed to be militant, fear of loss of respect had little influence on those who were predisposed to be militant. Since the general climate in the schools was one of support for the strike, fear of sanctions from colleagues was more likely to influence those who were predisposed

TABLE 17-13. Index of militant predisposition, fear of loss of respect, action on April 11 (New York sample)

Fear	Action on April 11			
	Punched time clock (percent)	Picketed (percent)	Called in sick (percent)	Number of teachers
Low IMP (0, 1, 2):				
Feared loss of respect	22	30	48	23
Did not fear loss of respect	69	14	17	77
High IMP (3,4,5):				
Feared loss of respect	14	58	28	76
Did not fear loss of respect	23	61	16	106

not to support the strike. Fear of sanctions from supervisors was more likely to influence those who were predisposed to support the strike.

Let us summarize our findings on the conditions which influenced the conversion of predisposition into action:

1. Those teachers who had a majority of their friends agreeing with them were more likely to convert predisposition into action than those who had a majority of friends disagreeing with them. Another type of social support was provided by union leadership. Where union leadership was active, the behavior of those predisposed to favor the strike was reinforced. Where local union leadership was absent or ineffective, those with favorable predispositions toward the strike were less likely to convert them into action.

2. When the strike was called, a teacher could cross the picket line and report for work, walk on the picket line, or call in sick. This latter alternative was a type of avoidance behavior. By calling in sick, the teacher was able to avoid making a clear commitment either in support of the strike or in opposition to it. We show how

four types of cross-pressure influence avoidance behavior. A teacher was under cross-pressure when (a) there was a conflict between a predisposition created by a status and that created by a social context, (b) there was a conflict between a status predisposing him to act one way and his subjective attitude toward the strike, (c) he had some friends who favored the strike and other friends who opposed the strike, or (d) he occupied two statuses which predisposed him to act in different ways. Each of these types of cross-pressure influenced the conversion of predisposition into action.

3. Those teachers who were afraid of sanctions from authorities were less likely to convert a favorable predisposition into action. Fear was an emotion which was not randomly distributed. Fear was related to age, the authority structure in the different types of schools, and the amount of social support. The presence of other individuals who openly supported the strike was the most important ingredient in overcoming fear.

4. If colleagues were a significant reference group, those teachers who were not predisposed to be militant but worked in schools where there was a heavy support for the strike were likely to give in to pressure and act contrary to their predispositions. Likewise, those teachers who were predisposed to be militant but feared punishment were most likely to overcome their fear if colleagues were a significant reference group. Those teachers who were favorably disposed toward the strike were more affected by fear of sanctions from authorities, whereas those teachers who were predisposed to oppose the strike were more affected by fear of sanctions from colleagues.

Perhaps the most significant finding of this paper is the one concerning the importance of reference groups as a factor mediating the influence of social context on the individual. It would seem that all studies making use of "contextual analysis" would benefit by including data on the reference groups of the individuals studied.[31] Knowing the salience of relationships with the people making up the social context will aid us in predicting the strength of the contextual variable.

Notes

This research was supported by a grant from the Columbia University sociology department. I would like to thank Jonathan R. Cole for his comments on an earlier draft of this paper.

1. An early use of contextual analysis may be found in Emile Durkheim's *Suicide* (Glencoe, Ill.: Free Press, 1951), p. 264, where he shows how the re-

lationship between marital status and suicide depends on the norms concerning divorce. This mode of analysis was independently rediscovered by Paul Lazarsfeld and his colleagues at the Bureau of Applied Social Research.

2. One area in which this disagreement may be seen is in the research on the effect of high school environment on the decision to go to college (see William Sewell and Vimal P. Shah, "Social Class, Parental Encouragement, and Educational Aspirations," *American Journal of Sociology,* LXXIII (March 1968), 559-72.

3. Seymour Martin Lipset, Martin A. Trow, and James S. Coleman, *Union Democracy: The Internal Politics of the International Typographical Union* (Garden City, N.Y.: Anchor Books, 1962), ch. xvi.

4. For discussions of the impact of the UFT success on the subsequent development of the teacher-union movement, see Myron Lieberman and Michael H. Moskow, *Collective Negotiation for Teachers* (Chicago: Rand-McNally & Co., 1966), p. 35; Stephen Cole, "The Unionization of Teachers: A Case Study of Change in a Profession" (Ph.D. diss., Columbia University, 1967), ch. i.

5. Statistics generated from a nonrepresentative sample cannot be used to make generalizations about population parameters. Thus, on the basis of the sample, we would not be able to say what percentage of the teachers in the population supported the strike or had any particular attitude. However, the fact that a sample overrepresents a particular group does not mean that the internal correlations among variables are not valid; e.g., even if our sample overrepresents Democrats, this does not mean that the correlation between political affiliation and support of the strike is not a valid one. For a comparison of sample statistics and population statistics and a further discussion of the problems involved in generalizing on the basis of a nonrepresentative sample, see Cole, "Unionization of Teachers," Appendix A.

6. I thank Professor Alan Rosenthal of Rutgers University for making these data available. Rosenthal reported some of his findings in "The Strength of Teachers Organizations: Factors Influencing Membership in Two Large Cities," *Sociology of Education,* XXXIX (Fall 1966).

7. For an analysis of why the response rate was so low despite a concerted effort to assure anonymity and several follow-up letters and phone calls, see Cole, "Unionization of Teachers." All tables specify whether the data are drawn from the New York sample, the Perth Amboy sample, or the aggregate data. All textual analysis refers to the New York survey unless otherwise indicated.

8. This procedure assumes that intensity of predisposition is reflected in action. Lipset *et al., Union Democracy,* adopt this same procedure when they use past voting behavior of "liberal" and "conservative" printers as the basis of establishing their predispositions.

9. I have analyzed the reasons for these correlations elsewhere (see Stephen Cole, "The Unionization of Teachers: Determinants of Rank-and-File Support," *Sociology of Education,* XLI (Winter 1968), 66-87.

10. The question was: "What proportion of your friends in school favored the strike? (a) none of them, (b) about one-quarter, (c) about one-half, (d) about three-quarters, (e) all of them."

11. Although, for the New York data, there is no direct evidence that the teachers' perceptions of the attitudes of their friends were correct, there is such evidence for the Perth Amboy survey. In Perth Amboy we know exactly how

many teachers in each school supported the strike. This information was reported in the local newspaper. The Perth Amboy teachers were also asked what percentage of their friends supported the strike. If we compare the actual number of teachers supporting the strike and the subjective view of the teachers of how many of their friends supported the strike, we find that only 14 percent of the teachers gave an estimate that was off by more than 20 percent. We do not imply that the 14 percent whose report varied from the objective condition had poor cognitive perception or were lying. The teachers were asked what percentage of "friends" favored the strike. It was possible for the teacher answering the questionnaire to give a broad or a narrow definition of this term. However, in general, we may conclude that the answer to this question is a fairly reliable measure of the actual amount of social support that the teacher received either in the school as a whole or among his special friends in the school. This latter definition of the term "friends" would be more likely to be given by teachers in large schools, i.e., secondary schools.

12. The figure 85 percent was arrived at by combining the data in cells 1 and 4 of Table 17-2. The 37 percent represents the combination of data in cells 2 and 3.

13. The figure 89 percent was arrived at by combining the data in cells 1 and 4 of Table 17-3. The 36 percent represents the combination of data in cells 2 and 3.

14. Lipset *et al., Union Democracy.*

15. This information was obtained from interviews with several union leaders.

16. Of course it is possible that there may be other differences between female teachers in girls' schools and in co-ed schools that would explain these data.

17. Here we are using the aggregate data provided by Alan Rosenthal, "Strength of Teachers Organizations."

18. The concept of cross-pressures was introduced by Paul F. Lazarsfeld, Bernard Berelson, and Hazel Gaudet in *The People's Choice* (New York: Columbia University Press, 1948). It was extended further in Berelson, Lazarsfeld, and W. N. McPhee, *Voting* (Chicago: University of Chicago Press, 1954). For a summary of other relevant literature, see Seymour Martin Lipset, *Political Man* (Garden City, N.Y.: Anchor Books, 1960), pp. 211-26.

19. For a similar table, see Lazarsfeld *et al., People's Choice,* p. 63.

20. Lazarsfeld and Wagner Thielens, Jr., found similar results in their study of the reaction of college teachers to McCarthyism. Those teachers who were the most conservative were the least apprehensive (*The Academic Mind* [Glencoe, Ill.: Free Press, 1958] , p. 239).

21. The teachers who were afraid and did not think the strike justified were probably being subjected to social pressure to support the strike. However, fear had very little influence on the behavior of those teachers who did not think that the strike was justified. The great majority of these teachers, whether or not they were afraid, crossed the picket line and reported for work. Teachers who did not believe the strike justified have been excluded from most of the analysis of fear of sanctions.

22. A teacher was classified as being afraid if he feared at least one of the following: loss of job, not being able to get a job in another school system, loss of pension benefits, that the principal would make things difficult, getting a black mark on his record, or loss of tenure. Only 19 percent of our sample

checked at least one of these items. Since these were not forced-choice questions, we believe that this technique resulted in a substantial understatement of fear. In Perth Amboy, where the same questions were used in a forced-choice format, 38 percent of the sample checked at least one item.

23. Among those teachers who believed the strike to be justified, 25 percent of those under thirty, 17 percent of those from thirty to fifty, and 31 percent of those over fifty were afraid.

24. The exact wording of the question was: "Do you think that the attitude of your principal was: (a) favorable to the strike, (b) unfavorable to the strike, (c) neutral, (d) I don't know what the attitude of my principal was?"

25. Twenty-six percent of the men and 21 percent of the women were afraid. Men are the primary breadwinners for their families and had more to lose than women if the strike failed.

26. Lipset *et al., Union Democracy.*

27. Teachers were asked to place a check next to the following statement if it applied to them: "I thought that if I *did* go to work I would lose the respect of some of my colleagues."

28. We thought it possible that fear of loss of respect might only be a valid indicator of whether colleagues were a significant reference group for those teachers whose attitudes toward the strike differed from the attitudes of their colleagues. This was not the case. If the majority of friends favored the strike, 44 percent of those believing the strike justified and 36 percent of those believing the strike was not justified feared loss of respect. The feeling of those not believing the strike justified needs little explanation. Their friends felt one way and they, another. The majority of their friends expected them to support the strike. If they did not live up to this expectation, they would lose the respect of their friends. But what about those who did think the strike justified, those who agreed with their friends? It is most likely that every teacher, no matter how militant, was to some extent worried about the strike. It was possible for a teacher to favor the strike, perceive his friends as favoring the strike, and still be afraid of negative sanctions from authorities. In such a situation fear of loss of respect might very well have been salient.

29. Just as fear of sanctions induced avoidance behavior, so did fear of loss of respect. Thirty-two percent of all those fearing loss of respect and 16 percent of those not fearing loss of respect called in sick.

30. Ideally we would run a five-variable table to demonstrate the validity of our assumption. However, this is impossible given the size of our sample.

31. The analysis in Lipset *et al., Union Democracy*, ch. xvi, might have been further perfected by including data on the extent of which the other printers in the shop were a reference group. Also, the analysis presented by James S. Coleman in "The Adolescent Sub-Culture and Academic Achievement," *American Journal of Sociology*, LXV (January 1960), 337-47, would have been more convincing had he broken down his student sample into those who had the "leading crowd" as a reference group and those who did not.

18 / Collective Negotiations and Teachers: A Behavioral Analysis

Don Hellriegel, Wendell French, and *Richard B. Peterson*

> Since the mid-1950's so much has happened in public school employer-employee relations that it should really be considered an entirely new field.
>
> . . . Prior to 1960, not a single state authorized collective, or any other form of, negotiations between teacher organizations and boards of education. There were, at that time, in the educational literature, only vague references to some sort of teacher negotiations and the improvement of staff relations.[1]

Although a body of literature is developing in this new field, there appears to be a lack of conceptualizing and of empirical evidence regarding classroom teachers' satisfactions and dissatisfactions with their organizational environment, attitudes toward teaching as a profession, perceptions of collective negotiations, and the interrelations among these variables.[2]

One manifestation of the strains which are occurring in the teacher-employer role relationship and of the growing willingness among teachers to take direct action is the upswing in teachers' strikes commencing with 1966. Prior to 1966, teachers' strikes were infrequent. "During the 26 years beginning in 1940, a total of 129 such stoppages occurred but only 35 of these were recorded in the decade im-

Reprinted from *Industrial and Labor Relations Review*, XXIII (No. 3, April 1970), 380-96.

mediately preceding 1966."[3] An official of the National Education Association estimated 140 teacher strikes occurred during the 1968-69 school year, an increase of 23 percent from the 114 strikes in the 1967-68 school year.[4] The growing militancy of teachers during the 1968-69 period of this study has been reported widely and discussed in the popular news media. However, Stieber has noted that "too often the strike in public employment has been treated as an unmitigated evil to be exorcized rather than the symptoms of a malady which needs treatment."[5]

This study provides a conceptual framework and empirical insights into such "symptoms" of one group of public employees—school teachers. The conceptual model presented is a means of identifying and portraying the assumed relationships among the key variables considered to provide the behavioral framework of teachers vis-a-vis collective negotiations. The research design and statistical findings which follow partially test the utility of the model.

THE MODEL

The underlying assumptions of the conceptual model and the research design are (1) attitudes affect the direction of the perceptual process, (2) this process may be related to particular motivational dispositions, and (3) these dispositions may be reflected in overt acts such as a strike or a vote against a strike.

The conceptual model (see Figure 18-1) of factors related to teachers' attitudes toward collective negotiations was developed on the basis of an extensive review of the literature from which the component variables and their assumed relationships were abstracted. Much of the available literature regarding teacher behavior and collective negotiations in education has not considered the form or degree of their interrelationships. The writings which have attempted such a synthesis typically are more limited in scope, i.e., they consider a few "behavioral" variables in relation to a few "negotiation" variables. Thus, the model is affected by some a priori reasoning.[6]

The model is assumed also to be a means of explaining and integrating the findings from the empirical investigation. Additional research may indicate that other variables need to be included or that the hypothesized relationships among the variables need to be altered. Thus, there is no attempt to conclude that this model provides a complete explanation of the relationships being investigated or that the sequence of relationships are as posited.

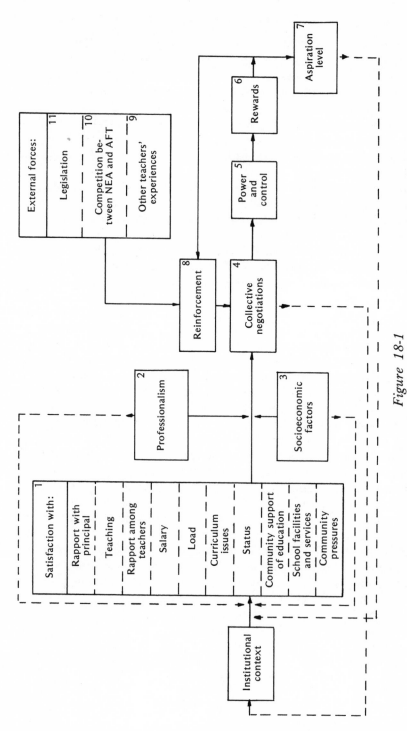

Figure 18-1

Conceptual model of factors related to teachers' attitudes
toward collective negotiations

THE MODEL: INTERNAL FORCES

Variable 1 in the conceptual model refers to the perceived satisfactions or dissatisfactions by the teachers with ten different dimensions of the institutional and environmental context within which they function. These dimensions of satisfaction include: rapport with principal, satisfaction with teaching, rapport among teachers, salary, load, curriculum issues, status, community support of education, school facilities and services, and community pressures. Thus, teacher satisfaction is analyzed as a multidimensional phenomenon. The model assumes varying satisfaction levels will have differential relationships with attitudes toward collective negotiations.

Variable 2 refers to the extent teachers support professional norms of behavior. Like satisfaction, professionalism is considered to be a multidimensional concept, consisting of the following elements: client orientation, colleague orientation, monopoly of knowledge, and decision making. It is assumed the nature of the professional role concept will have an interacting effect on the level of satisfaction as well as influence attitudes toward collective negotiations.

Corwin explains the process of professionalism for teachers as follows:

> For decades teachers have subscribed to the idea that they have professional obligations (such as staying late to work with students); now they are demanding professional rights as well (such as rights to select their own teaching materials and methods). . . .Militant professionalism, then is intended to compromise both the control that administrators have over public education and the control traditionally exercised by the lay public.[7]

This model, which attempts to conceptualize the frame of reference of teachers, infers the intervening variables to be both professional role conception and the socioeconomic characteristics of the teachers. These "interacting" relationships are portrayed by "feedback" loops to the satisfaction dimensions.

Variable 3 denotes socioeconomic factors which characterize the sample population: sex, marital status, teaching experience, educational level, and income. These characteristics are not of a particular explanatory value in themselves, but rather serve as operational criteria for evaluating the relevance of other behavioral dimensions. For instance, one might hypothesize that perceived low income on the part of a female teacher may result in dissatisfaction with respect to salary. But if the female in society has been conditioned to assume a more passive and nonaggressive role than the male, there may be a lower propensity for females to support strikes.

Variable 4 in the model refers to classroom teacher attitudes toward collective negotiations in terms of the following scales: (a) support of negotiations, (b) support of strikes, (c) support of penalties for striking, (d) support of arbitration, (e) support of broad scope to negotiations, (f) perceived similarity between NEA and AFT in terms of goals of the two organizations, and (g) teachers' perceptions of school boards' support of collective negotiations.

RELATION OF VARIABLES TO COLLECTIVE NEGOTIATIONS

The model connotes variables 1, 2, and 3 (i.e., satisfaction, professionalization, and socioeconomic factors) have differential and patterned relationships with variable 4 (collective negotiations). However, caution must be exercised in not assuming that this model or the research methodology proves causation because "correlational studies can sometimes disprove but never prove that a causal relationship exists."[8]

The feedback loop from variable 4 (collective negotiations) to the "institutional context" implies that this process may affect other parties in the total educational system in terms of the decision, communication, planning, control, and organization processes. For instance, the administrations in the three systems included in this study have created institutional positions to deal with negotiations.

Variable 5 (power[9] and control) connotes collective negotiations provide the means and serve the function of increasing the amount of power and control one subsystem (teachers) has within the total educational system. The state of mind of the leadership of NEA, with respect to the uses of power, is partially demonstrated in some of their statements. For instance, Elizabeth D. Koontz, president of NEA, stated at the 1968 convention:

We will use our power. In too many communities teachers have been handed a bill of goods. We intend to hand right back a bill of rights. . . .For too long teachers have worked under the theory, you educators do the teaching and leave the decisions to us.[10]

In summary, teachers may have an influence through collective negotiations on the amount and forms of control they can exercise. This ability to "control" may be facilitated through the use of various power tactics. For, as Horvat puts it,

Negotiation is a rapidly growing force in American education because it is a method by which teachers can gain some real control over decision-making in the schools. No longer can administrators and board members choose to, or afford to, reject out of hand or ignore the requests and demands of teacher groups. Collective negotiation processes create political, psychological, and in some cases legal pressures which force boards and administrators to listen to and respond to the demands of teachers of their districts.[11]

If such an increase in power actually occurs, the model posits that a means for increasing the rewards (variable 6) has been created. Generically, rewards may be thought of as desirable outcomes or returns. This is not to infer rewards are not, or would not, be available to teachers without the power and control which they may be able to create through collective negotiations. However, it is assumed one motivation for teachers engaging in collective negotiations is that it is perceived as a means to obtain increments of power and control. Concurrently, such increments of power and control may provide the means of gaining rewards which may be both intrinsic and extrinsic in nature. For, Blau has noted, "workers participate in unions not only to improve their employment conditions but also because they intrinsically enjoy the fellowship in the union and derive satisfaction from helping to realize its objectives."[12] Thus, the model indicates increases in rewards obtained from negotiations serve to reinforce (variable 8) the perceived legitimacy of this process by teachers.

Aspiration level (variable 7) refers to the concept that, as a consequence of obtaining rewards through collective negotiations, a potentially higher level of attainment for present goals, or a different set of goals, may be established. This propensity is indicated by the feedback loop from aspiration level to satisfaction (variable 1). Hypothetically, teachers initially may utilize collective negotiations primarily as a means to increase extrinsic rewards such as salary. Eventually, their span of attention may focus on the satisfaction of other perceived needs such as greater autonomy or participation in decision making.[13] The recognition of such possible changes in aspiration levels enables the model to be considered as "open" rather than "closed." However, it is not necessary to assume the changes in aspirations follow in a simple incremental pattern with changes in rewards (variable 6). The fundamental characteristics of open models are described by Alexis and Wilson as follows:

(a) Predetermined goals are replaced by some unidentified structure that is approximated by an aspiration level.
(b) All alternatives and outcomes are not predetermined, nor are the relations between specific alternatives and outcomes always defined.
(c) The ordering of all alternatives is replaced by a search routine that considers a relatively small number of alternatives.

(d) The individual does not maximize but seeks to find a solution to satisfy an aspiration level.[14]

Reinforcement (variable 8) refers to the primary "internal" and "external" forces which may be serving to shape the nature of and attitudes toward collective negotiations. The "reinforcement" concept may be thought of as having "positive" or "negative" valences. For instance, legislation could reduce or enhance the ability of teachers to engage in collective negotiations.

THE MODEL: EXTERNAL FORCES

The model posits three major external forces as generally having a reinforcing effect on collective negotiations: the perception of other teachers' experiences with collective negotiations in other school systems across the country (variable 9), competition between the NEA and AFT (variable 10), and legislation (variable 11).

The first external force hypothesized as having a reinforcing effect is the success teachers in other school systems across the country are having with this process. More importantly, it appears teachers *not* utilizing collective negotiations generally have not been able to make gains comparable to those made by teachers who *have* used the process. This may result in the perception of relative deprivation.[15] This reasoning assumes that one of the most important reference or comparison groups of teachers is their peers in other systems.

From a psychological perspective, it is known that behavior which is rewarded or perceived to be rewarding is reinforced and thus repeated. Zaleznik and Moment, in reviewing the work of Skinner, state, "any behavior followed by a reward which satisfies an active want is "learned" as an appropriate way in which to satisfy wants henceforth. Similarly, behaviors that are followed by deprivation of wants will tend to be avoided."[16]

In sum, teachers may have learned rewards can be obtained through collective negotiations, thereby reinforcing this process for those already engaged in it and increasing the likelihood of other teachers desiring to utilize negotiations.

Competition between NEA and AFT (variable 10) is assumed as having a reinforcing effect on collective negotiations and teachers' attitudes toward this process. Although such a causal relationship must be inferred, the reasoning does appear convincing. The successes of AFT in winning the right to represent teachers in several large metropolitan areas, commencing with New York City, may have stimulated NEA to aspirations for greater organizational growth.

Competition probably was initially created by AFT. For, as Muir states,

The AFT has acted as the spark to ignite the lethargic engine of the NEA in its drive to improve the economic welfare of the teaching profession. In this regard the impact of the AFT on the NEA can be compared to the impact of the CIO upon the AFL during the 1930's. . . .In much the same way the activities of the AFT have forced the NEA to change its position on bargaining, sanctions, and strikes and has caused them to seek protective legislation, exclusive bargaining rights and also to embark upon a campaign to organize the unorganized workers.[17]

Further, the current competition between NEA and AFT may partially explain the present militancy among some teachers.[18] The rationale for this assertion is developed by Brown.

The present teacher militancy, though rooted in economic conditions, is fed and fertilized by competition between the NEA and AFT. In the search for membership and support, each is attempting to demonstrate to prospective members that it can and does win greater benefits for teachers than the others.[19]

Dashiell and Schmidt provide case studies on the realities of this conflict in Michigan.[20] It appears some evidence exists for inferring that the competition between NEA and AFT is having a reinforcing impact on the process of and attitudes toward collective negotiations.

LEGISLATION REFLECTS LOBBYING EFFORTS

The last major external force in the model is legislation (variable 11). Much of the legislation concerning collective negotiations passed in recent years appears to reflect the lobbying efforts of both school boards and teacher associations. Moskow notes that the Washington Act (1965) was sponsored by the Washington Education Association and opposed by the AFT.[21] For the most part, legislation regarding collective negotiations has been enacted since 1962 and is, at a minimum, supportive of the concept of negotiations. Beyond this, there are wide differences among states. The states with legislation permitting or requiring school boards to engage in collective negotiations totaled sixteen as of 1968: Alaska, California, Connecticut, Florida, Maryland, Massachusetts, Michigan, Nebraska, New Hampshire, New Jersey, New York, Oregon, Rhode Island, Texas, Washington, and Wisconsin.[22] Lieberman anticipates

By 1972, 80% of the teachers will probably be in states which statutorily provide for some form of negotiations. . . .Statutes which have not resulted in meaningful negotiations are likely to be amended to result in more significant negotiations.[23]

Since the teacher attitudes reported were obtained in the State of Washington, it might be helpful to review some of the basic dimensions of the Washington Act.

Representatives of an employee organization, which organization shall by secret ballot have won a majority in an election to represent the certificated employees within its school district, shall have the right, after using established administrative channels, to meet, confer and negotiate with the board of directors of the school district or a committee thereof to communicate the considered professional judgment of the certificated staff prior to the final adoption by the board of proposed school policies relating to, but not limited to, curriculum, textbook selection, in-service training, student teaching program, personnel hiring and assignment practices, leaves of absence, salaries and salary schedules and noninstructional duties.[24]

The model purports this legislation probably affects (even though indirectly) and has been affected by teacher attitudes toward collective negotiations. Figure 18-2 attempts to conceptualize the interactional "tensions" between the legal context and the social-psychological context with respect to collective negotiations.

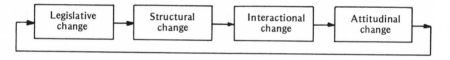

Figure 18-2
Simplified system of relations between the legal context
and social-psychological context

Thus, the generality of the findings to other states may be affected somewhat by the specific nature of the legislation in the State of Washington. The degree of such impact is a moot question. A priori, it is hypothesized that in the major industrialized sections of the country there may be more similarities in the "social" contexts analyzed in empirical portions of this study than in the "legal" contexts of the various states.

The analytical basis for this discussion has been that the conceptual model represents a particular "system" functioning within a given "environment."[25] It is felt the model assists in the cognitive process of identifying and tracing the nature of the relationships among the variables abstracted from this subsystem of the total educational system. Further, the use of a systems approach and an "open" rather than "closed" model is considered to have more utility to the researcher and practitioner than a simplified static approach.

The remaining discussion will be concerned with the empirical dimensions of the study.

RESEARCH DESIGN

The universe for this study comprised all counselors and classroom teachers at eight secondary public schools in three school systems within the Seattle metropolitan area. The eight schools represented a spectrum from lower to upper socioeconomic student backgrounds. The sample population specifically excluded full-time administrative personnel.

After approval of the study was obtained from the administrative cores in the three school systems, copies of the research proposal were distributed to the leaders of each of the four organizations representing the teachers. The teachers in one school system were represented by affiliates of both NEA and AFT. Teachers in the other two systems were represented exclusively by affiliates of NEA.

The leaders were told they had the right and power to veto the study since their members were directly involved and the subject being studied concerned their relationships to the administrative cores. Open and full support was sought from these leaders, since they could informally destroy the relevance of the study by simply requesting their members not to cooperate or, at a minimum, by creating hostility among some teachers toward the study. The positive support of these leaders was considered critical since teacher participation in completing the instruments was anonymous and voluntary. The leadership of all four teacher organizations approved the study. They also were willing to have the researcher express their support of the study to the teachers when he appeared at faculty meetings to explain the study and distribute the research instruments. The instruments were returned at the teachers' convenience in self-addressed stamped envelopes.

The rationale for limiting the study to secondary schools, and thereby eliminating representation of elementary and junior high teachers, represents a subjective balancing of goals. A male and female balance in the sample population was desired to facilitate testing the differences in the behavioral variables vis-a-vis sex. Some of these differences will be reported under the findings. The sex dimension is considered to have relevance because of the possibilities that males may experience more "relative deprivation" than females and may be an influence on female teachers' changing attitudes with respect to negotiations. Limiting the study to secondary teachers was also based on the following factors:

1. There is less turnover with secondary teachers than junior high or elementary teachers. There are two possible implications to this finding.

In a macro sense, there may be a stronger identification of secondary teachers with their roles and the concern with the long-run impact of possible changes in their role relationships. Second, it was desired to minimize the proportion of newer teachers among respondents since there was a stronger likelihood that they may be undergoing a process of attitude formation with respect to the variable being investigated.

2. Secondary teachers, as a whole, tend to have a higher level of formal education than elementary teachers. The assumption is that the level of formal education is a significant criterion in the development of professionalism, which is one of the intervening variables in the model. Thus, the level and diversity of professional role conceptions was assumed, a priori, to be greater with secondary teachers than with other groups.

3. Secondary teachers tend to be somewhat more diverse by virtue of their greater specialization, relative to elementary teachers.[26]

Several limitations with respect to the sample design need to be made. The findings of this study cannot be assumed to be representative of all secondary teachers in the United States or even in the Seattle area. For, as Chein has stated: "In nonprobability sampling, there is no way of estimating the probability that each element has of being included in the sample, and no assurance that every element has some chance of being included.[27]

Also, the exclusion of elementary and junior high teachers from the sample population may limit the applicability of the findings. But the research questions being investigated were of particular relevance to those segments of the teaching profession which may be "pattern setters." Thus, the exclusion of elementary teachers is not judged to be especially damaging; whereas the exclusion of junior high teachers, who may experience the greatest amount of frustration in teaching, suggests the need for replication with this segment of teachers.[28]

In evaluating the choices and consequences with respect to the alternative samples, the researchers opted for in-depth study of eight schools at the secondary level among three school systems.

The research instruments provided measurements on the following four variables in the conceptual model: satisfaction (variable 1), professionalism (variable 2), socioeconomic factors (variable 3), and collective negotiations (variable 4). The research instruments were distributed at faculty meetings at the schools during October and November 1968.[29]

The Purdue Teacher Opinionnaire[30] was utilized to determine the general level of satisfaction, as well as provide scores on ten dimensions to satisfaction. The professional role concept perceived by the respondents was measured by the Teacher Orientation Survey.[31] The four role segments which comprise the professional scale are (a) orientation to students, (b) orientation to the profession and professional colleagues, (c) belief that competence is based on knowledge, and (d) belief that teachers should have decision-making authority. The General Information Questionnaire was utilized to identify the socioeconomic characteristics of the respondents such as sex, income, marital status, age, teaching experience, formal education, organizational affiliation, discipline taught, etc.

The Collective Negotiations Survey was developed to determine the respondents' attitudes with respect to several dimensions of collective negotiations. The scales in this instrument included (a) support of broad scope to negotiations, (b) support of arbitration of disputes, (c) support of teacher strikes, (d) perceived similarity between NEA and AFT organizational goals, (e) teachers' perceptions of school boards' support of collective negotiations, (f) support of teacher penalties for striking, and (g) other items. The instrument was developed by recording on cards normative statements regarding collective negotiations made in articles, speeches, and books by academicians, school board members, superintendents, leaders of various teacher associations, and other public officials. The three hundred statements obtained were then classified according to their apparent content or meaning. The statements included within each of these classifications were compared, rewritten, and reduced in number. The criteria for revising or eliminating statements were redundancy between statements, the assessed degree of ambiguity in a statement, the extent to which statements about a phenomenon might be widely interpreted as a question of fact, and the extent of conflict between groups over ideas expressed in the statements. A number of other criteria, generally considered acceptable in the construction of attitude scales, were used in the development of the scales.[32]

FINDINGS: DESCRIPTIVE DIMENSIONS

The findings are based on usable returns from 335 secondary teachers, including 193 males and 142 females. The 335 returns represent

TABLE 18-1. Mean levels of satisfaction for all respondent teachers in descending order by satisfaction factor

Satisfaction factor	All respondents N = 335	
	$\overline{X}$	s
Satisfaction with teaching	3.4433	.4033
Community pressures	3.4184	.4308
Rapport among teachers	3.0976	.5254
Overall satisfaction	3.0375	.3739
Teacher load	3.0254	.5267
Teacher rapport with principal	2.9833	.6791
Community support of education	2.8887	.7047
Curriculum issues	2.7833	.7703
School facilities and services	2.7393	.7784
Teacher status	2.6860	.6682
Teacher salary	2.5042	.6704

Note: The categories are weighted in the following manner: a score of 4.0 indicates "agree" with satisfaction statements, a score of 3.0 indicates "probably agree," a score of 2.0 indicates "probably disagree," a score of 1.0 indicates "disagree." Thus, the higher the mean score the higher the mean level of satisfaction and vice versa.

about 55 percent of the 612 research instruments distributed. The most responsive school had a return rate of 67 percent, while the least responsive school had a return rate of 44 percent.

An analysis of the data from the thirteen socioeconomic characteristics warrants the conclusion that the respondents were a highly diverse group. This diversity tends to remain even when the respondents are classified by school. The major difference in the socioeconomic characteristics among schools appears to be that 42 of the 47 responding AFT members are found in only two schools.

The first set of attitudinal clusters to be reviewed are the ten satisfaction subscales plus the general satisfaction rating. The mean levels and standard deviations for the 335 respondents are presented for each subscale in descending order in Table 18-1. Satisfaction with teaching ($\overline{X}$ = 3.44) is the factor with the favorable and "high" satisfaction rating. By school, the rating on this factor is consistently favorable, varying between a mean of 3.62 and 3.29. Thus, the respondents at all eight schools like to teach, feel competent, and enjoy students. Another major finding is the relative dissatisfaction with both teacher status $(\overline{X} = 2.686)$ and teacher salary $(\overline{X} = 2.5042)$. These factors are defined as follows:

"Teacher Status" samples feelings about the prestige, security, and benefits afforded by teaching. Several of the items refer to the extent to which the teacher feels he is an accepted member of the community.
 "Teacher Salary" pertains primarily to the teacher's feelings about salaries and salary policies. Are salaries based on teacher competency? Do they compare favorably with salaries in other school systems? Are salary policies administered fairly and justly, and do teachers participate in the development of these policies?[33]

The satisfaction with status factor varies by school from mildly negative $(\overline{X} = 2.8845)$ to negative $(\overline{X} = 2.3967)$. The mean level of satisfaction with teacher salary $(\overline{X} = 2.5042)$ was negative and the lowest compared to the other ten factors. This low and negative mean level was found in all eight schools, with variations in means by school between 2.6872 and 2.1135. Summarizing, the respondent teachers are relatively satisfied with the role of teaching, while they are somewhat dissatisfied with the status and economic rewards

TABLE 18-2. Mean levels of attitudes toward collective negotiations in descending order of negotiation factors for all respondent teachers

Negotiation factor	All respondents N = 335	
	$\overline{X}$	s
Support of broad scope to negotiations	4.3149	.6690
Support of arbitration of disputes	3.6786	.5904
Support of teacher strikes	3.3512	.9538
Perceived similarity between NEA and AFT	2.9167	.9022
Teacher perceptions of school boards' support of collective negotiations	2.7374	.8678
Support of teacher penalties for striking	1.8584	.7925

Note: The response categories are weighted in the following manner: a score of 5.0 indicates "strongly agree," a score of 4.0 indicates "agree," a score of 3.0 indicates "undecided," a score of 2.0 indicates "disagree," and a score of 1.0 indicates "strongly disagree." Thus, the higher the score the greater mean "agreement" with the subscale.

available in the role. The literature is generally consistent with this finding.

The third major finding is that one school ranked as highest on six of the satisfaction factors, whereas another school ranked lowest on eight of the factors.[34] This may represent, to some degree, an operational manifestation of the concept of an organization as a system wherein the parts or dimensions of the system are continuously reinforcing one another. For example, in the high-ranking school, the writers found a high income and educational level of parents of the students, whereas in the lowest-ranking school just the opposite—with further problems of racial integration—was found.

LEAST VARIATION ON PROFESSIONALISM

Of the three attitudinal scales administered, professionalism provided the least amount of variation by school in terms of mean levels (and standard deviations). This is not a particularly surprising finding, since the respondents are relatively comparable to one another in terms of age, sex, formal education level, income, etc. The mean response for all respondents on the professionalism scale[35] was 3.64 (s = .4216), which is in the "positive" direction of the scale toward professional role orientation. Although the mean levels tend to indicate an orientation toward professional values, they do not warrant the conclusion that respondents articulate overwhelmingly strong sentiments toward these values. Data on teachers' attitudes toward various dimensions of collective negotiations are provided in Table 18-2.

With a mean of 4.31 for support of a broad scope for collective negotiations, it is evident most teachers are desirous of including within the negotiation process many of the dimensions of their relationships with the administrations. This subscale is constructed from statements which attempt to determine the extent to which the respondents felt the following areas should be included in the negotiation process: wages, working conditions, teacher responsibilities, procedures of appeal, and curriculum issues. At present, many administrations or school boards are concerned with limiting the scope of negotiations. Thus, a source of conflict between the parties may be the types of issues subject to negotiation in addition to conflicts over the issues per se.

There are generally supportive sentiments for use of neutral third -party arbitrators in disputes which do not appear to be subject to solution by other processes. A mean level of support for arbitration of 3.62 indicates the intensity of feeling is not quite as great as with the desired scope for negotiations. At a minimum, teachers are accepting the ideal of introducing an alternate decision mechanism which might be used on a limited basis. The difference in means between the "high" school and the "low" school on this factor is minor.

The mean support of teacher strikes of 3.35 is greater than expected considering the traditional antipathy most teachers have expressed toward the strike. However, the standard deviation of 0.90 for the mean indicates the dispersion of spread of attitudes on this factor is greater than for any other negotiation factor. The "high" school on this factor has a mean of 3.76 versus 3.11 for the "low" school, revealing a considerable difference by respondents between schools. The data tends to support the conclusion that a considerable range of attitudes exists among teachers with respect to the strike issue. The possible relationship of the socioeconomic characteristics of respondent teachers in relation to their attitudes toward the strike issue will be explored later.

Ironically, the mean level of perceived similarity between NEA and AFT was greatest in the school which had twenty-three respondents with membership in the AFT and thirty respondents with membership in NEA. In contrast, the school which had the lowest mean level of perceived similarity ($\bar{X} = 2.58$) between NEA and AFT had no respondents from AFT; thus, a sterotype situation may have developed. Conversely, the respondents from the school with members in both organizations perceived fewer differences in one another—this may be the result of daily interaction which leads to more "valid" data about each other.

The factor with the greatest variation in mean attitudes between schools is the teachers' perceptions of the degree to which they think their school board accepts the process of collective negotiations. The mean attitudes range from the evaluation of the school board as being mildly acceptant of the negotiation process at the "high" school ($\bar{X} = 3.26$) to one of definite disagreement with the process at the "low" school ($\bar{X} = 1.99$).

As expected, the respondents generally disagreed with penalizing teachers for engaging in strikes. For all respondents, a low mean of 1.86 was obtained, with a variation among schools from 2.26 to 1.62.

FINDINGS: ANALYTICAL DIMENSIONS

This section will discuss some of the significant relationships found among the previously described variables.

A dimension to the data which might be worth exploring is the relationship between support of teacher strikes and various satisfaction factors. It is assumed that the strike question continues to be a highly emotional issue; it is also assumed the ideology of the strike is more likely to be accepted by teachers under conditions of perceived dissatisfaction or frustration.

The results of testing this relationship through all the satisfaction factors for the 335 respondents are reported in Table 18-3.

There is a statistically significant relationship between eight of the satisfaction factors and support of teacher strikes. As expected, the direction of relationship between the variables is negative. The degree of negative correlation, at the .001 level of significance, is greatest (−.3639) between satisfaction with teacher salary and support of teacher strikes. By school, the power of this negative relationship tends to remain, and in one school increases to −.5145 (with a .001 level of significance). The second most powerful relationship is between satisfaction with status and support of teacher strikes. The correlation for all respondents is −.3073 (with a significance level of .01). Two schools have high negative correlation coefficients of

TABLE 18-3. Degree of correlation in descending order between satisfaction factors and support of teacher strikes by respondent teachers

Satisfaction factors	Correlation between satisfaction factors and support of teacher strikes
Teacher salary	−.3639
Teacher status	−.3073[a]
Overall satisfaction	−.2702[a]
Community support of education	−.1903[a]
Curriculum issues	−.1898[a]
Teacher load	−.1661[a]
School facilities and services	−.1643[a]
Teacher rapport with principal	−.1614[a]
Satisfaction with teaching	−.1052[b]
Community pressures	−.1005[b]
Rapport among teachers	−.0689[b]

[a] Indicates correlation significant at .01 level or better.
[b] Indicates correlation is *not* significant at .05 level or better
Note: No letter indicates correlation significant at .001 level or better.

—.4952 (.001 level) followed by —.4147 (.05 level). The coefficients for the remaining six sets of statistically significant relationships decline fairly rapidly to a low of —.1614 (.01 level).

In brief, the strongest negative relationships are found between salary and status and support of teachers strikes. The power of the relationships, although statistically significant, is weaker between overall satisfaction, teacher rapport with principal, teacher load curriculum issues, community support of education, and school facilities and services *and* teacher support of strikes.

Corwin and others[36] claim the drive to professionalism is a militant process. If this assumption is valid, those with a greater professional role orientation may express stronger and more favorable sentiments toward various dimensions of collective negotiations. On the other hand, the traditional ideology in the education field has been that professionalism and collective negotiations, particularly the strike, are inconsistent with one another.

A test of the data reveals a significant (.01 level) but low correlation (.2073) between professional role conception and support of teacher strikes by males (N = 192), while there is virtually no correlation for females (N = 143). Although this correlation indicates only a small amount of the variation in professional role conception is associated with variations in the support of teacher strikes, it is considered a relevant finding on the basis of three factors. First, the proposition in the literature, with few exceptions, is that those who are professionally oriented would not or should not support strikes. Second, there is a slight differential pattern between these two variables when evaluated on the basis of sex. Third, the general assumption that professional role conception and support of teacher strikes are incompatible is not confirmed. There is no evidence indicating professional role conception is antithetical to support of teacher strikes. In turn, there are no data indicating they are strongly and positively associated.

Statistically significant (.01 level) results were also obtained between professionalism and the negotiation subscales of support of binding arbitration (.2176) and support of broad scope for negotiations (.1700). Again, the correlations are quite low, thereby explaining a little of the variation, but the positive direction of the correlations is as posited.

In sum, the correlations between professionalism and the negotiation subscales provide mixed results. The negotiation factors and professional role conception are associated by low correlations, but it is considered significant that the general proposition which assumes support of strikes and professionalism as being incompatible is not confirmed. Further, the associations between these variables vary somewhat by sex. For males there is a statistically significant and and positive association between the two variables.

RELATIONSHIP BETWEEN SUPPORT OF STRIKE AND AGE, SEX, AND AFFILIATION

The last major domain to be investigated concerns the relationship between the support of teacher strike scale[37] and selected socioeconomic factors (variable 3 in the conceptual model). The three sets of comparisons presented in Table 18-4 were all significant at the .001 level.

TABLE 18-4. Support of teacher strikes by sets of socioeconomic factors

| Socioeconomic factors | Support of Teacher Strikes | | |
	N	$\bar{X}$	s
Males	193	3.5322	0.8591
Females	142	3.1087	1.0251
"Younger" teachers (40 or under)	183	3.5183	0.9048
"Older" teachers (50 or over	75	3.0553	0.9663
NEA members	255	3.2762	0.9583
AFT members	47	3.7933	0.7469

Note: Differences are significant at the .001 level or better. The significance levels are based on the F value.

The data confirms the assumption that males might be somewhat more predisposed toward strikes than females. Unfortunately, the findings do not provide their own explanation; several reasons may be given. For instance, this may be the result of different cultural socialization, wherein certain forms of aggressiveness by males tend to be more acceptable than for females. Or this finding may be a consequence of males experiencing greater frustration with respect to the available rewards, particularly economic ones. Another possibility is that males may perceive themselves as being more deprived in social status than are females, with the current manifestation being increased militancy. Of course, these "explanations" are only illustrative of others to which one might appeal. The younger teachers (under forty) had a mean level of support of teacher strikes of about 3.52, whereas this figure declined to approximately 3.06 for the older teachers (over fifty). This finding is of the form anticipated, because it is assumed, for the most part, the older teachers have worked many years in a social milieu in which the strike was anathema. Further, older teachers may be more adjusted or adapted to their environment and therefore may be less favorably responsive to the strike issue. However, these explanations are only generalities and may be quite irrelevant in specific situations and when combinations of variables are considered. For instance, the support of teacher strikes by the only four older male respondents from one school was a high mean of about 4.29.

The last set of relationships to be tested in this section concerns possible variations in support of teacher strikes on the basis of organizational affiliation. The AFT traditionally has represented a more militant or aggressive posture in its relations to various school administrations than has NEA. One manifestation of this militancy is assumed to be the ideological support of teacher strikes. Recently, the position of NEA (or at least some of its organizational units) on this tactic has altered, but AFT continues to be viewed as being more acceptant of the strike than NEA. Thus, it is assumed that teachers who are members of AFT will be supportive of teacher strikes. The further assumption is that teachers opposed to teacher strikes would tend not to join AFT because of the conflict it might create between personal and organizational values. The findings reveal a statistically significant difference (at the .001 level) in support of teacher strikes between the respondents based on their organizational affiliation. The mean level of support of teacher strikes is 3.28 for the 225 NEA respondents versus 3.79 for the 47 AFT respondents. But at two schools, the support of teachers strikes by NEA respondents is virtually as high as for AFT respondents.

CONCLUSIONS

For the most part, the model has been useful for conceptualizing and providing an understanding of the "internal" and "external" factors related to the various dimensions of collective negotiations. Some confirmation of this conclusion is provided by the insights acquired through the literature and by the knowledge generated through the empirical dimensions of this study. Some of the variables included in the empirical study revealed more substantial degrees of association with the negotiation factors than other variables. In brief, the model met its purpose of providing a framework of understanding, which was partially tested on an empirical plane.

A degree of speculation can be made with respect to the relationships between the theoretical assumptions and the empirical findings. First, the finding that lower levels of satisfaction with salary and status are significantly associated with several of the negotiation factors may indicate that some teachers perceive this process as a means of increasing their rewards, thereby leading to a reduction in their frustrations. Of course, these findings may contain necessary but not sufficient conditions for negotiations to be incorporated as a strategy of decision making by teachers. This is suggested through some deductive reasoning. Studies have shown that for years teachers were expressing dissatisfaction with their salary and social status, among other factors. But nothing happened! It is interesting to hypothesize that two shifts in the elements of the system were necessary for the emergence of negotiations. First, teachers had to reconcile themselves to the idea that collective negotiations were both a legitimate process and a potentially effective one for reducing their sources of dissatisfaction. Second, the officials of teacher organizations had to generate leadership and the philosophical conviction that this process could be functional for themselves, their members, and the educational system. Thus, with respect to the emergence of collective negotiations, other important variables may be shifts in leadership styles and in the goals of teacher organizations.

The positive, although mild, degree of association between support of teacher strikes and other negotiation factors with higher levels of professional role conception indicates a possible related effect with the sources of dissatisfaction. Thus, collective negotiations may be perceived by some respondents as a means of attaining professional goals such as participation in decision making and some control over task accomplishment. Support for this possibility also has been revealed in the literature which indicates that the drive toward professionalism for occupational groups may involve a degree of militancy as members attempt to change their traditional role relationships.

The third major conclusion is the possibility that some of the militancy expressed by certain respondents is a consequence of their perception of school board members as being hostile toward the process of negotiations per se. Therefore, the ability to resolve specific issues may be compounded by the distrust or lack of acceptance which one or both parties have toward the other.

Notes

1. James E. Allen, Jr., "Interest and Role of the State Education Department (of New York) with Respect to Employer and Employee Relations," in Robert E. Doherty (ed.), *Employer-Employee Relations in the Public Schools* (Ithaca, N. Y.: New York State School of Industrial and Labor Relations, Cornell University, January 1967), pp. 6-7.

2. For a discussion of the need for more research and theorizing in public employment, see Russell A. Smith and Davis McLaughlin, "Public Employment: A Neglected Area of Research and Training in Labor Relations," *Industrial and Labor Relations Review*, XVI (No. 1, October 1962), 30-44.

3. Ronald W. Glass, "Work Stoppages and Teachers: History and Prospect," *Monthly Labor Review*, XC (No. 8, April 1967), 43.

4. Data obtained from Howard Carroll, National Education Association, Washington, D. C., October 29, 1969. Mr. Carroll estimates 40 teacher strikes had occurred as of October 29 in the current academic year. These figures include both NEA and American Federation of Teachers (AFT) affiliates.

5. Jack Stieber, "Collective Bargaining in the Public Sector," in Lloyd Ulman (ed.), *Challenges to Collective Bargaining* (Englewood Cliffs, N. J.: Prentice-Hall, Inc., 1967), p.80.

6. For a synthesis and discussion of related literature, see Don Hellriegel, "Collective Negotiations and Teachers: A Behavioral Analysis" (D.B.A. diss., University of Washington, Seattle, 1969), pp. 32-117.

7. Ronald G. Corwin, "Professional Persons in Public Organizations," *Educational Administration Quarterly*, I (No. 3, Autumn 1965), 4-5.

8. Lyman W. Porter and Edward E. Lawler, *Managerial Attitudes and Performance* (Homewood, Ill.: Richard D. Irwin, Inc., 1968), p.41.

9. In this study, "the *power* of an individual [or organization] in a social situation consists of the sanctions others in the situation perceive that he [or the organization] has available to employ in ways that will affect them." See Winston W. Hill and Wendell L. French, "Perception of the Power of Department Chairmen by Professors," *Administrative Science Quarterly*, XI (No. 4, March 1967), 552.

10. "NEA Briefs Teachers for War on School Boards: Administrators Get a Reprieve," *The American School Board Journal*, CLVI (No. 2, August 1968), 26. See also S. Cole, "Teacher's Strike: A Study of the Conversion of Predisposition into Action," *American Journal of Sociology*, XIV (No. 5, March 1969), 506-20.

11. John J. Horvat, "The Nature of Teacher Power and Teacher Attitudes toward Certain Aspects of This Power," *Theory into Practice*, VII (No. 2, April 1968), pp. 53-54. Also see James A. Belasco and Joseph A. Alutto, "Organizational Impacts of Teacher Negotiations," *Industrial Relations*, IX (No. 1, October 1969), 67-79.

12. Peter M. Blau, *Exchange and Power in Social Life* (New York: John Wiley and Sons, Inc., 1964), p. 37.

13. Alexander Taffel, "The Principal and Teacher—School Board Negotiations," *The Bulletin of the National Association of Secondary Principals*, LII (No. 329, September 1968), 72.

14. Marcus Alexis and Charles Z. Wilson, *Organizational Decision Making* (Englewood Cliffs, N. J.: Prentice-Hall, Inc., 1967), p.161.

15. For several examples which tend to document this claim, see Edward B. Shils and C. Taylor Whittier, *Teachers, Administrators, and Collective Bargaining* (New York: Thomas Y. Crowell Company, 1968), pp. 32-92. For discussions of the import of reference group theory, see E. F. Jackson, "Status Consistency and Symptoms of Stress," *American Sociological Review*, XXVII (No. 4, August 1962), 469-80.

16. Abraham Zaleznik and David Moment, *The Dynamics of Interpersonal Behavior* (New York: John Wiley and Sons, Inc., 1964), p. 378.

17. Douglas Muir, "The Strike as a Professional Sanction: The Changing Attitude of the National Education Association,"*Labor Law Journal*, XIX (No. 10, October 1968), 627.

18. Robert W. Neirynck, "Teachers' Strikes: A New Militancy," *ibid.* (No. 5, May 1968), 293.

19. George A. Brown, "Teacher Power Techniques," *The American School Board Journal*, CLII (No. 2, February 1966), 12. Also see Stanley Elam, "The NEA-AFT Rivalry," *Phi Delta Kappan*, XLVI (No. 1, September 1964), 12-15.

20. Dick Dashiell, "Teachers Revolt in Michigan," *Phi Delta Kappan*, XLIX (No. 1, September 1967), 20-26; Charles T. Schmidt, Jr., "Representation of Classroom Teachers," *Monthly Labor Review*, XCI (No. 7, July 1968), 27-36.

21. Michael H. Moskow, *Teachers and Unions* (Philadelphia, Pa.: Wharton School of Finance and Commerce, University of Pennsylvania, 1966), p. 50.

22. "Comparison of 1966-67 and 1967-68 Negotiation Survey Data," *Negotiation Research Digest* (Washington, D. C.: National Education Association, June 1968), B-1.

23. Myron Lieberman, "Collective Negotiations: Status and Trends," *American School Board Journal*, CLV (No. 4, October 1967), 8-9.

24. State of Washington, *Laws of Washington*, Rev. Code (1965), c. 28, sec. 72.030, p. 23.

25. For an elaboration of the concepts of "system" and "environment," see A. D. Hall and R. E. Fagen, "Definition of System," in Walter Buckley (ed.), *Modern Systems Research for the Behavioral Scientist* (Chicago: Aldine Publishing Company, 1968), pp. 81-83.

26. Burton R. Clark, "Sociology of Education," in Robert E. L. Faris (ed.), *Handbook of Modern Sociology* (Chicago: Rand-McNally and Company, 1964), pp. 753-57.

27. Isidor Chein, "An Introduction to Sampling," in Claire Sellitz *et al.* (eds.), *Research Methods in Social Relations* (New York: Rinehart and Winston, 1959), p. 514.

28. This point was suggested to the authors by a reader of an earlier draft of this article, who stated "This [frustration] is in part due to the fact that the particular age level is most difficult to teach and handle, and secondly, because junior-high teachers who are nearly all certified to teach in the senior-high school are very often resentful of the fact that they have not been 'promoted' to their proper social and intellectual station." Of course, this reasoning lends further credibility to the model and research design, while noting the limitation in the sample.

29. The teachers who were not at the faculty meetings were given the instruments in self-addressed return envelopes by their principals. In no instance did the number of absent teachers exceed 12; the most typical figure was about 6.

30. Ralph R. Bentley and Averno M. Rempel, *The Purdue Teacher Opinion-*

niare (West Lafayette, Ind.: Purdue Research Foundation, 1967).

31. This instrument is a slight modification of a scale developed by Corwin. See Ronald G. Corwin, *Staff Conflicts in the Public Schools* (Columbus, Ohio: Department of Sociology and Anthropology, The Ohio State University, 1966), pp. 466-69

32. Alan L. Edwards, *Techniques of Attitude Scale Construction* (New York: Appleton-Century-Crofts, 1957), pp.13-14.

33. Bentley and Rempel, *The Purdue Teacher Opinionnaire,* p. 4.

34. The "low" satisfaction school was located in the central area of Seattle, serving a sizeable minority group of students from the lower socioeconomic strata.

35. The categories are weighted in the following manner: a score of 5.0 indicates "strongly agree" with the statements used to measure "professional role orientation," a score of 4.0 indicates "probably agree," a score of 3.0 indicates "undecided," a score of 2.0 indicates "disagree," and a score of 1.0 indicates "strongly disagree." Thus, the higher the mean score the higher the mean level of professional role orientation of the teachers.

36. Ronald G. Corwin, "Militant Professionalism, Initiative and Compliance in Public Education," *Sociology of Education,* XXVIII (No. 4, Summer 1965), 310-31. Also see Archie Kleingartner, *Professionalism and Salaried Worker Organization* (Madison, Wisc.: University of Wisconsin, Industrial Relations Research Institute, 1967).

37. This is the most "controversial" of the negotiation scales.

COMMENT / Thoughts on Collective Negotiations and Teachers

A. William Vantine

"Collective Negotiations and Teachers: A Behavioral Analysis" by Hellriegel, French, and Peterson seeks to identify factors that affect teachers' attitudes toward collective negotiations and work stoppages. A conceptual model developed from literature pertaining to collective negotiations and the social sciences was operationalized and field tested with secondary teachers in the Seattle, Washington, area.

A detailed, sequential review of Hellriegel, French, and Peterson's study appears to be of limited value. The conceptual framework advanced and the conclusions reported are intellectually sound. I will examine some of the notions presented and the conclusions reached in an attempt to provide the reader with additional insights into collective negotiations in general and the aforementioned study in particular.

Data for "Collective Negotiations and Teachers: A Behavorial Analysis" was obtained in the late 1960's when negotiations were still a relatively new phenomenon in public education. In the half decade since the study was published, negotiations in the public sector have been brought into sharper focus. Many of the ideas advanced five years ago are cogent today, but time has helped to clarify their utility. The notion, for example, proposed by the authors, that teachers' attitudes toward their profession, working conditions, job satisfaction, and economic welfare determine their propensity toward participation in strikes is an oversimplification of the complexities of relationships that exist in bargaining dyads. These concepts must be applied to the social and political arena in which a group of teachers and school officials cope. To achieve this, I developed a construct, based on concepts drawn from private sector bargaining, in which I identified a set of teacher-board relationships, forged by the collective bargaining process, along a continuum from predominantly "antagonistic" to basically "cooperative" relationships. Antagonistic relationships occurred most often in large, complex bureaucratic organizations where rank-and-file members were removed from decisions that affected them and where human interactions and wage patterns were generally thought to be substandard. Union-management accommodation relationships tended to occur in small organizations where working conditions and wage levels were equal to, or higher than, benefits in other organizations that were used as reference groups by employees and where decision making was relatively simple and both union and management shared an informal relationship in which mutual respect was evident and problems were handled jointly by the parties.[1]

These statements should not be construed to imply that large school districts can expect to have labor strife while their smaller counterparts can anticipate labor peace. Hellriegel, French, and Peterson contended that satisfaction and professionalism are multidimensional concepts affected by numerous social and political variables. They advance the proposition that teacher power will be directed not only toward economic goals but toward achieving greater autonomy and participation in decision making. These notions are supported by the fact that most school districts are rigid, hierarchical organizations that reflect Max Weber's "bureaucratic model" rather than "organic adaptive" systems.[2] Numerous studies have confirmed the contention that worker alienation toward a job and toward management is apt to increase in organizations where individuals perceive that they are mere functionary cogs than in those organizations that provide opportunities for employees to function as contributing, valued members of a viable, responsive enterprise. Organization climate, then, affects the union-management relationship that exists between the parties. (Relationships, as defined here, are not used to explain the end sought by the parties but rather the means employed to achieve ends.[3]) It is apparent, therefore, that the organizational climate that exists in a school district will determine, to some extent, the posture assumed and the priorities sought by the parties to a collective bargaining agreement.

Teachers' dissatisfaction with low salaries and status are causes for strikes, but I agree with the authors that such a notion does not adequately explain why secure, well-paid teachers from affluent suburban school districts choose to participate in work stoppages. The "Hierarchy of Needs Theory," developed by Abraham Maslow, provides some insight into this phenomenon. Maslow suggests that, once an individual fulfills his basic physical and security needs, his priorities shift toward the attainment of social and psychological goals.[4] Douglas McGregor, in *The Human Side of Enterprise,* reinforces this premise. McGregor's "Theory Y" contends that, once a need is met, it no longer serves as a motivating force.[5] These notions support the contention that teachers' attitudes toward strikes are based to some extent on teachers' feelings of relative deprivation. For example, a "poorly paid" teacher may strike to keep pace with the economic spiral whereas his well-paid, job-secure counterpart may strike in order to obtain control over areas that he perceives will enhance his personal ego and professional status. Many teachers no longer believe that areas of "professional concern" should be left to lay school boards and their "hand-picked" administrators. They reject "management rights" in favor of "professional rights" for teachers. An increasing number support the contention that educators should control their own professional destiny just as physicians control the medical profession. To some, then, collective negotiations are seen as a vehicle for waging a "holy war" that will change the social system. These teachers fail to recognize that they function as wage earners in controlled political service systems rather than as self-employed professionals. Their employment condition makes it difficult for them to obtain parity with other "learned professions." It is at least partly for these reasons that Seattle teachers sampled, who felt economically and socially deprived, were more willing to participate in a strike than those who experienced greater job satisfaction, and that well-paid teachers from privileged school districts strike for other than economic reasons.

A teacher group's disposition toward a strike must also take into account the faculty's knowledge of the issues bargained, the objectives and strategy of the leadership, and the support of the membership. Hellriegel, French, and Peterson assume that the needs and concerns of the faculties sampled generated the topics that their representatives chose to negotiate. This may be true in part, for every teachers' organization is a body politic that must be responsive to its members. However, my experience as president of a large teachers' organization and as chief negotiator for school boards reveals that many demands that are brought to the negotiating table by local teachers' groups are developed by state and national organizations. Such demands are designed to strengthen the role of the teachers' organization rather than to improve the condition of classroom teachers. This does not mean that teachers' organizations are not responsive to their clientele, but an examination of teachers' organizations reveals that few teachers are actually involved in establishing goals and carrying out the objectives of the organization. The leadership, as in any politically motivated organization, is responsible to the clientele, but the evaluative criteria used by the faculty to assess its leadership's performance is affected by the communications received from that leadership. One might postulate, then, that in large, complex organizations rank-and-file teachers will be more dependent on their bargaining agent for direction, information, and guidance than their colleagues in smaller, more simplistic school districts. These comments are not indictments of teachers' leaders. They are, rather, a reminder for the reader that the rank-and-file teacher, just as the teamster or steel worker, is manipulated by the communications he receives from his union leaders. In many school districts classroom teachers are not aware of the items that are offered up for negotiations in their name; nor do they realize that organized teachers' groups that have adopted collective negotiations as a procedure for expressing teachers' needs and exercising power have embarked on an industrial modus operandi.

Hellriegel, French, and Peterson contend that the applicability of their findings are affected by the specific nature of the legislation in the State of Washington as it affects collective negotiations. They also hypothesize that the major industrial sections of the country have more similarities in the social contexts analyzed in the empirical portions of their study than the legal contexts of the various states. One would agree that these were valid assumptions at the time the study was conducted, but the development of new state legislation adds a new dimension to these assumptions. There is little doubt that the absence of legislation leaves boards and teachers to their own devices. States that have enacted legislation have attempted to structure operating procedures and create public defense mechanisms. Yet, in so doing they have also legitimized collective bargaining as the officially recognized procedure for teacher-board interaction.

The creation of public employee bargaining laws has not only increased the bargaining power of teachers' groups, but in some states statute laws have been enacted that have created an imbalance of power between employees and public employers. In the states of Hawaii and Pennsylvania there are laws that provide teachers with a "limited right to strike." Pennsylvania enacted legislation in 1970 with the understanding that public employees would be restricted in their scope of bargaining. In practice, however, the strike has been used as an effective weapon to force negotiations on restricted areas. This condition cannot, however, be attributed solely to the inadequacy of public employee bargaining legislation. In Pennsylvania the problem rests squarely with the state legislature, which passed a public employee bargaining law but failed to develop the necessary machinery or to appropriate sufficient funds for adequate administration. During the first few years that this law was in operation, insufficient numbers of trained mediators were available to handle the onslaught of impasses that occurred. A fact-finding stage in the impasse procedure, designed as a step that could be used to reduce strikes, was practically nonexistent. Inadequate administration of the law was also coupled, until recently, with a phenomenon that placed local school districts in double jeopardy. Districts that were unable to complete 180 days of school because of work stoppages suffered state reimbursement reductions in the year following the strike, and their reimbursement factor was adversely affected for two years. Teacher leaders recognized that they could make up the days that they struck at another time during the school year. It is interesting to note that Pennsylvania has had more strikes in the past few years than all of the rest ot the states put together. It appears that in the "right to strike" states teacher leaders have demonstrated Skinnerian behavior patterns in that they have learned that their rewards could be increased without fear of effective negative sanctions by adopting a militant bargaining posture. As other states begin to move toward the adoption of collective bargaining legislation for teachers, one wonders, if alternative procedures for teacher-board interaction were mandated, whether they would be as successful in meeting human and professional needs and in reshaping educational institutions as collective negotiations have been.

The concepts of power and control as referred to by Hellriegel, French, and Peterson pertain to teachers as a professional body. The authors assume that teachers' power will be used to enhance a professional model rather than to nurture the teacher union movement. The steady growth of the AFT and the increased militancy of the NEA raise some serious questions about this assumption. Collective negotiations have provided teachers' organizations with greater decision-making power than they enjoyed in the past, but there are signs that the leadership of both national teacher groups has been so absorbed in the fervor of their newfound bargaining power that they have neglected to evaluate the substance of the direction they have been pursuing. These organizations have extended their power and influence, but have done little to take commensurate responsibility. It is evident that, if teachers' organizations obtain unlimited bargaining power, public education could be reshaped by self-serving teachers' groups.

In recent years the philosophical differences between the NEA and AFT have diminished. The success of the AFT in metropolitan areas forced the NEA to shed its "tea and cookie" image and assume a militant posture in order to ensure its survival. There are still basic differences between the organizations, but the chasm that existed in the 1950's and the early 1960's has begun to close. Indications of this phenomenon were recognized and noted by Hellriegel and others, and were identified in the Seattle sample. The teachers studied, who functioned in school districts that had active NEA and AFT units, perceived a significant degree of similarity between the two organizations. These perceptions lead me to hypothesize that, if competing organizations exist in a school district, they will be forced to modify their positions toward more commonly held teachers' goals in order to obtain support from the faculty. If this statement is valid, it gives rise to the notion that teachers who work in school districts where only one affiliated teachers' organization exists will be quicker to reject the ideals and programs of a rival organization because of preconceived notions about that organization and its goals than teachers who work in districts where they have been exposed to competing teachers' organizations.

Commonalities between teachers' organizations have increased NEA-AFT affiliate mergers not only at the local but at the state level. The historic merger of the New York State Teachers' Association and the state American Federation of Teachers last year is the crest of the wave for the future. I venture to guess that by 1975 the NEA and AFT will follow the example set by the AFL-CIO and unite to create a national teachers' union. This "United Teachers of America" will be the largest public employees' union in the country and the second largest union in the nation. Only the International Teamsters' union will be able to boast a larger membership. Such merger will provide teachers with political and collective bargaining power unprecedented in the history of the American labor movement.

If the unifying trend toward the elimination of differences continues, and there is every reason to believe that it will, it stands to reason that it will be only a matter of time before a strong centralized teachers' union will play an ever-increasingly dominant role in American education. The occurrence of such a condition is likely to produce greater emphasis on regional and state-wide bargaining. Master agreements, not unsimilar to those developed in the steel industry, are apt to control the educational enterprise. One can only guess that increased size and an emphasis on contract compliance will tend to decrease school district flexibility and strengthen factors that reward similarities rather than differences in the work force. If this hunch is correct, it follows that differentiated staffing patterns, career teaching ladders, and the like might give way to the industrial union notion of equal pay for equal time regardless of qualifications and performance. This pessimistic thought embodies the notion that the outstanding teacher, just as the master bricklayer, will be unable to fulfill his potential because of a system of rewards and punishments geared to levels of mediocrity. These notions are not to be construed as self-fulfilling prophecies. The fact that teachers are leaning toward the support of a monolithic representative system is evident, but the direction that this movement will take is still to be determined. The fact is, however, that teachers' organizations are fast approaching a crossroad that leads toward increased central control and adherence to an industrial model of collective bargaining, rather than to a more flexible and humanizing system. The direction taken will have a profound effect on education in the United States in the decades ahead.

Notes

1. A. William Vantine, "Toward A Theory of Collective Negotiations," *Educational Administration Quarterly,* VIII (1972), 40.

2. Warren G. Bennis, *Changing Organizations* (New York: McGraw-Hill, 1966).

3. Vantine, "Toward a Theory of Collective Negotiations," p. 40.

4. Abraham Maslow, *Motivation and Personality* (New York: Harper and Row, 1964).

5. Douglas McGregor, *The Human Side of Enterprise* (New York: McGraw-Hill, 1960).